# COMMENTARY ON ACTS 3

# COMMENTARY ON ACTS 3

## STEPHEN MANLEY

COMMENTARY ON ACTS 3
© 2015 by Stephen Manley

Published by Cross Style Press
Lebanon, Tennessee
CrossStyle.org

All rights reserved. No part of this book may be reproduced in any form without prior permission from the publisher, except for brief quotations.

*Scripture taken from the New King James Version®. Copyright © 1982 by Thomas Nelson, Inc. Used by permission. All rights reserved.*

Edited by Delphine Manley

ISBN-10: 0692439684
ISBN-13: 978-0692439685

Printed in the United States of America.

*CrossStyle.org*

# CONTENTS

## The Event – Acts 3:1-11

| | | |
|---|---|---|
| Acts 3:1-11 | A Spirit Sourced Pattern | 3 |
| Acts 3:1 | Cozy Comfortable Christian Cult | 11 |
| Acts 3:2 | A Lame Man's Testimony | 20 |
| Acts 3:3-4 | A Lame Man's Perspective | 28 |
| Acts 3:6 | What Do I Have? | 36 |
| Acts 3:5-6 | Expectation | 44 |
| Acts 3:6 | Destination | 52 |
| Acts 3:6 | Distinction | 61 |
| Acts 3:6 | Description | 69 |
| Acts 3:6 | Determination | 77 |
| Acts 3:6 | Development | 86 |
| Acts 3:7 | Let's Reach Out | 94 |
| Acts 3:7 | The Attitude of Jesus | 103 |
| Acts 3:8 | Let's Leap | 111 |
| Acts 3:9-10 | An Amazed Crowd | 119 |
| Acts 3:11 | A Clinging Convert | 127 |

# Exhortation from the Porch – Acts 3:12-26

| | | |
|---|---|---|
| Acts 3:12 | Paradox of Sourcing | 137 |
| Acts 3:13 | The Paradox of Servant | 145 |
| Acts 3:13 | Jesus, a Servant of God | 153 |
| Acts 3:13 | Jesus, the Attitude of God | 161 |
| Acts 3:13 | Jesus, the Delight of God | 169 |
| Acts 3:13 | Glorified Like Jesus | 177 |
| Acts 3:14 | The Holy One | 185 |
| Acts 3:14 | The Just | 193 |
| Acts 3:14 | Denied and Asked | 201 |
| Acts 3:15 | Substance of Life | 209 |
| Acts 3:15 | A Glorified Resurrection | 217 |
| Acts 3:15 | The Reversal | 225 |
| Acts 3:15 | Irreversible | 233 |
| Acts 3:16 | Let's Invoke | 241 |
| Acts 3:16 | Let's Live Invoking | 249 |
| Acts 3:16 | Source of Invoking | 256 |
| Acts 3:17 | Ignorance | 263 |
| Acts 3:17 | I Did Not Mean To! | 270 |
| Acts 3:17 | Two Causes | 278 |
| Acts 3:18 | All His Prophets | 286 |
| Acts 3:18 | God Foretold | 294 |

| | | |
|---|---|---|
| Acts 3:19 | Turn | 302 |
| Acts 3:19 | Repentance / Conversion | 310 |
| Acts 3:19 | Blotted Out Sins | 318 |
| Acts 3:19 | A Refreshing Presence | 326 |
| Acts 3:20 | A Focus on Jesus | 334 |
| Acts 3:21 | The Time of Restoration | 341 |
| Acts 3:21 | Word of the Prophets | 349 |
| Acts 3:22 | A Prophecy of Moses | 357 |
| Acts 3:22-23 | The Prophet Jesus | 365 |
| Acts 3:23 | To Be Removed | 373 |
| Acts 3:24 | The Prophets Again | 381 |
| Acts 3:25 | Who Are You? | 389 |
| Acts 3:25 | A Remaining Promise | 397 |
| Acts 3:26 | Who Is First? | 405 |
| Acts 3:26 | A Climactic Statement | 414 |

## About the Author    423

## PART ONE
### ACTS 3:1-11

# THE EVENT

Acts 3:1-11

# A SPIRIT SOURCED PATTERN

> Now Peter and John went up together to the temple at the hour of prayer, the ninth hour. And a certain man lame from his mother's womb was carried, whom they laid daily at the gate of the temple which is called Beautiful, to ask alms from those who entered the temple; who, seeing Peter and John about to go into the temple, asked for alms. And fixing his eyes on him, with John, Peter said, "Look at us." So he gave them his attention, expecting to receive something from them. Then Peter said, "Silver and gold I do not have, but what I do have I give you: In the name of Jesus Christ of Nazareth, rise up and walk." And he took him by the right hand and lifted him up, and immediately his feet and ankle bones received strength. So he, leaping up, stood and walked and entered the temple with them — walking, leaping, and praising God. And all the people saw him walking and praising God. Then they knew that it was he who sat begging alms at the Beautiful Gate of the temple; and they were filled with wonder and amazement at what had happened to him. Now as the lame man who was healed held on to Peter and John, all the people ran together to them in the porch which is called Solomon's, greatly amazed (Acts 3:1-11).

Luke presents a dramatic scene in the next two chapters. These exciting paragraphs are not filled with disconnected stories, but what happens revolves around one lame man. We

**Part One:** The Event

are introduced to this individual in his helpless condition. He is being carried to the temple gate *called Beautiful* on a daily basis (Acts 3:2). This man has been this way for more than forty years (Acts 4:22). In the first setting we see Peter and John's interaction with this man. He is healed (Acts 3:1-11). This healing is the introduction of a larger interaction with this man; we call this THE EVENT.

The immediate follow up to this miracle is the display in the temple. Being well known by the Temple community, this man created an excitement. The astonished crowd was receptive to THE EXPLANATION of Peter (Acts 3:12-26). He preached Jesus. The healed lame man held on to Peter and John. As Peter preached, the evidence of what he proposed stood by his side. Who could dispute the truth as it was applied?

An astounding result from this setting is twofold in nature, which probably shows us what happens when Jesus is presented. Luke relates, *"However, many of those who heard the word believed; and the number of the men came to be about five thousand"* (Acts 4:4). This number does not include the other influenced family members. However, there was a reverse response from the displeased leaders of Israel; consequently, they were *greatly disturbed* (Acts 4:2). So, as the day closed the apostles found themselves in jail. This is THE EFFECT (Acts 4:1-4).

The next morning the apostles were interrogated before the Sanhedrin. The leaders of Israel were greatly frustrated! With great risk they tried to absolve the religious influence created by Jesus. Their crucifixion of Jesus was not a small accomplishment. But much to their displeasure, Jesus' religious influence increased out of control. Even the interrogation of the apostles became a platform to authenticate His presence. The leaders of Israel recognize Jesus amid what is happening. This is THE EXAMINATION (Acts 4:5-12).

The leaders of Israel find it difficult to do more than merely threaten the apostles. What can they do when the healed beggar stands in their midst? How can they discredit what happened through the apostles? The leaders feel the pressure of people glorifying God for the miracle. God has a plan; the evil of men will not exceed His plan! This is THE ENCUMBRANCE (Acts 4:13-22). They threatened and then released Peter and John.

Immediately these leaders of the early church returned to the body of Christ. They reported everything that had happened and that was spoken. Instead of being discouraged they quoted Scripture, broke into praise, and prayed together. The Spirit of God honored their response with a fresh movement of His presence. This fresh movement resulted in additional evangelism as they boldly proclaimed Jesus throughout Jerusalem. This is THE EXALTATION (Acts 4:23-31).

You can see these two chapters are all tied together as the once crippled man is healed and then remains present. In the opening scene, he is presented as the crippled man at the Gate Beautiful (Acts 3:2). In the second scene, this healed beggar holds on to the apostles before the astonished crowd (Acts 3:11). In Peter's explanation before the Sanhedrin, he refers to this man standing before them as the evidence of the miracle (Acts 4:11). When the leaders of Israel desire to punish the apostles, the indisputable healing of this crippled beggar hinders them (Acts 4:22). The event is amazing!

Historic information is one of the values of the Book of Acts. The four Gospel accounts present fact about Jesus' life from His birth to His ascension. The Epistles inform us of the needs of the early Church and their interaction with their world. But how did we get from the life of Jesus to the establishment of the church? This bridge between the life of Jesus and the early church is the valuable contribution of the Book of Acts. This information must never be devalued.

But Luke presents much more than this. The Book of Acts is most often referred to as "The Acts of the Apostles." A better

## Part One: The Event

view is "The Acts of the Holy Spirit!" Jesus did not capture the world through the brilliant personalities of the apostles, but through the empowering of the Holy Spirit. The apostles were referred to as **uneducated and untrained men** (Acts 4:13), so to say higher education played a role would be inaccurate. It wasn't through their singing talent or charismatic personalities. No valid explanation exists except they were men sourced by the Spirit of Jesus.

A plan seems established as the sourcing Spirit moves through the apostles. The plan is not of man, but the plan is of the Spirit. No committee proposes or promotes a strategy, but it is initiated, instigated, and empowered by the Spirit of Jesus instead. The above material shows us the pattern. God astounds us with THE EVENT. He seems to always have someone present to give THE EXPLANATION. THE EFFECT is highlighted for all to witness. THE EXAMINATION by those critical is usually present. Boundaries are established; it is within these perimeters the Spirit of God chooses to work. The boundaries are THE ENCUMBRANCE. The heart of those filled with the Spirit cannot contain THE EXALTATION of the Spirit's movement.

You should recognize this pattern which was established in the previous studies of the Book of Acts. THE EVENT of the outpouring of the Holy Spirit is mind-boggling (Acts 2:1-4). A New Covenant is ushered into the world. The Old Covenant is fulfilled just as promised. The outside God comes to be inside the believer. The fall of mankind is reversed; people are intimate with God. This event is not confined to the Feast Day of Pentecost of that year, but an event of such magnitude it is continuing to this hour. Everything that happened then is promised to us now. We experience this event in this moment. We live in the fullness of the Spirit.

God is faithful in His witness. Peter is moved on by the Holy Spirit to address the Jews of the Dispersion with THE EXPLANATION of this event (Acts 2:5-39). Jesus is the explanation. He is a Spirit-sourced Man! God proves Pentecost through this Man by sourcing His life, His death, His resurrection, His ascension, and His exaltation. He receives from the Father the resource of the Spirit to pour out on us. He is sourced by the Father to be Lord and Christ of the Kingdom. Jesus is our new King!

THE EFFECT is the beginning of what God is going to do (Acts 2:40-41). ***About three thousand souls were added to them*** (Acts 2:41). A base is established that will thrust the growth of the church and encompass the world. The unstoppable power of God, proved in Jesus, is now manifested in three thousand additional Jews.

A critical group of Jews present THE EXAMINATION (Acts 2:13-15). They mock the original outpouring of the Holy Spirit by viewing it as drunkenness. God pays little attention to them. Only one verse of the explanation is given to them, and they are offered no spiritual insight. God appeals to their intellect to illustrate their foolishness.

The group who is added to the church operates within the boundaries established by the sourcing of the Spirit. But who wants to step outside those limits? Love, fellowship, unity, service, and the power of the resurrected Lord are the boundaries! These limits are THE ENCUMBRANCE of the sourcing Spirit (Acts 2:42-46).

No one is surprised when God is praised, and all are impressed with the love and kindness of the Christian community. THE EXALTATION affects their world for the Kingdom (Acts 2:47). Evangelism continues as the Lord adds to the church.

The sourcing of the Spirit establishes a definite pattern. As we continue to study the Book of Acts, we will see this manifested again in chapter five. This pattern reoccurs as Luke explains how God moves to win the world. The New Testament method for witnessing as used in the early church and a variety of other techniques are frequently taught in evangelism seminars. But the copying of structure, methods, or techniques will not bring

**Part One:** The Event

church growth to our day. Will we allow the Spirit of God to source His pattern through our lives and our churches?

As we apply this biblical pattern to our lives, let's construct a proposition. We must begin with GOD IS SOURCING. The key is not found by us in the latest marketing strategies or what the large, successful church does. What does God want to source? The Book of Acts promotes one theme, the sourcing of the Spirit of Jesus! A suggestion of any other idea is to miss the point. To grasp this theme is to focus on the spiritual rather than the physical. This sourcing is not an activity we can do but a spiritual position we must experience. The Jews of the Dispersion participated in a religion of doing and then crucified Jesus. They now repent (give up a former thought to embrace a new thought) as they respond to the Spirit of Jesus.

Perhaps we fail to win our world because our activities are filled with our own doing. We must become the stage on which Jesus can act. My mind may be so filled with my ideas that it has no room for His. My hearing may be so cluttered with the noise of my own creation that I cannot hear His whisper. My schedule may be filled with carrying out my solutions causing me to miss His solution. We strain our minds, energy, and lives to the breaking point when we could rest in Him. God sources!

In the opening event, God is sourcing. Forty years of self-sourcing brought a crippled man to the Gate Beautiful at the temple. Self-sourcing produced a few alms to pay towards his living. Peter and John, by their acknowledgment, are without resource to change this man (Acts 3:12). Jesus is their explanation of what happened.

This problem is spiritual not logistical. Our focus must be on Jesus not on success or accomplishments. We must seek intimacy with His heart not production from His power. Any hint of self-sourcing will destroy this beginning premise. We must be filled with Jesus. This sourcing cannot be overstated. The theme of the Book of Acts is the proposal that God must source.

A Spirit Sourced Pattern | **Acts 3:1-11**

Let us expand the proposition. GOD IS SOURCING THROUGH EVERY DAY LIVING EXPERIENCE. This proposition is startling! It may seem strange because our passage is filled with a wonderful event, the healing of a crippled man. We are not discrediting the unusual for it demands the attention of the crowd who listens to the explanation. It may be true that when God sources something it always becomes unusual. But let it be clear, the context of the sourcing is God in the everyday living experience.

Peter and John were following the normal tradition of their daily religious pattern. Luke says that they **went up together to the temple at the hour of prayer, the ninth hour** (Acts 3:1). The imperfect tense of this verb suggests it was their habit to go to the temple frequently. This is also verified by the description of the customs of the early Church. **So continuing daily with one accord, in the temple** (Acts 2:46). According to the Old Testament pattern, there were three times for daily prayer (Psalms 55:17). The hours were counted from sunrise according to Jewish reckoning. The third hour was in the morning at nine; the sixth hour was at noon. The ninth hour was at three in the afternoon and was also the time of the evening sacrifice, when the daily temple crowds would be at their peak.

When the lame man came to the temple, it was a part of his daily routine. **And a certain man lame from his mother's womb was carried, whom they laid daily at the gate of the temple which is called Beautiful, to ask alms from those who entered the temple;** (Acts 3:2). When the beggar sees Peter and John, he does what he always does. He asks them for alms. This is his daily routine. The movement of God through the apostles occurs in the usual, typical, and routine activities of everyday life.

Far too often we limit what God wants to source through us. We view our lives as too ordinary and mundane for God to act through us. We wait for the unusual moments such as a crisis, special revivals, or unusual spiritual moments. The

**Part One:** The Event

greatest spiritual witness of our lives flows through the daily routine of living as Spirit-sourced individuals. This type of witness is the consistency of Jesus in and through our lives when we are unaware. This kind of witness is what affects others for the Kingdom.

Pentecost describes of the New Covenant, intimacy of relationship between God and man. Pentecost is saturation, soaking, indwelling or welding of the spirit of man with the Spirit of God. The wonder of this experience is the consistency of His indwelling. Nor is it the Old Testament visitation of God on feast days. This is not the prophet coming in the crisis moment of our history warning us with the words of God. But this is the moment-by-moment influence and sourcing of the Spirit of God. Our daily lives become the platform for His revelation.

However, there is another thought in this proposition. GOD IS SOURCING, THROUGH EVERYDAY LIVING EXPERIENCES, THE OPPORTUNITIES TO EXPLAIN HIS GRACE. In other words, the focus of the sourcing is not us. The Divine activity is not just for our benefit. Yes, Jesus changes, enhances, and enlightens our lives. How can anyone be intimate with Jesus and not find their lives on a higher plane? The personal reward from the indwelling of Jesus is beyond description.

The motivation of the heart of God, which dwells in us, is "others!" Our lives become the display of Him for the sake of others. In those moments of daily living when His grace is revealed, we can point to Him. Jesus is present and sourcing every part of this proposition. God is sourcing our lives. The only explanation for us being is the uniting of our lives with Him. Jesus is the cause of a lame man's healing, love flowing from us when hatred is expected, and us caring when scorn would be normal. How are we to adequately penetrate the heart of the listener? We must be Spirit-sourced!

Acts 3:1

# A COZY COMFORTABLE CHRISTIAN CULT

*Now Peter and John went up together to the temple at the hour of prayer, the ninth hour (Acts 3:1).*

Among biblical scholars there is some difficulty with the translation and meaning of verse one. This verse presents a transition from what is happening in the early Church to this aggressive chapter on evangelism and persecution. My translation suggests the transition by the word *now* (de). However, this Greek word may be interpreted as a stronger contrasting transition.

The closing scenes of chapter two and the opening scene of chapter three present us with strong contrasts. Dominant in chapter two is Peter, the preacher. However, in this opening scene at the temple, Luke presents Peter as the personal worker. Peter explains Pentecost as he confronts the multitudes with the message of Jesus. As chapter two draws to a close, the ministry of Peter brings blessing and harmony among the believers in the early Church. Then in chapter three, through Peter, Jesus confronts a simple poor man, and the end result will be persecution and arrest.

The transition suggested in this verse may be much larger than understood thus far. It may reflect the Book of Acts and the important challenges confronting the early Church. Luke

Part One: The Event

presents to us the early formative years of the church. In our passage, the Church is a worldwide movement whose focus shifts from Jerusalem to winning the world. What were the problems facing them? How will the Spirit of Jesus lead them to fulfill the Great Commission (Matthew 28:19-20)?

We want to examine some challenges.

## Comfort Cluster
### (in Judaism)

We gain great insight when Luke links our passage with the description of the activities of the Jewish believers who experienced Pentecost. He paints an amazing picture of the interaction and fellowship of the believers forming the Church (Acts 2:42-47). They experience the teaching of the apostles. The **apostle's doctrine** is definitely a focus on the resurrection of Jesus (Acts 4:33). They are witnesses of Jesus as a resurrected Person; however, it is not simply an event that they testify. Their message is about the resurrected Jesus, One whom every individual can know and embrace. Every person can be filled with Him!

The unity of the church is strongly emphasized. The emphasis on being together highlights the close fellowship of the believers. The **breaking of bread** gives us a clear picture of their unity (Acts 2:42). This happens from **house to house** (Acts 2:45). Their concern for the needy in their fellowship is mentioned (Acts 2:45). Luke refers to them as **together, and** having **all things in common** (Acts 2:44). In fact, the Jewish citizens of Jerusalem were favorable toward this large fellowship (Acts 2:47).

Being a part of such a fellowship would be wonderful. The fellowship was the right size in number. High quality people held the responsible roles of leadership. Enough financial support was there to meet the needs of the group. God did miracles through the apostles, keeping excitement high. Everything was just right. Things needed to be kept in balance. If too many people are involved, there will be others who want to lead. They may not want to face the concerns that might begin to appear.

For instance, if the number increases too much, the Church will begin to contain various subgroups of our Jewish culture. Right now we experience good unity because we have the normal, basic Hebrews. But what happens if we get a group of Hellenistic Jews (Greek-speaking Jews) converted? Hellenistic Jews are not like us. They might eventually have some widows who feel as if they are neglected and will start complaining (Acts 6:1). Then there is division. Some of them might get roles of spiritual leadership and start preaching (Acts 7). They might not have the same opinion on things as we do. Maybe it is better to stay as we are.

Also, there is always the threat of the Jewish leaders. If we grow in number and create too much attention, we might be persecuted (Acts 4:18). You know what they did to Jesus. Keeping things the way they are would be better. We are all growing in Christ; our children are doing well. We have some great programs; the fellowship is good! Let's keep things balanced.

Will the Great Commission be fulfilled? Jesus said, ***"Go therefore and make disciples of all the nations, baptizing them in the name of the Father and of the Son and of the Holy Spirit, teaching them to observe all things that I have commanded you; and lo, I am with you always, even to the end of the age"*** (Matthew 28:19-20). ***"All the nations"*** is a big assignment to a group of disciples who has never been more than one hundred miles from home. Haven't we done well with this group of 3,120? We are adding a few new people occasionally.

Pentecost ushered in the New Covenant, and it was invigorating. Nothing would have happened if it hadn't been for Pentecost. Jesus told us, ***"But you shall receive power when***

**Part One:** The Event

*the Holy Spirit has come upon you; and you shall be witnesses to Me in Jerusalem, and in all Judea and Samaria, and to the end of the earth"* (Acts 1:8). Do you think He really meant that literally? He did not even mention Galilee, His home area. Perhaps He just got carried away.

Will the enthusiasm of the Spirit of Pentecost drive us to win the world? Will the faith of Pentecost sustain itself? Will the Church's mission requirement be fulfilled? Wouldn't it be all right to just stay as we are? We sure have a good group; we are pretty well balanced. We should not take on more than we can handle. But isn't this the main thrust of the Book of Acts? The Spirit-sourced individuals cannot survive in the cozy comfortable cluster! In the face of extreme persecution from the leaders of Israel in Jerusalem, the Church must advance (Acts 3:1-4:31). Amid disruption in the life of the Church, the mission is not aborted (Acts 4:32-5:11). Apostles are imprisoned and trials are held, but there is a growing momentum in evangelism throughout Judea (Acts 5:12-42). In fact, God develops fearless messengers, Hellenistic Jewish Christians who will not compromise the message or the mission (Acts 6:1-8:40). Besides all this the chief persecutor of the Christian Church, Saul of Tarsus, is converted and begins his ministry (Acts 9:1-31). If there were any members of the early Church tempted to try to preserve the cozy comfortable cluster of the first Pentecost group, they did not accomplish their goal. If anyone wanted to cultivate a club-like atmosphere or smother the Spirit's fire with exclusiveness, they failed!

But let everyone understand, the temptation is still present. A young pastor and wife were appointed to their first church. The church was an old established congregation of twelve members; they were the original twelve. With great enthusiasm the young pastor preached, sang, and evangelized the community. Young married couples were now coming. A nursery was required for the babies and toddlers. Children were causing distraction in the service. One Sunday morning, the original twelve confronted the pastor in his study before the service. They were obviously upset. The young pastor apologized for his sermons and promised to study more. They assured him it was not his preaching. Perhaps it was his singing; he promised to take voice lessons. They were not upset with the music. The problem must be the rate of church growth. So, the pastor promised to call more and work harder, but this was not the cause of their upset either. What could it be? They confessed, "We liked it better the way it was!" They explained that all these new people created too much noise; the children were constantly on the move. They wanted to go back to the original twelve. "What about all these new people?" the pastor asked. The original twelve advised that these people should attend one of the many other churches in town.

## A Confirmed Christian Cult
### (in Judaism)

One of the characteristics of the early Christians was their continued faithfulness to the temple (Acts 2:46). Luke said they *continued daily with one accord in the temple ... praising God and having favor with all the people* (Acts 2:46-47). This faithfulness is verified in our passage as well (Acts 3:1). Peter and John came to *the temple for the hour of prayer, the ninth hour*. The three selected times for prayer (Psalms 55:17) were morning, noon, and night. These were scheduled at the third hour (nine in the morning), the sixth hour (noon), and the ninth hour (three in the afternoon). The hour of prayer in the afternoon was also the hour of the daily sacrifice with the largest crowd present. Luke uses the Greek word "anabaino" translated *went up* in the imperfect tense. This word structure implies that going to the temple was a consistent activity for the believers.

The apostles did many signs and wonders. Luke said that

**Part One:** The Event

the multitudes came from the surrounding cities of Jerusalem. They brought their sick and those tormented by unclean spirits. The apostles continued the work of Jesus by healing them all (Acts 5:16). All these activities are done in the temple. ***And through the hands of the apostles many signs and wonders were done among the people. And they were all with one accord in Solomon's Porch*** (Acts 5:12). ***Solomon's Porch*** was a part of the temple complex.

Jews became Christians, but they did not give up or renounce any of their Jewish doctrines or traditions. But why should they? Jesus was a Jew, and He was the fulfillment of the prophecies of God for the Jews. Nothing in their activities violated their belief in Him. They were a group of Jews who embraced Jesus as the promised Messiah. They continued to live in their Jewish culture with their Jewish practices and traditions. There seemed to be no problem that all the people **added to the church daily** were Jews. Their leaders, the apostles, were Jews. Early Christianity was a Jewish movement.

But is Christianity going to be limited to the Jews? Again the Great Commission (Matthew 28:19-20) is a command to disciple **all the nations**. Saul, the persecutor, is transformed to the Apostle Paul; he is called to be an apostle to the Gentiles. Are we going to make Gentiles become Jewish proselytes before they can become Christians? Does this mean they will need to observe the Jewish traditions, laws, and ceremonies to be saved? Can Christianity exist outside the boundaries of Jewish traditions and influence? These are all questions facing the early church.

In our passage (Acts 3:1), the Christian faith exists within the framework of Judaism. In these beginning months of the Christian movement, this did not propose a problem. But some strange things were going to occur. Cornelius of Caesarea was a centurion of the Italian Regiment (Acts 10:1). He was a devout Gentile man; he prayed and feared God with his household. God honored his prayers; an angel spoke to him in a vision. He was instructed to send men to Joppa and find Peter who would tell him what to do. God told him exactly where to find Peter. Meanwhile, God prepared Peter with a vision, which appeared three times (Acts 10:9-16). The vision focused on clean and unclean animals, and each time God spoke, **"What God has cleansed you must not call common."** When Peter finally met Cornelius, the Gentile Pentecost took place (Acts 10:44-48). How will the Jewish Christians embrace this reality?

During this time God directed Philip, the evangelist. He was told by God to go to a specific road at an exact time. His instructions were to overtake a chariot in which **a man of Ethiopia, a eunuch of great authority under Candace the queen of the Ethiopians** (Acts 8:27). This man was reading the prophet Isaiah on his return from worshipping in Jerusalem. Philip explained the Scriptures to him; he was converted and baptized. An entire Gentile nation was touched with the Gospel.

When persecution began to occur, **those who were scattered went everywhere preaching the word** (Acts 8:4). Philip, the evangelist, also went into Samaria. Great revival broke out in Samaria. In fact, Peter and John were sent by the church in Jerusalem to oversee this new work in Samaria.

Meanwhile, Paul started his missionary journeys where he established the new Gentile churches. This ministry was born from the church at Antioch. God spoke to the leaders of this church. **"Now separate to Me Barnabas and Saul for the work to which I have called them"** (Acts 13:2). Evangelism began to reach all the nations! This evangelism was not the work and dream of a man; it was the directed plan of God.

Christianity was new wine which could not be contained in old Jewish wineskins. It became a major problem and a special council was called in Jerusalem (Acts 15:6). What a gathering it must have been! God directed the council to release the Gentile Christians from the Jewish traditions and laws. Christianity could not and would not be a sect of Judaism. What God proposed in

**Part One:** The Event

the Old Covenant is now fulfilled in the New Covenant. We are released to live in Jesus and Jesus in us!

The Jerusalem Council was held and recorded in the Book of Acts, and that council would be held repeatedly throughout the history of the church. It may need to be held several times in our hearts and lives. When our relationship with Jesus is lost in the details that surround its existence, it is tragic. When we become so bound by the circumstances and activities of the relationship, we miss intimacy with Him. We begin to convert individuals to our circumstances and activities rather than to Him. They become our converts not His! They are brought into our group not His family. They become puppets of the religious cult instead of sons of God!

Jesus strongly addressed this problem. After three years of extreme conflict with the leaders of Israel, He spoke openly to the multitudes. This speech was His final message preached publicly. In this message He pronounced "the seven woes to the scribes and Pharisees." Each one of these "woes" describes the essence of removing the Christian faith from an intimate relationship with Jesus to a structured, legalistic, form to which I must adhere. He begins with PROHIBIT (Matthew 23:13). Not only do we not win people to the Kingdom of God, but we stand in their way. We are also filled with PRETENSE (Matthew 23:14). We destroy individuals while we pretend to rescue them. We focus on PROSELYTES (Matthew 23:15). Our new converts never know the transformation of inner relationship with Jesus, but only our religious structure. He becomes *twice as much a son of hell as yourselves*. You PROFANE the heart of Jesus' death (Matthew 23:16). You adjust your structure for your own comfort instead of allowing your relationship with Jesus to shape your life. You PAY tribute to minor things that should be done, and you ignore the important things (Matthew 23:23). Your PROCEDURE is reversed (Matthew 23:25). You concern yourselves with the outward while neglecting the inward. The result is PUTREFACTION (Matthew 23:27). You simply spill death and rot everywhere you go.

The one deterrent to this trap is Jesus. We must embrace Him; He must embrace us. We must live in the aliveness of His Person. He is our safeguard.

## Acts 3:2

# A LAME MAN'S TESTIMONY

*And a certain man lame from his mother's womb was carried, whom they laid daily at the gate of the temple which is called Beautiful, to ask alms from those who entered the temple (Acts 3:2).*

One of the strange things about the Scriptures is its reflective ability. It acts like a mirror, allowing me to see deep in my own life. If we simply look in our lives, we will not comprehend ourselves, but by viewing the Scriptures we are painting an understandable picture of ourselves. Of course, this is strictly because of the Living Word acting through the Written Word. James states some strong conclusions concerning this truth. "Don't be **like a man observing his natural face in a mirror; for he observes himself, goes away, and immediately forgets what kind of man he was**" (James 1:23-24).

Such a reflection is granted to us in the lame man at the gate called Beautiful. He is the main actor in the drama of these two chapters (Acts 3 & 4). Luke gives no details to his continued faithfulness to Jesus, but he must have a key role in the early Church's evangelism. This assumption is made from his consistent demonstration. He did not receive a miracle and then disappear. He remained at the heart of the action in the midst of threats and persecution.

After receiving his healing **he, leaping up, stood and walked** *and entered the temple with them — walking, leaping, and praising God* (Acts 3:8). Don't ignore the phrase **with them**. The crowds in the temple recognized him with wonder and amazement. The people crowded around Peter and John in Solomon's Porch; because **the lame man who was healed held on to Peter and John in that location** (Acts 3:11). Peter was able to preach about Jesus to the audience. He made indisputable reference to the healed lame man because he was standing right there. "Jesus **has made this man strong, whom you see and know**" (Acts 3:16).

Such a strong movement of God was present that it affected the priests, the captain of the temple, and the Sadducees (Acts 4:1). The officials arrested Peter and John. After spending the night in prison, Peter and John were brought before the rulers, elders, and scribes *as well as Annas the high priest, Caiaphas, John, and Alexander, and as many as were of the family of the high priest,* (Acts 4:6). When Peter was allowed to address this group, he preached Jesus. In his message he stated, **"Let it be known to you all, and to all the people of Israel, that by the name of Jesus Christ of Nazareth, whom you crucified, whom God raised from the dead, by Him this man stands here before you whole"** (Acts 4:10). How did this healed man get in this meeting? Was he arrested with Peter and John? Did he simply refuse to slip into the crowd and go his way? He is still with the apostles!

The healed beggar's presence influenced the judgment of the leadership of Israel toward the apostles. Luke restates it again: **And seeing the man who had been healed standing with them, they could say nothing against it** (Acts 4:14). They find no way to punish the apostles. The crowd is affected by this man's healing because they have known him for more than forty years (Acts 4:22). What a testimony this man has!

Join me in examining this man's condition in detail.

Part One: The Event

# This Was His Place

In the study of the first chapter of Acts, a Greek word (topos) translated *place* appears twice in a key verse (Acts 1:25). Before the Pentecost event, the one hundred and twenty disciples were conducting the first recorded business meeting of the early church. Peter led the meeting (Acts 1:15). Through prayer and the Scriptures, it became apparent replacing Judas was necessary. After his betrayal of Jesus, Judas hanged himself. The disciples revealed their thinking on the matter through prayer. They prayed, **"You, O Lord, who know the hearts of all, show which of these two You have chosen to take part in this ministry and apostleship from which Judas by transgression fell, that he might go to his own place"** (Acts 1:24-25).

The Greek word "topos" is translated *part* and *place* in this text. The word is used figuratively as a place, spot, space, or room, which is occupied or filled by any person or thing. In other words, they viewed the ministry of Judas as a place, office, or space; God put Judas in this *place*! This approach is a phenomenal concept of ministry. Ministry is not something I create or build; it is a *place* built by God in which He puts me. The sin of Judas was not simply an act of betrayal; he was not satisfied with his *place*. Instead of remaining in the *place* built by God, he vacated that *place* in order to build **his own place**. The indication is that **his own place** was hell. Could it be that hell is any*place* other than God's designed *place* for us? If we are not in His *place,* we must build our own, and it always ends up being hell.

While the Greek word "topos" is not used in our text (Acts 3:2), the same concept is indicated by the words written. Luke, the author of the Book of Acts, was a doctor. Often he interjects important details, which others would consider unimportant. This interjection is especially true with physical details involving sickness and healing. Luke informs us this lame man was more than forty years old (Acts 4:22). This detail is especially important in light of the fact he was **lame from his mother's womb** (Acts 3:2). No help was for him all of this time. A great sense of helplessness is expressed in this description.

In our sentence (Acts 3:2), the subject is "***man***" (aner). The verb is "***was carried***" (bastazo). Several words are clustered around the subject. "***A certain***" (tis), "***lame***" (cholos), "***from***" (ek), "***his***" (autos), "***mother***" (meter), and "***womb***" (koilia) give content to the main subject. However, another Greek word, "huparcho," is in this same cluster which is not translated. This Greek word emphasizes the helplessness of the situation and means "to be" or "to exist." The word is a present tense participle which makes it a continuous action. Luke emphasizes the continuing state of his lameness for more than forty years. If any chance of a change in this man's condition were possible, it would have already taken place.

According to the verse, this lame man **was carried** (bastazo) daily to **the gate of the temple, which is called Beautiful**. This Greek word is in the indicative mood, which means a statement of fact, and in the passive voice, which means the subject is not responsible for the action of this verb. The word is in the imperfect tense, which means it is an action of the past, which affects the present. This way of life has been the lame man's continual routine since childhood, emphasized with the word **daily**.

However, the real significance of this Greek word (bastazo) comes from its root, "basis." We get our English word for basis or base from this root word. It means "the foundation of something." It refers to the sole of the foot, or in a more general meaning, the foot of a man, which is the base on which he stands and goes. It is used as a part of the miracles' description. ***And he took him by the right hand and lifted him up, and immediately his feet and ankle bones received strength*** (Acts 3:7). While this is the root word of "bastazo," in this form it gives us the idea of "to raise

**Part One:** The Event

upon a basis" or "to support." "Bastazo" is used twenty-seven times in the New Testament, and it is generally used to describe "taking up," "hold," or "to bear." The word is used to describe Jesus carrying His cross (John 19:17). It symbolizes discipleship as a disciple bears his cross (Luke 14:27). Paul reports that he carried in his body the marks of Jesus (Galatians 6:17). It was used by Jesus to describe the work of the Apostle Paul as he was sent to be a missionary to the Gentiles (Acts 9:15).

With this as a background, we come to our passage. Those who daily carried the lame man to the temple formed the foundation or basis of his life. His existence depended on others. He was helpless. The level and quality of his life was determined by the quality and level of help others offered to him.

This helplessness is further highlighted with the Greek word (tithemi) translated *laid* (Acts 3:2). This word is in the imperfect tense, which means an action in the past with a continuous affect in the present, and in the indicative mood, which is a statement of fact. This dependence was the lame man's place. He was dependent on others, and they daily placed him here to beg. What other choice did he have?

The insight into the attitude of his place increases as we continue to read in this verse. He was daily laid in this place **to ask alms from those who entered the temple** (Acts 3:2). The Greek word (aiteo) translated **to ask** is very focused. Considering that several other Greek words are translated "ask" helps us better understand the passage. For instance, "putho" means "to question" or "ascertain by inquiry." This word's focus is on information or data. "Erotao" is the Greek word used for requesting or asking a favor. The Greek word "zeteo" expresses a more severe asking as in seeking or searching for something hidden. "Deomai" is used in the sense of asking for an urgent need, to petition, to beseech, or pray. This brings us to the Greek word (aiteo) used in our passage. This word is used in the sense of demanding, and carries the idea of demanding something due. Jesus never uses this Greek word to His own prayer life. This word lacks the idea of intimacy.

The lame man is daily carried and laid in his place. His place is a place of helplessness and dependency on others. Yet his place is a platform for demanding what is due him. It absolutely amazes me. Self-sourcing is such a survivor, and it will twist, connive, adjust, compensate, and adapt in order to stay in control. In the midst of such helplessness, one would think this beggar would be broken of all pride. He sits before the community of people who come to the temple daily. Would he not humbly, with gratitude, receive from their hand the alms? He has been doing this for forty years. Would he not have an attitude of submission and surrender? But self-sourcing refuses to relinquish; it justifies and demands.

Is this indicative of the spiritual condition of each of us without Jesus? In our helpless state, haven't we demanded, justified, and controlled? We have dwelt in a place of self-sourcing. We are like the "lukewarm church." We **say, "I am rich, have become wealthy, and have need of nothing'—and do not know that you are wretched, miserable, poor, blind, and naked"** (Revelation 3:17). Have we self-sourced our own place, as did Judas?

## This Is His Place

The radical change in this man's life is best described in a change of place. We will never again find him sitting at the Gate Beautiful begging for alms. No one will ever carry him to the old place. He will sit no longer with the attitude of something is due him, how life mistreated him, or how others owe him. He did not decide to change places. His change was not stimulated by taking several theological courses from the seminary. This change was not a result of a self-improvement seminar. Jesus presented Himself to this man through the apostles!

**Part One:** The Event

The Greek words Luke uses to describe what activated this change are fascinating. Luke writes: ***And he took him by the right hand and lifted him up, and immediately his feet and ankle bones received strength*** (Acts 3:7). As the lame man was fixed in his place, someone **took** (piazo) **him**. The Greek word (piazo) means "to compress, hold fast, squeeze, seize, or lay hold of." If we join the crowds in thinking it was Peter who seized him, we will be strongly corrected by Peter (Acts 3:12). Peter is a Spirit-sourced man, the hand of Jesus!

Luke highlights this truth by relating "***and lifted*** (egeiro) ***him up.***" This is the Greek word used consistently in the New Testament for the resurrection of Jesus from the dead. The spiritual content of this statement pictures Jesus reaching into a man's life through Peter. He literally removes the lame man from his former place to plant him in a new place. Paul related this same truth when he wrote: ***He has delivered us from the power of darkness and conveyed us into the kingdom of the Son of His love,*** (Colossians 1:13). The words Paul uses in his description give the same impact as Luke. Paul tells us that God **has delivered** (rhuomai). This Greek word means, "to draw or snatch from danger, to rescue, or to deliver." However, it carries with it the meaning of drawing to oneself, not merely rescuing from someone or something. We were in our place, the place of darkness. Our self-sourcing acted, was in control, and considered adequate. But Jesus came to us. We were helpless and could not even seek Him. He sought us out! He **conveyed** (methistano) ***us into the kingdom of the Son of His love***. The Greek word "methistemi" is a compound word. "Meta" means "to change places." "Histemi" means "to place or stand." Jesus received us from our old place. He reached out and snatched us from where we were to put us in our new place. He is our new place!

Luke describes this new place. Something happened in the body of the lame man. Luke said: ***So he, leaping up, stood and walked and entered the temple with them — walking, leaping,*** *and praising God* (Acts 3:8). Continuing his description he wrote: ***Now as the lame man who was healed held on to Peter and John, all the people ran together to them in the porch which is called Solomon's, greatly amazed*** (Acts 3:11). The healed man is pictured as "holding on" to Peter and John. The Greek word (krateo) translated ***held*** is very suggestive. The word contains great physical strength and emphasizes the idea of seizing.

In this beginning stage of the healed man's spiritual journey, he recognized the source of his change as Peter and John. Peter quickly points him to Jesus. This man was not going to let go of the source. His place was to stay in the source. The answer to every spiritual need of your life is being Spirit-sourced. This sourcing is your new place. We must seize and hold on with all of our strength to the Source. All of our efforts and our concentration must be focused on this one thing. We must hold on to the Source.

Luke continues to describe the healed man's new place. As the leaders of Israel interrogated the apostles, ***they saw the man who had been healed standing with them, they could say nothing against it*** (Acts 4:14). The Greek word (histemi) translated ***standing*** means "to place or to stand as if being in a place." Notice the location is ***with them***. This new place is a new identification. What is indwelling the apostles and sourcing them is now indwelling and sourcing this man! He is standing in a new place.

This sourcing is an example of what Jesus wants to do in all of our lives. He alone can correct whatever sin brought us to helplessness. We have all self-sourced ourselves amid our helplessness. Jesus takes us by the hand. Will we respond to Him?

Acts 3:3-4

# A LAME MAN'S PERSPECTIVE

*Who, seeing Peter and John about to go into the temple, asked for alms. And fixing his eyes on him, with John, Peter said, "Look at us," (Acts 3:3-4).*

A strong emphasis on "hearing" is in the Pentecost event (Acts 2:1-4). Many activities that occurred during this event have to do with focus. Luke describes the coming of the Holy Spirit on the believer as **a sound from heaven** (Acts 2:2). The Greek word (echos) translated **sound** is used only four times in the New Testament, and it is the root word for our English word "echo," and emphasizes "hearing." In this event, the first demonstration of the Holy Spirit through the lives of the disciples is "speaking" (Acts 2:4). The Jews of the Dispersion were astounded when they heard Galileans speak in their native languages (Acts 2:6).

When Peter stood to explain this event, he began the body of his message with: **"Men of Israel, hear these words"** (Acts 2:22). These words are a translation of the Greek word "akouo." This word often expresses more than physical hearing, and it can mean to "obey." Jesus exhorted the multitudes: **"He who has ears to hear, let him hear!"** (Matthew 11:15). He encouraged the crowds to embrace the truth beyond a simple physical hearing. This exhortation is the same as Peter's exhortation to the Jews of the Dispersion at Pentecost. At the close of his message, he reminds them of **this which you now see and hear** (Acts 2:33).

He urges them to learn by hearing, being informed, or knowing.

The result of what they heard is declared with great conviction. ***Now when they heard this, they were cut to the heart,*** (Acts 2:37). Peter continued to converse with them. ***And with many other words he testified and exhorted them,*** (Acts 2:40). They ***gladly received his word*** (Acts 2:41). The early church continued to grow. They continued to listen as they were ***steadfastly in the apostles' doctrine*** (Acts 2:43).

Now Luke changes the method without changing the emphasis. As we find ourselves amid of the practical experiences of the early Church's ministry, the emphasis becomes one of "seeing." "Seeing" is what astounded the crowd in the temple. As the crowd at the Pentecost event was amazed at what they heard, this crowd is amazed at what they see. A lame man is healed! He has been lame for more than forty years. He undoubtedly is well known in Jerusalem because he sits daily at the Gate Beautiful for forty years. Everyone living in Jerusalem knows his desperate situation. Now they see ***him walking and praising God*** (Acts 3:9). This man is instantly made well. He is ***walking, leaping, and praising God*** (Acts 3:8).

Luke emphasizes the physical seeing. As the physical hearing was a call to know, grasp, and comprehend the movement of God in Pentecost, so the physical seeing is a call to know, grasp, and comprehend as well. Luke weaves this message into Peter and John's encounter with the lame man. Peter and John go to the temple for the three o'clock hour of prayer (Acts 3:1). The daily routine of the lame man is to be carried to the Gate Beautiful for this time. He comes early to maximize his exposure to the crowd. This hour of prayer is also the time of the daily sacrifice at the temple and attracts the largest crowd of the day. The lame man is in his place at the proper time begging for alms (Acts 3:2). Then Luke describes the interaction between the lame man, and Peter and John. He begins with the lame man "seeing" Peter and John (Acts 3:3). Then he puts a strong emphasis on Peter's response (Acts 3:4). Peter voices a command to the lame man, which involved "seeing" (Acts 3:4). In the interaction of "seeing," the Spirit of Jesus is released to heal the man.

## Perception

The first aspect in the story highlights the lame man "seeing" Peter and John (Acts 3:3). What is his impression of them? How does he perceive them? According to <u>Vine's Expository Dictionary of the New Testament</u>, there are eleven different verbs Luke could have used for "see." The one used is not in the cluster of words meaning "to see," but is in the word group for "to know." The verb used is the Greek word "eido." Luke highlights a truth. The lame man not only sees Peter and John physically as they pass, but he perceives, grasps, comprehends, thinks about, or sees them. In other words, he sees them or understands them within the framework of his perspective.

This statement is not a criticism or an attempt to belittle him. For nearly forty years, he sat at the Gate Beautiful. He saw hundreds of people pass as they rush into the temple. He comes to view them as "marks," someone who will give him alms. He never sees them as people he can help; they are seen by him as people who can help him. He does not live in the perspective of how can he minister; he lives in the perspective of being ministered to. His attitude is never "what can I give," but it is always "what can I get." Don't be too critical! How can you blame him? After all, look at his situation. How can he minister to anyone? It demands all his energy and time to survive.

He is a vivid picture of the self-sourced man! To maintain who I am, it demands every effort focused on myself. My job, my emotional stability, my plans, my family, my finances, my dreams, my physical health, and even my education are about sustaining me. Maybe I do help some people, but it only is because it makes me feel good. Even my involvement with Jesus becomes self-focused. I want peace, joy, and forgiveness. I must be ready for eternity. I want to go to heaven. After I am sure of my salvation, I will want to serve and work for Jesus as much as I can. This work will determine how much reward I will get in eternity. My motives are about me. This lame man is a type of who we are.

Perception is an amazing thing. Each one of us lives in a world produced by our own perception, all have their perception of the world, and it is differs from everyone else's world. What you perceive in your framework may not be true, but it is true for you because it is your perception. The truth you see in your view determines your actions, attitudes, and responses. They can be wrong if your perception is wrong. An old saying is, "There is your view, my view, and the real view."

The lame man lives in the world of his perception. He is always at the Gate Beautiful just outside the temple. He never goes into the temple. During this time, the Jews did not allow the poor or physically handicapped people to enter even the Court of the Gentiles. This man has never experienced what other Jewish men assumed. Worship, feast day ceremonies, and being close to the presence of God are not in his perception. He does not see those who pass as "fellow worshippers." He only sees them as "marks."

## Peering

Peter and John rush into the temple for the hour of prayer. People are everywhere and these two men know many of them. They are fellowshipping, talking, and laughing with joy. Luke makes a strong point of an interruption in their schedule. ***And fixing his eyes on him, with John,*** (Acts 3:4). Beggars are everywhere; this man is just one more. How can he possibly become a concern in my self-sourced perception? But Peter and John do not live in a self-sourced perception; they live in a Spirit-sourced perception. They come to a stop, and they focus directly on the man. The Greek word (atenizo) translated *fixing his eyes* presents a focus. Luke uses this special word a total of twelve times. Paul is the only other writer in the New Testament to use this word, and he uses it only twice (2 Corinthians 3:7, 13).

As Jesus began His Galilean ministry, He came to Nazareth. On the Sabbath Day He went to the synagogue to worship. He was handed the book of the prophet Isaiah where He read prophecies about Himself. The passages related how the Spirit of the Lord was on Him to do a variety of ministries (Luke 4:18-19). The prophecies were Messianic. Luke records: **Then He closed the book, and gave it back to the attendant and sat down. And the eyes of all who were in the synagogue were fixed on Him** (Luke 4:20). Luke also uses this word "atenizo" to describe the attention a servant girl gives to Peter who is sitting by a fire. Jesus was arrested and taken to the high priest's house. This young girl sees Peter and identifies him as one of the disciples. Luke writes: she **looked intently at him and said, "This man was also with Him"** (Luke 22:56). The Greek word translated **looked intently** is the same used to describe the staring of the disciples at the ascension of Jesus (Acts 1:10).

Sense the strong atmosphere in each of these situations. Everyone present is staring with full attention. This is the strength of how Luke uses this term in our passage. Peter and John's full attention is focused on this lame man. Time stands still; nothing else matters. All plans are set aside. This one beggar has their full concern! How can this be? They are Spirit-sourced men! This moment is divinely appointed in the life of this lame beggar. Peter and John passed this lame man dozens of times and paid no attention to him. But not true on this day. The Spirit of Jesus focuses them.

The perception of this spirit-sourced focus differs from the lame man's. The beggar's perception is self-sourced; what can I get. The Spirit-sourced focus is: *"Silver and gold I do not have, but what I do have I give you: In the name of Jesus Christ of Nazareth, rise up and walk"* (Acts 3:6). This man became the instrument of evangelism through which 5,000 men were won (Acts 4:4). Also, the leaders of Israel did not persecute the apostles because of this man (Acts 4:14, 21). However, even all these benefits were a focus on others.

This focus is a duplication of the life of Jesus. No wonder the leaders of Israel *marveled. And they realized that they had been with Jesus* (Acts 4:13). The style of the cross is the focus. The Holy Spirit sources it. Jesus is amazing! He did not have a leaning toward ministering to others; it was the consistent pattern and flow of His being. He never thought about Himself, but He always thought of others. We have only one record where Jesus requested prayer for Himself. Even then, He requested, *"Stay here and watch with Me"* (Matthew 26:38). If the prayer request was focused on Him, it was a focus on His redemption of the world.

The nature of the Father indwelt Jesus; the nature of Jesus indwelt Peter and John. The motive of the Father was the motive of Jesus, and it was now the motive of Peter and John. As Jesus became a Spirit-sourced Man, so Peter and John became Spirit-sourced men. This Spirit-sourcing was evident by the expression of their perception.

But there is something more in this passage than simply a "giving spirit." Peter and John became the "eyes of God" on this man, evident by the miracle that only God could do. This is not a call to become more selfless nor a proposal for spiritual discipline, but it is the wonder of becoming the body of Christ. We are not encouraging you to think more of others and less of yourself. Can Jesus live through me? Will I allow Him to express, speak, and see through me? Can I become the eyes of God?

The healed man quickly recognizes this! *So he, leaping up, stood and walked and entered the temple with them — walking, leaping, and praising God* (Acts 3:8). He did not praise Peter and John, but he praised God. Did he not recognize that this healing was the work of God? The crowd in the temple was amazed by this miracle. They knew this man and his desperate need. Peter became anxious lest they attribute the miracle to him. *So when Peter saw it, he responded to the people: "Men of Israel, why do you marvel at this? Or why look so intently at us, as though by our own power or godliness we had made this man walk?"* (Acts 3:12). He immediately began to speak to them about Jesus!

I know that God can see everything, but wouldn't it be amazing if He wants to see my world through my eyes? He knows my family circumstances, but does He want to see them through my eyes? This means that His perception of my situation will become mine. His perception is not my view, your view, nor the real view, but it is His view! Can I become the eyes of God? Can I see the world as He sees it? But even more importantly, can my world recognize that God sees them through me?

## Pay Attention

Peter's reply to the lame man adds another ingredient to the "seeing language" of this passage. *And fixing his eyes on him, with John, Peter said, "Look at us"* (Acts 3:4). In the event, Peter's command seems overboard. The lame man is already engaged with Peter and John. He sees them, and he asks them for alms. They stop abruptly in front of him and stare down at him. This lame man expects that Peter and John will give him money. Will he not stare back at them? Will Peter and John not have his full attention? Yet, Peter tells this man: *"Look at us."*

The Greek word (blepo) translated *look* is used 137 times in the New Testament. Some of these times promote the idea of "understanding" or "perceiving;" however, this is not the case in our passage. This time it is in the imperative mood,

A Lame Man's Perspective | **Acts 3:3-4**

a command, is evidenced by being followed by, ***on us***, which is in the accusative, an object. Peter does not order the lame man to figure, calculate, or comprehend what is going to happen. Will the lame man simply focus and experience the Person of Jesus in his life?

This unexplained divine involvement is illustrated forcibly in an Old Testament story (2 Chronicles 20). Three outraged countries, Moabites, Ammonites, and the people of Mount Seir, form their armies together. They are determined to defeat Israel. King Jehoshaphat declares a fast throughout Israel. God gives this king instructions for the coming battle. What a victory it will be! King Jehoshaphat reports to the people: *"Thus says the Lord to you: 'Do not be afraid nor dismayed because of this great multitude, for the battle is not yours, but God's. Tomorrow go down against them. They will surely come up by the Ascent of Ziz, and you will find them at the end of the brook before the Wilderness of Jeruel. You will not need to fight in this battle. Position yourselves, stand still and see the salvation of the Lord, who is with you, O Judah and Jerusalem!' Do not fear or be dismayed; tomorrow go out against them, for the Lord is with you"* (2 Chronicles 20:15-17).

The secret is not having faith in our faith; it is not in our comprehension. Victory is not found by us in our theology. Victory is in Jesus alone! We are called to focus exclusively on Him.

Acts 3:6

# WHAT DO I HAVE?

*Then Peter said, "Silver and gold I do not have, but what I do have I give you: In the name of Jesus Christ of Nazareth, rise up and walk" (Acts 3:6).*

Matthew records the story of the Rich Young Ruler (Matthew 19:16-22). Questions are raised from this story, which concerns us all. These questions have to do with materialism. When we are self-focused, materialism is important. Self-centeredness seeks the comfort of materialism. Materialism has power. Materialism dominates our schedules, relationships, and spiritual lives. The moment someone suggests "denying yourself," we immediately think of materialism. How can anyone possibly deny themselves while satisfying every materialistic desire? The Rich Young Ruler was so mastered by his materialism that **he went away sorrowful, for he had great possessions** (Matthew 19:22).

The struggle in the young man moved Jesus to say, **"Assuredly, I say to you that it is hard for a rich man to enter the kingdom of heaven"** (Matthew 19:23). The Greek word (duskolos) translated **hard** is an adverb modifying the main verb (**to enter**). It means "with great difficulty." In other words, materialism is a huge obstacle in the path of salvation. To clarify and emphasize this statement, Jesus adds, **"And again I say to you, it is easier for a camel to go through the eye of a needle than for a rich man to enter the kingdom of God"** (Matthew 19:24).

Several explanations lessen the severity of this statement. However, the camel was the largest animal known to the Jews. They understood the darning needle with an eye for the thread. This illustration startled the disciples. They considered rich people extremely blessed by God. If those blessed by God have a difficult time getting into the Kingdom, what chance do those not blessed by God have to enter? Jesus concludes, ***"With men this is impossible, but with God all things are possible"*** (Matthew 19:26). It will take a Divine intervention in our lives. The grip of materialism is strong in the self-sourced life; it is impossible for self to free itself to be saved.

In these thoughts, let's enter the scene of the begging lame man. Surely materialism does not have a hold on him? We do not want to assume more from the passage than is spoken. However, the brief discussion between Peter and the lame man is focused on materialism. The lame man is daily laid at the Gate Beautiful for materialism. This beggar daily desires materialism. The single request he makes to the apostles is for materialism. Peter recognizes this fact; he diverts the lame man's attention from materialism to the flow of God in them (Acts 3:6).

This passage becomes the heart of the story! Peter commands the lame man to ***"Look at us"*** (Acts 3:4). He wanted this man's full attention. Getting the lame man's attention, Peter said, ***"Silver and gold I do not have"*** (Acts 3:6). This statement is contrasted with another statement, ***"but, what I do have I give you"*** (Acts 3:6). The contrast is much greater than it appears in the English translation. The Greek word (huparcho) translated *have* is related to materialism (***silver and gold***). The Greek word (echo) translated *have* is related to the sourcing of the Spirit of Jesus. In other words, Peter uses two different Greek words to describe what he does and does not *have*. One does not have materialism as one may have the Spirit of Jesus! What is the difference between these two? I want to attempt to describe two differences.

Part One: The Event

## Self-covering – Spirit-revealing

Materialism is self-covering. The Greek word (huparcho) translated **have** is related to materialism (***silver and gold***), and is a compound word. "Hupo" expresses the idea of coming from under. "Archo" expresses the idea of being first; thus, it expresses the idea of ruling. It carries the same thrust as "eimi," translated "I am." It highlights the idea of "to be, live, or exist." Materialism is not something one carries in their wallet or checkbook; rather, materialism is so masterful it covers your life. It carries you in its wallet.

I never see you as you are because of your materialism. The authentic "you" is never known, because "you" are marred and covered with the hypocrisy and veneer of materialism glitter. Let us be clear. The amount of materialism is not the determining factor. One may have such little ***silver and gold***, he is homeless. The materialism in which he lives covers who he is. The person God dreamed him to be is never seen by others or developed. Materialism becomes a costume covering him; he never flourishes because of the confines of materialism. Such a person may feel the answer is in more money. This emphasis only highlights and verifies our proposition. He lives in the state of materialism. His life is covered by it, and how thick the covering does not matter.

The Gate Beautiful mentioned in our passage may be a picture of this truth. This gate is not mentioned elsewhere in the New Testament. Neither Josephus nor the Jewish Mishnah mentions this gate. It evidently was immense and made of Corinthian bronze. All the other eleven gates of the temple were made of wood and covered with gold and silver. The bronze of the Gate Beautiful was so stunning it did not need to be covered. Its real substance was manifested for all to see.

The lame beggar lived in a house of materialism. He saw everything through the lens of materialism. People rushing by him were objects of his materialistic view. Peter stopped in front of this lame beggar. *And fixing his eyes on him, with John, Peter said, "Look at us"* (Acts 3:4). Peter said, "We do not live in your materialistic world with the covering of silver and gold. We are authentic like the gate at which you beg." Perhaps Peter cast a glance or even pointed to the magnificent doors that towered above the poor beggar. Those doors had no silver or gold either, but were crafted in solid Corinthian bronze. They were too precious to be marred with an overlay that would only detract from their beauty. To be healed the lame man must shed his materialistic covering, and be real.

In one of his epistles, Peter exhorted the women: *Do not let your adornment be merely outward — arranging the hair, wearing gold, or putting on fine apparel — rather let it be the hidden person of the heart, with the incorruptible beauty of a gentle and quiet spirit, which is very precious in the sight of God* (1 Peter 3:3-4). In times past, we spoke of these verses as statements against makeup and jewelry. The truth of these verses applies to the men of our day. Don't allow materialism be your covering. Whatever the amount, do not let materialism be the state in which you live.

The contrast to this covering is given in Peter's next statement. Allow the Spirit to reveal who you are to your world! The Greek word (echo) translated *have* is connected to Jesus, and it paints a different picture. It defines something that "one has in, or about him, including the idea of to bear, carries in oneself, as in the womb." Matthew describes the natural Father genealogy of Jesus as *she was found with child of the Holy Spirit* (Matthew 1:18). The Greek word (echo) translated *have* is at the heart of this description. Having silver and gold is similar to a veneer covering while having Jesus is more like pregnancy. What is present in you is not covering you, but is shaping, manifesting, and participating with you in life! Even though it is not always pleasurable, it contributes to purpose, life, and privilege.

Part One: The Event

## Possessed – Possessing

Another contrast between these two words Peter uses, and is possessed — compared to possessing. When Peter speaks of ***silver and gold*** he uses the Greek word, "huparcho." It denotes "to be or in existence." It points to an "existence" or condition before the circumstances mentioned and continuing after it. This word is not always a negative but highlights the eternal status of Jesus. ***Let this mind be in you which was also in Christ Jesus, who, being*** (huparcho, existing) ***in the form of God, did not consider it robbery to be equal with God,*** (Philippians 2:6-7). This character is the state of being in which Jesus dwells. Paul expresses Jesus as ***being*** (huparcho, existing) ***in the form*** (morphe), the essential and specific form and character) ***of God***. This statement describes the deity of Jesus! This statement highlights His state before His incarnation, and the continuation of His Godhood at and after the event of His birth. Jesus lives in this state!

However, "huparcho" is used in many negative statements. In the early church ***Ananias, with Sapphira his wife, sold a possession*** (Acts 1:5). The possession was a piece of property (Acts 5:3). They brought the money to the church to help the needy. However, they kept part of the proceeds for themselves as they proclaimed giving it all. The consequences for each were severe. Peter said to Ananias, ***"While it remained, was it not your own? And after it was sold, was it not in your own control?"*** (Acts 5:4). Owning the property was not negative. Before it was sold, there was no spiritual problem, but after the reference to selling the property, Peter introduced the Greek word "huparcho." Ananias and Sapphira changed in their hearts after the sale of the land. Materialism entered into their state of being. What they knew in the fullness of the Spirit was replaced with the domination of materialism.

Paul wrote to the church of Corinth proclaiming Jesus. Paul

believed the only answer to every church problem is Jesus. One of the many problems of the Corinthian church was division. Paul wrote: *For first of all, when you come together as a church, I hear that there are* (huparcho) *divisions among you, and in part I believe it* (1 Corinthians 11:18). The Corinthian congregation dwelt in a state of division. They did not have divisions; divisions had them. The corporate division among them in the church was a result of the individual state of division in the people. The framework of their lives was being expressed in their corporate gathering.

Now the force of this word (huparcho) is used with materialism. This condition is far beyond possessing material things. Materialism is not an accumulation of physical items; it is a spiritual attitude. The spirit of materialism may engulf our lives until it becomes the state of being in which we dwell. As Jesus dwelt in the state of being (God), so we can dwell in the state of materialism. As the Corinthian church dwelt in the state of division, so we can dwell in the state of materialism. Materialism becomes our existence. Do not dismiss this as impossible for your life. Do not use the excuse that you are not rich. The focus of your life is more important than how much you own. Those who have no materialism can dwell in the state of materialism. The wrinkles on our brows are as dollar signs. Everything is gauged by materialism. We see the circumstances of our lives through the eyes of our possessions.

Materialism becomes the spiritual state of our being. It becomes our dwelling place. I want you to picture materialism as a house in which you live. A house exists to meet your needs. You arrange your living room and design your kitchen according to your desires. You keep your house at a comfortable temperature for your pleasure. The house is not bad or evil, but it does perform a function. Materialism is this way. No one proposes the elimination of materialism because it is necessary.

However, let's broaden the picture. Let's give the house life and make it an organism. Instead of a house existing for your

**Part One:** The Event

sake, it begins to exist for its own sake. You exist to serve and minister to the needs of the living house. It sucks the life from you for its own survival. The house grows more powerful as you become much weaker. All your actions are determined by and contribute to the house. You are worse than a slave because the house feeds off you.

*And fixing his eyes on him, with John, Peter said, "Look at us"* (Acts 3:4). Once he had the lame beggar's full attention, he said, *"Silver and gold I do not have,"* (Acts 3:6). The lack of funds is not the indication of this statement. According to Luke's account, no one in the early Church lacked. *Nor was there anyone among them who lacked; for all who were possessors of lands or houses sold them, and brought the proceeds of the things that were sold, and laid them at the apostles' feet; and they distributed to each as anyone had need* (Acts 3:34-35). Peter had funds at his disposal to distribute to the needy. He is not denying the presence of funds to meet the material needs of the beggar. But he says that the realm in which he dwells is not materialism. He is not an individual who distributes money the needy. This way of life is not what possesses him. The function of the early Church was not an institution caring for the physical needs of the community. The Church had a higher calling!

This higher calling is expressed in Peter's completed statement. *Then Peter said, "Silver and gold I do not have, but what I do have I give you: In the name of Jesus Christ of Nazareth, rise up and walk"* (Acts 3:6). The Greek word (echo) translated *I do have* establishes the basis for this calling. We have discussed the usage of this Greek word (echo) in other studies (Acts 2:44). This word (echo) has a dominant role in Christian understanding, and it is used 700 times in the New Testament with various items. The word is thoroughly and distinctively Christian. The basic meaning of this word is "to possess or own," and it distinguishes Christianity as a "religion of having."

We could go through a long list of Scriptural references

describing the various spiritual aspects one could have. In John's account of the Gospel, it is stressed repeatedly that we have (echo) eternal life here and now. This truth elevates the richness of the Christian life from the realm of hope to the realm of present possession. We have God's love (John 5:42), peace (John 16:33), grace (John 17:13), light (John 8:12), and life (John 3:15). However, what is most startling of all is that we have (echo) God. Jesus is the heart of this possession. Two verses in John's epistles are paramount. **Whoever denies the Son does not have** (echo) **the Father either; he who acknowledges the Son has** (echo) **the Father also** (1John 2:23). **Whoever transgresses and does not abide in the doctrine of Christ does not have** (echo) **God. He who abides in the doctrine of Christ has** (echo) **both the Father and the Son** (2 John 9). This possession of the Father and the Son is an amazing thought.

"Having Jesus" must be seen by us as Him "having us." His possession of us is understandable. He is the Creator and the Redeemer. He has every right to claim us as His possession. However, the only reason we can claim Him as our possession is because He gives Himself to us! In this interaction between "Him having us" and "us having Him" that ministry happens. This relationship describes the fullness of the Spirit. The early Church accomplished the Great Commission due to this possession. No ministry takes place without this relationship.

One can argue that the only reason we can "have Him" is because "He has us." Jesus can "have us" without "us having Him." In fact, this argument is a picture of the devil and his relationship with us for us to possess Him. He can possess us, but he never gives Himself to us; we never possess him. Love is the only motive for God sharing Himself with us. Think of our unique position among all His creation. You and I alone are the receivers of such love. The old song says, "Now I belong to Jesus; Jesus belongs to me. Not for the years of time alone, but for eternity!"

## Acts 3:5-6

# EXPECTATION

*So he gave them his attention, expecting to receive something from them. Then Peter said, "Silver and gold I do not have, but what I do have I give you: In the name of Jesus Christ of Nazareth, rise up and walk" (Acts 3:5-6).*

What if God had a plan and called you to be a part of it? Would you respond? If you say, "It depends on the plan's details," you are indicating that you must know all the workings of the plan before you get involved. What if His plan for you is greater than He can explain or you can comprehend? How do you explain to a toddler the wonder of marriage, career, or a fulfilled life? Perhaps God gives you the knowledge you can comprehend, and you must trust Him for the rest!

The grammar structure of verse five hints at a fundamental truth. The main subject of the verse is the opening word of the sentence; it is a Greek word (ho), not translated in our verse. This Greek word places the emphasis of the sentence on the begging lame man. The word is not simply a pronoun combined with the main verb, but is the Greek word (ho), normally translated "the" or "this one." When (ho) this is combined with the singular third person indicated in the main verb, it becomes "the he." It gives us a strong focus on the beggar.

The main verb of the sentence is the Greek word (epecho) translated **gave his attention**, and is a combination of two words.

(Epecho) is "epi," which means "upon" and "echo," which means "to have or hold." The word is often used in the New Testament for the mind. For instance, Paul urges us to stay focused by **holding fast the word of life** (Philippians 2:16). In our verse, the verb is in the active voice, which means the beggar is responsible for the action of this focus. Again our attention is drawn to this lame beggar and his response.

We are given one other important bit of information about this lame man's response. Luke says that the lame man was ***expecting*** (prosdokao). This Greek verb is a participle in the nominative case. It gives content to the main subject, the lame man. It expresses the idea of "expecting," "looking for," or "waiting." We can understand this from the progression of the story. As Peter was rushing into the temple, he stopped. He fixed his eyes directly on this man and spoke to him. He gave a command, ***"Look at us"*** (Acts 3:4). Immediately the lame beggar gave his full attention to Peter. He expected a generous gift from such an encounter.

What he received was far beyond his expectation. In fact, he could not have dreamed of such deliverance. His daily routine became a 40 year pattern. Why would today be any different? He had no unusual expectation in his heart. Let's examine three aspects of the pattern.

## Conjecture

Consider this fact; he will not receive what he expected from them. The reason for his daily pattern is to ask for alms. He was carried daily to the Gate Beautiful because it was where the crowds passed. He thought through and adapted a pattern to receive the most from his begging. No doubt his dress and mannerisms are all designed to make his begging more appealing. When Peter and John pass by to enter the temple, he ***asked for***

**Part One:** The Event

*alms* (Acts 3:3). When Peter confronts him saying, **"Look at us"** (Acts 3:4), he expects to receive alms from them. His thinking, pattern, and efforts are focused on receiving alms.

The lame man is like the disciples during the three years of Jesus' ministry. They had difficulty grasping the idea that Jesus would "bleed, suffer, and die." Jesus spent the last six months of His life attempting to prepare them for the cross. He predicted His death and resurrection three times. They were focused on a great king, like David, who would overthrow their enemy, Rome. Their vision was limited to their own time and experience. The values of the eternal Kingdom of God differed from the values of this world. They wanted relief from the immediate problems. Even after Jesus' resurrection, they would have been thrilled with the restoration of the kingdom to Israel (Acts 1:6). What God had planned was so far beyond their expectations. Who could have visualized an eternal Kingdom?

When you pray continually about a concern, don't be surprised at how God answers. Paul wrote to the church in Rome about his prayers. He mentioned the Christians of Rome always in his prayers without ceasing. One of those constant requests was that by some means he might find a way in the will of God to come to them (Romans 1:9-10). When he finally arrived in Rome, he was a prisoner (Acts 28:16). Paul did arrive in Rome but only after being arrested, slapped in the face, shipwrecked, and bitten by a venomous snake. Probably none of these elements were requested in his prayer. When we sincerely pray, God will answer; however, it is not always in our timing or how we expect.

I seldom, if ever, receive what I expect from Jesus. My intention is not to discourage you in your prayer life. You might seldom recognize the answer to your prayer. Some proponents are fore praying specifically and in great detail for what they desire. I would not say this is wrong. The difficulty is in the limitation. We try to place God in a box where He cannot be contained.

Expectation | **Acts 3:5-6**

A time of persecution came on the church. King Herod killed James, the brother of John, with the sword (Acts 12:2). This was so pleasing to the Jews that the King increased his efforts. He seized Peter also. Herod *delivered him to four squads of soldiers to keep him* (Acts 12:4). Each squad contained four soldiers. Throughout the night Peter was chained between two soldiers with a guard before the door to the prison.

The church offered constant prayer for Peter (Acts 12:5). We do not know what they said in their prayers. Because James was martyred, they probably prayed for Peter's protection and safety. In the middle of the night, an angel of the Lord came to Peter, and he was released from his chains. He followed the angel through the first and the second guard posts. *They came to the iron gate that leads to the city, which opened to them of its own accord; and they went out and went down one street,* (Acts 12:10). The church was having a prayer meeting in the house of Mary. Peter came and knocked on the door of the gate. Rhoda answered the knock. In her excitement she left the door closed and ran to tell everybody in the prayer meeting. *But they said to her, "You are beside yourself!" Yet she kept insisting that it was so. So they said, "It is his angel"* (Acts 12:15). So Peter continued to knock on the door. When the church discovered he was really there, *they were astonished* (Acts 12:16). Does God always answer our prayers beyond what we expect?

## Comprehension

Consider this fact; the lame man did not comprehend what was happening. This is evident in the passage. He did not grasp the power of God in the apostles. Did he even recognize them as apostles of Jesus? *Many wonders and signs were done through the apostles* (Acts 2:43). The lame man's request to Peter and John was for alms and not for Divine grace. which indicates his lack. After he received the miracle, he held on to Peter and John as if they were responsible (Acts 3:11). If God only moves in our lives to the level of our comprehension, we will experience no grace!

God is not limited to our knowledge! What an amazing truth! Isn't it significant? Childhood is the most likely age for an individual to experience Jesus. Those who have lived in fear and the darkness of paganism may hear the simple message of Jesus. Then they respond without understanding theology or doctrinal theories. God is not limited to their level of comprehension. Paul's cry was **to know the love of Christ which passes knowledge; that you may be filled with all the fullness of God** (Ephesians 3:19). Paul also spoke of love, which is the nature of God. **Love never fails. But whether there are prophecies, they will fail; whether there are tongues, they will cease; whether there is knowledge, it will vanish away** (1 Corinthians 13:8).

I am not pleading for ignorance. A simple statement is: despite the amount of your knowledge, Jesus is greater! He is always stretching us beyond what we know. He is always moving in our lives beyond the boundaries of our established knowledge. Dare we limit Him to our logic? "Theology" is always what you have contrived, reasoned, and thought. Jesus is bigger than your theology, your mind, and your limits. Do not forget what Paul taught us. He wrote to the Ephesians, **"Now to Him who is able to do exceedingly abundantly above all that we ask or think, according to the power that works in us,"** (Ephesians 3:20).

Think of the safety in this truth. The reality of being Spirit-sourced is to rest in the hands of God, infinite love. He cares more about you and your situation than you do. He knows the complete details of your circumstances. His knowledge of what needs to be done far surpasses yours. He knows the past, present, and future with all its influences. His power can make **all things work together for good to those who love God, to those who are called according to His purpose** (Romans 8:28). His motive is pure; His knowledge is complete; His power is adequate. What more could we desire? We can trust in Him above our own thinking, perception, or comprehension!

## Concentration

Consider this fact; the lame man did not have the proper focus. Luke states that the lame man *gave them his attention expecting to receive something from them* (Acts 3:5). The Greek word (para) translated *from* is different in this verse. The normal two Greek words (ek and apo) translated "from" focus on "a change of location." It is about movement. "Para" has a focus on "the source, author, or director." It means, "from whom something proceeds." The lame man was focused on Peter and John as the source of what he expected.

This focus is verified further in the story. After receiving the miracle, *he, leaping up, stood and walked and entered the temple with them — walking, leaping, and praising God* (Acts 3:8). Luke indicates the lame man's focus was Peter and John during this time. He actually *held on to Peter and John* (Acts 3:11). The temple crowd focused its attention on Peter and John. Peter was abhorred by the crowd's focus. *So when Peter saw it, he responded to the people: "Men of Israel, why do you marvel at this? Or why look so intently at us, as though by our own power or godliness we had made this man walk?"* (Acts 3:12). He proceeds to preach a sermon that focused on Jesus! The miracle resulted in the conversion of about five thousand men (Acts 4:4).

The heart of a demonic plot is "misdirection." If the devil can divert our focus from Jesus, the victory is won. The diversion is done in a variety of ways. Every habit is a diversion of our focus from Jesus to that habit. A person becomes consumed by drugs or alcohol. Pornography and lust become the deciding feature of someone's life.

**Part One:** The Event

However, the deed is not the problem, but the focus is. Even good deeds can become evil if the focus is wrong. We can be "church" focused instead of focused on Jesus. How well we are doing, our performance, or our success in ministry becomes the focus. We can focus on our ministry education, experiences, or traditions. While there is nothing wrong with any of these things, it is misdirection.

Legalism is a wrong focus. The moment one focuses on rules, Jesus is pushed into the background. "Causes" become misdirection. Abortion is unthinkable; it should be eliminated. However, when it becomes our focus, we have missed the correct answer; Jesus is the solution. Pornographic materials are not the real issue; the real problem is the lack of Jesus. Premarital sex is not the problem; we must focus on Jesus. We must never be "against" more than we are "for!" If any one of these problems mentioned were to be eliminated, the problems of our world would not be resolved. Jesus is our only chance.

Peter immediately speaks to the crowd and to the healed man. They must focus on Jesus as the only source. The idea of Peter as the source of this miracle is appalling to Peter, because it would be self-sourcing! Self-sourcing is often our focus. In fact, any focus other than Jesus is a product of self-sourcing. All the above deeds, each good and bad, can be self-sourced, and the moment this happens our focus is on us instead of Jesus.

Self-sourcing affects every problem in the lame man's life. He does not receive from Peter and John what he expected. He expected alms, but he received a miracle. Why did he not recognize the power of God moving through the lives of these men? They lived in the sourcing of the Spirit. Why would he settle for a few dollars when his life could be changed? He is so self-sourced that he is self-focused. He cannot see beyond what he can produce. For more than forty years he has been ***daily at the gate of the temple, which is called Beautiful*** sourcing a meager income. Begging is the best self-sourcing can produce.

Expectation | **Acts 3:5-6**

Why didn't he comprehend that the purpose of his life is way beyond begging for alms? How could he be satisfied with his daily routine at the Gate Beautiful? If you asked him, he would undoubtedly say, "Is this the best I can do in my condition?" He cannot comprehend anything beyond this state. Acceptance into the temple with all its worship is unthinkable to him. Having a meaningful life with family is a fantasy. A productive job fulfilling his life is beyond his reach. How can he possibly minister to anyone else? All his energy is demanded to supply his needs. He is self-sourced; therefore, he is self-focused.

The answer in his life is not just solving his physical problem with a miracle. He must see Jesus as the center and source of his life. If this does not happen, he will continue to be disabled in every way. Peter is desperate to call his attention to Jesus. Jesus must become the source of His life. Peter will preach in Solomon's Porch (Acts 3:11-26). His message will focus on Jesus. The healed man is by Peter's side listening intently. Peter is filled with the Spirit. The Spirit sources a message through him to the leaders of Israel (Acts 4:7-12). When he finishes even the leaders are focused on Jesus (Acts 4:13). ***The man who had been healed standing with them, they could say nothing against it*** (Acts 4:14). He heard again the message of Jesus. If he is not focused on Jesus, some greater disabling will occur in his life. Peter brings us all back to Jesus!

Acts 3:6

# DESTINATION

*Then Peter said, "Silver and gold I do not have, but what I do have I give you: In the name of Jesus Christ of Nazareth, rise up and walk" (Acts 3:6).*

You cannot ignore the consistent pattern of the early Church. They focused on the "name of Jesus." This pattern was prophesied through the Prophet Joel, **"And it shall come to pass that whoever calls on the name of the Lord shall be saved"** (Acts 2:22). This pattern is established in the beginning movements of the Spirit of Christ through Peter. The pattern is determined by how we approach and resolve the questions or difficulties of life. When guilt strikes the human heart, forgiveness can be experienced in only one way. **"Repent, and let every one of you be baptized in the name of Jesus Christ for the remission of sins; and you shall receive the gift of the Holy Spirit"** (Acts 2:38). When a lame man needs healing, there is only one way. **"In the name of Jesus Christ of Nazareth, rise up and walk"** (Acts 3:6). When a crowd needs clarification and spiritual guidance, one provision is enough. **"And His name, through faith in His name, has made this man strong, whom you see and know"** (Acts 3:16).

When the power of God is manifested, even the skeptics question: **"By what power or by what name have you done this?"** (Acts 4:7). When such skeptics accuse, there is only one adequate answer. **"Let it be known to you all, and to all the** *people of Israel, that by the name of Jesus Christ of Nazareth, whom you crucified, whom God raised from the dead, by Him this man stands here before you whole"* (Acts 4:10). In fact, the universal truth is very plain!

*"Nor is there salvation in any other, for there is no other name under heaven given among men by which we must be saved"* (Acts 4:12). The enemy of the Gospel has only one focus and defense. *"But so that it spreads no further among the people, let us severely threaten them that from now on they speak to no man in this name." So they called them and commanded them not to speak at all nor teach in the name of Jesus* (Acts 4:17-18). The heartbeat of the prayers of the early Church was for evangelism. They prayed that it *"may be done through the name of Your holy Servant Jesus"* (Acts 4:30).

The number of Christian songs highlighting the "name of Jesus" is astounding. *"There is a name I love to sing, I love to tell its worth. It sounds like music in my ears; the sweetest name on earth! Oh, how I love Jesus." "Jesus, Jesus, Jesus, there's just something about that name!" "All hail the power of Jesus' name!"* But His name is more than a poetic form or a sentimental reference. His name is not a buzzword to be used as a magic formula. It is not to be treated as a slogan or bumper sticker. The name is contained in the person of Jesus Himself! You cannot reference His name without referencing Him. His name is never separated from His person.

The seriousness of cursing is because of the relationship of His name to His person. You cannot say, "I did not mean anything by it; it is just a word." The name of Jesus is never just a word. If the word you use in cursing doesn't mean anything, please use another word. When you swear, say, "finger" or "toe." You might say, "bridge" or "meat." No one ever uses meaningless words. When cursing, they say, "Jesus." It means something! If it means something in cursing, certainly the name means something in prayer.

When a lame man is in need, will a magic chant be the answer? Could you without embarrassment offer him a religious formula to be spoken? Will a religious cliché work? Why would you not go to the source of spiritual power to meet the need, "the name of Jesus?" No wonder Peter said, **"Silver and gold I do not have, but what I do have I give you: In the name of Jesus Christ of Nazareth, rise up and walk"** (Acts 3:6). Peter was a Spirit-sourced man. He did not live in the sphere of **"Silver and gold."** His resource was not located in physical materialism. The Spirit of God was birthed in him. He begins to describe such a state for us.

## Destination

If you are going to minister to me, I want to know where you are taking me. If you place your arm around me to lift me, where will I be placed? Think of the contrast in the passage between those who have helped this lame man. The contrast is plainly stated. He has been lame for more than forty years (Acts 4:22); it started at his birth. In describing this lame man, Luke writes: **And a certain man lame from his mother's womb** (Acts 3:2). The lame man was carried daily to the Gate Beautiful at the temple. Who was responsible for such a kind gesture? Did his parents perform this helpful act until they were physically unable to help him? Have some close relatives or friends now taken their place? The best they could offer him was to carry him to the temple. They daily placed him at the gate so he could beg for his life's support.

Contrast those friends with the Spirit-sourced men. They reach down and take **him by the right hand and lift him up** (Acts 3:7). They will not place him by the temple to beg. He will be put into a new place; it is Jesus! Jesus is the final resting place. This is where every aspect of our lives must come. Victory and healing are found here.

Notice the three important ingredients regarding the new dwelling place.

LOCATION — You can't misinterpret the intent of Peter's statement: *"In the name of Jesus Christ of Nazareth, rise up and walk"* (Acts 3:6). Jesus is the new location for the lame man! The emphasis or focus in these beginning chapters of the Book of Acts amazes me. The focus is on our need to change locations. Three to five thousand Jews of the Dispersion are absolutely captured and amazed by the coming of the Holy Spirit. The Holy Spirit moves upon Peter to bring revelation to them. His final instruction to them is: *"Be saved from this perverse generation"* (Acts 2:40). The emphasis is a call to be removed from one location and be placed in another. They are to be subtracted from one group and added to another group.

<u>The Message</u> translates this statement as: *"Get out while you can; get out of this sick and stupid culture!"* (from THE MESSAGE: The Bible in Contemporary Language © 2002 by Eugene H. Peterson. All rights reserved.) Their Jewish traditions and culture led them to crucify Christ. They blindly follow their leaders. They must find a new location. The location is not physical, but a spiritual reality. It will take repentance (giving up a former thought to embrace a new thought). The physical representation of this is baptism. Embracing a new thought (Jesus) will be displayed in *"be baptized in the name of Jesus Christ"* (Acts 2:38). He will be their new location. Luke proclaims that **the Lord added to the church daily those who were being saved** (Acts 2:47).

Now a lame man who dwells in one place for more than forty years is to be relocated to a new place. He has never gone to the temple, only laid at its gate. Now he will run through the porches; he will join the praise gathering at Solomon's porch (Acts 3:11). He will see the world from a new height, his full standing capacity. No longer will he be groveling in the dust as he crawls from place to place. *So he, leaping up, stood and*

**Part One:** The Event

*walked and entered the temple with them — walking, leaping, and praising God* (Acts 3:8).

All of these things are mere benefits of his new location. His new location is Jesus. He has found all this *in the name of Jesus Christ of Nazareth*! Paul's declaration of this truth is forceful. More than two hundred times in the New Testament the phrase *"in Christ"* is proposed. Paul uses it eight times in Galatians. Ephesians thunders its truth for thirty-four times. In Colossians, he manifests it another eighteen times. It becomes the bumper sticker slogan of the Christian faith. This is our new location; we are *"in Christ!"*

The power of God worked in Christ to raise Him from the dead. It did not give Him life among the dead, but *seated Him at His right hand in the heavenly places,* (Ephesians 1:20). We can only imagine what a place in the *heavenly places* will be like. Paul tells us that *it is far above all principality and power and might and dominion, and every name that is named, not only in this age but also in that which is to come* (Ephesians 1:21). If you marvel at that, think on this. You and I are dead in our sins. The same power of God that raised Jesus *made us alive together with Christ (by grace you have been saved), and raised us up together, and made us sit together in the heavenly places in Christ Jesus,* (Ephesians 2:5-6).

We are lame men who have found a new location *in the name of Jesus Christ of Nazareth*. The new location is a place of leaping, walking, running, and praising God, and it is a place of victory, shouting, and adoration. A place described as "up." A place above all that would tear us down, a place of safety and security. This place is a new location; it is Jesus!

**LOCKED LOCATION** is the second ingredient of our new location. We are placed *"in"* the name of Jesus. This is a translation of the Greek word "en." The word is a primary preposition denoting a fixed position in place, time, or state. It expresses primarily the idea of resting. The Greek word (eis) translated "into" indicates motion. The Greek word (ek or apo) translated "from" indicates motion. The Greek word "en" is between "into" and "from," and it means remaining in place.

"In" is the most frequently used preposition in the Greek language. This preposition is used around two thousand seven hundred times. This means there are a variety of ways it is used. The Greek word (onoma) translated *name* is in the dative case, and it has two different usages that may apply. The "instrumental dative" indicates how the verb's action takes place. It corresponds to the English prepositions "with" or "by." You can easily see that usage in our text. The means or instrument by which the lame man will ***rise up and walk*** will be ***Jesus Christ of Nazareth***.

This is verified by Peter's message to the great crowd on Solomon's porch in the temple. The lame man held on to Peter and John, attracting a crowd. The crowd was ***greatly amazed***. It appears the crowd attributes the miracle to Peter and John. Peter is horrified and proclaims, ***"Or why look so intently at us, as though by our own power or godliness we had made this man walk?"*** (Acts 3:12). Peter will not tolerate anyone thinking he is the instrument of this miracle. He further explains, ***"And His name, through faith in His name, has made this man strong, whom you see and know. Yes, the faith which comes through Him has given him this perfect soundness in the presence of you all"*** (Acts 3:16).

Jesus must be recognized as the sole instrument for the need of our lives. We must never add Jesus to a list of answers. He is not one among many other solutions. We cannot isolate Him to certain categories in problem areas. How easy it is to believe He is the answer to my eternal salvation, but He is not adequate to care for my finances. Certainly Jesus can forgive my sins, but can He solve the conflict in my home. Perhaps Jesus can control the planets and stars, but can He control my temper. The Gospel message is very simple. ***Jesus Christ of Nazareth*** is the sole instrument or means for the solution of every need of

### Part One: The Event

the human life! You and I need to look nowhere else.

Another usage of the dative case is the "locative dative." It indicates the place or when the verb's action occurs. It corresponds to the English prepositions "in," "at," or "on." ***Jesus Christ of Nazareth*** is the location in which the lame man will ***rise up and walk***. This is indicated by Peter's statement to the lame man, ***"Silver and gold I do not have, but what I do have I give you:"*** (Acts 3:6). In a previous study we highlighted the two locations or realms proposed in this statement. ***Silver and gold*** represent the realm of materialism. The Greek word (huparcho) translated ***I have*** expresses "to be" or "to exist." Peter informs the begging lame man that he does not dwell in or have access to the power of materialism. But there is a realm in which he does live. He is a Spirit-sourced man. He dwells in the location of ***Jesus Christ of Nazareth***. He is possessed by and possesses this realm. The sourcing of the Spirit of Jesus will supply what he needs. Peter refers to this location as ***what I do have I give you***. The Greek word (echo) is translated ***I do have***. The word selection that Peter uses to express "having" is very significant. This Greek word (echo) is used for a woman having a baby in her womb.

The miracle verifies the change in a location. This lame man is not allowed into the temple. He knows nothing of the fellowship of worship. He never experiences the wonder of the sacrificial lamb, prayers or singing. His existence is from the lowly location of the ground with all its limitations. Now he is relocated. He leaps and runs through the temple. He dwells in a new location of praise. He dwells in ***Jesus Christ of Nazareth***.

This is our fixed location. This is not a place we visit; it is not a place to come to fulfill the religious obligations of our lives. This is not just a haven when the storms of life threaten us. This is the "permanent," "never leave," "always stay," location for our lives. This dwelling place is as the body is to the heart. The heart finds purpose, value, and safety in continuously dwelling in the body. To leave the body is certainly death. Jesus is my place.

Destination | **Acts 3:6**

**LINCHPIN LOCATION** is the third ingredient of this new location. A linchpin is the pin passed through the end of an axle to keep a wheel in position. It is a person or thing vital to an enterprise or organization may be considered a linchpin. The piece of evidence around which an entire criminal court case revolves may also be considered a linchpin. Without the linchpin everything falls apart.

*"Jesus Christ of Nazareth"* is the linchpin and without Him it will not happen. This is not a vacation spot. It is the only place. This is a deal-breaker. If you do not embrace Jesus, there is no solution for the need of your life. The answer to the need of the lame man is found in Jesus.

Peter is very strong on this matter. In speaking to three to five thousand Jews of the Dispersion, he leaves no room for options. They must **"Repent, and let every one of you be baptized in the name of Jesus Christ for the remission of sins; and you shall receive the gift of the Holy Spirit"** (Acts 2:38). The message Peter preached in the temple to the crowd surrounding the once lame beggar was about Jesus. The leaders of Israel were extremely upset because **they taught the people and preached in Jesus the resurrection from the dead** (Acts 4:2).

The apostles were arrested and placed before the leaders for examination. The leaders asked this question. **"By what power or by what name have you done this?"** (Acts 4:7). Peter's unrelenting answer was, **"let it be known to you all, and to all the people of Israel, that by the name of Jesus Christ of Nazareth, whom you crucified, whom God raised from the dead, by Him this man stands here before you whole"** (Acts 4:10). The leaders of Israel were hindered in their desire to punish the apostles. They finally threatened them **not to speak at all nor teach in the name of Jesus** (Acts 4:18).

Jesus is the only solution. Anything added to Him is a deal-breaker. Adding anything undermines the very solution we seek. There is nothing beyond Him. He is our only location. Neither

**Part One:** The Event

a backup lane nor second agenda exists. We are confronted with Jesus alone!

Acts 3:6

# DISTINCTION

*Then Peter said, "Silver and gold I do not have, but what I do have I give you: In the name of Jesus Christ of Nazareth, rise up and walk" (Acts 3:6).*

Some Bible scholars speak of "the personalization of the Bible." They refer to the quiet way in which the Bible presents "people." The biblical writers do not see people as a mass, as a fraction of a mass, or as cases for study, but as people. This view is verified by their "name!" The proper name in the Bible is the symbol of the person. When a person is addressed by name, they are given significance, meaning, dignity, and worth.

In the Bible, a name is not just a label but part of the personality of the one who bears it. Various rites were used to find names for children. Often new names were given to children as their personalities were revealed. The name carries will and power. The name conjures up the person. In fact, there is no way to separate the name from the person.

If the preceding facts are true for humanity, it must be true for God. No wonder God demands, **"You shall not take the name of the Lord your God in vain, for the Lord will not hold him guiltless who takes His name in vain"** (Exodus 20:7). In the Ten Commandments, this command ranks number three. The Hebrew word (lashaaw) translated *in vain* always refers to "emptiness or vanity." It designates anything that insubstantial, unreal, or worthless, either materially or morally. Speaking the name of God in a moment when one is unaware of the greatness of His person is breaking this commandment. "Oh, my God!" is a favorite phrase of many people. In a moment when they have no desire for His presence, they speak this name. If you confront them, they reply, "I didn't mean anything by it." This reply validates the point! Don't speak His name unless you mean something by it!

The devil aggressively campaigns against this name, which verifies this truth. He wants everyone in his kingdom to belittle, treat as worthless, and take this name *in vain*. A man smashes his thumb with a hammer; he yells, "Jesus Christ." Why did he connect a smashed thumb with the Redeemer of the world? How did God, who is love, merciful, and always strengthens and helps, become connected to a smashed thumb? Is this not belittling, lowering, and speaking His name in vain? Why not say, "rock," "chair," or "use your friend's name?" Is this not a demonic campaign against the person of God?

If so, the opposite must also be true! Peter comes to a lame beggar at the Gate Beautiful. He focuses entirely on this man; he demands that this man give him his attention as well (Acts 3:4). In this moment Peter invokes the power of the Name (the Person) of Jesus. He said, **"In the name of Jesus Christ of Nazareth, rise up and walk"** (Acts 3:6). All the wonder in the person of Jesus is now focused on this man.

In our previous study, we investigated "The Destination." The lame beggar found a new location. He went from crouching on a mat to standing erect. He moved from begging the worshippers outside the temple to a worshipper. However, all these things were benefits of his new location in Jesus! We are to dwell in this new location, **the name of Jesus Christ of Nazareth**. Everything we need is in Him. A need to look elsewhere does not exist. In our present study we are investigating "The Distinction."

Distinction | **Acts 3:6**

# Linkage
(Reference)

Many times Peter and John have gone through the Gate Beautiful into the temple. They passed this lame beggar before without confrontation. This time is radically different. The difference is the Spirit-sourcing in Peter and John. God decided it was time to do something about this lame man. Peter and John stop right in front of the beggar and give him their full attention. They demand his full attention as well. Peter boldly declares his absence from materialistic domination. The material realm is not the sphere in which he lives; rather, he possesses has ***Jesus Christ of Nazareth***. This possession is only possible because Jesus gives Himself to us. In the dynamics of this relationship, that Peter can offer to the lame man everything found ***"In the name!"***

You could make a strong case for this statement being a formula. Peter challenged the Jews of the Dispersion to ***be baptized in the name of Jesus Christ*** (Acts 2:38). Peter clarified the source of the miracle to the crowd gathered at the temple. He said, ***"And His name, through faith in His name, has made this man strong,"*** (Acts 3:16a). Peter immediately ties this name to the person of Jesus. He continues, ***"Yes, the faith which comes through Him has given him this perfect soundness in the presence of you all"*** (Acts 3:16b). Even "faith in His name" comes from the person of Jesus. His name and His person are inseparable.

Throughout the years, theologians have given a variety of opinions at what stimulated this formula to be so popular. The statement was a favorite in baptism (Acts 2:38), miracles (Acts 3:6), teaching (Acts 4:18), preaching (Acts 9:27), assembling of the church (1 Corinthians 5:4), salvation (1 Corinthians 6:11), thanksgiving (Ephesians 5:20), deeds (Colossians 3:17), anointing with oil (James 5:14), and believing (1 John 5:13).

**Part One:** The Event

Some propose this formula comes from "the language of money transfers." During the Hellenistic era, this formula was used. *In the name* would express a "transfer" from one account to another. An individual in baptism is transferred to the Lord's account; therefore, he becomes God's possession.

Other scholars trace this formula to the instruction of the rabbi. The phrase was used in relation to the recipient of a sacrifice; therefore, it referred to dedication. A sacrifice would be dedicated in the name of a person. Jesus is our sacrifice; He is dedicated to our name. We can claim His sacrifice as ours because it belongs to us. Jesus makes a sacrifice in His name dedicated to us. All the benefits of this sacrifice become ours!

Other scholars think the phrase, ***"In the name of Jesus Christ,"*** constitutes the event of salvation through Christ. When this statement is fully experienced in one's life everything present in the person of Jesus becomes ours. The lame beggar experienced much more than physical healing. If he remained spiritually the same, he would never have stayed with the apostles. His self-sourced attitude of continually using others for his own benefit was changed. He became Spirit-sourced.

Each of these ideas concludes in experiencing Jesus. We find everything we need in Jesus. His name is not a magic formula, a religious token, or a theology. ***In His name*** does not invite us to join a church movement. The phrase is not an additional influence in our lives. His name is not another idea to add to our list of philosophies. Well, I am a Catholic; I am a Baptist; I am a Methodist. These are unimportant statements compared to His name. Being an Indian, Latino, African American, or a Caucasian is not an element in the embrace of His person. I have been in prison; I am a murderer, sex offender, a Pharisee, a scribe, or a Bible college graduate. It does not matter. Jesus is all that matters. You must embrace His name, the fullness of His person.

The story of the New Testament is about the Kingdom of God. The Kingdom came to Israel, and was not a new political

Distinction | **Acts 3:6**

system, a correction of religious practices, or a reform to an old system. Jesus was the Kingdom. The woman who had an issue of blood was desperate to touch the hem of His person (Matthew 9:21). The cry of the blind man addressed Jesus whom they followed (Matthew 9:27). Matthew, a tax collector, was challenged by Jesus to ***"Follow Me!"*** (Matthew 9:9). The clear-cut cause of the miracle of the lame beggar is Jesus.

## Love Linkage
(Relationship)

The Greek word (onoma) translated ***name*** highlights the beginning of this closing sentence (Acts 3:6). This word placement is the author's method of placing great importance on it. **Strong's Greek Hebrew Definitions** proposes an interesting insight. He says, "Onoma is from a presumed derivative of the base of 'ginosko.'" "Ginosko" is one of four Greek words translated "to know." "Onoma" is a relational term, and is used for the most intimate relationship in marriage (Matthew 1:25). It does not focus on data or information, but on intimacy. It means to know something through experience. This idea seems to be interwoven in the usage of "onoma."

For instance, the ***name*** of a person is intimately related to their person. In the New Testament it is never just a title, but it establishes a relational link between the name and the person. This link is understandable in our culture. When an individual speaks about a "chair," he is not saying a formula or a term. A direct reference and link to an object exists. The title is never separated from the object, and this is certainly true with "Jesus!" The moment I mention His name, His person is highlighted. I cannot use His name without His person being involved. Often in prayer, we desire to use His name without His person. This approach would enable us to get what we desire without His

**Part One:** The Event

involvement or control. This can never be accomplished. A direct relationship between the name of Jesus and His person exists.

The blessings and qualities of the person of Jesus are implied in the mention of His name. The name of Jesus and His Person are so related that they become identical. All the qualities in His Person are implied by using His name. To notice the identification Peter included with the name is important. He says, "**In the name of Jesus Christ of Nazareth**" (Acts 3:6). No misunderstanding should exist about the Jesus upon whom we call. Far too often, we manufacture our own Jesus. We ascribe qualities and conditions that are not present. In Peter's statement, he verifies the Jesus to whom he calls. It is interesting to trace the name of Jesus through the sermons Peter preaches to the Jews. He specifically describes in detail the person to whom he refers. He does this again it this passage. Jesus is the One they crucified; Jesus is the One God raised from the dead. Jesus is from Nazareth. No other can be **Jesus Christ of Nazareth**. As the church grows and is farther away from the crucifixion event, there will be a tendency to lose sight of **Jesus Christ of Nazareth**. He may come dressed in a suit and tie conducting the great business of redemption. He may come dressed in a Santa Claus' suit and pass out gifts to the children. He may become a gigantic rabbit's foot or a genie in a religious bottle. He may take the form of the Old Testament law. All of these views of Him twist our relationship with Him. It destroys our relationship with the real Jesus. All that can be found in Him, **in the name of Jesus Christ of Nazareth**, is missing.

In the Old Testament, the name of God could not be pronounced. God was holy and far removed from mankind. His name could not be formed on the profane lips of even the high priest. When reading the Holy Scriptures, God's name was set aside for a substitute word such as "Lord" or "heaven." This substitution was an expression of the relationship between God and humanity. Only a few men people had direct contact with God. The judges and prophets of the Old Testament at various times interacted with Him. Oh, the New Covenant brought amazing changes. These changes are found in Jesus. He brought us into intimacy with God. Not just a few select people, but each one can know God. Every person speaks the name of Jesus. Not only do we freely speak His name, but He also gives us His new name. In the Book of Revelation, Jesus said to the church in Philadelphia, *"He who overcomes, I will make him a pillar in the temple of My God, and he shall go out no more. I will write on him the name of My God and the name of the city of My God, the New Jerusalem, which comes down out of heaven from My God. And I will write on him My new name"* (Revelation 3:12). This passage is a statement of relationship. To know the name is to know the Person!

## Liaison Linkage
### (Reconciliation)

A liaison communicates, coordinates, or facilitates a close working relationship between individuals or organizations. Is this not the person of Jesus? We can find reconciliation *in the name of Jesus Christ of Nazareth*! A genuine mediator with opposing parties attempts to bring reconciliation. If reconciliation is to occur, parties must compromise and change their position. However, the New Testament reconciliation is different. God is never reconciled to us. He does not make compromises or adjustments to include us. The New Testament message is clear: *Now all things are of God, who has reconciled us to Himself through Jesus Christ, and has given us the ministry of reconciliation, that is, that God was in Christ reconciling the world to Himself,* (2 Corinthians 5:18-19). The sin of mankind was not an item God could dismiss. Humanity was so radically changed in their nature that there could be no relationship between God and mankind. God did not change; God made it possible for

**Part One:** The Event

mankind to change! This change happens in mankind *in the name of Jesus Christ of Nazareth*. God reconciled the world to Himself through Jesus. We can crawl into the presence of God on the coattails of Jesus. We can come boldly into the throne room of God through Jesus. He reconciled us!

Peter, a Spirit-sourced man, confronts a lame beggar. This beggar never worships in the temple. God dwells in the Holy of Holies, a short distance from this man's begging place. He has no contact with his Creator. His life is consumed with materialism. All his energy is focused on his survival. This man is trapped in his situation. He cannot start reconciliation with God. But God cannot reconcile this man to Himself as he is. What can be done? Jesus is the answer. God became man!

Jesus is Peter's message to the lame beggar. *In the name of Jesus Christ of Nazareth,* God made the way out. This man can enter into the presence of God; in fact, he can be filled with God. Everything holding him is released, and he is free. He is reconciled to God. All this is found *in the name* (the person) *of Jesus Christ of Nazareth.*

God does not accept you as you are. You cannot know Him in your present position. *In the name of Jesus Christ of Nazareth, rise up and walk.* Jesus comes to take you by the hand and bring you to where you need to be. *In the name* is the new location. Do not stay where you are!

# Acts 3:6

# DESCRIPTION

*Then Peter said, "Silver and gold I do not have, but what I do have I give you: In the name of Jesus Christ of Nazareth, rise up and walk" (Acts 3:6).*

One of the fears in analyzing any passage is to be so enamored with the details that the truth is neglected. This must not happen with our passage. The truth spoken by Peter to the lame beggar builds as phrase is added to phrase. He begins with what he does *not have*, a translation of the Greek word "huparcho." It highlights the idea of existing or being within a set of circumstances. It also promotes the idea of ruling or being first. Peter does not suggest that money is not available for the beggar. He boldly declares that he does not live in the controlling realm of "things." What he does **have** (echo) is more significant? This Greek word (echo) expresses possession as a woman with a child in her womb, which influences everything about her life. Peter is not controlled by the realm of materialism, but has the wonder of the influencing, life-giving Spirit of Jesus!

Because Peter is a spirit-sourced man, he can invite the lame beggar to move to a new location, DESTINATION. He can now live **in the name of Jesus Christ of Nazareth**. Jesus is the dwelling place. The DISTINCTION of the new location gives us the exact position. The distinction is **in the name**!

However, the difficulty is that the "name" becomes generic.

**Part One:** The Event

To speak to God is acceptable because. "God" fits into every world religion. In our weekly Kiwanis Club meetings, we participate regularly in three important items. We normally sing a song focused on the United States of America. We pledge allegiance to the flag of our country. We also pray. In one such meeting, I was asked to offer the prayer. My prayer addressed Jesus, praised Jesus, requested Jesus, and ended in Jesus' name. In sincerity one member raised a question about my prayer. If there had been Muslim Kiwanis members present, would they have been offended? The concern raised was not about the offense of prayer. Asking God to bless our country was not offensive. Jesus was the concern! The problem with Jesus is that He is never generic.

The Jews in the context of our passage found the name of Jesus offensive. No offense is found in God. Even the proposal of a Messiah being promised by this

God is not offensive. The problem is with Jesus as the Messiah! *"These are the days of Elijah"* can be sung in evangelical and Jewish services, without offense. The Native American is not averse to the Great Spirit of the sky. Meditating on God does not upset the meditation techniques of the Eastern Religions. Praying to God for our troops is acceptable to all on Memorial Day. As the dead are memorialized and the living are threatened daily are remembered, no one objects to a prayer being offered to God. The saved and unsaved, the godly, and the ungodly will stand tall with closed eyes in reverence for God.

Social actions are a blessing to all. All decent people embrace feeding the hungry, standing against abortion, and fighting pornography. No one rejects programs for the children. Those concerned about family embrace Easter egg hunts, Christmas parties with a visit from Santa Claus, and Fall Harvest Trick or Treat. The problem is with Jesus. He is troublesome. No one is against scavenger hunts, free pizza, and games for the young people. The problem is Jesus.

One of our associates had the privilege of meeting for many

Description | **Acts 3:6**

hours with a retired Christian and his pastor son in Hawaii. The father was one of the original three men who started the twelve-step program embraced by our court system. Recovery programs are in abundance based on this one program. One of the twelve steps calls for the recognition of a higher power. People who recognize their helplessness in addictions of every kind are not threatened by calling on a higher power. But this elderly man declares that in the original twelve-step program Jesus is the higher power. Through the years it has changed from Jesus to the higher power. A higher power is acceptable to many more people than acknowledging Jesus.

You will note in our passage, Peter is not satisfied with a generic God. He declares the answer to the need of the lame beggar is *in the name of Jesus Christ of Nazareth*. This declaration eliminates any confusion about his reference. Jesus is the One crucified with His title attached to the cross. *Now Pilate wrote a title and put it on the cross. And the writing was: JESUS OF NAZARETH, THE KING OF THE JEWS* (John 19:19). Peter declared Jesus repeatedly. In his sermon to explain Pentecost, he boldly declared, *"Men of Israel, hear these words: Jesus of Nazareth, a Man"* (Acts 2:22). In the same message he confronted the Jews of the Dispersion when he said, *"Therefore let all the house of Israel know assuredly that God has made this Jesus, whom you crucified, both Lord and Christ"* (Acts 2:36). This reference highlights one person. He does the same confrontation with the Jews gathered at Solomon's porch. He cries, *The God of Abraham, Isaac, and Jacob, the God of our fathers, glorified His Servant Jesus, whom you delivered up and denied in the presence of Pilate, when he was determined to let Him go"* (Acts 3:13). When interrogated by the leaders of Israel after being placed in prison, Peter refuses to soften the confrontation. He said, *"Let it be known to you all, and to all the people of Israel, that by the name of Jesus Christ of Nazareth, whom you crucified, whom God raised from the dead, by Him this man stands here before you whole"* (Acts 4:10). He is relentless in his clarity about Jesus.

Will you join me in a consideration of the three ingredients of this description?

## Logos

His identification is not a new term for us. One of the consistent references to **Jesus Christ of Nazareth** is the **Word**. *In the beginning was the Word, and the Word was with God, and the Word was God* (John 1:1). *And the Word became flesh and dwelt among us, and we beheld His glory, the glory as of the only begotten of the Father, full of grace and truth* (John 1:14). The **Word** is a translation for the Greek word "logos." It refers to the idea or rational thinking of the mind. In other words, Jesus Christ is the idea that God has in His mind about us. God's dream for mankind is fulfilled and manifested in Jesus.

The name **Jesus** is used nine hundred and nineteen times in the New Testament. Nine hundred and thirteen times the reference is to **Jesus Christ of Nazareth**. Six times this name refers to other people. In Jesus' culture this name was frequently used; therefore, it was necessary for the New Testament writers to distinguish the exact individual. In the Old Testament the name of God was so sacred it could not be spoken. Death by stoning was the penalty for violating this law. Now God takes on flesh and becomes one of us. He takes on our name and is identified with us! Jesus is a common name that everyone speaks. Seventeen times in the New Testament He is identified as **Jesus of Nazareth**. He must be identified and distinguished from all others.

The name **Christ** is directly connected to the Old Testament. It comes from the Greek word "Christos" meaning "to smear or anoint." The Hebrew word "messiah" has the equivalent meaning.

In the noun form it means "the anointed one." Some argument among biblical scholars exists about using this term. Is it a "name" or a "title?" Regardless, Jesus is the Man who is selected by God to establish the Kingdom of God. He will blaze a trail for us into this Kingdom. He is the author of salvation. *Jesus Christ of Nazareth* is the human being who is the idea God has for all humanity. He is the first One to be what we are destined to be. He is God who set aside all He HAD as God to become all He wanted us to be. The very nature of being this "idea" brought about an open door for us. Such terms as *"captain of their salvation"* (Hebrews 2:10), and *"He is not ashamed to call them brethren,"* (Hebrews 2:11) give expression to the "Logos." He is "the anointed One."

    The Father made Him King of the Kingdom. He is not King of the Kingdom because He is God; He has this position because He is the first man to be sourced by God. The Kingdom is established through Him. He has the authority to describe the nature of the Kingdom as presented in the Sermon on the Mount (Matthew 5, 6, and 7). In Him we experience the blessings of the Kingdom (Ephesians 1:3). We are chosen by God in Him to be a part of the Kingdom (Ephesians 1:4). In Him we become acceptable people in the Kingdom (Ephesians 1:6).

    During His time before Pilate, the Jews accused Jesus of claiming to be the King of the Jews. This accusation placed Him in rebellion against the Roman Empire. Pilate quizzed Jesus,

    *"Are You the King of the Jews?"* (John 18:33). Jesus questioned his sincerity. Was this his question or was it the question of the Jewish leaders? Pilate quickly reported that he was not a Jew. Jesus answered, *"My kingdom is not of this world. If My kingdom were of this world, My servants would fight, so that I should not be delivered to the Jews; but now My kingdom is not from here"* (John 18:36). Pilate continued to question Him, *"Are You a king then?"* Jesus answered, *"You say rightly that I am a king. For this cause I was born, and for this cause I have come into the world,"* (John 18:37). He is *Jesus Christ of Nazareth*.

Part One: The Event

## Logo Logos

A logo is a symbol which represents an organization, product, or movement. It comes from the Greek word "logos." When developing a logo, one wants to take the heart of the organization or product and symbolize it. Everything at the core should be found in the logo. Jesus is the logo of Christianity. Everything found in the heart of Christianity is Jesus. If it is not found in Him, it is not included in Christianity. Jesus sets the perimeters. You must not establish a theology and shape Jesus according to your ideas. Our theology must come from Him. You must not allow your desired way of life decide your beliefs. Jesus must decide your beliefs. Do not allow your attitude to be shaped by your circumstances or disappointments; Jesus must be the deciding element. He decides who we are!

Jesus is the Word, the Logos. He is the manifested idea in the mind of God concerning out identities. He is the example of what God dreamed for us. He is the logo, and any deviation from His person destroys God's dream of God for us. Paul cries, ***"And you are complete in Him,"*** (Colossians 2:10). The boundaries for our existence are Jesus. The Law was the boundary in the Old Covenant. The provision of God, the fulfillment of His dream for us, was found within this boundary. Mankind could not earn this provision by keeping the law. We were to abide within the boundaries of the law to experience God's provision. The difficulty is humanity was incapable of remaining within those restrictions. In the New Covenant, God graciously changed the boundary of His provision. The boundary is Jesus. We experience the God's provision in the fullness of Jesus.

But we must progress beyond thinking that Jesus is someone to be like. Christ likeness is not us imitating Him. Christ-likeness is a state of being. We possess the same Source He has. What is present in Him is now present in us. We are filled with the same

Spirit. We look like Him, act like Him, and think like Him. We live in the boundaries of His Spirit. He is our logo!

Peter made this statement in our text. *"In the name of Jesus Christ of Nazareth, rise up and walk"* (Acts 3:6). The lame beggar comes into a new location. The *name* cannot be separated from the person. *Jesus Christ* is the person. Within the boundaries of this Person, the lame beggar will *rise up and walk*. His wholeness is found in this Person. Any attempt to step outside this Person results in lameness again. Jesus must be his existence. A message to our lives Jesus is our new location. We must abide in Him as the branch abides in the vine (John 15). He must be our focus because there is nothing for us outside of Him.

## Literal Logo Logos

*Jesus Christ* is the "logos." He is the idea of God manifested among us. He is the rational thought of God concerning all mankind. The source of the life of God in Jesus is now to be in us. Thus, Jesus is the "logo" of all Christianity. Relationship with Him establishes the boundaries of my existence. I can *rise up and walk* in Him. I am lame and begging when I am outside of Him. Everything in Him can now be in me as I am in Him. Peter offers this to the lame man.

But be assured, this relationship is not an emotional feeling, sentimentality, and certainly not a doctrine open for discussion or disagreement. Nor is it a proposal to come together to work on a relationship, or an investigation of a new philosophy or idea. There is something literal about the relationship. Peter makes this plain by telling the lame beggar that his is found *"in the name of Jesus Christ of Nazareth."* This proclamation distinguishes Jesus from all other personalities. It identifies Him! He is not Jesus Christ of Heaven living a heavenly life. He is not Jesus Christ of the mystical world living beyond the physical realm. He is not

**Part One:** The Event

Jesus Christ of the philosophical thought who does not struggle with body drives. NO, He is Jesus **Christ of Nazareth.** He lives on my streets; He works at my job; He experiences my temptations.

If He is Jesus Christ of Heaven, I will feel more at ease because that enables me to idealize Him. He becomes the goal towards which I strive. His way of life is my example as I stumble through life. Phrases like "I am trying" and "I am doing my best" symbolize my attempt. I can then tolerate failure and compromise because I am not from "heaven" as He is. After all, I live in an imperfect world.

But ***Jesus Christ of Nazareth*** changes everything! He was from my world; He lived with my limitations; He knew my pressures and heartaches. He was sourced by the Spirit of God and fulfilled the dreams in the mind of God. He was the idea (logos) of what God intended for all mankind. My way of life must match His after I am sourced with the same Spirit of God. I am in Him; everything found in Him is now mine. I can forgive like He forgave; I can love like He loved. His attitude can be mine. As the Spirit of God fills and sources Him, so I can be filled and sourced. I dare not settle for anything less and be called Christian.

# Acts 3:6

# DETERMINATION

*Then Peter said, "Silver and gold I do not have, but what I do have I give you: In the name of Jesus Christ of Nazareth, rise up and walk" (Acts 3:6).*

One of the exciting elements about the story of the lame beggar is the continued commentary on the results of the miracle. Many accounts of people receiving miracles in the Gospels exist; however, we never hear from or see them again. How did God use them in ministry? What affect did they have in the community? Was it just a physical miracle or did they fall in love with Jesus? These kinds of questions express our concern.

We have the same kind of concern for each other in the church. A person begins attending our services. They show interest in religious things. They may come to an altar of prayer. Our concern is long range. What will be the effect of this in six months? Was this just immediate relief for a present problem? Will we see changes in their way of life? How does one measure the spiritual success of an encounter with Jesus?

The lame beggar encounters Jesus through the Apostles. The encounter is much deeper than a simple medical correction. The physical aspect of the miracle is exciting and a large attraction. **So he, leaping up, stood and walked and entered the temple with them — walking, leaping, and praising God. And all the people saw him walking and praising God** (Acts 3:8). No one

#### Part One: The Event

plays down or belittles such a miracle. But what does this mean long range? Is this a "fix" of just a physical problem allowing a selfish way of life to continue on an increased level? Evidently the answer is "No!" He **entered the temple with them**. As they spent time in the temple area, **the lame man who was healed held on to Peter and John** (Acts 3:11). In fact, Peter is so sure of the change in the beggar's life that he refers to him throughout his message to the crowd that has gathered. He speaks twice to **this man** (Acts 3:12, 16). The leaders place the apostles in jail and the morning after interrogate them about **what power or by what name** they accomplished the miracle. Peter again refers directly to the healed beggar who stills stands with them (Acts 4:10). His presence sways the leaders' decision about the apostles. Luke writes, **"And seeing the man who had been healed standing with them, they could say nothing against it"** (Acts 4:14).

In our passage (Acts 3:6), Luke, a medical doctor, gives us insight into the physical miracle but also into the spiritual effect. The anklebones and feet of the lame beggar received strength and this outcome is worthy of applause. It had a large effect on the temple crowd. But Jesus never isolates His presence to just the physical correction in our lives. He meets the needs of the whole person or He will not meet any needs. Don't think for a moment you and I can segment His touch on our lives to one area. In the first proposition of Peter to the lame beggar, the elements of the entire life are highlighted. He said, **"In the name of Jesus Christ of Nazareth, rise up and walk"** (Acts 3:6).

## Cause
### (In the name of Jesus Christ of Nazareth)

The cause of the physical and spiritual miracle in the lame beggar is Jesus! There is no "My part and His part" language do not exist, but it is all His part. Through the prevenient grace of

Jesus, the encounter begins. Peter attended the hour of prayer hundreds of times and he passed this lame beggar repeatedly. He saw the beggar out of the corner of his eye as he rushed by. This time he stops directly in front of the beggar and demands his attention (Acts 3:4). Peter never before spoke with this lame man. This time he engages the lame beggar with an explanation and a command (Acts 3:6). Physical contact never happened before this day, but this time **he took him by the right hand** (Acts 3:7). The explanation for this new encounter is Jesus. Peter is a Spirit-sourced man directed by the Spirit of Jesus.

Wait! Didn't the lame beggar have a choice in this matter? The statement being made by Peter is in the imperative mood. The Greek word (egeiro) translated *rise up* and the Greek word (peripateo) translated *walk* are each commands. The assumed subject is "the lame beggar." Each commanding verb is in the active voice. This means the subject is responsible for the action of the verbs. Peter engages the will and response of the lame beggar to participate in the miracle. He does not have to respond to the Divine power acting on his behalf. But if he does respond, the Divine power will produce the intended result.

The cross style message is not one of indifference or non-involvement. We are intimately involved in desiring, seeking, responding, and participating in what God is doing. We are involved as a glove participates in the action of the hand. We are involved like an engine is fueled by gasoline. We are involved as a suit worn by a man. The breakdown in all these illustrations is the lack of a "will." We have a will! We must respond! We have a choice! A glove, engine, and suit do not have a will involving choice. We do!

Our response is called "faith," which is invoking the activity of the second party. This response means we do not wait until God does something before we get involved. We are not dependent on what we see. We are intimate with the Divine Person. He acts in us and we respond. This occurs before the physical act

**Part One:** The Event

of the miracle. The lame beggar is NOT brought to his feet with full strength, and then he responds. He responds, and then he is brought to his feet in the miracle.

Jesus feeds the crowd of five thousand men besides women and children. The multiplication of the bread is a result of the power of God. It is a miracle. The issue of the miracle is found in the method of the miracle. Matthew is specific in his statement. ***"Then He commanded the multitudes to sit down on the grass. And He took the five loaves and the two fish, and looking up to heaven, He blessed and broke and gave the loaves to the disciples; and the disciples gave to the multitudes"*** (Matthew 14:19). He highlights the reality that the miracle was not in the hands of Jesus but in the hands of the disciples and the multitude. How long would it take for Jesus to break enough bread to feed nearly twenty thousand people? He took the bread and broke it; He gave it to Peter. He instructed him to break it and pass it to the crowd. Can you see Peter start with the first man of the group who looks as if he could eat the entire loaf in one bite? If Peter passed the broken loaf and said, "Just break off a little piece and pass it on," it would be easy to believe. As Peter and the crowd responded to Jesus, they broke and passed the bread. It multiplied in their hands. Jesus did not multiply the bread and then the disciples passed it. The disciples responded to Jesus and the bread multiplied.

A significant time in the history of Israel was when Joshua led the people into the Promised Land. They were ready to cross the Jordan and possess the land. God instructed the priests to go first with the Ark of the Covenant. They came to the edge of the raging river. They were told to place their feet in the Jordan and the waters would part. We prefer God to part the waters before we march. God told them to march (respond) then He would part the waters before we march. ***And as those who bore the ark came to the Jordan, and the feet of the priests who bore the ark dipped in the edge of the water (for the Jordan overflows all its*** *banks during the whole time of harvest), that the waters which came down from upstream stood still, and rose in a heap very far away* (Joshua 3:15-16).

The New Testament and the New Covenant pattern is the responding first in faith! The Spirit of God reaches out to take us by the right hand. Will we respond? We must not wait for God to strengthen our anklebones and feet and respond. When we respond His strength will be there for us. The act of faith is invoking the activity of the second party.

## Content
### (rise up)

*Rise up* (egeiro) speaks to the response (cause) and also to the "content." This Greek word (egeiro) comes from a root word that focuses on "collecting all of one's facilities." All the Greek lexicons begin their definition of this word (egeiro) with the examples of a sleeping man being awakened. For instance, *then Joseph, being aroused from sleep, did as the angel of the Lord commanded him and took to him his wife* (Matthew 1:24). A man slumbering at night is the picture. His entire body is relaxed and asleep. Suddenly, he jumps out of bed; his mind is alert; His emotions are high. His physical structure is tense, and he is ready for action. Joseph had determined the course of his action. He knew that Mary was pregnant, and he was not the father. He did not want to stone her to death; therefore, he decided to get a divorce and secretly put her away. He went to bed that night content with his decision. Suddenly an angel of the Lord appeared to him in the night hour and *aroused* him. The arousal was like a bucket of cold water dumped on his head. He was brought to his feet in attention. Every muscle of his body was tense for action. All his faculties are pulled together into one focus.

Part One: The Event

This Greek word (egeiro) is used for the resurrection of Jesus. He is dead and wrapped in grave clothing. Suddenly His entire being is invigorated by the resurrection of the Father pulling Him with one focus. Interestingly, when translating this Greek word (egeiro), the word "up" is often included. This word (up) is not a prefix, and it is not in the Greek word. However, the meaning of the word lends itself to describing something that was down and is now coming up. The word describes; going from sleeping to awakening, dead to resurrected, sitting to standing, and sickness to health. In each case, there is the emphasis of coming "up." This word is the command of Peter to the lame beggar. *In the name of Jesus Christ of Nazareth, rise up and walk.*

"Egeiro" seems to be a favorite Greek word of Luke. He uses it four times in the context of this miracle. In our passage we find this word in the COMMAND. Peter cried, *In the name of Jesus Christ of Nazareth, rise up and walk* (Acts 3:6). God calls us "up" as a part of our lives. Do not stay where you are; you must come up! Also, it is found in the CONNECTION. *And he took him by the right hand and lifted him up, and immediately his feet and ankle bones received strength* (Acts 3:7). In the physical connection between Peter and the lame beggar, the impact will be "up." Have you been around people who are always putting you "down?" Do you shy away from those who have a negative spirit and are "down?" The Spirit-sourced man is an individual whose influence is "up."

Peter proceeds to use this Greek word (egeiro) two more times in his sermon. Each relate to Jesus being raised from the dead. The first is a declaration of COMPREHENSION. Peter preaches, *"But you denied the Holy One and the Just, and asked for a murderer to be granted to you, and killed the Prince of life, whom God raised from the dead, of which we are witnesses"* (Acts 3:14-15). This passage is a personal testimony of the resurrection. Peter sees, experiences, and comprehends the action of this word (egeiro) in Jesus; he now transfers that Divine action into the lame beggar. What an opportunity you and I have! Our comprehension of the Spirit of God's action brings us "up." We can now expose those around us to the lifting power of God. Peter also uses this word (egeiro) while addressing the leaders of Israel. He preaches, *"Let it be known to you all, and to all the people of Israel, that by the name of Jesus Christ of Nazareth, whom you crucified, whom God raised* (egeiro) *from the dead, by Him this man stands here before you whole"* (Acts 4:10). This passage is a proclamation of CERTAINTY. This lame beggar who now stands with Peter is the proof of the resurrection of Jesus. The same power of God working in Christ to bring Him "up" is now working in the lame beggar bringing him "up."

The call of God on our lives is contained in this emphasis. We are called "up." We *were dead in trespasses and sins,* (Ephesians 2:1). We are lifted to life. He *raised us up together, and made us sit together in the heavenly places in Christ Jesus,* (Ephesians 2:6). The old law with its burden of guilt and duty is lifted. Jesus took *the handwriting of requirements that was against us, which was contrary to us. And He has taken it out of the way, having nailed it to the cross* (Colossians 2:14). Jesus took it "up" on the cross giving us liberty. *If then you were raised* (up) *with Christ, seek those things which are above, where Christ is, sitting at the right hand of God* (Colossians 3:1). In fact, *set your mind on things above* (up), *not on things on the earth* (down), (Colossians 3:2).

## Condition
### (walk)

The command of Peter is specific. The "*rise up*" is followed by "*walk*," and it is a translation of the Greek word "peripateo." It comes from two Greek words combined. One word is "peri" which means "about." The other word is "pateo" which means "to walk." We desire to be raised to "sit." But we much prefer to be raised to be "problem free." A much more acceptable status would be to have good health and wealth. We hate to be misunderstood, and we desire to have "fame" or at least "acceptance."

This word takes on the content of the new location's boundaries into which the lame beggar has been placed. Because he is in the person of Jesus, all the acts of his life must be acceptable within those boundaries. The idea in this word "*walk*" is highlighted in the epistles. Paul seems to give it content. He says, **"Let us walk properly, as in the day, not in revelry and drunkenness, not in lewdness and lust, not in strife and envy"** (Romans 13:13). Paul reflects on the CONDUCT of our living. He urges us to cast off all works **of darkness, and let us put on the armor of light** (Romans 13:12). In fact, we are to **put on the Lord Jesus Christ, and make no provision for the flesh, to fulfill its lusts** (Romans 13:14). These are the two statements that sandwich his call to **walk properly**. It is a new location, with new boundaries, demanding a new conduct of life.

The reality of "walking within the new boundaries" also refers to CONDITIONS of our living. Paul said, **"But as God has distributed to each one, as the Lord has called each one, so let him walk"** (1 Corinthians 7:17). He speaks of a variety of conditions in this chapter. Wives with unbelieving husbands and husbands with unbelieving wives are two of these. He mentions those circumcised and those uncircumcised. The condition of a slave or being free is suggested. You are to stay in whatever condition God calls you; you are to live out (**walk**) within the boundaries of Jesus. These new boundaries will change your world!

Paul exhorts the Ephesians, **"I, therefore, the prisoner of the Lord, beseech you to walk worthy of the calling with which you were called,"** (Ephesians 4:1). This scripture refers to the

CALLING of our lives. The Greek word (klesis) translated *calling* expresses the wonder of an invitation as to a banquet. The Greek word (kaleo) translated *called* focuses on "a summons to come." He continues in this chapter to express various aspects of that invitation. He speaks of ***apostles, some prophets, some evangelists, and some pastors and teachers***. We are to walk *worthy* of the calling. The Greek word (axios) translated *worthy* is literally "appropriately." What is an appropriate manner of living for one who is called of God? It is ***lowliness and gentleness, with longsuffering, bearing with one another in love, endeavoring to keep the unity of the Spirit in the bond of peace*** (Ephesians 4:2-3). This passage explains the attitude of the Spirit-sourced person walking within the boundaries of the person of Jesus.

We are no longer lame sitting by the Gate Beautiful begging for alms. We are on our feet with the full strength of the Spirit of Jesus; we will leap, run, and *walk* in the boundaries of our new location. Jesus is our place; we are home!

## Acts 3:6

# DEVELOPMENT

*Then Peter said, "Silver and gold I do not have, but what I do have I give you: In the name of Jesus Christ of Nazareth, rise up and walk" (Acts 3:6).*

Peter said, **"Silver and gold I do not have, but what I do have I give you:"** (Acts 3:6a). *I give* is a translation of the Greek word "didomi." The word is in the active voice, which means Peter is responsible for the act of giving. Peter uses this same word (didomi) in his sermon to the crowd. His explanation is, **"Yes, the faith which comes through Him has given him this perfect soundness in the presence of you all"** (Acts 3:16). The word is in the active voice in this statement, which means **the faith which comes through Him** is responsible for the action of the **perfect soundness**. Peter is not taking personal credit for this miracle. He accredits this miracle to be a result of his own faith and the faith of the lame beggar, which each are from Jesus.

Think of the significance of Peter's action. He stands before a lame beggar more than forty years of age (Acts 4:22). Peter boldly declares victory for this lame man. Luke writes, **"And he took him by the right hand and lifted him up,"** (Acts 3:7). What was the risk involved? Suppose the lame man collapses in weakness? If the lame man's feet and anklebones are not strengthened, will the early church be embarrassed? Peter's faith in Jesus is bold. However, intimately linked with his faith is the strong willingness to give it away.

Peter has not always been this way. As Jesus approached the last six months of His ministry and life, He desired to capture His disciples with His true mission. He pointedly asked them, *"But who do you say that I am?"* (Matthew 16:15). Peter's faith was bold and secure. He exclaimed, *"You are the Christ, the Son of the living God"* (Matthew 16:16). Peter gives no hint of doubt in His statement. The most important point quickly became, not the certainty of his faith, but the focus of his faith. The focus of his faith is for himself and his benefit. Jesus gave His first prediction about His death and resurrection (Matthew 16:21). He is a "bleeding, suffering, and dying Messiah." Peter immediately **took Him aside and began to rebuke Him,** (Matthew 16:22). A focus on "bleeding, suffering, and dying" would not benefit Peter. In fact, it would require him to have the same focus.

This picture is exhibited in the upper room at the close of Jesus' life. In distress, Jesus predicts a stumbling among all His disciples (Matthew 26:31). Peter does not accept this statement. In faith and determination he says, *"Even if all are made to stumble because of You, I will never be made to stumble"* (Matthew 26:33). Jesus continues the conversation by giving Peter details of his denial. Peter reacts again by saying, *"Even if I have to die with You, I will not deny You!"* (Matthew 26:35). His expression seems to testify of his strong faith in Jesus. His faith is focused on himself. He is not focused on pouring his life out for others. He is focused on his own standing among the disciples.

The change in Peter's life is amazing as proved in the confrontation with the lame beggar. The engagement proves a Spirit-sourcing. Peter and John have hurried to the hour of prayer often. The lame beggar was begging alms during those times as well. They are in no less a hurry today than on any other day. Why have they stopped to focus on the lame beggar? Is it not Spirit-sourced? Peter has no hidden motive; He will gain

**Part One:** The Event

no advantage. In fact, it will create friction with the leaders of Israel. Why take time for a lame beggar now? The encounter is a Spirit-sourced matter!

This brings us to the surface of several questions about faith.

## What is Faith?

This question will not require a long discussion. Faith is defined as "invoking the activity of the second party." Faith is not a feeling. Faith always engages and brings results, but its activities are focused. The activities of faith must not be confused with the results of faith. Faith never produces results; it always engages the activities of someone else. The focus of the faith produces the results.

This reality may be more important than it first appears. If faith were the source of the results, then we would develop a faith in our faith. If we "invoke the activity of the second party," we expect the second party to bring the desired results. When the second party is our "faith," the source of the results will be our "faith." No one is ever saved by their faith; it is a means by which we embrace a saving source. Therefore, it becomes obvious that all people have faith. All people are invoking the activity of a second party. The difference between us is not in faith, but in the object of our faith.

The question about faith is not amount, but focus. Jesus empowered and sent the disciples into Galilee to minister (Matthew 10). After their return, Jesus takes three disciples to the Mount of Transfiguration. The remaining nine disciples find themselves helpless in the face of a demon-possessed boy. After ministering to the boy, Jesus explains the situation to His disciples. Their inability to help is because of their **unbelief** or "little faith" (Matthew 17:20), and at first glance, this seems to emphasize the amount of their faith. Jesus continues His explanation, *"For assuredly, I say to you, if you have faith as a mustard seed, you will say to this mountain, 'Move from here to there,' and it will move; and nothing will be impossible for you"* (Matthew 17:20). The *mustard seed* was the smallest seed in Jewish culture. It was the size of a dot made by a sharp pencil when pressed against a paper. Consequently, if their faith is less than a *mustard seed* they have no faith. The emphasis is not on the size of one's faith but on the focus of that faith.

All of us have the faith we need; the problem resides in the object of our faith. In other words, we are all "invoking the activity" of some "second party." For instance, Peter had faith from the beginning. When he stood tall and gave his confession, *"You are the Christ, the Son of the living God"* (Matthew 16:16), it was an expression of faith. When they departed the upper room, was Peter's response to Jesus' statement an expression of faith? He said, *"Even if all are made to stumble because of You, I will never be made to stumble"* (Matthew 26:33). Does he not believe to the point of giving his life? Is there any doubt of his intention? No one could view Peter and criticize him for uncertainty. Peter has enough faith; his difficulty is in the object of his faith.

Once Peter's object of faith is properly understood, it becomes clear the object of our faith sources the results. Faith cannot take credit for any activity; it only points to the source responsible. The results will always have the characteristics of the source, and this is evident in Peter's experience. When he gave his confession, it seemed his faith was focused on Jesus, but in reality his faith was focused on himself. He did not embrace the activity of Jesus when He revealed His coming death and resurrection. This objection was opposite of what the object of his faith proposed. He thought of thrones, ruling, prosperity, and success. These thoughts were all evidence of self-sourcing. With confidence he declared his loyalty to Jesus. But Jesus was not the source of his faith, because Peter denied Him three times. The results of his faith had the characteristics of the self-sourcing.

Now, there is a difference in our passage (Acts 3:6). Peter is going to *give* (didomai) what he has. He boldly declares it to be an act of faith (invoking the activity of the second party), Peter says, *"And His name, through faith in His name, has made this man strong, whom you see and know"* (Acts 3:16). The results have the characteristic of the source, Jesus. A lame beggar's life is radically changed with no personal benefit to Peter. Peter gives himself away. He invokes the activity of Jesus, and Jesus presence in the lame beggar brings him transformation.

## What is the Source of Faith?

Another question in the passage is present. Where may I receive this faith? I would love to affect the lives of people like Peter. You and I are not the first to have had such thoughts. Simon, the sorcerer, desired the power of God to do as the apostles were doing (Acts 8:14-15). He offered money for the power of God. *Peter said to him, "Your money perish with you, because you thought that the gift of God could be purchased with money!"* (Acts 8:20). Simon, the sorcerer, had no comprehension of the fullness of the Spirit of Jesus.

No one can buy or earn faith, because it is already given to all people. Peter explains, *"And His name, through faith in His name, has made this man strong, whom you see and know. Yes, the faith which comes through Him has given him this perfect soundness in the presence of you all"* (Acts 3:16). The Greek word (dia) translated *through* is a primary preposition meaning the channel of an act. The word can be used to mean an instrument or how something happens. All people have faith provided to themselves by Jesus. This gift is in the provision of "prevenient grace." You need no concern over having faith or the amount of faith. Jesus has already met that need in your life.

Development | **Acts 3:6**

All the faith (invoking the activity of the second party) is yours.

Well, how do I respond to the faith that I have? My ability to respond is not a concern either. Your "responder" is working well! A responder is ingrained into the nature of your being. You are constantly living a life of faith. Every decision, every movement of your being is an act of invoking the activity of the second party. You are created to depend on someone; you are constantly living by faith. Therefore, having faith and using that faith are not concerns. You can dismiss them from your mind.

## What is the Object of My Faith?

The object of your faith is the primary concern for your life. You have an important decision to make about this issue and only this issue. We are surrounded with many choices. We end confused because there are so many choices. But confusion should not exist concerning the object of your faith. There are only two choices which are "self" or "Jesus;" you will either be self-sourced or Spirit-sourced.

Let's clarify again; the question is not the amount of faith, but the object of faith. When you come on Sunday morning, you head for your favorite pew. Let's say it is the third row from the back on the isle. Every time you come to church you sit there by faith. Sunday after Sunday you plop down in your favorite spot. You do this by faith; you invoke the activity of the pew to hold you. You do not test the pew; you do not require your wife to sit first to be sure. You do not shake the pew. You sit in the pew by faith. Then comes the Sunday when you sit by faith and experience the collapse of your pew. You end splattered on the floor. Someone rushes to help you to your feet saying, "If you only had more faith!" You now see this as impossible. For many months in absolute faith, you have plopped onto this pew. There was never a doubt or question in your mind that this pew would not hold you. You had all the faith you needed. The problem was not in the amount of faith, but in the faith's object. You had an unworthy object of your faith.

If I am self-sourced, it means I am the object of my faith. I invoke the activity of me. Faith in me expresses my self-confidence. It allows me to achieve things. I do not hide in the corner as if I am unable. I boldly step forward to act. No one can say I am lazy, because I trust in me to do everything. I participate with self to work, accomplish, and achieve. I invoke my activity to produce. I receive the applause; I am responsible and deserve it.

If I am Spirit-sourced, it means the object of my faith is Jesus. I invoke the activity *of* Jesus on my behalf. Faith *in* Jesus expresses itself in confidence *in* Jesus. It allows me to accomplish things. I do not hide in the corner as if I am unable. I boldly step forward to act in His power. No one can say, "You are lazy, for you trust in Jesus to do everything." I participate with Jesus to work, accomplish, and achieve. I invoke His activity to produce. I refuse the applause; I am not responsible and do not deserve it.

If I have faith in me, I am limited in the results. My failures are caused by my limitations. My inabilities are apparent because of my tremendous stress and pressure. I am responsible for solving my problems, making right decisions, and accomplishing results. The limits of my resources are the limits of my faith. There is nothing beyond me. I am my only hope. The chief characteristic of self-sourcing is self-focus. All my energies and resources are focused exclusively on me. I do not have any resource to spare. All my relationships are for helping me. I invoke the activity of me. Therefore, it demands self-focus to barely maintain what I need.

If I have faith in Jesus, He is the limit to the results. I only need to be anxious if my needs are beyond His inabilities. He is now responsible for solving my problems, making right decisions and accomplishing results. There is nothing beyond Him. He is my only hope. The chief characteristic of Spirit-sourcing is

Jesus-focus. All my energies and resources are focused exclusively on His will. I have resource to spare. I can be extravagant with love and forgiveness. All my relationships are for helping others. I am invoking the activity of the second party; the second party is Jesus. Therefore, it demands focus on Him every moment. The constant is *"Silver and gold I do not have, but what I do have I give you."* The chief concern of my Source is now my ultimate concern. What He is like, I have now become by His grace. If He is a bleeding, suffering, and dying Messiah, I hunger for this way of life. His heart is now my heart. I invoke His activity on my behalf. I live by faith.

Acts 3:7

# LET'S REACH OUT

*And he took him by the right hand and lifted him up, and immediately his feet and ankle bones received strength (Acts 3:7).*

The New Testament is filled with parallels. The parallels teach and emphasize the same truth repeatedly, highlighting a particular truth as important. Many concepts or ideas may not matter, but the idea about the fullness of the Spirit of Jesus does matter. In the long-range view of life, many concerns may have little effect, but this is false about the fullness of the Spirit of Jesus. This truth is fundamental and must be present and acknowledged in all truth. In fact, this truth may be the source of all considered truths.

This infilling is first viewed by readers in the Gospel accounts as parallel with the Book of Acts. Would anyone dare argue against Jesus as the focus of the four Gospel accounts? Only two of the Gospel writers give an account of His birth (Matthew and Luke). All four writers give an account of Jesus' baptism by John the Baptist. During His baptism He experiences Pentecost. His baptism establishes the Source by which the entire ministry of Jesus is explained. Jesus does not do what He does because He is God, although He is indeed God. Jesus is going to do what He does because He is a Man sourced by God. The Gospel accounts are focused on one Man. He is the first Man;

the beginning Man of a new kind of humanity. He is the start of the Kingdom of God, which will be formed by Spirit-sourced beings. The Gospel writers declare the activities, attitudes, and advances of a Spirit-sourced Man. After reading these writings, you will be startled by this one Spirit-sourced Man.

You may question the possibility of being another Spirit-sourced man; however, this sourcing is the point of the Gospel accounts. Jesus, a Spirit-sourced Man, is sourced by the Father to start something new. The Father will not only source the life of Jesus but also His death. In fact, God will source His resurrection and ascension. Jesus will be sourced as the King of the new Kingdom. Jesus, the Spirit-sourced Man, establishes redemption, a way for others to come into this sourcing. How is this possible?

The Book of Acts is not a focus on one Spirit-sourced Man, but on a multitude. We see initially 120 people receiving what Jesus received. This sourcing quickly expands into a worldwide movement. People everywhere are being Spirit-sourced. The purpose of this expansion is to include you and me. What happened in Jesus and the early disciples, you and I can experience. Jesus, the early disciples, and now you become the explanation of Spirit-sourcing. The emphasis of the explanation is not a theology or doctrine, but a "life." What was launched in Jesus was not a "belief system" but a "life system." We are to be this "life system"!

As the story of the lame beggar unfolds, this life system is revealed by the response of the apostles. After placing the apostles in jail and now interrogating them, the leaders of Israel **perceived that they were uneducated and untrained men, they marveled. And they realized that they had been with Jesus** (Acts 4:13). These apostles acted like Jesus; they responded like Jesus. They seemed to have the same desires as Jesus. The conflicts between the leaders of Israel and Jesus are now present between the leaders of Israel and the apostles. The conflicts are as if Jesus is present again!

The miracle received by the lame beggar could have taken

place in the Gospels. Instead of this miracle coming through Peter, it could have come through Jesus. In fact, it is a duplication of the activities of Jesus, the Spirit-sourced Man. Let us look at the parallel evidence.

## Attribute of Spirit-sourcing

Something is happening in verse seven of the story that gives us the heart of Spirit-sourcing. ***And he took him by the right hand and lifted him up, and immediately his feet and ankle bones received strength*** (Acts 3:7). The main subject of the sentence is the pronoun, ***he***. The main verb of the sentence indicates this subject. The Greek word (egeiro) translated ***lifted him up*** is the verb in the indicative (simple statement of fact). The Greek word (piazo) translated ***took*** is a verb in the participle form, and in the nominative case, which relates the participle to the subject of the sentence.

The antecedent of the pronoun ***he*** is Peter. The Greek word "piazo," (***took***) gives content to Peter, the same one as before the Pentecost event. But he seems to have a different character or attitude. He is a leader now as he was then. He does most the talking now as he did then. He continues to have bold ideas. But he has a different focus which changes the impact he has on others. This attribute can be described by many possible terms; it has many expressions. We are going to call it "redemptive attribute"!

We see this attribute in Jesus throughout the Gospel account. Even thought there are many, will recall a few examples. After a busy day of ministry, Jesus slipped away ***into Peter's house***. He was confronted with the desperate need of the household. Peter's ***wife's mother*** was ***lying sick with a fever***. Everything in Jesus demands redemption. ***So He touched her hand, and the fever left her*** (Matthew 8:15). The story is simple, but it expresses the chief characteristic of a Spirit-sourced life. The Greek word (haptomai) translated *touch* is not "piazo." However, it expresses something of the same attitude.

Two blind men follow Jesus. The news that Jesus raised the ruler's daughter from the dead has spread everywhere. They cry to Jesus, **"Son of David, have mercy on us!"** (Matthew 9:27). After a brief conversation with them Jesus **touched their eyes, saying, "According to your faith let it be to you"** (Matthew 9:29). Again *touched* is not the Greek word (piazo) as in our passage. This word is "haptomai," which gives an expression of the same attribute.

Out in the Sea of Galilee, in a boat, in the middle of the night, the disciples are battling a storm. The disciples are frightened as someone walking on the storm waves approaches their boat. The walker is Jesus! Peter requests the privilege of walking on the water with Him. Jesus invites him. He starts well but quickly begins to sink. **And immediately Jesus stretched out His hand and caught him,** (Matthew 14:31). The Greek word (epilambanomai) translated *caught* is another expression of the same "redemptive attribute."

These stories of Jesus, a Spirit-sourced Man, are many. Now Peter, a Spirit-sourced Man, is involved in the same activity. What flowed through Peter is an expression of what flows through Jesus. Sourcing is the common denominator! Does this not give you hope? Could it happen through you and me? Perhaps the primary attribute is not about discipline, training, or experience; it is about sourcing!

What is the attitude of Spirit-sourcing? What is a "redemptive attribute"?

## Aggressive
### (Tone)

The tone in this encounter and those of Jesus is one of aggression. Peter confronted the lame beggar (Acts 3:4). Peter insisted this man encounter *Jesus Christ of Nazareth* (Acts 3:6). Peter commanded this man to move to a new place with new actions (Acts 3:6). This command was not a relaxed, casual invitation; it was a bold, aggressive encounter. Peter does not speak with soft tones, "I do not want to hurt your feelings, but could I suggest to you a change of location"? Peter is boisterous with a bold command to *rise up and walk* (Acts 3:6).

At first one might attribute this to personality. Peter has always been aggressive and domineering. When Jesus asked the disciples, *"But who do you say that I am?"* (Matthew 16:15), Peter was the first on his feet to give expression. He was aggressive in speaking for the rest of the disciples. His bold declaration about Jesus will be remembered. When Jesus declared the reality of the disciples stumbling because of him, Peter was the first to boldly deny such a possibility. He could see the other disciples falling into such a trap. *"Even if all are made to stumble because of You, I will never be made to stumble"* (Matthew 26:33). When the Rich Young Ruler left sorrowfully, Peter aggressively asked, *"See, we have left all and followed You. Therefore what shall we have?"* (Matthew 19:27). Isn't this just his personality?

Perhaps it is. Carefully notice that his aggression and boldness changed from a self-focus to a focus on others. Through the Gospel accounts he is aggressive; it is always about him. We do not want to focus on him; the other disciples were also aggressive about their desires. *At that time the disciples came to Jesus, saying, "Who then is greatest in the kingdom of heaven?"* (Matthew 18:1). A constant power struggle among this group existed. An incredible change took place as they stepped into the New Covenant! It only can be explained by a change in their sourcing.

This "aggressive attribute" is highlighted generally in the early church. The early Christians, illustrated by individual cases, appeared bold. In describing the relationship between the Christians and the community, Luke writes, *"So continuing daily with one accord in the temple, and breaking bread from house to house, they ate their food with gladness and simplicity of heart, praising God and having favor with all the people"* (Acts 2:46-47). The preceding passage indicates a direct, aggressive penetration into the Christian's local community. After the apostles were threatened and released, they returned to the church reporting everything the leaders of Israel had said. *And when they had prayed, the place where they were assembled together was shaken; and they were all filled with the Holy Spirit, and they spoke the word of God with boldness* (Acts 4:31).

The same attribute is strongly suggested by Jesus in His promise to His disciples. Just before His ascension, Jesus again related to them the heart of the New Covenant, *the Promise of the Father* (Acts 1:4). He said, *"But you shall receive power when the Holy Spirit has come upon you; and you shall be witnesses to Me in Jerusalem, and in all Judea and Samaria, and to the end of the earth"* (Acts 1:8). The self-absorbed, self-focus of the Jewish tradition would change in the New Covenant to an aggressive movement encompassing the world! The isolation and elimination of all "others" except "us" would be replaced by the expression of the love of God for a world. This new characteristic would burn in the heart of the believer; he would become aggressive under the power of the Spirit.

## Actual
### (Touch)

Do you not marvel at the involvement of Peter with the lame beggar? His involvement is startling because the man is lame and a beggar. Peter gave the man his full attention. *And fixing his eyes on him, with John, Peter said, "Look at us"* (Acts 3:4). The conversation was one-sided as Peter aggressively and boldly challenged the lame beggar to respond to the movement of Jesus.

**Part One:** The Event

Peter's physical connection with the lame beggar is amazing. ***And he took him by the right hand and lifted him up*** (Acts 3:7). The Greek word (piazo) translated ***took***, is much stronger than a simple touch. It means "to press, to squeeze, to seize, to hold fast, to compress." This same physical condition moves from being initiated by Peter to the response of the lame beggar. ***Now as the lame man who was healed held on to Peter and John*** (Acts 3:11). The Greek word (krateo), translated ***held on***, means "to take hold of, grasp, to hold fast." It is a different Greek word from our passage; it gives us the same impact.

During the late 70's I was involved in a pastor's meeting in my home area. For several sessions we listened to a CEO of a major corporation. I became aware of a gradual change occurring in our approach to overseeing the church. We started being CEO's administrating the corporation of our church world from behind a desk. The statement that we are in big business is true. But remote control by proxy cannot be the policy. In the business segment of the church we must respect the requirements of our culture. Redemption requires that we have personal and physical involvement.

Many of us are willing to admit this truth and take part in its reality; however, the Scripture takes it further. To be redemptive, our involvement requires "bleeding, suffering, and dying"! The life of Jesus reveals it. The Book of Acts thunders with it. The Greek word translated "witness" is "martus" in the noun form and "martureo" in the verb form. This word as used in the early church gathers the idea of suffering. It gained the thought process of giving your life to Christ. No one could be a witness for Jesus without suffering was apparent. The suffering is produced by the physical interaction with others in our world. Jesus equated our physical interaction with the needs of our fellowman and how we treat Him (Matthew 25:31-46).

## Acceptance
(Together)

Luke emphasizing the **right hand** appears significant. Several uses of this imagery in the Scriptures are present. One applies to our passage and the "right hand of fellowship." Paul writes, *"And when James, Cephas, and John, who seemed to be pillars, perceived the grace that had been given to me, they gave me and Barnabas the right hand of fellowship, that we should go to the Gentiles and they to the circumcised"* (Galatians 2:9).

In our passage, Peter **took him by the right hand and lifted him up, and immediately his feet and ankle bones received strength** (Acts 3:7). How shocking this must have been to some of those watching. Peter is an acceptable Jew; he has the right to all the privileges of the temple. Being lame this beggar is not acceptable in the temple; he has no right to enter any part of the temple. Peter has owned and operated a fishing business; he has been financially responsible for his life and family. The lame beggar relies on the charity of others; he does not contribute to the betterment of society. Peter is a spiritual individual who has been steadfast in his Jewish faith. This lame man has deep spiritual problems which are evidenced by his handicapped state. A reason for Peter to notice or get involved with this beggar does not exist. The Spirit of Jesus has removed the barriers between them. A miracle is experienced in the acceptance. Without the **right hand** there would not have been a miracle.

The **right hand** in the passage goes further than this. Accepting this man without prejudice is not the only sign; the joining with him in his need and experiencing the miracle is also a sign. Peter takes part in the acts of the Holy Spirit in this man's life and physical being. The question must be raised. Would this man receive such a marvelous miracle of physical and spiritual change without the participation of Peter? This man did not

**Part One:** The Event

receive a miracle done to him; he participated with Peter in the joint movement of the Spirit of Jesus! This joint participation is true evangelism. Evangelism is not simply telling others the message but accepting their person and joining them in their deliverance. What a privilege to live in the flow of the Holy Spirit, meeting the needs of people around us!

## Acts 3:7

# THE ATTITUDE OF JESUS

*And he took him by the right hand and lifted him up, and immediately his feet and ankle bones received strength (Acts 3:7).*

Every believer appears to have a strong desire to be like Jesus. However, there is difficulty with this ever-present desire. No one ever seems to claim its achievement. I have heard hundreds of testimonies and have never heard, "I am exactly like Jesus!" What would you conclude from this? Is this an unachievable goal? Is it unrealistic? Is the resource of the crucifixion lacking? Is Christ-likeness only available to the believer after arrival in heaven? Perhaps this quality type is like the quality of humility. If you *think* you have achieved humility that is evidence that you have not. The truly humble do not recognize themselves as having humility; those Christ-like do not know they are such.

A big distance between the culture of Jesus' day and our present setting exists. Christ-likeness must be understood in our culture, and we must view Jesus in His culture; but we must go beyond the surface of His activities to the heart-source. Techniques and methodology are not our primary concerns. The principle or principles determining all applications must be experienced. What motivated Jesus must motivate us. Many Scriptures pressing us to this reality exist. Paul writes, **"Let this mind be in you which was also in Christ Jesus,"** (Philippians 2:5).

#### Part One: The Event

**The Amplified Bible** says it this way. ***"Let this same attitude and purpose and** [humble] **mind be in you which was in Christ Jesus:** [Let Him be your example in humility:]."* Paul emphasizes that the disposition or temperament of the believer must be that of Christ! The Greek word (phroneo), translated ***mind***, has to do with "to think, have a mindset, and be minded." The activity represented by this word involves the will, affections, and conscience.

Believers often concentrate on imitating the actions of Christ. Some people have willingly duplicated a personal beating and crucifixion to be like Jesus. The merit is never discovered in the activity, but it is found by us in the attitude. This truth was Peter's message explaining Pentecost to the Jews of the Dispersion. What happened to 120 believers? The disposition of Christ came to indwell them. What was driving, motivating, and sourcing Jesus was now in the believer. A new day is here where the Spirit of Jesus captures us!

Peter and John confront a lame beggar. A miracle happens, which gains the attention of the temple crowd, and it is a spectacular event! A lame man leaps, walks, and praises God. Being captured by the miracle is natural. To be like Jesus would require doing such miracles. But the miracle is the surface glitter of the story. Look at the attitude of Peter and John. Discover what drives them, which is an expression of the Spirit of Jesus. Peter and John are Christ-like!

In our previous study we recognized the parallel between this miracle and the miracles of Jesus. Because the same Spirit sourced each, it is not a surprise. A "redemptive ATTRIBUTE" present in these miracles. In this present study, we desire to investigate the ATTITUDE of this "redemptive act, is the attitude of Spirit-sourcing. A dictionary definition of "attitude" is "a settled way of thinking or feeling about someone or something, typically one that is reflected in a person's behavior."

## Aspiration

In this miraculous event, there is "intent" behind all the action. Peter and John rush into the temple for the ninth hour of prayer. The temple is crowded because the daily sacrifice is offered during this time. The course of their purpose is interrupted by a lame beggar. He did not interrupt their pattern, but their Spirit-sourcing did! The prevenient grace of God attributed to this moment an opportunity for a lame beggar. Peter and John stop directly in front of this beggar. They "fixed their eyes on him!" (Acts 3:4). This eye contact was not a casual glance but was their full attention. Everything else is set aside; there is no other concern. They demand the same from him.

This encounter is not a moment for advice or counsel, but it is a moment for the full power and presence of Jesus to be brought to bear on this man. *"In the name of Jesus Christ of Nazareth, rise up and walk,"* said Peter (Acts 3:6). Notice carefully the procedure of their actions. The apostles encounter this man. They demand (imperative) that he move to a new location, *in the name of Jesus Christ of Nazareth*. Doesn't this complete the transaction? Isn't this as far as they need to go? The responsibility is now up to the lame beggar; he has a choice to make. Perhaps it will be best to let him think about his need and the tremendous possibilities in Jesus. They can have a meeting with him later.

But Peter cannot let him go! *And he took him by the right hand and lifted him up* (Acts 3:7). The Greek word (piazo), translated **took,** means "to press, to squeeze, to seize, to hold fast, to compress" and is a verb in the participle mood. The word in this case acts as an adjective giving content to the main subject, **he.** The main verb is *"lifted him up"* translated from the Greek word "egeiro." This word is in the indicative mood, a simple statement of fact. Therefore, the action of the sentence is found by us in the lifting of the lame beggar to his feet. Luke gives us content to the attitude of Peter as he describes him with the adjective ***took***.

The Spirit-sourced man cannot be satisfied in giving spiritual advice; he cannot give the Gospel message and walk away. He cannot allow the lame beggar to stay where he is in helplessness. The Spirit of Jesus in Peter pushes him to further involvement. This does not negate the freewill of the lame beggar, but it does highlight the earnestness and desperation felt in the heart of Peter for this man.

How easy it is to become accustomed to lame beggars sitting by the gates. We can walk by them day after day. We become desensitized to their desperate need. Is this why we need the mind of Christ? The plea is not to just care about the world or lame beggars in general, but is about one lame beggar at the Gate Beautiful. It is about caring for him at this moment when prevenient grace flows to his life in a new way. This sensitivity requires us being Spirit-sourced by walking continuously in union with the Spirit of Jesus.

Was this not expressed in the life of Jesus repeatedly? After delivering the Sermon on the Mount, Jesus came down from the mountain. Great multitudes were attracted to Him. A leper, at risk, came close enough to speak to Jesus. He worshipped Him, saying, **"Lord, if You are willing, You can make me clean." Then Jesus put out His hand and touched him, saying, "I am willing; be cleansed"** (Matthew 8:2-3). The Greek word (thelo) translated **"I am willing"** speaks to the attitude and love of Christ. It means, "to will, wish, desire, implying active volition and purpose." Jesus expressed His heart's desire toward this man. This one leper on this one particular day experienced the love of Christ, which would not let him go!

This call is not an encouragement for us to love others more. We are called to be Spirit-sourced. It is in this sourcing we experience the attitude or mindset of Jesus. The Spirit of

Jesus must source us. It is in knowing Him we experience His heart. This way of life was the purpose of God for us from the beginning. He brings us into the heart of the Trinity; He wants us to experience His nature.

## Action

This way of life is, however, much more than a "feel good about you" religious emotion. There seems to be a progression in the event. An initial contact occurs between the apostles and the lame beggar. The apostles share great spiritual truth with the lame beggar. Personal involvement occurs as Peter takes the beggar by the right hand. If this were the conclusion, it would be an immense tragedy because something solid, physical, and seeable needs to occur. Otherwise the lame beggar goes on begging; the Gate Beautiful continues to be cluttered with a man who cons the worshippers at the temple.

Luke reports, *"And immediately his feet and ankle bones received strength"* (Acts 3:7). The Greek word (parachrema), translated *immediately,* is an adverb and is two Greek words, "para" and "chrema." Para means "to" or "at." Chrema means "in the course of the event." The idea of the Greek word is not focused on "quickly" or "how fast" something occurs but focuses on a sequence of acts in the event. In other words, if the lame beggar's feet and anklebones had not received strength, the event would be incomplete. The physical evidence was a natural flow of the entire event.

It astounds me that this adverb occurs 18 times in all the New Testament. Luke uses this word 16 times in his writings (ten in Luke and six in Acts). He is much more detailed in his writings than the other authors. Most uses of this word are connected with miracles. He is concerned about the consequences of the event; otherwise, it is simply theological words spoken. A lame

**Part One:** The Event

beggar is given good counsel about something impossible for him to accomplish.

Perhaps a positive consequence is the need in the religious movement of our day. We have many words with little positive action. Love is often spoken but love is little felt by people. We argue for forgiveness but we seldom embrace it. We preach selflessness but live selfishly. Unless someone runs, leaps, and praises God in the temple, the temple crowd will never be attracted. Unless someone stands on his or her feet in front of the leaders of Israel, these opponents will win their judgment against the apostles (Acts 4:16). Victory is not found by others in our theology or our preaching; it is found in our ***walking, leaping, and praising God***.

This victory may appear to be an emphasis on "performance." This idea must be kept in the perspective of the passage. Many people walked in the temple, but they did not have the impact of this lame beggar. His walk was not a result of **the ninth hour** of prayer. He was not fulfilling the Jewish ceremonial tradition of the afternoon sacrifice. This walk was a natural physical expression of the movement of Jesus in his life. No instructions or laws were given to the healed beggar. His walk was spontaneous from his heart.

I deeply desire a natural, spontaneous, and motivational expression of my embrace with Jesus. I detest "working things up" or "making things happen." I tire of thinking of what should be and then responding accordingly. I do not want to ask, "What would Jesus do?" I want to be in harmony with Him until the physical expression of my life looks like Him. "Calculate," "figure it out," "make it happen" Christianity produces no joy, leaping, or praising. I want my expression to be the result of the full focus of the person and power of ***Jesus Christ of Nazareth***. Five-thousand men were won to Christ through the influence of this lame man's walk. The accomplishment of a duty never produces such impact. Our world will be affected with only "I cannot help myself" actions. This effect is a by-product of the movement of Jesus in our lives. Let us focus on Him.

## Aim

The miracle was awesome! The purpose of God for the movement of the Spirit in this man's life is beyond description. But as it is described in our passage, Luke writes, *"and immediately his feet and ankle bones received strength"* (Acts 3:7). The Greek word (stereo), translated **received strength**, is a verb meaning to make solid, firm, strong, or stable. This same word is used by Peter to describe what took place in the life of this lame beggar. Peter explains, *"And His name, through faith in His name, has made this man strong, whom you see and know"* (Acts 3:16). The noun form of this word (stereoma) is translated *firmament*. In the creation event it is written, **Then God said, "Let there be a firmament** (stereoma) **in the midst of the waters, and let it divide the waters from the waters"** (Genesis 1:6). Luke describes the movement of the Spirit among the churches, *"So the churches were strengthened* (stereo) *in the faith, and increased in number daily"* (Acts 16:5).

Luke, a physician, describes stability and firmness in the foundation of the lame man's life. What he stood on became strong. We see this developing in this man's life. Stability came to the foundation of his life. He stood among the temple crowd and then he stood in the presence of the hostile Israel leaders. This stability (standing) produced an unquestionable witness. *And seeing the man who had been healed standing with them, they could say nothing against it* (Acts 4:14).

James relates this reality to our intimacy and communication with Jesus. We must live in faith (invoking the activity of the second party), and doubt must not exist. *He who doubts is like a wave of the sea driven and tossed by the wind. For let not that man suppose that he will receive anything from the Lord; he is a double-minded man, unstable in all his ways* (James 1:6-8). Have you known *"unstable"* people? You meet them with fear

**Part One:** The Event

and trembling. You never know how they are going to respond. They appear controlled by their circumstances, which controls their emotions. One moment they are on top but another moment are depressed.

The person of ***Jesus Christ of Nazareth*** came to focus on this lame man. A new stability gripped his life. He is standing! Would this not be desired for every aspect of our lives? One man says, "I am not on the mountain top; I am not in the valley. I am on the WAY!" Can Jesus be the stabilizing factor in every circumstance of our lives? He is unmovable, unshakable, and the solidifying factor for our lives.

Acts 3:8

# LET'S LEAP

*So he, leaping up, stood and walked and entered the temple with them — walking, leaping, and praising God (Acts 3:8).*

**The hour of prayer, the ninth hour** (Acts 3:1) was here. This **hour of prayer** attracted the largest crowd. This crowd was the reason the lame beggar was brought daily to the Gate Beautiful at this exact hour. Besides prayer attracting the crowd to the Temple, it was also the hour when sacrifices and burnt offerings were offered daily. God established this practice when giving the Law, the Ten Commandments, and the instructions for the tabernacle. God said, **"Now this is what you shall offer on the altar: two lambs of the first year, day by day continually"** (Exodus 29:38).

The first lamb was to be offered in the morning and the other lamb was offered at twilight; (Exodus 29:39). "Twilight" was "between the two evenings," and it was associated with **the ninth hour**, three in the afternoon. The second lamb was to be offered with **the grain offering and the drink offering, as in the morning, for a sweet aroma, an offering made by fire to the Lord** (Exodus 29:41). The specific purpose of this offering was fellowship. This offering was to be done at the **door of the tabernacle of meeting before the Lord** (Exodus 29:42). God promised, **"I will meet you to speak with you"** (Exodus 29:42). The burnt offering would be in the atmosphere of a **sweet aroma**

**Part One:** The Event

in which God and man would communicate.

The lamb was to be skinned, and the blood sprinkled over the altar. The body of the lamb with the grain offering and the drink offering was to be burned. The grain offering was **one-tenth of an ephah of flour mixed with one-fourth of a hin of pressed oil** (Exodus 29:40). An "ephah" is estimated to be one and one-twelfth bushels. A "hin" is about five quarts. The drink offering was **one-fourth of a hin of wine** (Exodus 29:40). These were burned together on the sacrifice altar giving forth a sweet aroma.

This offering was daily sacrificed from the time of Mt. Sinai, the giving of the law, to the day Peter enters the temple at **the ninth hour**. During the periods of exile, this practice would be hindered. But from the return of Israel to Jerusalem at the end of the Old Testament and the establishment of the law, this practice would be consistent. During the 400 years between the Old and New Testaments, this sacrifice was made daily. Peter experienced this daily.

God's presence was experienced in this moment. His presence was an assurance of deliverance and victory. But the "presence" was missing during the intertestamental period. The ceremony was routine. It became a ritual to complete. One cannot meet with God without being changed, but there was no change. No one ever leapt for joy; there was no voice disturbing the silence with praises to God. Ritual and duty never shout for joy; routine religious practices never produce spontaneous praise. We come to the temple at the hour of prayer. The sweet aroma of the burnt offering fills our nostrils. But where is the presence of God?

It happened outside the temple at the Gate Beautiful! God came, but He did not come in the stale, routine patterns of our ritual. He came in the miracle power of changed lives. A lame beggar is on his feet! A lame beggar who was never allowed to participate in the ritual now experiences the presence. One who

Let's Leap | Acts 3:8

was never allowed to enter the temple brings the presence of God into the temple. ***So he, leaping up, stood and walked and entered the temple with them — walking, leaping, and praising God*** (Acts 3:8).

If you know nothing about grammar, still you must be affected by the structure of this sentence. The constant repetition of the action words ***leaping*** and ***walking*** must impress you. These words are surrounded by the action words of ***stood, entered***, and ***praising***. This activity happens through a lame beggar who for years sat by the Gate Beautiful. Understanding the grammar makes the sentence even more startling.

The subject of the sentence is ***he***, indicated by the three main verbs. They are ***stood, walked***, and ***entered***. The basic structure of the sentence reads, "He ***stood, walked***, and ***entered***. Four additional verbs are in the sentence, but they are participles. These participles are verbs acting as adjectives modifying the subject, ***he***. The sentence could read as follows: "The leaping up, walking, leaping, and praising God one (***he***) stood and walked and entered the temple with them."

There appears to be three extreme emphases throughout this sentence structure.

## Walk

The original command of Peter to the lame beggar was given as he took him by the right hand. The command was, ***"In the name of Jesus Christ of Nazareth, rise up and walk"*** (Acts 3:6). The verb, ***rise up***, in the imperative mood making it a command. It focuses on the physical. The consequence is he "leaped up" from his sitting position, he "stood" to his feet; he ***walked*** (Acts 3:8). Note the physical progression in these statements. All three steps in the progression are focused on the physical. Upon actually entering the temple, the lame beggar is *walking* (Acts 3:8). He continues "leaping, and praising God." This action is definitely a physical demonstration of what took place in his physical life. Luke makes a strong point of revealing that **all the people saw him walking and praising God** (Acts 3:9). Again, this highlights the physical activity being accomplished.

To diminish the physical effect of Jesus on a person's life is impossible. Who would want to? Every generation always has those who attempt to departmentalize their lives. They separate their physical lives from their spiritual. Some people in the church at Corinth embraced this philosophy. They embraced and tolerated immoral activities in the physical while they claimed their spiritual lives felt the embrace of Christ. Paul admonished them about the impossibility of such. He said, **"For you were bought at a price; therefore glorify God in your body and in your spirit, which are God's"** (1 Corinthians 6:20). How can one possibly separate a physical act from the spiritual involvement? Do not forget, Jesus died physically on a cross to affect the spiritual life of mankind. These two areas of man are one!

The Old Testament structure of man's creation is a dichotomy not a trichotomy. **And the Lord God formed man of the dust of the ground, and breathed into his nostrils the breath of life; and man became a living being** (Genesis 2:7). The living being, a living soul, was constructed of body (**dust of the ground**) and spirit (**breath of life**). You do not have a soul; you are a living soul. Your eternal state is not a spiritual state without the physical. Heaven is not the removal of our physical bodies, but a removal of the curse of sin from the physical. We are a whole unit made by God.

The Greek word (peripateo), translated **walked**, and is from "peri" (about) and "pateo" (walk). This word is used figuratively throughout the New Testament for the way an individual lives his or her life. Paul uses the analogy of "baptism." **Therefore we were buried with Him through baptism into death, that just as Christ was raised from the dead by the glory of the Father, even** *so we also should walk in newness of life* (Romans 6:4). Christ was raised from the dead with a new body, and it was physical. So we are to "walk" in our present bodies in the newness of His life. The picture is strong. What Jesus did in our spiritual lives is so powerful it spills forth into our physical lives. No one has a spiritual life not manifested in his physical life. How you feel, what you believe, and your commitment in the spiritual realm will automatically display itself in the physical. The physical is the stage on which the spiritual acts!

The tense of the verbs "***walked***" and "***walking***" in our passage is very significant (Acts 3:8). The first time it is in the imperfect tense. This tense gives the understanding of something which took place in the past but continues its affect into the present. Many times it is translated "kept on." The second usage of "***walking***" in our passage is in the present tense. In the Greek, the present tense means "now with continual action." As is indicated in the narrative, the lame man did not walk for a brief time then go back to his beggar position. He walked and continued to walk. He is described throughout chapters three and four. This miracle continued in his life. But we also understand the "figurative walking" of this man's life was just as continual. We see him holding onto Peter and John (Acts 3:11). He was with them in the ministry in the temple as Peter preached. He was the real demonstration of Peter's sermon (Acts 3:16). He was with the apostles as they stood before the leaders of Israel (Acts 4:10). He lived out this miracle physically in his flesh and spiritually in his spirit.

## Whole

The three main verbs of the sentence are ***stood, walked***, and ***entered***. As noted above, the Greek verb (peripateo), translated ***walked***, is in the imperfect tense. This tense indicates the continuous action of an event happening in the past. In other words, the lame man kept on walking. However, the Greek verb (histemi), translated ***stood***, and the Greek verb (eiserchomai), translated ***entered***, are both in the aorist tense. The aorist is a "non-tense." The verb is not regarded as occurring in the present, or the past, or the future. A focus is on the event being complete.

Based on the passage, there is nothing more needed than for the lame beggar to be physically whole. Luke, the author, is a doctor and often gives us medical insights into the miracles. He does so now. He parallels the Greek word (exallomai), translated ***leaping up***, with the Greek word (hallomai), translated ***leaping***. The Greek word "exallomai" is the same as "hallomai" except the prefix "ek." This word is an ancient medical term for the "socketing of the heel and ankle" and used only here in the New Testament. The process would have taken corrective surgery and months of prolonged healing; the patient would need to learn to walk again. It took place in a split second! The Greek prefix "ek" means "from" or "coming forth." The lame man came forth from his lame place to a place of wholeness.

The Greek word (hallomai), translated ***leaping***, and is a rare word for "jumping." "Hallomai" is used in the Old Testament Greek translation in Isaiah. The prophet speaks of the Messianic hour when ***the lame shall leap like a deer*** (Isaiah 35:6). Now is the time! The fullness of the Spirit of Jesus is moving. All God dreamed for mankind is now available to them. Now is the time for leaping and praising God. The purpose of God for humanity is now whole.

As the study of chapter three develops into Peter's explanation to the crowd, there is an exciting verse, which will require much study. Peter forcibly says that all has taken place through faith in the name of Jesus. At the end of his statement he describes the condition of the lame man as ***perfect soundness*** (Acts 3:16). The Greek word (holokleria), translated ***perfect soundness***, means "to be whole in every part." The passage is the only place this word is used in the New Testament. It rings with the truth of completeness in Christ. No wonder Paul cries, ***"And you are complete in Him"*** (Colossians 2:10).

Do not interpret ***complete in Him*** to mean "arrival" or "absolute." The lame beggar had much to learn from the apostles. We must adhere to the admonition of Peter. ***"But also for this very reason, giving all diligence, add to your faith virtue, to virtue knowledge, to knowledge self-control, to self-control perseverance, to perseverance godliness, to godliness brotherly kindness, and to brotherly kindness love"*** (2 Peter 1:5-7). When compared with this list, we realize a sense of lack. However, do not belittle what you can find ***in the name of Jesus Christ***. A state of existence described as "wholeness" exists.

## Worthy

Everyone else has been rushing in and out of the temple on a daily basis. But the lame beggar has not. He has gone only outside the Gate Beautiful, the entrance to the temple. In the oral interpretation of the Jews, they were guilty of adjusting the laws of God to fit their prejudices and desires. Jesus boldly pointed this out to them. The leaders of Israel accused Jesus and His disciples of transgressing the traditions of the elders because they did not wash their hands when they ate bread. ***He answered and said to them, "Why do you also transgress the commandment of God because of your tradition?"*** (Matthew 15:3). Then He proceeded to give two illustrations regarding God's command about your father and mother (Matthew 15:4-5). In His final public message delivered to His disciples and the multitude, Jesus pronounced seven woes on the leaders of Israel (Matthew 23). Each of these pronouncements struck a blow at this procedure.

The Jewish prejudices were very strong concerning the Gentiles. Many of their defilement laws were developed from

**Part One:** The Event

this prejudice. They were also prejudiced against their fellow Jews. They considered poverty, sickness, and a physical handicap a result of sin either in the individual or his family. Any sacrifice offered to God had to be whole. Any sacrificial lamb must be without spot or blemish. Although this requirement was the law of God concerning sacrifices, the leaders of Israel transposed this toward people as well. The lame beggar was dismissed as unworthy based on two accounts, his handicap and his poverty. He would not be worthy to enter the temple and worship God.

But the amazing truth is he is found by the leaders worthy *in the name of Jesus Christ of Nazareth.* All that could keep him from worship is removed. In Jesus we are found worthy to have access to God. *Therefore, brethren, having boldness to enter the Holiest by the blood of Jesus* (Hebrews 10:19). In Jesus we are found worthy to be *accepted in the Beloved* (Ephesians 1:6). In Jesus, *when we were enemies we were reconciled to God through the death of His Son, much more, having been reconciled, we shall be saved by His life* (Romans 5:10).

The Book of Acts is going to unfold with story after story of those unworthy individuals going to be found worthy of Him. *A man of Ethiopia, a eunuch of great authority under Candace the queen of the Ethiopians, who had charge of all her treasury* (Acts 8:27) was found worthy to rejoice in Jesus. Saul of Tarsus *breathing threats and murder against the disciples of the Lord* (Acts 9:1) was found worthy to be the apostle to the Gentiles. *Cornelius, a centurion of what was called the Italian Regiment* (Acts 10:1) was found worthy to receive the fullness of the Spirit of Jesus. The truth is manifested repeatedly as the story goes on and on throughout the histories of our world. Even your life is found worthy in Him! "But you do not know what I have done," you cry. He does, and you are found worthy in Him.

Acts 3:9-10

# AN AMAZED CROWD

*And all the people saw him walking and praising God. Then they knew that it was he who sat begging alms at the Beautiful Gate of the temple; and they were filled with wonder and amazement at what had happened to him*
*(Acts 3:9-10).*

Luke is an amazing writer, especially as the Spirit of Jesus sources him. As with all writers of the New Testament, he does not simply relate a series of stories. He writes with purpose and interprets all passages in light of that theme. We encourage "saturation" in the Scriptures to grasp the theme. The theme of the Book of Acts highlights the acts of the Holy Spirit. In chapter one Luke introduces the possibility of Pentecost; in chapter two, Pentecost explodes. Every following event gives purpose to the character of the Spirit-sourced life. Luke proposes the standard for the Spirit-sourced person.

Through the process of "saturation," established patterns are easily seen. For instance, the Jews of the Dispersion are witnesses to the entire Pentecost Event (Acts 2). God attempts to win them by pouring out His mercy on them. They are attracted by the loud sound connected with the coming of the Spirit (Acts 2:22). The Galilean disciples begin to speak in 15 different languages related to this group (Acts 2:4). During this account, Luke emphasizes five times, with four different Greek words, the

Part One: The Event

response of the Jews. He begins with the Greek word (sugcheo), translated "confused" or "bewildered" (Acts 2:6). Then he says, ***"They were all amazed** (existemi) **and marveled** (thaumazo)"* (Acts 2:7). He continues, ***"So they were all amazed** (existemi) **and perplexed** (diaporeo)"* (Acts 2:12).

The primary characteristics of this group of Jews were openness and seeking. They came to Jerusalem annually during the feast days, a period of three or more months. They came expecting God to do a "new thing." They immediately recognized the Pentecost Event as this "new thing." They prompted the question, ***"Whatever could this mean?"*** (Acts 2:12). Peter, moved on by the Holy Spirit, responded with an explanatory sermon (Acts 2:14-39). Over 3000 Jews of the Dispersion repented and were added to the Church (Acts 3:41).

What a phenomenal pattern! God initiates a movement by His presence and brings about an overwhelming miracle in someone's life. This miracle astonishes the people around them. This astonishment establishes a platform for the explanation of the Gospel. People respond to the message and are saved. What a pattern!

One leaves this scene gasping for breath. Now the same pattern appears in our passage. A phenomenal miracle has just occurred. No question or argument about the source of the miracle exists. God initiated this miracle! Peter and John have passed the lame beggar hundreds of times on their way to the temple. Why did they stop this time? ***And fixing his eyes on him*** (Acts 3:4), Peter responded in a Spirit-sourced moment. In the unfolding of the event, no one could dispute this healing was a miracle of God. The lame beggar recognized it as he gave praise to God (Acts 3:9). Peter explained this to the crowd in the temple (Acts3:16). Around 5000 men recognized this truth and responded to the explanation (Acts 4:4). Even the leaders of Israel ***could say nothing against it*** (Acts 4:14).

The second aspect of the pattern brings us to our passage.

# An Amazed Crowd | Acts 3:9-10

*And all the people saw him walking and praising God. Then they knew that it was he who sat begging alms at the Beautiful Gate of the temple; and they were filled with wonder and amazement at what had happened to him* (Acts 3:9-10). Luke gives such vivid details to this matter that it is impossible to miss his emphasis.

He begins with, *"And all the people saw him walking and praising God."* The Greek word (eido), translated *saw*, becomes important when connected with the Greek word (epiginosko), translated *they knew* (Acts 3:10). Four or more Greek words (gnostes, eido, ginosko, epiginosko) are translated and mean "to know." "Eido" means "to know" or "to see." It bespeaks perception or understanding. The crowd at the temple saw with their physical eyes and understood with their minds that the lame beggar was walking and praising. They related the "person walking and praising" with the "person begging and lame at the Gate Beautiful."

Then Luke deepens the relationship of this knowledge with the crowd. "Ginosko" is a relational term. It emphasizes the idea of knowing by experience and is used to describe the most intimate relationship in marriage (Matthew 1:25). Luke uses "epiginosko" to describe the involvement of the crowd. The word is "ginosko" with the prefix "epi" included, and is used for increasing, strengthening, and magnifying the relationship. Luke says, *"Then they knew that it was he who sat begging alms at the Beautiful Gate of the temple"* (Acts 3:10). The greatness of the miracle began to permeate the depth of their minds and understanding. They now have no doubt about this man, where he has been, or what has happened to him.

Luke continues to give emphasis to the depth of this knowledge by using the Greek word (pletho), translated *filled*. A "sponge" best describes this Greek word (pletho) which is "saturation"! The knowledge of what is demonstrated in the life of this lame beggar permeates the depth of their beings. All doubts are erased. To dispute what God did in the lame man would be futile. This man is the demonstration of the miracle and the power involved in the change. Peter needs to spend no time convincing them of the miracle; he can focus on who is responsible for the miracle.

Luke connects "filling" with two Greek words to describe the emotional quality of the feelings in the crowd. He begins with the Greek word (thambos), translated *wonder*. It means "to surprise, to astound, or to dumbfound." No one could dispute the reality of the lame man walking; his walking was beyond explanation and shocking to see. He was more than 40 (Acts 4:22); he was in a lame condition from birth (Acts 3:2). What *wonder* filled their lives!

Luke also uses the Greek word (ekstasis), translated *amazement*. This word describes an ecstasy in which the mind is for a time carried, as it were, out of or beyond itself and lost. It could be translated "out of my mind." This miracle so gripped their inner lives, they questioned each other, "Are we losing our minds?"

It seems Luke could not help but continually comment on what was happening in the lives of the crowd. He says, **"Now as the lame man who was healed held on to Peter and John, all the people ran together to them in the porch which is called Solomon's, greatly amazed"** (Acts 3:11). The Greek word (ekthambos), translated *greatly amazed*, and is the basic Greek word "thambos" with the prefix "ek." This prefix strengthens the basic word that means "astonished or amazed." This is the same basic Greek word used in verse 10, **and they were filled with wonder** (thambos).

Luke continues by noting Peter's recognition of this condition in the crowd. Peter responded to the people, **"Men of Israel, why do you marvel at this?"** (Acts 3:12). It means "to wonder, marvel, be struck with admiration or astonishment. This miracle was a shocking surprise to the crowds. If they knew the truth about Jesus and the fullness of His Spirit, they would rejoice and praise. This power and presence could also dwell in them. He is going to call them to repentance.

What an amazing story! To keep everything in proper perspective, let's view the basic ideas.

## Method

We will spend little time on this point because it is well covered in the above material. The heart of the miracle is Jesus. He is the source by which the lame man is now walking. The healed beggar is deeply aware of this fact as evidenced by his praise to God (Acts 3:9). Peter becomes concerned that the crowd doesn't understand this. The crowd gathers around Peter and John as the healed man holds onto them (Acts 3:11). Peter cries, **"Or why look so intently at us, as though by our own power or godliness we had made this man walk?"** (Acts 3:12). He immediately launches into a discourse describing what God did for them and this beggar. 5000 men become convinced the source of this miracle is Jesus. They believe in Him (Acts 4:4).

The heart of the Book of Acts displays the Spirit of Jesus as the only source for life. No other addition to Him can be. The source is not a combination of powers; it is only Jesus! The education or training of the apostles is not it (Acts 4:13). A personality enabling them to attract the crowd is not mentioned. No talent, such as singing, is highlighted. We hear nothing of an organized committee meeting to brainstorm about new methodology. No study is initiated to establish the demographics or cultural adaptation of the message. The entire Book of Acts is filled with "God is moving"! He is the only explanation for what is happening.

Does this mean education is evil or wrong? Certainly not! However, when I depend on my education instead of Jesus as the Source, education becomes my god. The Apostle Paul was one of the most highly educated men in his day. He used his education in the writing of much of the New Testament. He mentions his education a few times, but it is never highlighted as the source for ministry. He says, ***"For you see your calling, brethren, that not many wise according to the flesh, not many mighty, not many noble, are called. But God has chosen the foolish things of the world to put to shame the wise, and God has chosen the weak things of the world to put to shame the things which are mighty;"*** (1 Corinthians 1:26-27). We are to depend on Jesus alone!

## Means

If we are thoroughly convinced the source of ministry is exclusively Jesus, then we can consider the instruments He might use to accomplish this ministry. We are the instruments. Jesus did not just do the miracle; He did it through Peter and John. Peter was the one who confronted the lame beggar (Acts 3:4). Peter was the one who spoke to him (Acts 3:4). Peter was the one who commanded him to ***"rise up and walk"*** (Acts 3:6). Peter was the one who seized him by the right hand (Acts 3:7). Peter was used by Jesus to give the explanation that convinced the crowd (Acts 3:12). Peter and John were the ones arrested and threatened for their witness (Acts 4:3, 21). Peter and John had no lack of involvement. No one could accuse them of being "lazy." They did not passively sit back in idleness; they were instruments for Jesus' use. They became the platform on which the resource of the Spirit of Jesus was displayed.

Pride is a grave danger for the "instrument." The glove might consider it is accomplishing feats without the source of the hand. The moment this idea is considered, defeat is inevitable. If the disciples had taken credit for the miracle, the leaders of Israel would have ignored them. The single factor upsetting the leaders was Jesus. Luke writes, *"So they called them and commanded them not to speak at all nor teach in the name of Jesus"* (Acts 4:18). It seems easier to learn the language than to learn the activity of faith. I say all the words, know all the phrases, and speak the correct language, but do I completely depend on Him?

The leaders of Israel released Peter and John, then they returned to the early church. They *reported all that the chief priests and elders had said to them* (Acts 4:23). This report contained the displeasure and threats of the most powerful men of Jerusalem. These threats must be seen by all the disciples in light of the recent crucifixion of Jesus. The early Church embraced these threats with prayer and Scripture (Acts 4:24-30). The prayer was a request for the continued flow of the resource of Jesus to use them as instruments. Their prayer was answered; *the place where they were assembled together was shaken; and they were all filled with the Holy Spirit, and they spoke the word of God with boldness* (Acts 4:31). When confronted with threats, they returned to and focused on Jesus!

## Motivation

If Jesus is moving through the apostles, what is the purpose? If a lame beggar is restored, what is the purpose? Jesus is always concerned about the individual. We must not generalize the truth. To say that God wants to win the whole world is easy. Therefore, the motive for His death, resurrection, and ascension is to evangelize. Jesus heals a lame beggar because He wants to win 5000 men. He wants to grow a great church.

Although these facts may contain truth, they are not the complete truth. God is interested in winning the whole world (John 3:16). However, the world must be understood in terms of people. The miracle of the lame beggar is not a means to an

**Part One:** The Event

end. Jesus is genuinely interested and concerned over this one man. Even if evangelism had not been the result, Jesus would still have stopped Peter and used him as an instrument to change this lame beggar!

But we must note the progression here! Once the lame beggar is healed and responds, Jesus immediately uses him to affect another life. Jesus is desperately concerned about life. Although we may not know his name, Jesus does. This individual comes to the temple for the ninth hour of prayer. He does not know about the New Covenant instituted by Jesus. He has not embraced the wonder of the fullness of the Spirit of Jesus. He is steeped in the traditions of his upbringing and culture; he must be shaken into reality. The miracle of the lame beggar will become the instrument of this shaking.

The fact that there may be 5000 people shaken does not discount the truth of this motive. God would have used Peter for just one person, the lame beggar. God would use the lame beggar for one person or 5000 "one persons." The same involvement Jesus had in the life of the lame beggar is the same involvement in each life of those in the temple. He plots, moves, and acts on behalf of each person.

One might immediately wonder how they can get involved in the lives of others. Our focus is not on the motive because that belongs to Jesus. Our focus is to be on intimacy and being an instrument. This means we receive no credit, because we did not plan it, we did not initiate it, or we did not do it. Look what He did!

## Acts 3:11

# A CLINGING CONVERT

*Now as the lame man who was healed held on to Peter and John, all the people ran together to them in the porch which is called Solomon's, greatly amazed (Acts 3:11).*

In this verse Luke highlights something we cannot miss. In the Greek text of this passage, the subject is ***people***. The main verb is ***run together***. This group of people was ***greatly amazed*** over the miracle in the lame beggar's life. Although all this information is present in this verse, it is not the focus. Because this information is found by the reader in the first word of the text, it is what Luke highlights in the verse and considers the most important information about the lame beggar.

***"Now as the lame man who was healed held"*** is actually translated from two Greek words. The first Greek word is the conjunction "de," translated ***now***. This gives us additional information from what is told in the preceding verses. The second Greek word is "krateo" and is a verb in the participle form, which modifies and gives further content to the healed man. Thus the words ***"as the lame man who was healed"*** are added to the translation to identify what is modified. The Greek word "krateo" conveys "to have power over, to grasp, or to hold firmly."

This miracle is contrasted with the miracle at the Pool of Bethesda. A man ***had an infirmity thirty-eight years*** (John 5:5).

Jesus commanded him, ***"Rise, take up your bed and walk"*** (John 5:8). Immediately this man walked with his bed on his shoulder. However, it was the Sabbath and the Jews decided to stone him. The healed man defended himself by blaming Jesus though he did not know Him. John writes, **but the one who was healed did not know who it was, for Jesus had withdrawn,** a multitude **being in that place** (John 5:13).

The healed beggar **held on to Peter and John**. He "adhered" to them" and "joined himself" to them; he was desirous of "remaining" and "participating" with them. Other translations use words such as "clinging," "firmly clung," "kept his hand on," "wouldn't let go," "holding tightly to," and "threw his arms around."

As we have noted in previous studies, this new condition was not a temporary state for this healed man. As Peter begins his message to the gathered crowd, he refers to the healed man present (Acts 3:6). After the message and the positive response of the people, the apostles were put in jail for the night. The leaders of Israel interrogated them the next morning. In response Peter says, ***"Let it be known to you all, and to all the people of Israel, that by the name of Jesus Christ of Nazareth, whom you crucified, whom God raised from the dead, by Him this man stands here before you whole"*** (Acts 4:10). How did the healed beggar get there? Did he refuse to leave the apostles and end in jail with them? How did he attend a private meeting among the leaders of Israel? Luke writes, **and seeing the man who had been healed standing with them, they could say nothing against it** (Acts 4:14). He was definitely there!

This attitude and spirit is highlighted throughout this story. Luke presents it to us quite naturally. Is it automatically ingrained in an experience with Jesus? When He captures us does His presence cause that in us? Is Jesus so wonderful that we "adhere" to Him? We "join ourselves" to Him. We desire to "remain with Him" and "participate" with Him! We "cling," "firmly cling," "keep our hands on," "won't let go of," "hold tightly to," or "throw our arms around!" May I assure you this response is normal in experiencing Jesus.

Join me in examining this thought in light of our passage.

## Attraction

I desperately want to be true to the passage. Could I start with my personal testimony about Jesus? He is so attractive to me. What is it about Him that causes my entire self to respond? The consistency of His nature reassures me. His holiness pulls me to goodness. His love embraces me and will not let me go. His wisdom challenges me to know more. His attitude draws me to all that is positive. His emotional stability presents to me a foundation for stable living. His wholeness assures me that I can be complete in Him. The light of His countenance brightens my life. His resurrected life allows me to live in Him. His serenity brings rest to my soul. The boundaries of His arms will not let me stray. His crucifixion assures me of His love. His reigning Lordship tells me nothing can harm me. His authority over all things shrinks all obstacles. His generous heart gives me all I can ever need. Why does He attract me? I was made for Him. I cannot live without Him; why would I want to try?

Is that what is happening to this healed beggar? Let's go back to the Greek word (krateo), translated **held on to**. It appears 47 times in the New Testament. Its uses vary from an individual being held as a prisoner (Mark 6:17) to the women clinging to the feet of their risen Lord (Matthew 28:9). An element of force and aggression is contained in the word, and it can be used in the negative or positive sense. Jesus **took** (krateo) Peter's mother-in-law by the hand and healed her of the fever (Mark 1:31). This force and aggression is no doubt present in the interaction of the healed beggar and the apostles.

However, we must not just focus on the physical aspect

of this involvement; look at the attitude, the aggressive heart causing this seizing! I was strangely moved by Jesus using the same Greek word (krateo) as He spoke to the churches. It rings throughout His messages as if this aggressiveness is what He really desires for them and us. He openly confesses this attitude is how He feels and what He does. He says, *"**These things says He who holds** (krateo) **the seven stars in His right hand, who walks in the midst of the seven golden lampstands**"* (Revelation 2:1). The way a healed beggar is drawn to and holds onto Jesus shining through an apostle is the same way Jesus is drawn to and holds on to us, the church.

Three of the seven churches to which He speaks He calls to this "attraction." He compliments the church in Pergamum. ***And you hold*** (krateo) ***fast to My name*** (Revelation 2:13). However, there are others in this church who **hold** (krateo) **the doctrine of Balaam** (Revelation 2:14), and others **who hold** (krateo) **the doctrine of the Nicolaitans, which thing I hate** (Revelation 2:15). Jesus challenges the church in Thyatira, **"But hold** (krateo) **fast what you have till I come"** (Revelation 2:25). Jesus delivers the same message to the church in Philadelphia. **"Behold, I am coming quickly! Hold** (krateo) **fast what you have, that no one may take your crown"** (Revelation 3:11).

Look closely at each of these encouragements. They cannot possibly be interpreted as activities, rules to keep, or ceremonies to observe. The heart's passion is highlighted in each. He calls upon desire and delight. This call echoes from the Old Testament. Listen to the Psalmist, **"I delight to do Your will, O my God, and Your law is within my heart"** (Psalm 40:8). He continued, **"Whom have I in heaven but You? And there is none upon earth that I desire besides You. My flesh and my heart fail; but God is the strength of my heart and my portion forever"** (Psalm 73:25-26). Although the (krateo) is not used, the same aggressive call exists.

The same spirit captured the early church. ***So continuing*** *daily with one accord in the temple, and breaking bread from house to house, they ate their food with gladness and simplicity of heart, praising God and having favor with all the people* (Acts 2:46-47). God gives us all a burning heart of seeking, passion, openness, and response, and it is a heart that just cannot stay away.

## Adjustment

One might respond, "Well, the healed beggar just received a miracle. No wonder he is excited and focused." Are you indicating this excitement will not last long? Are you basing this on your experience? How often we have looked at those who receive a fresh touch from Jesus and say, "They will get over it!" Is this because we have? But the significance of the passage is that he did not get over it! We see him as the story unfolds throughout chapters three and four. He is still **holding on** (krateo).

This **holding on** is not only evident in the rest of the story, but also in the grammar of the Greek word (krateo), which is in the present tense. In the Greek language this means "now with continual action." When you couple this with his continuation with the apostles during the persecution, it is apparent his passion is not fading. This truth gains more force as we realize the main verb of the sentence (syntrecho) is not present tense but aorist. Thus, the focus of the sentence is on the continuing action of this healed man's passion.

But the excitement and experience of a miracle can fade. One can easily get into the routine and forget the marvelous change. One fits into a new way of life. This way of life is new and thrilling, but even this will grow into an ordinary, everyday living experience. Remember there will be problems and difficulties in the new way of life. He will have to get a job; he cannot beg

**Part One:** The Event

any longer. He will need sandals to wear, so his expenses will increase. Life will get more complicated, and the luster of his new miracle will soon fade.

But it did not! The answer is found by the reader in the "adjustment" made our passage. This passage is not about a miracle; indeed, the luster of such a miracle could fade. This passage is about Jesus, and this does not fade! As one views the rest of chapter three, the adjustment is made by Peter in his sermon of explanation. The focus of the healed beggar may have been on the miracle. But Peter very forcibly said, *"In the name of Jesus Christ of Nazareth, rise up and walk"* (Acts 3:6). They were amazed by the miracle because *they knew that it was he who sat begging alms at the Beautiful Gate of the temple;* (Acts 3:10).

Peter is absolutely horrified at the thought that this man or the crowd might focus on him. He cries, *"Men of Israel, why do you marvel at this? Or why look so intently at us, as though by our own power or godliness we had made this man walk?"* (Acts 3:12). Immediately he begins to promote Jesus. He boldly identifies Jesus as the One they *delivered up and denied in the presence of Pilate, when he was determined to let Him go* (Acts 3:13). He leaves absolutely no room for any misunderstanding concerning the identity of Jesus, his focus.

Peter continues his identification of Jesus by referring to the prophets. Jesus is the fulfillment of the prophecies of Moses. He said, *"The Lord your God will raise up for you a Prophet like me from your brethren. Him you shall hear in all things, whatever He says to you. And it shall be that every soul who will not hear that Prophet shall be utterly destroyed from among the people"* (Acts 3:22-23). It was not just Moses (who was enough) but it was *all the prophets* (Acts 3:24). Samuel and everyone was from the time of Moses until this (Acts 3:24). In fact, Peter proclaims they are the first to receive this revelation of Jesus (Acts 3:26). God is blessing them!

This promotion is not a focus on doctrine, although there is a doctrine involved. This promotion is a focus on a living, functioning, historic person named Jesus. This promotion is not about an experience, although there was a miracle in this man's life. This promotion is not about tradition, although previous patterns of history are recalled. This promotion is not about promises of the past, although God's promises are highlighted. This promotion is not about their guilt, although it is stated that they are guilty. This promotion is not about the customs and culture of their generation, for, as in a previous explanation, they must *be saved from this perverse generation* (Acts 2:40). This promotion is about Jesus!

## Amazement

This verse is the second mention of "amazement" in this story. People saw the once lame beggar walking and leaping in the temple. This sighting was magnified by the fact he was praising God for this miracle. They knew who he was because he had been at the Gate Beautiful for nearly 40 years. Luke writes, and *they were filled with wonder and amazement at what had happened to him* (Acts 3:10). This sighting stimulated a movement of the crowd to gather around Peter, John, and the healed man. Luke records, *all the people ran together to them in the porch which is called Solomon's, greatly amazed* (Acts 3:11). We must place this amazement of what has taken place since Pentecost. The crucifixion of Jesus has been spoken everywhere by everyone. The rumor of the resurrection has also spread throughout Jerusalem. The general population has no reason to accept this as fact. The Pentecost Event has stirred the city again; in addition 3000 of the population accepted Jesus and were added to the church. Daily they were in the temple as witnesses to Jesus. *Many wonders and signs were done through the apostles*

**Part One:** The Event

during these days (Acts 2:43). The news of awesome miracles and incredible wonders must have spread daily throughout the city.

Now the temple crowd sees a miracle with their eyes which is not just this one amazing miracle. This miracle points to all the other miracles, which point to the resurrection and truth about Jesus. Peter, in his message to them, clarifies what they are already thinking. This miracle serves the purpose for which miracles are designed. They do not focus on themselves but are "signs." This miracle is a finger pointing towards of Jesus. This crowd is awestruck with the wonder of all flowing from the Spirit of Jesus.

This miracle alone is a momentary interruption in the temple worship for that day. It is a curious event, which draws attention for a moment. But place it in the revelation of Jesus with what has taken place, and our lives are permanently changed. We are brought back to Jesus who alone is the amazing element. Anyone who loses his passion or amazement has lost focus on Jesus. Everything else from church work, ministry involvement, or stardom fades in its thrill. Only Jesus can maintain and increase the constant wonder and amazement in my life!

# PART TWO
## ACTS 3:12-26

# EXHORTATION FROM THE PORCH

Acts 3:12

# PARADOX OF SOURCING

*So when Peter saw it, he responded to the people: "Men of Israel, why do you marvel at this? Or why look so intently at us, as though by our own power or godliness we had made this man walk?" (Acts 3:12).*

What an event! The early Church is growing and demonstrating the life of Jesus throughout Jerusalem. The witness is strong enough to find **favor with all the people** (Acts 2:47). Volumes of writings would have to offer all the evidence of this. Luke selects one great illustration (Acts 3:1-11). He chooses a lame man placed daily at the Gate Beautiful to beg. He has been lame since birth and is now more than 40 years. He is always there at the ninth hour, three o'clock in the afternoon, which is the hour of prayer when the crowd greatly increases. Throughout these many years he developed the skills and discernment to work the crowd to receive the greatest financial reward.

The Holy Spirit moves on Peter and John to confront this lame man. This confrontation becomes a special occasion as the lame man is healed. The details of the miracle revolve around Jesus. Peter has the person of Jesus; he amply gives Him to this man. The power showed in the miracle is all **in the name of Jesus Christ of Nazareth,** (Acts 3:6). Jesus links with Peter as he reaches forth his right hand to lift the man to his feet. The lame man is healed and does not lazily slip off, but he leaps, walks, and praises

**Part Two:** Exhortation from the Porch

God. All people in the temple become aware of this man's miracle.

As Peter and John move in the temple area, they arrive ***in the porch which is called Solomon's,*** (Acts 3:11). Because of the crowd's state of amazement, Peter chooses to "exhort" them. His delivery is not a sermon in the proper sense. He does not select a text as he did in the sermon at Pentecost (Acts 2:16-21). His message is a response to a great concern he has over the focus of the crowd. He points them to Jesus. He reveals the empowerment and nature of Jesus in the form of "paradoxes." A paradox is a seemingly absurd or self-contradictory statement or proposition that when investigated or explained may prove to be well founded or true. One such example is Jesus is the "***glorified***" One, a "***Servant***" (Acts 3:13). He is "***the Holy One and the Just***," but Barabbas, a murderer, is the one they prefer to free (Acts 3:14). Jesus is the "***Prince of life***" and is killed (Acts 3:15). These are a few of the paradoxes.

Verse eleven becomes a transitional sentence between the miracle and our present study, "Exhortation from the Porch" (Acts 3:12-26). We are going to begin with the Paradox of Sourcing (Acts 3:12).

## Paradox of Sourcing

***The lame man who was healed held on to Peter and John*** (Acts 3:11). "Krateo" is the Greek word translated "***held on to***." It comes from the root word for "strength." It means, "to seize, grasp with strength." The idea of the verse is that this healed man was physically holding onto Peter and John. While he was doing this, the crowd began to run to the area of the porch to see what was happening. You can understand the crowd's focus on Peter and John. Peter understood that he was the instrument for the movement of Jesus' power to this man. The difficulty for the lame man and the crowd is recognizing Peter's power source.

Paradox of Sourcing | **Acts 3:12**

Peter spoke the words of deliverance. Peter reached out his hand and inspired the first movement of the lame man to healing. It was Peter who rejoiced with the man in his miracle. Why the healed man held on to Peter is not a question!

Peter and John's awareness of the situation presented in verse eleven is highlighted in the first Greek word of our verse. This verse begins with the Greek word "eido." It comes from the root word "oida," one of the four Greek words meaning "to know." It means to grasp, perceive, or understand. The disciples were not just seeing with their eyes, but they understood what was happening in the hearts of the healed man and the crowd. A correction must occur. This understanding is further emphasized by the Greek word "aprokrinomai," translated "*he responded.*" This word portrays the sense of evaluating, judging, or discerning. Peter does not answer a question that the people ask. He responds to what he discerns the crowd is thinking.

Peter asks two questions. The first one is **"Why do you marvel at this?"** This question corresponds to how he greets them, **"Men of Israel."** You are the people of God. You read and memorize the great Old Testament stories of deliverance. The Old Testament is about a contrast between the Living God Jehovah and the dead gods of the pagans. How do we know our God is alive? He acts. God's actions are revealed in the stories of His deliverances on our behalf. The people of Israel celebrate these Divine acts annually. They know the details of every story because they are told by other Israelis repeatedly.

Besides this, they hear about the remarkable things Jesus is doing in their midst (Acts 2:42). Why wouldn't the healing of a lame man stir them to this height of wonder? Why wouldn't they praise and thank God as He moves again before them? Instead, they wonder and are amazed at this miracle. They focus on the miracle instead of the God doing it. They are like little children who get more excited about the gift than the one who gave it. You should not marvel at all, but you should praise. Jesus

Part Two: Exhortation from the Porch

just does these things. ***"Why do you marvel at this?"***

The second question Peter asks is equally penetrating. ***"Or why look so intently at us, as though by our own power or godliness we had made this man walk?"*** The first part of this second question, ***"Or why look so intently at us,"*** is a translation of "atenizo." The first letter "a" is a particle of union and brings intensity to the word. The second part "tenizo" means "to strain or to stretch." The crowds could not help staring at these two apostles. They fixed their attention on Peter and John.

The rest of the question tells us why they are staring at the apostles; it forms the basis of the question that Peter asks, ***"As though by our own power or godliness we had made this man walk?"*** A strong emphasis is on "***own***." Does this crowd think it is the self-sourcing power of Peter and John that caused this miracle? Do they think any man could have this kind of power in himself? Is it by self-sourcing?

In addition, did this miracle happen through the "***godliness***" of these two men? The crowds thought this man was lame because of the sin of his parents. It would take pure holiness or godliness to invade the demonic territory of sin and change the consequences of sin. This miracle is not only physical, but this is also a redemptive miracle. Are the persons of Peter and John so strong in their self-sourcing or so righteous in their nature, they could restore this lame man?

Do you and I think we are exempt from this controversy? This sourcing controversy is a fundamental paradox of our lives. This sourcing deals with the core of all our activities; it speaks to the attitude and focus of our lives. In fact, it may reveal whether we are Christian. This point is so valuable and important that when settled the flow of all Christianity naturally happens. To miss this available sourcing is to miss it all! Am I going to trust in Jesus or in myself? Will I allow Him to source my future or do I need to step in and give direction? Can Jesus heal my relationships or do I need to guard and protect myself? This question is as old as the healed lame man and the crowd of two thousand years ago but is as up to date as your life and mine!

We might find ourselves in several approaches. They are revealed in Peter's exhortation.

## God is Acting and We Think it is Us

This opening statement of Peter's exhortation is bold. *So when Peter saw it, he responded to the people: "Men of Israel, why do you marvel at this? Or why look so intently at us, as though by our own power or godliness we had made this man walk?"* (Acts 3:12). Jesus is responsible for this miracle. When this man showed **perfect soundness in the presence of you all,** it was because of **His name** (Acts 3:16). God acted! There is no other explanation. God's capability to do such a miracle is not astonishing. No one is surprised in God's ability to straighten bones and strengthen limbs. So **why do you marvel at this?**

The answer is in thinking it is us! If a mere human has the resource to heal this lame man, it would be astounding. You look at us as if you think we did this miracle. We do not have the power, and we do not have the godliness to conquer Satan's work. We are exactly like you! Peter must have told them of his earlier denial of Jesus. He did not have the power to even stand up to one servant girl in the night hour. He cursed the name of Jesus in failure. This miracle of healing was only a few months after the demonstration of what self-sourcing produces. Now this crowd looks at Peter as if he is responsible for this miracle.

Paul and Barnabas confront a man in Lystra crippled in his feet from his mother's womb. Jesus healed this man through Paul; **he leaped and walked** (Acts 14:10). The crowd sees this miracle and immediately cries out, **"The gods have come down to us in the likeness of men!"** (Acts 14:11). When Paul and Barnabas recognize what is happening, they tear their clothes and cry out to them, ***"Men, why are you doing these things? We also are men with the same nature as you,"*** (Acts 14:15). God does something great, and somehow we think it is us.

Perhaps you feel as if this does not apply to you. You have never accredited a miracle from God to any man. But the reality of the case is we all have! We live out of ourselves daily; we accomplish many things and accredit them to our own knowledge and skill. We make ourselves feel better from the encouragement of our own achievements. Do you realize the involvement of God in your life? If His resources were removed from you, your life would fall apart. This need is true whether you belong to Him. Where do you get your ability to get out of bed in the morning? Who gave you the ability to make money? Why do you have a job? Your capacity for love, family, and feelings of contentment come from Him. We live as if it is us! We should all fall on our faces in repentance. We are self-sourced.

This recognition is the loud call of Christianity! Will we recognize "God is acting?" He is the source, but we think it is us. Is it not the height of folly? Will you make a new commitment in your heart to never take credit for another thing? Are you willing to recognize that He is your source? The removal of His supplying hand will mean absolute ruin. To be Christian is to embrace Him as the source!

## The Devil is Acting and We Think it is Us

Don't you hate to be conned? When someone manipulates, uses, and deceives you, it is upsetting. In his exhortation to the Jewish crowd, Peter reveals that this deception is what happened to them. God's intent was to glorify His Servant Jesus (Acts 3:13). He did this despite them. They were being used by the devil. Peter says that it was through ignorance. He says, ***"Yet now, brethren, I know that you did it in ignorance, as did also your*** *rulers"* (Acts 3:17). Paul admits this about himself by testifying, **"Although I was formerly a blasphemer, a persecutor, and an insolent man; but I obtained mercy because I did it ignorantly in unbelief"** (1 Timothy 1:13).

This mercy is good news. If we did it ignorantly, then we are not to blame. But revelation has come! You know now! This new knowledge is why Peter calls these people to *repent* (Acts 3:19). They thought they were acting when they were actually being used by the devil. Peter even lists the physical activities resulting from the demonic sourcing. He says, **"You delivered up and denied in the presence of Pilate, when he was determined to let Him go"** (Acts 3:13). To study the three religious trials and the three secular trials of Jesus is surprising. Each trial was filled with the sourcing of the kingdom of darkness. The trial of Caiaphas, illegally held at night by their Jewish law, is called "a mock trial" (Matthew 26:57). It is held at night which is illegal by their Jewish law. No human can be tried for his or her life at night. This kind of decision must be made when men are rested and alert. In that trial, they enter into a demonic frenzy and beat Jesus nearly to death. They pull his beard out by demonic strength. They drag Him to Pilate for the secular trial. Pilate desperately wants to release Him. The Jewish crowd has a chance to glorify God in Christ, but they do not. They think it is their choice, but all the time they are under the control of the devil.

Peter reminded them, **"But you denied the Holy One and the Just, and asked for a murderer to be granted to you"** (Acts 3:14). God gave them a chance to choose between Barabbas, a robber, and Jesus, their Messiah (Matthew 27:16-17). They preferred anyone other than Jesus. How could it be? The question was consistently asked, **"Why, what evil has He done?"** (Matthew 27:23). They were instruments of the devil warring against God. Peter continues by saying, "You **killed the Prince of life**" (Acts 3:15). This statement by Peter is a startling truth! Each

**Part Two:** Exhortation from the Porch

time I act, sourcing myself, I am an instrument of the devil. Self-sourcing is the devil's nature.

## Jesus Acts and We Know it is Him

Peter's exhortation of repentance to the Jewish crowd is his high point. If they would only ***repent therefore and be converted, that your sins may be blotted out, so that times of refreshing may come from the presence of the Lord,*** (Acts 3:19). The "refreshing" of His presence comes in the recognition that He is acting. We live in the flow of His Spirit who accomplishes His will through our lives. Oh, the wonder of living moment by moment in the active sourcing of His power. Our attitude, action, expressions, purpose, and intent are all in cooperation with His Spirit. He is acting, and we know it.

Do you sense the safety and security of living in His action, His sourcing? Despite what the Jews did to Jesus, they could not stop the accomplishment of God's plan. ***The God of Abraham, Isaac, and Jacob, the God of our fathers, glorified His Servant Jesus*** through the demonic sourcing of the crucifixion (Acts 3:13). Through the devil's sourcing, they ***killed the Prince of life, whom God raised from the dead, of which we are witnesses*** (Acts 3:15). I must live in the sourcing of Jesus!

## Acts 3:13

# THE PARADOX OF SERVANT

*The God of Abraham, Isaac, and Jacob, the God of our fathers, glorified His Servant Jesus, whom you delivered up and denied in the presence of Pilate, when he was determined to let Him go (Acts 3:13).*

The commotion is overwhelming! Crowds of people are on the move. The news spreads like a wave rolling from person to person. Everyone is gathering at Solomon's Porch to see the latest miracle from that group called "Christians." Many folks had only heard of the miracles; now they have the chance to actually witness one. If some miracles are suspicious, this one is definitely not. The lame man was born this way. He lived in this community for more than 40 years. Everyone knows him; he is a permanent fixture at the Gate Beautiful, his spot. If you come to the temple at three o'clock, you will find him there. Can this man be healed?

As you arrive at Solomon's Porch, it is easy to spot the lame beggar who has been healed. He is holding onto Peter and John, the apostles. Does he think they are responsible for his miracle? If they go away, will the miracle vanish as well? Everyone thinks this event will bring Peter and John fame and wealth.

What is Peter saying? He rebukes the crowd for being surprised at this miracle. After all, the time is an hour of prayer when such prayer requests are made. Surely, someone in this

**Part Two:** Exhortation from the Porch

crowd prayed for this lame man. Why should anyone "marvel" at the movement of God? Are not the Old Testament stories filled with such deliverances?

Peter says something else, continuing his rebuke. He says he is not any different than from other men, denying any claim to power or godliness resulting in this miracle. Did he or did he not do the miracle? Was not it his hand that reached out and raised the lame man to his feet? He spoke the words that stirred something deep inside the lame man. Surely we are going to think he had something to do with it.

If he is not responsible, then who is? Peter just said, **"The God of Abraham, Isaac, and Jacob, the God of our fathers,"** (Acts 3:13). Everyone in the crowd voiced the same words in the past hour because it is **the hour of prayer, the ninth hour** (Acts 3:1). They came to the temple to offer the sacrifice and make the prayers. They were taught to repeat this phrase in their recited prayers. Peter is speaking about their God! Jehovah is the God of their forefathers; He is the One in whom they believe. He proved Himself repeatedly in the deliverances of the Old Testament. They celebrate His Divine power in all their feast days.

What does our great God have to do with this miracle? What did Peter say? He said, **"The God of Abraham, Isaac, and Jacob, the God of our fathers, glorified His Servant Jesus,"** (Acts 3:13). Wait a minute! The crowd begins to question what they have witnessed. Is this miracle an act of our God "glorifying" Jesus, the One we crucified? Is our God connected to this One called Jesus? How can that be? We heard that Jesus of Nazareth was a criminal; after all, He died with a criminal on each side. We may be confused about Jesus of Nazareth, but we are certainly not confused about **the God of Abraham, Isaac, and Jacob, the God of our fathers.** If **the God of Abraham, Isaac, and Jacob, the God of our fathers** is the basis of the new Christian faith, it is not new at all. Is Peter saying that the roots of Jesus are in our Old Testament? Jesus has not started something new but is completing what was begun by our forefathers.

What exactly is the connection between our God Jehovah and Jesus? Peter seems to think our God **glorified His Servant Jesus** through this lame man whom he healed. The Greek word "doxaso," translated **glorified**, means "to render or esteem glorious." The root word (doxa) means "to think or suppose." It emerges from the idea of thought or opinion, especially favorable human opinion. Therefore, secondly it means reputation, praise, splendor, light, perfection or rewards. The "doxa" or glory of man is human opinion, which is shifty, uncertain and often based on error. Man pursues glory for his own safety and personal gain. The glory is unworthy. On the other hand, God's opinion highlights the true value of things as they seem to the eternal mind; God's favorable opinion is true glory.

Our human opinion of Jesus is a very low opinion. We **delivered** Him **up and denied** Him **in the presence of Pilate, when he was determined to let Him go** (Acts 3:13). In fact, we **denied the Holy One and the Just, and asked for a murderer to be granted to** us (Acts 3:14). Actually, we **killed the Prince of life** (Acts 3:15). How can one describe our opinion? We viewed Him as a criminal and treated Him like one. He angered us and threatened our traditions. We were totally ignorant (Acts 3:17).

God's opinion, the Trinity's view, of Jesus is far different. Jesus' presence within a lame man will not allow anklebones to remain weak. His power and godliness invades demonic territory and releases every demonic hold. God's view of Jesus is one of honor and high value. He is the **Holy One and the Just**. Our God did not glorify Jesus through the golden temple or our ceremonies. He did not use the elaborately dressed high priest or any of his associates. Jesus was **glorified** through a lame beggar.

But look at Peter's description of Jesus. Jesus is God's Servant, and this is a paradox because it is not how we think. A paradox is a seemingly absurd or self-contradictory statement or proposition that when investigated or explained may prove to be well founded or true. Why would God glorify a *Servant*? This decision of God certainly parallels the idea of God using a lame beggar instead of someone important. God thinks this way.

The Greek word (pais), translated *Servant,* is used 24 times in the New Testament, and there is an interesting study connected to the word. Matthew consistently uses this word to refer to a boy or a child. However, Luke interprets the "pais" as a slave (doulos) in order to express or emphasize a non-family relationship between the one who commands and the one who obeys. In the Book of Acts, Luke calls Jesus a *Servant* ("pais" meaning "doulos") four times (Acts 3:13, 26; 4:27, 30). In other words, Luke does not deny the family relationship within the Trinity; instead he highlights the complete obedience of Jesus to His Father. He does not focus on just the activity of the obedience, but on the attitude and state of being. Jesus has the very nature of a *Servant*. What is this state?

## Servant Role

Paul highlights this state in his great "Kenosis passage" (Philippians 2:5-2:11). He encourages us to have the same state of being, attitude, and mind as Jesus. In describing this state, he uses the word *servant* (doulos). He uses the description of **obedient to the point of death, even the death of the cross.** In each part of the description, Paul relates the lowering of oneself to showing "humility." In the high position of being God, Jesus did not have the right to maintain such a state. Rather, He set aside all of the advantages of being in that position and took on the position of one dying on a cross. This denial of divine advantages was obedience to the plan established by the Trinity.

When Peter calls Jesus as the **Servant** of **the God of Abraham, Isaac, and Jacob, the God of our fathers,** he is referring to the redemptive plan of crucifixion. In other words, Jesus is obedient to the nature of the Triune God. Whatever thunders in the heart of the Trinity thunders through the member of that Trinity who became a man. What will the nature of God look like if planted into the heart of man? It will look like Jesus. In describing this nature, Peter relates it to the cross. This description is why we consistently speak of the cross style because it is the role of a servant!

We must understand this deep principle in the heart of God. In God's opinion or perspective, Jesus is glorified when a lame beggar is healed; a lame beggar restored to life and purpose is the glorification of Jesus. This restoration is God's desire. Jesus is not glorified because He is a star; His fame is spread everywhere. He is not glorified because of the action of a miracle or because Jesus had the resource to do miracles. The glorification is the lame beggar's **walking, leaping, and praising God** (Acts 3:8). When an individual in his absolute helplessness is embraced by the unlimited resource of Jesus, a new thing, the Kingdom of God, is created, and it the glorification of Jesus is displayed.

Our talents manifested for Jesus do not glorify Him. Our intellect displayed through our education does not glorify Him. Our organizational abilities, operating the large corporation called the "church" do not glorify Him. Jesus is glorified through the cross style. Have you ever been the glorification of Jesus? Glorifying Jesus is not something you do; it is something the **God of Abraham, Isaac, and Jacob, the God of our fathers** does through you. In His servant nature of total helplessness, God can be glorified through Jesus. Through the lame beggar's absolute inability, God could glorify Jesus through him.

# Servant Relationship

There is another important aspect to the state of glorification is. In our verse Peter exhorts, *"The God of Abraham, Isaac, and Jacob, the God of our fathers, glorified His Servant Jesus,"* (Acts 3:13). The Greek word "autos," translated **His,** is in the genitive, which establishes relationship between two words. The relationship between the Trinity and *Servant Jesus* is far beyond ownership as might be indicated in the English translation. The intimacy and oneness between Jesus and the Father is better felt than explained.

The Jews whom Peter exhorted may be contrasted with this Divine relationship. They **delivered up** (paradidomi) Jesus (Acts 3:13). This Greek word is used consistently in the Gospels for the betrayal by Judas. They *denied in the presence of Pilate, when he was determined to let Him go* (Acts 3:13). They stood in the way and denied Jesus the freedom Pilate wanted to grant Him. These same Jews had a better relationship with Barabbas, a murderer, than they did *the Holy One and the Just* (Acts 3:14). Their only connection with Jesus was to kill *the Prince of life* (Acts 3:15).

But *the God of Abraham, Isaac, and Jacob, the God of our fathers* did none of these things to Jesus. He *glorified His Servant Jesus*. Jesus became the lame beggar. In this *Servant* position the Trinity can embrace Jesus in His helplessness. Jesus can walk, leap, and praise God. He can be the flow of the demonstration of God among men. He will step on the head of the devil and deliver the final blow of defeat. As a helpless man, the Trinity can *glorify His Servant Jesus*. He can even raise Him *from the dead, of which we are witnesses* (Acts 3:15).

Because this took place through Jesus, God can *glorify His Servant Jesus* through the lame beggar. The same empowerment, flow of the Spirit of God, manifested in Jesus would now be manifested in this beggar. How can the change in this man's life be explained? Peter said, *"And His name, through faith in His name, has made this man strong, whom you see and know. Yes, the faith which comes through Him has given him this perfect soundness in the presence of you all"* (Acts 3:16).

Jesus is glorified!

Can you and I embrace Him in this kind of relationship? Can the Trinity embrace me in my helplessness and **glorify His Servant Jesus**? Jesus will not be glorified through my self-discipline or reformations. He will not be applauded because of my cleverness. The long hours of dedicated service and sacrifice for the church do not glorify Him. My positions and powers do not highlight His greatness. In my brokenness, my helplessness, I can experience His embrace. As a lame beggar without hope, I find He comes to me. In this oneness with Him, He is glorified. What a privilege to be the platform for Him to make Himself known to my helpless world! The display of His Person through my helplessness is the visibility of His glory.

## Servant Related

I always thought we were no longer servants, but we became sons of God. A variety of Scriptures certainly say this. In the very heart of Jesus' discourse on the fullness of the Holy Spirit, Jesus said, ***"No longer do I call you servants, for a servant does not know what his master is doing; but I have called you friends, for all things that I heard from My Father I have made known to you"*** (John 15:15). Jesus is in an upper room with His disciples. They are deeply disturbed at the consistent talk of His death. He is within a few hours of the cross. His complete focus is on preparing them for this event and the good news that it will produce. They will be intimate with God as He is intimate with the Father. This means we will not be considered *servants* by Jesus; we are elevated to a new level of *friends*, sons of God.

Jesus equally taught, ***"Yet it shall not be so among you; but whoever desires to become great among you, let him be your servant. And whoever desires to be first among you, let him be your slave"*** (Matthew 20:26-27). It is interesting that Paul begins the Book of Romans with the presentation of his name, **Paul**. He immediately describes himself as ***a slave of Jesus Christ*** (Romans 1:1). He opens the Book of Philippians with the same statement. In writing to Titus, He repeats the phrase. James' book to the twelve tribes scattered abroad opens with his claim to be ***a slave of God and of the Lord Jesus Christ***. Peter's second epistle introduces him as ***a slave and apostle of Jesus Christ***.

Are we slaves, or are we sons of God? Is Jesus a Son or a Slave? Does it have to be one or the other? Could it be that from God's viewpoint He is glorifying Jesus as a Son? However, from Jesus' view as man, He is a slave. God views me as His son. I must consistently see myself as a servant. It is the prodigal son returns with the attitude and determination to simply be a slave to the Father. However, the Father's love will not allow such because he is a son. What will keep the son from becoming an elder brother? What will keep the prodigal son from returning to the pigpen? The continual consciousness that he is a servant will.

## Acts 3:13

# JESUS, A SERVANT OF GOD

*"The God of Abraham, Isaac, and Jacob, the God of our fathers, glorified His Servant Jesus, whom you delivered up and denied in the presence of Pilate, when he was determined to let Him go"*
*(Acts 3:13).*

In our previous study we fell short of grasping the full impact of whom Jesus is as a **Servant**. The paradox of **the God of Abraham, Isaac, and Jacob, the God of our fathers** glorifying **His Servant Jesus** is beyond comprehension. Even more amazing is that the Jews of that hour missed what God was doing despite the fact that they were told of this repeatedly.

The title of **Servant** applying to Jesus is remarkable. The New Testament does not reveal this as a common title for Jesus. Peter uses it twice in his exhortation from Solomon's porch (Acts 3:13, 26). Twice again it is repeated in a prayer in the following chapter (Acts 4:27, 30). The difficulty with the term is that the Greek word "pais" from which **Servant** is translated is more often translated "son." It appears in our translation that the "son of God" concept became so dominate that this translation of **Servant** was seldom used. The translation is notable in this passage because of its apparent connection to the prophecy of Isaiah. Isaiah presented the coming Messiah as "the Suffering Servant" (Isaiah 52, 53). Peter refers to the foretelling of the prophets that Jesus would suffer (Acts 3:18). The most likely

**Part Two:** Exhortation from the Porch

prophecy for this reference is Isaiah.

I want to encourage you to read the prophecy of Isaiah (Isaiah 52:13-53:12). Many Jewish scholars ignore this Messianic prophecy. It did not fit their desires; they could not comprehend a "suffering servant" bringing any kind of deliverance to Israel. Some Jewish scholars attempted to include this prophecy by proposing there would be two Messiahs. Still, their focus was on a military Messiah who would bring political freedom. They missed **His Servant Jesus**.

There seems some elements are connected to this suggested servant role. They are highlighted in the prophecy of Isaiah. Peter underlines them by saying initially in his exhortation that Jesus is a **Servant,** and then he begins to describe the content of this service.

## God Chose Him

To maintain a clear and adequate picture, we must understand completely who God is. Many Evangelical Christians confine their reference to God as the Father, the first member of the Trinity. A biblical emphasis does not allow this. In the Old Testament, a Hebrew word "Elohim" is translated God. Throughout the Old Testament this reference is always plural, a direct reference to the Trinity, the Three in One. The Triune God is seen in the creation of man, *"Then God* (Elohim) ***said, 'Let Us make man in Our image, according to Our likeness;'"*** (Genesis 1:26).

In the New Testament Greek language, ***God*** is a translation of "Theos," which is singular. Even in the Old Testament Greek translation, it is the same. The Greek translators knew the Greek culture with its multitude of gods. If they referred to the God of the Old Testament as plural, the culture would consider it a reference to several gods. So the Greek translators focused on the "oneness" of our God, the Trinity. Although He is three, He is one! Throughout this discussion we will highlight the Trinity, the Three in One.

The Trinity chose Jesus. In the sovereignty of their unity, Jesus was chosen to be the Redeemer. As a member of the Trinity, Jesus was a part of the decision. This participation was not forced on Him; He embraced the choice. He openly and voluntarily placed Himself as **Servant** of God, the Trinity!

Understanding the SINGULAR element in this choice is imperative. No other was qualified to enter this role. The Trinity was driven by their "holiness nature." The style demonstrated on the cross was the motive behind for the development of the plan of the Triune God. They desperately needed a man who could qualify to take humanity back to what was intended for them. The Apostle Paul pictured it as two arenas (Romans 5). Adam was created in the arena of holiness, dependency, and intimacy with God. As the representative of this arena, he opened a door to another arena. The other area was of self-sufficiency, self-sourcing, and sin. Through this one man, Adam, we were all placed in the second arena, the kingdom of darkness.

The Trinity needed another man to open the door to reenter the arena of intimacy with God. He would need to be a man from the arena of holiness who could enter into the arena of sin and lead humanity back. He needed to open a door of Spirit-sourcing. The Trinity could not find such a man. Every man had embraced and participated in the arena of self-sourcing. No one qualified to lead the way back. The Trinity decided One of their members would become this qualified Man. He would become the **Servant Jesus**, a Man who had never participated in humanity's sin. He would be a man with only abilities known to humanity. He would be a man without sin and always dependent on the Spirit of God.

Listen to the language of Peter's exhortation. ***"The God of Abraham, Isaac, and Jacob, the God of our fathers, glorified His Servant Jesus,"*** (Acts 3:13). The statement that the Triune

God of the Old Testament "glorified *His Servant Jesus*" refers to the crucifixion/resurrection event. John, in his Gospel account, continually relates the "glorification" of Jesus to the crucifixion. Jesus is glorified in the accomplishment of the Trinity's plan! He is the *Servant*.

The most significant aspect of this *Servant* is His heart. He is a SHARER of the heart of the Triune God. Can you imagine the Three in One discussing this plan? The Father and the Holy Spirit did not outvote Jesus. He is not stuck with the job. No one is reluctant. The passion of each heart is linked in oneness. What the Father feels is what the Son feels. Each of them feels as the Holy Spirit feels. They are all driven by love for you. This love is a huge sacrifice; the response is spontaneous as they cry in unison, "Whatever the cost!"

We must try to comprehend the omniscience of the Trinity. They all knew what would happen. This adventure was not an attempt or experiment to see what would happen. They knew every detail of the adventure. They saw the full extent of being *delivered up* (Acts 3:13). They understood the depth of being *denied in the presence of Pilate* (Acts 3:13). They all felt the blow of the loved ones denying *the Holy One and the Just* and asking *for a murderer to be granted* (Acts 3:14). Can you imagine a Sovereign Triune God loving men who *killed the Prince of life*? (Acts 3:15). No wonder Jesus cried out, *"For God* (The Triune Godhead) *so loved the world that He gave His only begotten Son, that whoever believes in Him should not perish but have everlasting life"* (John 3:16).

Peter cries, *"The God of Abraham, Isaac, and Jacob, the God of our fathers, glorified His Servant Jesus, whom you delivered up and denied in the presence of Pilate, when he was determined to let Him go"* (Acts 3:13). He expresses the heart of the Triune God. God, the Father, pours out His heart and life through the Son. The Holy Spirit is active and alive in the service of Jesus. The Son emptied Himself to become the *Servant* that

Jesus, a Servant of God | **Acts 3:13**

He might lead man back into the heart of the Triune God. Jesus is the visible expression of the loving heart of God, the Trinity.

Another key element is SACRIFICE. In discussing these elements, we are emphasizing various aspects of a single truth. As said in the introduction, the core of the title Servant is suffering. One story that highlights this core characteristic is in Matthew's Gospel (20:20-28). The study of this story changed my life. James and John, sons of Zebedee, make a political move regarding the coming Kingdom. They solicit the help of their mother, Jesus' aunt. Because they are family, Jesus' cousins, they should occupy the right and left hand positions in the coming Kingdom? Of course, this upset the other ten disciples. They were displeased because they did not think of asking this for themselves.

Jesus must confront the self-sourcing of the disciples. He begins by comparing these Jewish disciples with the Gentiles. The Gentile world, such as Rome, is always fighting for position. The **rulers of the Gentiles lord it over them, and those who are great exercise authority over them** (Matthew 20:25). But Jesus declares, "**It shall not be so among you**" (Matthew 20:26). No room for compromise or adjustment is in this statement. Jesus will not tolerate this attitude of desiring position over others. This attitude is contrary to His heart and the heart of the Triune Godhead who sent Him. Everything about Jesus stands opposite to this attitude.

Jesus immediately paints the portrait of Himself. "**Whoever desires to become great among you, let him be your servant**" (Matthew 20:26). Is not this the picture of Jesus, the second member of the Trinity? Is not He the greatest among us? But when you are the **Servant,** it does not matter, because it is a different greatness with a different attitude. The disciples wanted a greatness based on the service rendered to them. The Trinity "glories" in greatness based on how much service one can render to others. In fact, Jesus goes on to strengthen the statement. "**And whoever desires to be first among you, let him**

**Part Two**: Exhortation from the Porch

*be your slave"* (Matthew 20:27). If you were a person's slave, being first would not matter.

This idea may sound good in theory. In a theological discussion, one might embrace this lowly servant idea. But Jesus immediately takes His disciples into the practical reality. He gives the illustration of the One who leads the way into this arena. He says, ***"Just as the Son of Man did not come to be served, but to serve, and to give His life a ransom for many"*** (Matthew 20:28). Here is the intent of the Divine choosing. Jesus became the **Servant** of the Trinity, the Three in One. His heart and Their heart could do no other! This concept is Their perspective of greatness and being first. It is the cross! The cross is the glory They embrace.

All three of these elements are aspects of the Trinity choosing Jesus to be the **Servant**. So far the entire discussion has been about Jesus, and what He does for you and me. Peter says all this with a purpose. The healed lame man is holding onto Peter and John. An amazed crowd gathers at Solomon's porch. They focus on Peter and John. From Peter's response to them, we can conclude everyone is giving the credit for this miracle to Peter and John. In absolute determination, Peter separates himself from any glory and places it all on Jesus. He highlights Jesus and His purpose, which is to bring them to repentance. Instead of embracing Jesus, they **delivered up and denied** Him. Instead of accepting Him, they **asked for a murderer to be granted to** them. Instead of experiencing His life, they **killed the Prince of life**. They must now repent.

Although repentance is the overall response required, there is an underlying element in Peter's statement. God (the Trinity) has chosen Jesus to be the suffering Servant and glorified Him. What Jesus became for us is a prototype of what God (the Trinity) wants us to become. Jesus is opening the door to the arena of service as a servant. We will be an extension of this glory to our world.

The Scriptures is filled with passages relating to how we are CHOSEN. We are not the "only begotten Son of God," but we are "sons of God." A distinct selectivity has taken place toward you in the mind and heart of the Trinity towards you. The uniqueness of your person, both in fingerprints and DNA, demands recognition of the full attention of God's selective ability. Paul says, *"Just as He chose us in Him before the foundation of the world,"* (Ephesians 1:4). The Trinity choosing Jesus was such a massive choice that it included you. Jesus so identified Himself with us that when the Godhead chose Jesus we were also chosen. Paul continues to say that everything present in Jesus is contained in that choice. The purpose and destiny for which Jesus was chosen now becomes ours in the same choice of God.

This means the element of SINGULAR is present for us and for Jesus. As Jesus was the only One who qualified to fulfill the purpose of which He was chosen, so you too are the only one who qualifies. God (the Trinity) has a significant purpose in you. You must play a role; you were especially designed and destined for this.

This means the element of SHARER is present for us and for Jesus. Jesus shares the very heart of the Trinity. He is the second member of the Three in One. Oh, the wonder of such a thought! The Trinity has opened its hearts to us. How He feels, thinks, and cares is now in us! Indeed, we are *partakers of the divine nature* (2 Peter 1:4). Jesus, the second member of the Trinity, emptied Himself of all that made Him different from us. He became what we are that we might become what He is.

This means the element of SACRIFICE is present for us and for Jesus. His perspective on glory is now ours. His style is now our style. As Jesus is *His Servant Jesus,* you are now His servant (your name). You are privileged to participate in the fulfillment of the dream of God. No one has the qualities you have; no one can fulfill the dream as you can; no one has the destiny you have. The uniqueness of your intimacy and oneness with the Trinity

**Part Two:** Exhortation from the Porch

fulfills the dream of God; it is glorification.

What should you do? The call is to you as it was to the Jews of Peter's hour. ***"Repent therefore and be converted, that your sins may be blotted out, so that times of refreshing may come from the presence of the Lord"*** (Acts 3:19). We must surrender everything that hinders the uniting of our hearts with His. As Jesus was in total submission, so we must submit. We are His servants!

## Acts 3:13

# JESUS, THE ATTITUDE OF GOD

*"The God of Abraham, Isaac, and Jacob, the God of our fathers, glorified His Servant Jesus, whom you delivered up and denied in the presence of Pilate, when he was determined to let Him go"*
*(Acts 3:13).*

The temple crowd was **greatly amazed**. God had healed the lame beggar and created a new sensation. The people gathered around Peter, John, and the healed beggar at Solomon's porch. Peter begins to exhort the crowd; his primary concern is the concentration of the crowd. They are enthralled by what they think is the instrument of the miracle and the miracle itself. Peter desperately wants them to focus on Jesus, the author of the miracle.

In this exhortation, Peter, in a remarkable statement, links Jesus with all that these Jews know about God. He says, **"The God of Abraham, Isaac, and Jacob, the God of our fathers, glorified His Servant Jesus,"** (Acts 3:13). I must remind you that **the God of Abraham, Isaac, and Jacob, the God of our fathers** is the Trinity, the Three in One Godhead. The Hebrew word "Elohim," translated "God" in the Old Testament, is always plural. **His Servant Jesus** is a member of that Triune Godhead.

In our previous study we viewed the amazing plan of God for redemption. God cannot redeem humanity due to the nature of sin. It was a man, Adam, who opened the door into the arena of darkness. He brought all people into such a realm. It will take another man to open the door to reenter the arena of light. But it will require a man of equal stature with Adam. He will need to be on the spiritual level of all God intended man to be in Adam. The Trinity cannot find such a man, *for all have sinned and fall short of the glory of God,* (Romans 3:23). Man got us into this mess; man will have to get us out. But it will take a man not in the mess! Jesus is the Man!

God, the Trinity, CHOSE Jesus to become a man. He is the only One qualified to open the door to the new arena. He shares the heart and nature of God. Out of Him, a new species of humanity is born. We are brothers with Jesus; we are sons of God. Jesus became the *Servant* who accomplished the task. The Trinity *glorified* Him. However, those who have the perspective of the world will not recognize this glorification. We think of applause, power, and ruling others. His glory is the cross. The nature of God, the Trinity, is focused on pouring out His life. The cross style is an outward focus. In our passage, we quickly discover the link with the prophecy of Isaiah (Isaiah 52-53). It is a prophecy focused on the "suffering Servant" to come. The prophecy is a description concerning the glorification of Jesus.

## God Consigned Him

A second aspect in this Servant role of Jesus is the mission. God, the Trinity, CHOSE Jesus to CONSIGN Him. This consignment is a strange "paradox" as Peter suggests in his exhortation. He presents the grand picture of Jesus the Great Servant (*His Servant Jesus*). We can easily see in this picture that God, the Trinity, chose Jesus for a mission. He will be the fulfillment of all the prophecies of the Old Testament. He will march into a downtrodden nation and restore people to the greatest heights. Why the Jewish scholars looked for a military

Messiah is easily understood.

Peter gives us the content of Jesus' mission. He says, **"Whom you delivered up"** (Acts 3:13). The Greek word "paradidomi" is used consistently for Judas' betrayal of Jesus, and is in the active voice, which places the responsibility for the action solely on the Jews at the porch. You might think God had a mission for Jesus and the Jews interfered. But look at his further description, **"Whom you delivered up and denied in the presence of Pilate, when he was determined to let Him go"** (Acts 3:13). Was God using Pilate to keep Jesus from the cross, but the stubbornness of the Jews would not allow it? From this statement, no blame can be placed on Pilate; he (krino) evaluated, judged, discerned, and wanted to do the right thing.

In fact, Peter adds weight to the responsibility of the Jews. He says, **"But you denied the Holy One and the Just, and asked for a murderer to be granted to you"** (Acts 3:14). They did not just deny but *asked* (aiteo). This Greek word refers to the seeking by an inferior from a superior. It is often translated "begging." These Jews begged for and preferred a murderer to the Son of God. Is there any excuse? Are they not responsible? Peter climaxes his accusation by saying, **"And killed the Prince of life"** (Acts 3:15). In the active voice, which means they are responsible.

But this is the paradox. These Jews are directly responsible for what Jesus experienced. But this experience was the mission of the Trinity on which this Holy One was sent. Experiencing this from the hand of the Jews was the essence for which He was chosen. He was sent on this "consignment." God, the Trinity, is responsible for the cross. In Peter's sermon on Pentecost, he gloriously says this, **"Him, being delivered by the determined purpose and foreknowledge of God, you have taken by lawless hands, have crucified, and put to death;"** (Acts 2:23). Evil people, filled with their self-desires, strutted around as if they had accomplished *their* will. In reality, they accomplished the plan of the sovereign God. What a paradox! The **Servant Jesus**

**Part Two:** Exhortation from the Porch

carried out the plans of the Trinity in submitting to the evil of man. He was *glorified*. A sovereign Trinity dreamed and planned for the redemption of humanity on a cross. Jesus fulfilled this plan in obedience as a *Servant*. God must be praised. Man will forever be responsible for the cross, the death of Jesus. How evil and dark was the moment of his sin! Each statement is true; it is a paradox.

A distinct SINGULAR element about the consignment of Jesus exists. The Trinity chose Him because He was the only One who qualified for the mission. No one else could be the "second Adam" to open the door to the lost arena. God became the redemptive Man. But Jesus is "singular" in His consignment because He is the only one *glorified*. Remember the mission of Jesus is contained in this word. "**Glorified**" comes from the Greek word "doxa." It refers to perspective, opinion, or viewpoint. Jesus is not *glorified* because of position, applause, or fame. This perspective would be the viewpoint of the world. The nature of God values the cross style. God does not think about how important He is or how much He should get. He lives in the perspective of how may I minister and how much may I give. The nature of God is displayed in a single person, Jesus!

This singularity is easily discovered in our passage. Peter exhorts, **"The God of Abraham, Isaac, and Jacob, the God of our fathers, glorified His Servant Jesus"** (Acts 3:13). "*Glorified*" is a main verb in the third person "singular." "*His*" is a pronoun in the third person "singular." Without knowing any Greek grammar, you would conclude from the rest of the verses that the focus is on a single Person. The Jews were guilty of "delivering up" a single Person. Pilate was determined to let this single Person go, but the Jews rejected this single Person. They asked for Barabbas instead of this single Person. The *Prince of life* is this single Person; they killed Him.

The Trinity is not "glorifying" a role or position, but a Person. If Jesus does not fulfill this role, no one else will. This is not the case. Only one chance is in this single Person. The Scriptures consistently bring us back to this one Person. God, the Trinity, does not have a back-up plan, or a second agenda. Listen to Peter's explanation, *"And His name, through faith in His name, has made this man strong, whom you see and know. Yes, the faith which comes through Him has given him this perfect soundness in the presence of you all"* (Acts 3:15).

The leaders of Israel will confront Peter with a demand for an explanation. They want to know, *"By what power or by what name have you done this?"* (Acts 4:7). No hesitation is in his answer. *"Let it be known to you all, and to all the people of Israel, that by the name of Jesus Christ of Nazareth, whom you crucified, whom God raised from the dead, by Him this man stands here before you whole"* (Acts 4:10). He then continues, *"Nor is there salvation in any other, for there is no other name under heaven given among men by which we must be saved"* (Acts 4:12).

All the hopes of the Trinity focus on the success of this single Person. He is not one among many; He is the only One! He is not one attempt among many; He is the only attempt! This hope is not a single doctrine or theology; this is a single Person. This dream is not a plan of God several can fulfill; Jesus is the plan of God, the Trinity. You and I need look no further than Jesus. *"You are complete in Him"* (Colossians 2:9).

In the consignment of Jesus by the Trinity, the element of SHARER is present. In the "glorification" of Jesus, **His Servant**, is the demonstration of the nature of God, the Trinity. Paul makes a strong observation about God. He places it in the framework of *"a faithful saying"* (2 Timothy 2:11). He says, *"If we are faithless, He remains faithful; He cannot deny Himself"* (2Timothy 2:13). Paul's declaration is a statement about the absolute steadfast consistency of God. Who He is does not change!

If God, the Trinity, is "glorifying" **His Servant Jesus**, we can be assured the nature of God is demonstrated in that "glorification."

The "glorification" is an expression of the opinion, viewpoint, or perspective on God, the Trinity. What God sees as valuable is going to be expressed in the "glorification." "Glorification" is always focused on the crucifixion, the cross style. Jesus shares the heart and nature of God, the Trinity.

When an individual designs a plan as a solution to an important problem, the plan will be an expression of his nature. For example, if much money is needed, the plan to secure that amount will reflect the nature of the one making the plan. If cheating, robbing, and conning are a part of the plan, the nature of the one planning is declared. Jesus is the Trinity's solution to redeeming a world. The nature of the Trinity is revealed in the display of the solution.

The idea of Servant bespeaks the nature of God who has the plan. The content of that Servant is revealed in Peter's exhortation. He was **delivered up and denied in the presence of Pilate, when he was determined to let Him go** (Acts 3:13). He is the **Holy One and the Just**, yet He is rejected so that a murderer could be granted (Acts 3:14). He is **the Prince of life** only to be killed (Acts 3:15). Because this is His plan, what does this reflect about His nature? Is He not the selfless, self-sacrificing Lover of our souls? Is He not the God who **so loved the world that He gave His only begotten Son** (John 3:16)?

John reported, **"No one has seen God at any time. The only begotten Son, who is in the bosom of the Father, He has declared Him"** (John 1:18). No one **has seen**, meaning "perceived, known intimately, comprehended" God at any time. The Greek root word is "oida," one of four Greek words for "know." It expresses much more than physical sight or data. No one has grasped the heart and nature of God, not just physically seen Him. This verse expresses the "singular" emphasis as well. Jesus is the **only begotten Son**. He is from and is in the heart of the Father. He is the singular declaration because He is the singular Son. He is the singular Person who **has declared Him**. The Greek word (exegomai) translated *has declared* means "to exegete." Exegete is what a Bible scholar does to the Scriptural text. Jesus is the *Servant* who exposes, interprets, and reveals the inner being of God, the Trinity.

We have not had a clear picture of God until Jesus. All the confusion about our God in the Old Testament revelation must be rethought in light of Jesus. Any interpretation of how God feels and what He may have done must be re-examined in light of Jesus. Make no judgments about the nature of God until you have thoroughly embraced and known Jesus. He is the complete and final revelation of the Trinity. All previous revelations or thoughts about God must be adjusted by this one revelation, Jesus!

Jesus was "consigned" by the Trinity. He is the SINGULAR plan; there is no additional plan. He is the SHARER of the nature of God; the Trinity *glorified His Servant Jesus*. Jesus is the SACRIFICE of the heart of God. When we view this "sacrifice" as described in the context of our passage, it is remarkable. Its emphasis is on "extremes." Everything involving Jesus is to the extreme, and it is an element of His "glorification."

He was not born in comfort, but in a stable.

He was not born of acceptable parents, but born an illegitimate babe.

He was not born to wealthy parents, but was born to a peasant couple.

He was not raised in the best Jewish environment, but was raised in the worst town in Palestine.

He did not just become a man, but a homeless man. *"Foxes have holes and birds of the air have nests, but the Son of Man has nowhere to lay His head"* (Matthew 8:20).

He was not handsome among men, but *He has no form or comeliness; and when we see Him, there is no beauty that we should desire Him* (Isaiah 53:2).

His ministry was not to respectable Jews, but to those who

bore the physical evidence of sin. ***And they brought to Him all sick people who were afflicted with various diseases and torments, and those who were demon-possessed, epileptics, and paralytics;*** (Matthew 4:24).

He did not just experience persecution, but was treated as a criminal.

He did not just die, but experienced the death of the cross.

He did not just take on the sins of a few people, but took on the sins of all generations.

He did not just embrace the idea of sin, but felt all your sins as if He committed them Himself.

He did not just pay a token penalty, but he went to the worst of hell.

Why did He do this? So no one is excluded! Whatever the extremity of your life might be, He has been there. He has covered all needs. This is His "glory!"

## Acts 3:13

# JESUS, THE DELIGHT OF GOD

*"The God of Abraham, Isaac, and Jacob, the God of our fathers, glorified His Servant Jesus, whom you delivered up and denied in the presence of Pilate, when he was determined to let Him go" (Acts 3:13).*

We are slowly making our way into the heart of this paradox of "a glorified Servant." The reason for the time spent is twofold. God has it ingrained into His nature. Therefore, if we are to share His nature, it becomes who we are to be! In other words, it is not a side, minor, or insignificant issue. It looms as the core of all we call Christian.

Re-establishing our focus is important. **His Servant Jesus** does not proclaim a role. As the Trinity moved into the necessary activities to redeem our world, God is not play-acting to fulfill a task. Jesus did not become a servant, which means adjusting His attitude and nature to fit such a role. Rather, Jesus is a **Servant,** and the role reflects the qualities of His nature and attitude. In fact, it does not matter what title you give Him, the servant qualities will be reflected in that position.

Jesus is King, an exalted position of high authority and power. But notice on His coronation day He rides into Jerusalem on a donkey (Matthew 21). A stallion would bespeak the magnitude of His status but Jesus rides on a beast of burden, which is His servant nature. But He is exalted to the right hand of the Father to receive the fullness of the Promise that He will distribute to the world (Acts 2:33). He dwells there in confidence, *since He always lives to make intercession for them* (Hebrews 7:25). He dwells to serve!

Jesus was CHOSEN to be the *Servant*. Because it is the Three in One who chose Him, He participated in the selection. All humanity was swept into the arena of self-sufficiency, self-sourcing. "Sin," with its heart nature of "I," dominated every human. Jesus was the only Man qualified to take us back to the arena of a "servant." Jesus was CONSIGNED for redemption. Some details are declared in Peter's exhortation. He was *delivered up*; He was *denied* freedom and a murderer was preferred. He was killed, and this is all contained in the title, *His Servant Jesus*!

Jesus was not just CHOSEN (selected) and CONSIGNED (sent), He was CELEBRATED. The atmosphere of our text is based on this celebration. *"The God of Abraham, Isaac, and Jacob, the God of our fathers, glorified His Servant Jesus,"* (Acts 3:13). I searched carefully throughout the Scriptures to see the consistency of this "celebration." Each Scripture exposing the "servant" idea exposes the "exaltation." It seems embedded or ingrained into the nature of the servant principle. Contained in the essence of breathing is living. If you are breathing, we assume you are living. If you are living, we assume you are breathing. Living is not necessarily the reward for breathing; one does not breathe as a job, duty, or obligation. One does not get paid "life" as wages for the work of breathing. So it is with "celebration." "Exaltation" is not a reward for self-sacrifice. The servant attitude is not a duty or obligation to earn recognition. You cannot be a servant and not be exalted.

This exaltation is portrayed in the tone of our passage (Acts 3:13). Peter proclaims that *they killed the Prince of life, whom God raised from the dead, of which we are witnesses* (Acts 3:15). When the early Church heard the threats of the leadership of Israel, they broke into praise. They referred to Jesus as

*"Your holy Servant Jesus, whom You anointed"* (Acts 4:27). They prayed for boldness to proclaim *"Your word, by stretching out Your hand to heal, and that signs and wonders may be done through the name of Your holy Servant Jesus"* (Acts 4:29-30). In each case there is celebration connected to the servant-heart.

In the great "Kenosis Passage," Paul describes Jesus as the servant. He says, *"But made Himself of no reputation, taking the form of a bondservant, and coming in the likeness of men. And being found in appearance as a man, He humbled Himself and became obedient to the point of death, even the death of the cross. Therefore God also has highly exalted Him and given Him the name which is above every name"* (Philippians 2:7-9).

A group of Greeks attending the feast asked to speak to Jesus. They might have wanted to start a new school of study in Athens under the direction of Jesus, the great Teacher. Jesus' answer to them was quite abrupt. He proclaimed, *"The hour has come that the Son of Man should be glorified"* (John 12:23). He described this glorification in an illustration from nature. He said, *"Most assuredly, I say to you, unless a grain of wheat falls into the ground and dies, it remains alone; but if it dies, it produces much grain"* (John 12:24). This describes natural process. We have become so used to this process that we take it for granted. "Glorification" is a natural part of the death experience.

To speak of "celebration" as it relates to being a *Servant* is dangerous. The danger is in our carnal minds. The nature of our world is to exalt self-sourcing. The pattern is simple. If an individual excels beyond the ordinary, we give him applause, honor, and exaltation. The level of the exaltation is equal to the level of their service. For instance, in a church organization, if an individual sacrifices, gives their time, and produces a successful program, we honor them. They earned it. We give them a sense of accomplishment from the church body. This idea is so ingrained into our thinking; it is a product of our self-sourcing nature.

**Part Two:** Exhortation from the Porch

To speak of "exaltation" as it relates to a *Servant* is dangerous. In the name of Jesus, can you and I refuse that thought process? Can we enter into the mind of the Trinity? Can the Divine heart direct us to the natural process of being in Him? Can He cleanse all our remaining patterns of self-seeking until we think like Him?

# Singular

In our passage Peter proclaims the life of Jesus. In our minds it is an extreme paradox. He speaks of "*glorified*" in the same breath as "*Servant.*" He does so that one would think they are the same. However, in our self-sourcing reality they are vastly different. "Servant" speaks of the sacrifices one makes. It insinuates that an individual works hard. It highlights what a person is willing to go through to accomplish a task. It describes the product or result. Once that aspect is in place, then we consider another aspect, "*glorified.*" The degree of "glorification" is determined by the value of the service rendered.

However, this is not the biblical approach. Peter makes this bold statement: **"The God of Abraham, Isaac, and Jacob, the God of our fathers, glorified His Servant Jesus"** (Acts 3:13). He immediately begins to describe, in brief detail, this statement, as if it was a "whole unit." In other words, He is not saying that Jesus is a servant but fulfills that obligation. Now the Father will glorify Him as if this was different from being a servant. "Being *glorified*" and "being **His Servant Jesus**" are equally present the entire time. They are ingrained in each other. One does not exist without the other.

Jesus was **delivered up and denied in the presence of Pilate, when he was determined to let Him go** (Acts 3:13). We can easily see the servant aspect of this trial event. Jesus has the goal of crucifixion before Him. He sets His sights and will not be detoured. In the Garden of Gethsemane prayer time, He settles the direction; it will be the accomplishment of His Father's will. What a *Servant* He is! But where is the "glorification?" That is the point! The glorification is just as much present in the sacrifice as is the "servant."

Let me remind you that the Greek word "doxaso," translated **glorified,** comes from the idea "to think, or suppose." We must crawl out of our self-sourcing thought process and enter into the mind of Christ. What does He value? In the Divine logic of the Trinity, what is lifted and exalted is the loss of your life. The loss is the act of **being delivered up and denied**, or the grain of wheat falling to the ground and dying.

But wait, they **denied the Holy One and the Just, and asked for a murderer to be granted**. They **killed the Prince of life** (Acts 3:14). **His Servant Jesus** is being obedient. He gives Himself without reservation to the will of the Father. If He endures to the end, He will be exalted. No! You must not miss the heart of the matter. Contained in the moment of the sacrifice and service is the exaltation. They are one and the same. The glory is not in a separate moment of reward, it is contained in the heart of the sacrifice itself. The two are one, making them singular.

How will this change our state of living? Through the Book of Acts it is the heart of evangelism. In a Philippi jail the "servant aspect" is highlighted. Paul and Silas are in stocks with bleeding backs. If they will hang on and be faithful, God will exalt them. No! God will not ultimately glorify them for this reason. Paul and Silas realize the glory is in the opportunity of service at the midnight hour. They are not divided. The opportunity of bleeding for Jesus is the essence of glory itself. In realizing this, they break forth in praise. An earthquake happens. Evangelism occurs in the lives of a key family. It may be that we have not won our world because we have not seen the truth. We have groaned while waiting for our moment of relief. We wait patiently for God to glorify us after He delivers us from our moment of suffering. We have not realized that the suffering is the glory.

Part Two: Exhortation from the Porch

The heroes of faith are listed in the Book of Hebrews. As the chapter closes, the writer lists the deliverances that come through faith. They *subdued kingdoms, worked righteousness, obtained promises, stopped the mouths of lions, quenched the violence of fire, escaped the edge of the sword, out of weakness were made strong, became valiant in battle, turned to flight the armies of the aliens. Women received their dead raised to life again* (Hebrews 11:33-35). All these are positive acts; we will consider acts of victory. He goes on to say: *"Others were tortured, not accepting deliverance, that they might obtain a better resurrection. Still others had trial of mockings and scourgings, yes, and of chains and imprisonment. They were stoned, they were sawn in two, were tempted, were slain with the sword. They wandered about in sheepskins and goatskins, being destitute, afflicted, tormented — of whom the world was not worthy"* (Hebrews 11:35-38). We look at these acts as defeat, as if their faith did not work. But the Hebrew writer makes no distinction between them. If they are delivered or not delivered, neither determines the glorification of the "servant." In the heart of God, the glory is in the movement of God through the servant.

## Sharer

How can this be? A natural result of the servant nature, the nature of the Spirit of God, is present. *His Servant Jesus* shares the heart nature of the Trinity. In sharing this nature, the glory of God is displayed despite the outcome of the activity. The glory is not contained in the outcome; it is in sharing His nature.

*"The God of Abraham, Isaac, and Jacob, the God of our fathers, glorified His Servant Jesus"* (Acts 3:13) is the statement of our passage. Peter immediately describes the demonstration of the Spirit of God glorifying Jesus. The Spirit of God moved through a man when He was *delivered up and denied in the*

*presence of Pilate, when he was determined to let Him go* (Acts 3:13). Jesus did not do what self-sourced men do. He did not fight back; He did not blame or accuse. His life was a platform for the glorification of the Father amid the trial. Look what Jesus went through. They **denied the Holy One and the Just, and asked for a murderer to be granted to** them, **and killed the Prince of life** (Acts 3:14-15). He did not complain; He forgave. He did not rant about the unfairness of the situation. He was a platform for the glorification of the Father through His death. He shared the nature of God and was glorified.

We realize that self-sourcing is always destructive, which is evident in the home falling apart. Arguments and division are continual. Drunkenness and filth are destroying the family and lives of its members. The nature of sin shows destruction on the stage of each life in that family. But it is equally true for the family who appears to be successful. They have more than enough money. The children have all the advantages of education and wealth. But the home is a product of self-sourcing, which is always destructive. What determines the destruction is not the consequence, but the nature showed while living!

We must be gripped by this truth. Our focus and energy must not be for the outcome and apparent success of the service. We must be focused on sharing His nature, being energized by His power, and flowing with His presence! When we are sourced by His Spirit the glory is equally present in the crucifixion and in the deliverance from the crucifixion. If we know this, really know this, it will change our attitude in all things. We will become people who cling to Him.

## Sacrifice

In this reality of truth, we discover a new definition for sacrifice. It brings us back to the Greek word (doxaso) translated

***glorified.*** Again the root Greek word is "doxa." It has to do with opinion or perspective. It is amazing how your perspective determines what and how you define "sacrifice." A father works hard each day. He leaves early in the morning and often stays late at night. He provides for his family. Is it a sacrifice? Does he gripe and complain over the need to support his children? Does love fill his heart until he views all he does as a privilege?

The early Church viewed the persecution as a privilege. They were considered worthy to suffer for Christ's sake. Paul often repeated the idea of joining Jesus in His death, so we will know Him in His life. The fellowship of His suffering is the power of His resurrection (Philippians 3:10).

The New Covenant is intimacy with the Spirit of Jesus. How can He indwell us and be separate from us? In the Old Testament God was aside from us. In the New Testament, He came to indwell us. However, we often treat Him in the New Testament time as if we remain in the Old Testament time. He is in us, but He is still not a part of us. Our lives are intertwined with Him. His purpose and plan is acting through us. May we view everything that happens in our daily lives as a part of the Divine plan of God to fulfill His dream in and through us? We get to be a part of the accomplishment of God's purpose. Jesus knew the cross, and all its involvement was to accomplish the Divine plan through Him. Thus the Hebrew writer said, ***"Looking unto Jesus, the author and finisher of our faith, who for the joy that was set before Him endured the cross, despising the shame, and has sat down at the right hand of the throne of God"*** (Hebrews 12:2). The glory is in being the servant!

## Acts 3:13

# GLORIFIED LIKE JESUS

*"The God of Abraham, Isaac, and Jacob, the God of our fathers, glorified His Servant Jesus, whom you delivered up and denied in the presence of Pilate, when he was determined to let Him go"*
*(Acts 3:13).*

As I saturate in this paragraph of "The Exhortation from the Porch" (Acts 3:12-26), I am haunted. It has to do with my identification with the Jews of that hour. I feel certain I would have joined them in their position against Jesus. The base of this feeling stems from the reality of how I respond to the personal situations in my life. Although the circumstances differ from those of the Jews, the consequences are the same. I have **delivered up** and **denied**. I have participated in choosing a murderer over Jesus and **killed the Prince of Life**. How can it be?

Our passage is not a sermon in the proper sense, but a response to the need of people. Peter discerns their state of mind and directs them to correction. Two major sections to the passage are giving proper instructions. The first section is the "Paradoxes of Jesus" (Acts 3:12-17). Peter's exhortation begins with a focus on Jesus. The Jews gathered on the porch must see Jesus, or they will not allow change in their lives. They have been led astray by their perspective on the Messiah and their traditional training. A part of the "ignorance" is causing their problem. **His Servant Jesus** is nothing like the military

Messiah they expect. In this section, Peter establishes a genuine view of Jesus.

On the foundation of these "paradoxes," Peter calls them to the "Prerequisite of Repentance" (Acts 3:18-26). They must "give up a former thought to embrace a new thought!" The **blotting out of their sins** will be determined by their response. Repentance will open the door for the **times of refreshing** from His presence in their lives. It will be through only repentance these Jews will experience all the prophets proclaimed for this hour. In fact, God has come to them first with His great offer (Acts 3:26).

Peter begins with the "Paradox of Sourcing" (Acts 3:12). What looks like the product of two men is really the movement of Jesus! How can this crowd miss it? The two questions Peter asks penetrate the depth of their souls. Why do they **marvel at this** lame beggar's healing? They miss the reality of Jesus, the fulfillment of all the God of their fathers desired! How can they **look so intently at us, as though by our own power or godliness we had made this man walk**? They miss Jesus, who alone is the power and godliness of the Trinity God of their fathers, and is a call to embrace Him.

Then Peter speaks of the second paradox. It is the "Paradox of **His Servant Jesus.**" **The God of Abraham, Isaac, and Jacob**, the God of our fathers is a phrase these Jews used in the hour of prayer. They came to the temple for prayer at the ninth hour, the hour of this healing. The Trinity God to whom they prayed **glorified His Servant Jesus** in that hour through a lame beggar. What a paradox! No one glorifies a servant. We have looked extensively at this paradox. However, there is a contrast in this paradox, which continues to investigate my soul. The contrast is between God's (the Trinity's) perspective on Jesus and the Jews' perspective (or mine).

## Partnership

Peter proclaimed, *"The God of Abraham, Isaac, and Jacob, the God of our fathers, glorified His Servant Jesus,"* (Acts 3:13). The language of this statement declares a "partnership." We discovered "*The God*" is the Triune God of the Old Testament. He is the "Elohim," which is always plural. He is the "Three in One" or the Trinity. These three Persons have always been in partnership with each other. This partnership is so tightly linked that they are actually one. If you accuse us of believing in three gods, we will immediately and strongly correct you. We do not believe in three gods, for the three Persons of the Trinity are One. We have one God.

"How can this be?" The answer is "holiness." The nature of these three Persons is so holy that unity is felt. This "holiness" is often called "perfect love," and it is the essence of the cross. The cross was at the heart of the Trinity long before the event. Each member of the Trinity died to Himself and lives for the other members. This living is "agape" love, the nature of God that never thinks of itself but always of others.

The most unbelievable element of this partnership is that God included us! He included us in creation. He created us in His image (Genesis 1:26-27). For generations, theologians have attempted to explore the depth of what this means. We are not gods! We have none of the Divine attributes of the Trinity. But we have the capacity to experience, dwell in, and link with the nature of God. We are designed so our completeness is in this link. Man is in his fullness only when he is intimate with God.

When man decided to link with someone else other than God, redemption was required. Man became independent instead of dependent. Man began to source himself rather than be sourced by God. To some extent, God decided to start over with a new breed of humanity. Instead of creating another man

**Part Two:** Exhortation from the Porch

as He did the first Adam, He became a man, the Second Adam. The second member of the Trinity took on a startling role. He became a man! He became all contained in the **Servant**. God, the Trinity, **glorified His Servant Jesus**.

The link of Jesus, the Man, with God was intended from the beginning of creation. Whatever connection Jesus has with God is intended for this new breed of humanity. This new breed is born from a cross, and is expressed in this term **Servant**! A Servant has the opportunity to be infused with the person of God. Our humanity becomes a platform on which God can show Himself. Humanity living is elevated to a level impossible in himself. Who would not want such a life?

The answer is in the demonstration of the Jews. What a contrast the Jews are to Jesus, **His Servant**. They want no link with what the Trinity is doing in Jesus. Peter describes their link with Jesus as **you delivered up** (Acts 3:13), meaning "to surrender." The Greek word is "paradidomi," written in the active voice and the indicative mood. The indicative means is a simple statement of fact. The active voice places the responsibility of the action on the Jews. "Para" presents the emphasis of "to the side of or over to." "Didomai" means "to give." These Jews are responsible for delivering Jesus over to the power of someone.

They are caught in the dilemma of the condition resulting from Adam's fall. They do not have partnership with God as was intended in creation. They source themselves. The relationship they have with God is far removed. They believe in God and want His good favor when there is a problem they cannot handle. They want a god they can manipulate and use on demand. They are willing to maintain religious ceremonies and laws that are conducive to fostering this remote relationship. But none of this remote relationship is an intimate relationship of sourcing and oneness. The Jews source their lives and their religion. If God gives them anything, it is because they deserve it and He owes them.

Jesus proposes a new relationship of intimacy with God. The Jews want nothing to do with it. It requires an elimination of Jesus, the new breed of humanity. The Jews do this with and under the jurisdiction of Pilate. Pilate attempts three times to release Jesus. Each time the Jews rebuff him. They bring Jesus to Pilate as one who misleads people. Among the Jews, Pilate examines Jesus and finds Him not guilty. He tells the Jews, "I will ***therefore chastise Him and release Him***" (Luke23:16). But they will not allow it and fill the court with shouts of ***"Crucify Him, crucify Him!"*** (Luke 23:21). Luke records, ***Then he said to them the third time, "Why, what evil has He done? I have found no reason for death in Him. I will therefore chastise Him and let Him go"*** (Luke 23:22).

I now hang my head in shame. I joined that crowd; my voice of rejection can be heard. I am guilty of the same. The partnership God places in the Man, Jesus, I have rejected for my own self-sourcing. I do not want to become a "servant." I want God to be my slave. I do not want to be the flow of His life; I want to use His power to fulfill the flow of my life. I do not want my life used for the fulfillment of His dreams; I have my selfish dreams. Let us crucify ***His Servant Jesus***. Let us go back to the God in the temple building that I can manipulate and use for my own selfish ends. The contrast found in our passage is in our lives!

# Perspective

The heart of the idea of "***glorified***" is perspective. The Greek word "doxa" is the root Greek word for ***glorified*** and refers to perspective, opinion, or viewpoint. We have highlighted this idea repeatedly in this study. It is the key to understanding what Peter presents to the Jews from the porch. Who is it that is "***glorifying***" Jesus? Peter says, ***"The God of Abraham, Isaac,*** *and Jacob, the God of our fathers, glorified His Servant Jesus,"* (Acts 3:13). The God of the Old Testament is the God of these *"Men of Israel"* (Acts 3:12). He is "Elohim," the Three in One God. He is the Trinity. This Trinity holds Jesus in high esteem. Their perspective on Jesus is one of great value and worth.

On at least two occasions, this God comes down to give His confirmation on Jesus. Listen to the words of God. ***And suddenly a voice came from heaven, saying, "This is My beloved Son, in whom I am well pleased"*** (Matthew 3:17). All three members of the Trinity are present in this scene. The Holy Spirit baptizes Jesus while the Father states the opinion of God's heart.

On the Mount of Transfiguration, the Trinity states their approval once more. Moses and Elijah carry on a conversation with Jesus. The discussion focuses on the glorification of the cross. Moses, the representative of the Law, and Elijah, the representative of the prophets, encourage Jesus to stay focused on the cross. Even in this sacred scene Peter proposes a ridiculous idea. But God has something more to say. ***While he was still speaking, behold, a bright cloud overshadowed them; and suddenly a voice came out of the cloud, saying, "This is My beloved Son, in whom I am well pleased. Hear Him!"*** (Matthew 17:5).

This statement comes at the end of at least six days of argument with Jesus about His position as **Servant**. Jesus informed them His first prediction of His death and resurrection (Matthew 16:21) beginning the six-day argument. Their perspective is different from the Trinity's. They do not want a **Servant Jesus** who will bleed, suffer, and die. If Jesus the Master is a servant, these disciples will need to be servants as well. However, something radical happens to Peter's viewpoint. He embraces the **Servant Jesus**.

Now he speaks to thousands of Jews who have the same opinion he had. Although they are not disciples, they are resisting God's perspective on Jesus. Instead of holding Him in high esteem, they **delivered up and denied** Him intentionally. They forcibly resist all God did in Jesus. A pagan judge who has no connection with their God has a higher opinion of Jesus than they do. They miss all God is doing through Jesus. The **Holy One and the Just** is rejected, and a murderer is preferred. They **killed the Prince of life**. Peter's use of the emphatic of "humois," is translated "*you*" is significant. It places the responsibility squarely on the Jews.

But how can I be critical of them. I must hang my head in shame. I value my own life more than I value Jesus. I repeatedly push His will aside in favor mine. I decide my destiny instead of fulfilling His dream for my life. I crucify Him repeatedly in open shame. I choose those "things of murder" as more valuable than the **Holy One and the Just**. The call to "repent" comes loud and strong in my life. My perspective on Jesus is wrong!

## Passion

A third element in this contrast is PASSION. This scene is saturated with it. The emotion of the healed lame beggar reaches into the crowd of Jews who rush into Solomon's Porch. The healed man holds onto Peter and John. Luke chooses Greek words containing passion to describe the gripping embrace of this man. Peter responds to the healed man and the crowd with equal passion. He is horrified to think they accredit him with the miracle. What is the tone of his voice? Is he shouting as he pleads with them?

But more than Peter's passion in his exhortation is the emphasis of God's passion for Jesus. To understand the word "*glorified*" without feeling and experiencing the strength of the heart of God for Jesus is impossible. One must consistently remember to think of God as the Triune Godhead. What Jesus does as a **Servant** fulfills the passion of the heart of God. From before the foundations of the world God planned, dreamed,

**Part Two:** Exhortation from the Porch

and focused on the appearance of Jesus, the **Servant**. He cannot think of Jesus without glorifying Him.

In the heart of the rejecters, there is equal passion. You cannot read of the trials, scourging, and crucifixion without feeling the passion. We refer to this week of events as "The Passion." Peter reminds these Jews how passionate they are about rejecting and eliminating Jesus. He uses words such as ***delivered up***, ***denied***, and ***determined*** (Pilate). They pursue Jesus and push Him to His death. As we read the account, there is a distinct awareness of demonic involvement. The force required to rip a man's beard out by its roots points to demonic empowerment. The bloodthirsty, relentless beating of the stripes seemed to go beyond ordinary. The soldiers inventing their crown of thorns mixed with their laughter and ridicule point to demonic inspiration.

My role in this drama is equally passionate. I aggressively reject and dishonor Him. You and I have never been innocent bystanders along the way. We participate with our entire beings. Oh, could I repent and join the heart of God? Could every nerve of my being, every thought of my mind, and every emotion of my feelings passionately express a love for Jesus?

## Acts 3:14

# THE HOLY ONE

*"But you denied the Holy One and the Just, and asked for a murderer to be granted to you," (Acts 3:14).*

Speaking from Solomon's Porch, Peter is determined to highlight and focus on Jesus. He will not diminish or lower his concentration to appease the crowd. In fact, he does an amazing thing; it is the heart of evangelism. He uses the cultural setting of his audience to promote Jesus. He begins his exhortation by addressing them as **"Men of Israel."** He reminds them of who they are in the fulfillment of Old Testament's plan. Peter says, **"The God of Abraham, Isaac, and Jacob, the God of our fathers, glorified His Servant Jesus"** (Acts 3:13).

Jesus is not a new entity. He is the accomplishment and fulfillment of every movement of God Jehovah in the Old Testament. The **Servant Jesus** is not the result of the sovereign tyrant God who forced Jesus into service. The God of the Old Testament is named "Elohim." In the Hebrew language, as said in previous studies, this name is plural. It refers to the Triune God, the Three-in-One Trinity. We do not believe in three Gods; these three Divine Persons are One! Peter refers to **"The God** (Elohim) **of Abraham, Isaac, and Jacob, the God** (Elohim) **of our fathers."** Jesus is one of these Divine Persons. The nature and heart of the Trinity is singular. Jesus is the expression of that passionate heart. He renders the service of becoming man, but not just a man because He dies on a cross. The Trinity controls everything in our passage. Jesus embraced it in service.

The Trinity holds Jesus in high esteem. The Three-in-One God glorifies Him. This opinion comes from the core of God. His nature delights in the sacrifice of Jesus. We discover the heart of God through Jesus. We must repent (give up a former thought to embrace a new thought.) Our opinion is the opposite of God's. We joined the Jews in their denial of Jesus. We also want a military Messiah to come and rescue us from all of our sufferings. We **delivered up** the **Servant Jesus**. We can hold Him in high esteem; we sell Him cheap for the temporary and meaningless. We choose ourselves instead of Him. We must repent!

Peter also expresses two titles for Jesus. He is **the Holy One and the Just** (Acts 3:14). This title was not shocking to the Jews gathered on the porch because it was a common title for the coming Messiah. What was shocking was its application to Jesus. In the Gospels the demons often accredit this title to Jesus. ***Now there was a man in their synagogue with an unclean spirit. And he cried out, saying, "Let us alone! What have we to do with You, Jesus of Nazareth? Did You come to destroy us? I know who You are — the Holy One of God!"*** (Mark 1:23-24, see also Luke 4:34). The angels of God also recognized Him as such. In an encounter with Mary, the angel Gabriel said, ***"The Holy Spirit will come upon you, and the power of the Highest will overshadow you; therefore, also, that Holy One who is to be born will be called the Son of God"*** (Luke 1:35). Peter understood this title as used in the Old Testament. In his sermon on Pentecost, he quoted one of the Psalms, ***"For You will not leave my soul in Hades, nor will You allow Your Holy One to see corruption"*** (Acts 2:27; Psalms 16:10). Peter settled this in his heart as a disciple of Jesus. Jesus preached a strong sermon. Some disciples responded, ***"This is a hard saying; who can understand it?"*** (John 6:60). It appears all the disciples except the twelve left Him. Jesus inquired of them their intention. Peter's response for the group was, ***"Lord,*** *to whom shall we go? You have the words of eternal life. Also we have come to believe and know that You are the Christ, the Son of the living God"* (John 6:68-69).

In the Old Testament's Hebrew language, the term "**Holy One**" highlights "one who is tenderly and piously devoted to another." This term corresponds to the expression used in the New Testament, *"My Beloved Son"* (Matthew 3:17; 17:5). This use of the phrase gives us the same picture as the phrase, ***glorified His Servant Jesus***. The Trinity is expressing a strong appreciation, esteem, and support of Jesus. Their approval is found in what the nature of God causes Him to be! This view is contrasted with the attitude of the Jews who viewed Jesus as more contemptible than Barabbas, the murderer.

However, there is a second use for the term, **Holy One**. It is used in the Old Testament to denote "one who is holy, set apart to God." Again, this phrase gives content and additional expression to the phrase "***His Servant Jesus***." The positive element of these words, **Holy One**, must be emphasized. Most often we highlight the negative aspect. "Holiness" is thought to be as a separation from something that is evil. Words such as "separation" or "isolation" express negative content. Holiness is not separation "from" but separation "unto!" A dedication to God consuming an individual until all other things are set aside is holiness. Therefore, holiness is found in the surrender and intimacy with God, not in the separation. ***The Holy One*** is tenderly and piously devoted to another; therefore, He is separated "from." He does not separate Himself "from," then become tenderly and piously devoted to another.

This expresses the heart of the content of ***His Servant Jesus***. Jesus shares the nature and heart of the Trinity. He burns with the passion of God, the Triune God. This oneness with the Trinity expresses the separation and to the servant role. Jesus is not set apart for God and becomes one with the Trinity. He is one with the Three in One Godhead and is set apart. His holiness is an

**Part Two:** Exhortation from the Porch

expression of His oneness.

In viewing the inner connection with Jesus, the **Servant** and Jesus, the **Holy One**, we are confronted with a basic principle. We will view this spiritual principle in three parts. We begin with ONENESS PRODUCES HOLINESS. We said this in the previous paragraphs. Now we must highlight this for an understanding of practical holiness in our lives. Personal holiness is only produced from "oneness" with Divinity. This oneness is the thrust of Peter's exhortation. For the Jews of the Old Testament, the Trinity Godhead was the God of their forefathers. This Trinity glorified **His Servant Jesus**. This glorification bespeaks the intimate relationship existing among these three members of the Trinity. One became Jesus of Nazareth, the Man. This intimacy was experienced in the fullness of the Holy Spirit. This nature of God flowed in oneness in Jesus, producing the holiness He experienced.

In the Old Testament setting, God alone is holiness. No one else possesses this quality of nature. He is so holy that those who worship Him constantly say: *"Holy, holy, holy"* (Isaiah 6:3). In this setting, the existence of man is threatened when he walks clumsily into the presence of such holiness. A rope had to be placed around the base of Mount Sinai. The warning was severe. **"Whoever touches the mountain shall surely be put to death"** (Exodus 19:12). No one dared to enter the Holy of Holies, the dwelling place of the Holy One. The High Priest could enter only once a year after an extensive purification process. Even then it was a fearsome encounter! God being holy beyond anything man can be is obvious.

It becomes evident in the New Covenant that the holy nature of God is to indwell man. Man derives holiness from the presence of God, and there are many "types" of this in the Old Testament. Moses stands on mountain ground he has walked often with his sheep. But on this occasion the voice of God cries: **"Take your sandals off your feet, for the place where**

***you stand is holy ground"*** (Exodus 3:5). The logical thinking rejects the idea of this ground being holy, because it is the same as in previous days. The difference is in the presence of a Holy God. This ground derived holiness from God's presence. This illustration is repeated again and again. The temple, the ark, utensils used in the temple, the altars, and many other things are examples of this. They are holy because they are set apart and have connection with the Presence of a Holy God.

This explanation and illustration is the key to understanding our passage (Acts 3:12-26). Jesus, **His Servant**, experiences the holiness of God. The Trinity God embraces Jesus in oneness. God glorifies Jesus by the expression of His nature through Him. This expression is dominant in His servant role. All He experienced from the Jews is allowed and utilized in the servant role. The Trinity embraces these events that are a product of the ***determined purpose and foreknowledge of God*** (Acts 2:23). In this oneness, Jesus is the **Holy One**.

Although this oneness is exciting to discover in Jesus, to comprehend its application is overwhelming. If it is true of Jesus as a man, it is true for us also. This oneness has been the plan of God from the beginning of His creation of man. What was lost in the fall is restored to us in Jesus. He is the first One to experience it. He introduces us to the New Covenant. We are to be in oneness with the Trinity. We are to be intimate with the Spirit of Jesus. We are to derive holiness from His presence in us. We will never be holy outside His presence. Our being is to be saturated and mixed with all He is. Thus, who He is in His nature can be who we are!

The lie of religion must be exposed. We must become holy to come to Him is a falsehood. Our religious system attempts to shape and discipline us into the kind of people who can be accepted by God. Our best actions on our best days are far removed from His holy nature. Jesus' servant act on the cross brings us into the presence of God. In His indwelt presence, we

**Part Two:** Exhortation from the Porch

will experience forgiveness, cleansing, renewal, and holiness. Holiness derives from His nature!

We must also say that ONENESS PRODUCES HOLINESS EXPRESSING PURPOSE. This means holiness is never a feeling or the lack of specific activities. The Greek word "hagios," translated **holy** carries with it the idea of being set apart. The word "consecrate" is often connected to this idea. This idea is what makes religious items "sacred." They are set apart for the function and use of God. Thus, an item in the temple would be holy because it has the purpose of being used by God.

In the New Covenant as introduced by Jesus, the idea of holiness is expanded. Just to be set aside for a sacred, religious purpose is not enough. You might consecrate your life for religious work and never be holy in the New Covenant reality. The combination of your oneness with the nature of God and you allowing this nature to express itself in the plan designed for you is New Covenant holiness. If any element of this combination is removed, holiness dissipates. No one can claim to be holy when he is fulfilling his own desires and lust. Neither can anyone propose to be holy when he is experiencing self-fulfillment through humanitarian activities. Holiness is only known through oneness with God. This intimacy with God must be allowed to dominate, saturate, and shape the direction of your life. Holiness is in the expression of the Spirit of God through the purpose of man's life.

This holiness is dramatically visible in our passage. Jesus is the **Holy One**. He is the human expression of the Trinity. He is **the image of the invisible God** (Colossians 1:15). This holiness is not declared by the shape of His features, the height of His physical body, or the dress of His culture. This holiness is in the fulfillment of the nature of God through purpose. He is the **Servant Jesus**. He is subordinate to the flow, desire, and passion of the heart of God. He is in oneness with the Trinity and gives physical expression to what that heart expresses. Physical activities are involved. However, you can do the physical activities and not be the expression of the heart of God. Many men died on crosses. Some people gave their lives for others yet this may not be an expression of holiness.

Our passage distinctly highlights the oneness of Jesus with the Trinity. He is esteemed and embraced by God, the Three-in-One. Jesus is *glorified* in the flow of the nature of God through the oneness. It manifests itself in healing a lame beggar. Glorification is found in being **delivered up and denied in the presence of Pilate, when he was determined to let Him go**, and is blaringly expressed in being **denied** as **the Holy One and the Just**. In fact, a **murderer** was granted His place. The evil of man was expressed in all these activities. But the sovereign plan of God fulfilled His purpose through **the Holy One**. He was in oneness with the Trinity; this oneness flowed in purpose.

These qualities and conditions must be felt in us. It is the New Covenant possibility. We can be in oneness with the Spirit of Jesus. He paved the way for us. This oneness with His Spirit can saturate and flow through us to achieve the purpose of God for our lives. We are uniquely made. View your DNA; look at your fingerprints. Would not oneness with God express the unique purpose of God for your life? This expression of oneness in purpose is holiness.

A third element is ONENESS PRODUCES HOLINESS EXPRESSING PURPOSE THAT DEFINES YOUR PERSON. Jesus is the **Holy One**. He is intimate with the Trinity and filled with the Spirit. The nature of The Three-in-One Godhead flows through Jesus expressing the purpose, which is redemption. This purpose gives definition of the person of Jesus. Jesus is defined by this nature of God. It permeates every action, thought, and intent of His heart and mind, and is strongly evident in the Scriptures. We call it a "style," the style of the cross.

What is happening on the cross is happening in the life style of Jesus. It defines His person. His intent in doing miracles

**Part Two:** Exhortation from the Porch

was to help others. He had no hidden agenda. His leadership was that of "washing feet." The presentation of His position as King was to ride a donkey, the beast of burden. Jesus was not fulfilling a role; He was not performing an act. What He is in His person is expressed in His actions. He is a man expressing the nature of God.

Here is an important note! Jesus is not defined by His actions, but His actions are defined by His nature. We are identified by our actions. When someone continually talks about fishing; spends all of his spare time fishing; his dress, home décor, and money are focused on fishing, he is known by most as a "fisherman." Our actions define our identity. This correlation is not so with Jesus. His identity is the result of fulfilling His role and His actions. He is the Savior, which is the nature of His person. This nature defines every act of His ministry. He did not do anything outside the perimeter of His nature. His nature defines His actions.

What a challenge for us! Oh, to be filled with the heart and nature of God. Is it a possibility for my life? Can holiness flow from my person because He has me? In this flow, there will be purpose. The destiny of my life is contained in His nature. My life will not be defined by what I do, but what I do will be determined by my life possessed by Jesus. I must experience this!

## Acts 3:14

# THE JUST

*"But you denied the Holy One and the Just, and asked for a murderer to be granted to you," (Acts 3:14).*

The contrast between the activities of the Jews and Jesus is astounding. Peter describes the reality of the case without hesitation. The awfulness of the Jews' actions is startling when viewed against the backdrop of the purity of Jesus. The stark contrast is almost beyond belief. Jesus is **the Holy One and the Just** (Acts 3:14). These are two additional titles given to **His Servant Jesus**. To see these two titles together is necessary. "**The Holy One**" describes the nature and character of Jesus. God is the only one holy. There is no avenue for any human being to be holy. Holiness is derived only from God. God designed man to depend on Him. He wants to fill, saturate, and intertwine His nature into the being of man. Thus, man would be holy, but it is a derived holiness. This lack of holiness is not a condition resulting from the fall; it is the state of man because of creation.

Once man is filled with God and is holy, righteousness becomes possible. The Greek word "dikaios," translated ***Just,*** is often translated "righteous." This term describes the actions of the individual consistent with his character. For instance, God is holy and righteous. His character or nature is holy and His actions are always in alignment with His nature. In the Mesopotamian area, the word came from a river reed. This reed was used as a

**Part Two:** Exhortation from the Porch

construction tool to judge the horizontal straightness of walls and fences. God chose in His Word to use this term for His nature. He is the straight edge or ruler by which all things are evaluated. His actions set the rule for "righteousness." Because God is holy and every act corresponds to His nature, He expects this standard for all filled with His nature.

In our passage, Jesus is **glorified** as **His Servant Jesus**. He is a man filled with the nature of God. This nature brings Jesus into a state of holiness. He is the first person since Adam to live in the new arena of the Kingdom of God, the fulfillment of the New Covenant. Nothing blocks the permeating nature of God in Jesus' life. He is **the Holy One**. What God the Father is doing in Jesus is His design for you and me. Intimate relationship with us has been His intent from the beginning. He never intended to share His omnipresence, omniscience, or omnipotence with us. He wants to share His nature.

This sharing of His nature was never intended to be partial. As Jesus lived without hindrance to the nature of God, so we are to live without hindrances. Christianity was never just about forgiveness and going to heaven. It has always been about fullness and intimacy. The plan was the removal of all rebellion and resistance to the sourcing of His Spirit in us. We are restored to oneness with God. John Wesley called this oneness "perfect love," but it was not perfection in the sense of the elimination of misjudgments. We lack knowledge; therefore, we make wrong decisions. This lack of knowledge is why we keep insurance on our vehicles. Perfection happens in our hearts when we are filled with God's love. **God is love** (1 John 4:8, 16), which is the character and nature of God. We are to be filled, permeated, and saturated with this love.

Samuel Logan Brengle was the founder of the Salvation Army. God did something amazing in his life. He testified: "I walked out over Boston Common before breakfast, weeping for joy and praising God. Oh, how I loved! In that hour I knew

Jesus, and I loved him till it seemed my heart would break with love. I was filled with love for all His creatures. I heard the little sparrows chattering; I loved them. I saw a little worm wriggling across my path; I stepped over it; I didn't want to hurt any living thing. I loved the dogs, I loved the horses, I loved the little urchins on the street, I loved the strangers who hurried past me, I loved the heathen, I loved the whole world." (*They Found the Secret*, V. Raymond Edman, Zondervan, p. 29). This verbalizes holiness.

Jesus is **the Holy One**. But it is not enough to be "holy." He was also **just**. This means that His character, the nature of God, is in alignment with His actions. As Jesus is filled with the character of God, so it is demonstrated in His activities. As there is no blockage to the nature of God, so there is no hesitation to the performance of the desires of that nature. This performance is why the writers of the New Testament could acclaim Jesus as **the image of the invisible God** (Colossians 1:15). Every action of Jesus demonstrated the nature of Jesus derived from the Trinity. He is "righteous."

What about our lives? After all, I am not Jesus, the Second Member of the Trinity. I was not born of a virgin with Divine intervention. I have never been involved in a miracle production. I live in a cursed world; I have many faults and come from an abusive background. I cannot be expected to demonstrate the nature of God as Jesus did. If God's righteousness is the standard and Jesus matched that standard, where do I stand? What is expected of me?

Perhaps we should take another view of Jesus. He is the Second Member of the Trinity. However, He emptied Himself of all that He possessed as God. He became a person like all of humanity. He possessed all the limitations of knowledge, strength, and disciplines you and I have. Everything that made Him different from us, Jesus set aside. He was involved in doing miracles, but He continually made us aware that He did not do those miracles. They were demonstrating the nature of God that filled Him at His baptism. In fact, He lived in a cursed world with all the limitations connected to the fall. He came from an abusive background. He was raised in Nazareth, the worst town in Palestine. Even into His adulthood, He was accused of being an illegitimate child. As an adult, He was homeless without a family except the disciples. One betrayed Him and the rest forsook Him. Yet He was filled with the nature of God and was **the Holy One**. He demonstrated that holiness in His actions. He was **Just**.

Does this leave me without excuse? Am I able to live as God intended? Will I be the demonstration of the nature of God in my actions and be "holy" and "just?" Will I embrace the standard of God? The answer is "yes!" Jesus is the living proof! Because being "holy" is not a quality I manufacture, I can qualify. I derive it from intimacy with God. I can surrender as Jesus surrendered. I can experience the same "holiness" Jesus had. If I respond to the nature of God as Jesus did, I can be "just" as He was!

How will such an experience be demonstrated in my life? It will look exactly like Jesus, Christ-like. We can see it in our passage.

## Submitted

*"The God of Abraham, Isaac, and Jacob, the God of our fathers, glorified His Servant Jesus, whom you delivered up and denied in the presence of Pilate, when he was determined to let Him go"* (Acts 3:13). Jesus was a **Servant**. The Greek word is "pias," not the slave "doulos" owned by a master. Luke uses "pias" in his writings to emphasize a state beyond the relationship of the family that focuses on an individual who is submitted and subordinate to another. Jesus dwells in the spiritual state of being submitted to God.

In the practical everyday world that means Jesus was ***delivered up and denied***. The sound of those words repels us. "***Delivered up***" speaks of the loss of control. The end result is crucifixion and shame. "Paradidomi" is the Greek word, translated "***delivered up***," used most often for Judas betraying Jesus. The practical demonstration of the holy nature of God living in Jesus was submission to all that took place in the crucifixion event. Surely the crucifixion is completed and should be viewed by us as in the past. Then why does Jesus say, ***"If anyone desires to come after Me, let him deny himself, and take up his cross, and follow Me. For whoever desires to save his life will lose it, but whoever loses his life for My sake will find it"*** (Matthew 16:24-35). This sounds as though He is expecting this of me.

Jesus is filled with the nature of God. This nature burns with the passion of redemption of the world. The cross characterizes this nature. This nature never thinks about itself, but always others. This nature constantly gives itself up for what is better for others. How can this nature not result in the practical activities of the crucifixion? Jesus submitted Himself to this nature. Please attempt to understand the difference between obedience to this nature and submission to this nature. "Obedience" means the Father told Jesus what to do and He submitted in doing it. "Submission" means this nature permeated the core of Jesus existence; He could not help Himself. The nature of God produced through Jesus the practical intent of the cross, which is the heart of the New Covenant.

Jesus was the first to experience the New Covenant; He established it for us. We can be filled with the nature of God. We are not filled as a coffee cup is filled; we are filled as a sponge is filled. We are soaked, saturated, and overcome with the nature of God. His Spirit becomes our spirit; His mind becomes our mind; His will becomes our will. Resistance, reluctance, and hesitation are no longer factors. We do not struggle to obey;

we cannot help ourselves. We have submitted to the nature of God. All our actions become "just." The actions of our lives match the nature of our being. We are the image of the invisible God. He is demonstrated in our world. We move beyond duty, obligation, and law.

## Substitute

Another strong element in the "servanthood" of Jesus demonstrated in our passage is the wonder of "substitution." Peter proclaims: *"But you denied the Holy One and the Just, and asked for a murderer to be granted to you,"* (Acts 3:14). This verse is a vivid illustration of what is happening in the spiritual world. By Roman law, the Jews could have their courts and administer their laws and penalties. Their method of execution was stoning. However, just a few years before the death of Jesus, the Roman government decided to require all executions to be approved and executed by Roman courts. The method of Roman execution was crucifixion. If this had not been changed, prophecy would not have been fulfilled.

Therefore, the leaders of Israel must bring Jesus to Pilate for legal execution. They had already conducted their Jewish trials; at the first light of dawn, they brought Jesus to Pilate. Pilate saw through their accusations. John's account of the Gospel says: *"From then on Pilate sought to release Him"* (John 19:12). However, the Jews would not allow it. According to John there was a custom that a prisoner would be released at the Passover (John 18:39). Pilate found the worst, most hated prisoner to stand by Jesus. The crowds could choose Jesus or Barabbas. Then *they all cried again, saying, "Not this Man, but Barabbas!"* (John 18:40). Barabbas was released; Jesus took his place. He was a substitute.

The people's choice is one of the great aspects of the

atonement. Listen to Paul's thought. *"For when we were still without strength, in due time Christ died for the ungodly. For scarcely for a righteous man will one die; yet perhaps for a good man someone would even dare to die. But God demonstrates His own love toward us, in that while we were still sinners, Christ died for us"* (Romans 5:6-8). This love is symbolized consistently through the sacrifice for the sins of people. The writer of the Book of Hebrews relates that the animal bodies of the sacrifices had to be burned outside the camp (Hebrews 13:11). The sins of people were placed on those bodies. The priest could not eat these animals as they could other sacrifices. They must be destroyed. *Therefore Jesus also, that He might sanctify the people with His own blood, suffered outside the gate* (Hebrews 13:12). Jesus is our substitute; He took our place. All that we deserve, He experienced. *For He made Him who knew no sin to be sin for us, that we might become the righteousness of God in Him* (2 Corinthians 5:21).

Do we dare consider our intimacy with Jesus in this light? Does not the nature of *the Holy One* demonstrate itself in the One who is *Just*? His daily activities are aligned with His nature. The redemptive love of Jesus flows forth; it embraces me. He takes my burdens as if they are His own. Does He not want to do this through me to my world? Think of Jesus identifying with me so completely that my needs become His needs. In that moment, He lifts those needs from me and a moment of clarity results in my life. I can respond to His truth in that moment. Will I be that in the life of someone else? Are there people around me burdened; they are blinded (2 Corinthians 4:4). Will I embrace them in the spiritual realities? Will I carry their burden for a moment of clarity in their lives?

The nature of Jesus saturating in us produces an activity expressing His nature of redemption. Every action of my being must be redemptive. Would you consider the hundreds of situations in which you must make decisions? How will you respond? What will you decide concerning others? The guiding force of all those decisions must be redemption. You must always be redemptive. Anything else will run contrary to the nature of Jesus that fills you.

## Sacrificial

No one can read our passage without being deeply moved by the sacrifice involved. The sacrifice is beyond the comprehension of my finite mind. What did it mean for **the Holy One and the Just** to replace Barabbas and me? I cannot go to the depth of such a question. From the incarnation to the exaltation of Jesus, it is characterized by "sacrifice," the cross style of His nature. All that can be placed in the category of "unfair" is here. It is not right; it should not be! However, we who are so needy have no problem accepting the unfair then expressing gratitude. We know that all we experience as good comes because of that sacrifice. We gather weekly to praise and honor Jesus, the sacrifice.

However, our passage is pulling us into a deeper understanding. While the sacrifice of Jesus intimately and directly affects us, how does it change us? Now we are the body of Christ, the physical expression of His nature. **The Holy One** fills us and we are to be **Just**. His being flows forth in the manifestation of activities aligned with this nature. They will always have the evidence of sacrifice. If I am intimate with Him, I am "holy." If this derived holiness is sourcing all my activities, I am "just." All my activities will be saturated with the motive of sacrifice. The cross style of life will be expressed and lived. I will without effort fulfill the words of Jesus, *"deny* myself, *and take up his cross, and follow* Him*"* (Matthew 16:24).

I am afraid because embarrassment is always present in speaking of sacrifice. I know so little of it. My closing prayer must be for an alignment of my activities with His indwelling nature!

## Acts 3:14

# DENIED AND ASKED

*"But you denied the Holy One and the Just, and asked for a murderer to be granted to you," (Acts 3:14).*

Peter is given an astounding opportunity. The healed lame beggar clings to him; the crowd five thousand men will be saved is staring at him. They are all gathered at Solomon's porch. What do you say to a crowd this size, especially the crowd responsible for the death of Jesus? Perhaps it is a time for the truth! Truth may be earth shaking; it may cut them to the heart. A line in the sand will be drawn, and they will have to choose. Let us hear that truth!

At the end of one of our previous studies, we highlighted "extremities." Extremities are an amazing part of Peter's description of God. Peter said, **"The God of Abraham, Isaac, and Jacob, the God of our fathers, glorified His Servant Jesus"** (Acts 3:13). We must see the content of the service of Jesus in "extremes." His service in redemption cannot be called mild. He did not take a mediocre approach. His nature will not allow it. He touched the limits. Consider the suggested list again:

He was not born in comfort but in a stable.

He was not born of acceptable parents but born an illegitimate babe.

He was not born to wealthy parents but was born to a peasant couple.

**Part Two:** Exhortation from the Porch

He was not raised in the best Jewish environment but was raised in the worst town in Palestine.

He did not become a man but a homeless man. *"Foxes have holes and birds of the air have nests, but the Son of Man has nowhere to lay His head"* (Matthew 8:20).

He was not handsome among men, but *He has no form or comeliness; and when we see Him, there is no beauty that we should desire Him* (Isaiah 53:2).

His ministry was not to respectable Jews but to those who bore the physical evidence of sin. *And they brought to Him all sick people who were afflicted with various diseases and torments, and those who were demon-possessed, epileptics, and paralytics;* (Matthew 4:24).

He did not experience persecution but was treated as a criminal.

He did not just die but experienced the death of the cross.

He did not take on the sins of just a few people but took on the sins of all generations.

He did not just embrace the idea of sin but felt all your sins as if He committed them Himself.

He did not pay just a token penalty but he actually went to the worst of hell.

This experience is the reason the writer of Hebrews cried out: *"For we do not have a High Priest who cannot sympathize with our weaknesses, but was in all points tempted as we are, yet without sin"* (Hebrews 4:15). Jesus dealt with all the possibilities. No one despite guilt or circumstances is left untouched. Jesus is the complete *Servant*.

Our passage is startling (Acts 3:14). Peter not only describes the "extremes" of Jesus, but also the "extremes" of sin. He paints a picture of the worst of the worst, no one will ever go beyond the sin these Jews committed. He never mentions drugs, alcohol, or sexual perversion. Yet the description is the outer limits of sin. Adultery, rape, or stealing is not mentioned. Yet his description of sin makes one cringe.

One reason it is so horrible is that it is described in a contrast. Our sin is placed against the backdrop of the righteousness of Jesus. His character and service is so brilliant it exposes sin at its core. We are viewing the depth of evil. Jesus is the *"glorified... Servant Jesus"* (Acts 3:13). He is *"the Holy One and the Just"* (Acts 3:14). *"The Prince of life"* is *"raised from the dead"* (Acts 3:15). Our actions must be seen in light of His nature. Our sins are blaring and seen in the extreme!

In our passage, Peter presents Jesus as **the Holy One and the Just**. Holiness is the quality of the nature of Jesus that is perfect love. Perfect love bespeaks the complete lack of selfishness. The cross is the consistent beat of His heart and emotions. He is "just," His actions are in alignment with His character. He never acts contrary to His nature of perfect love. Against this specific picture, our sin is displayed.

*"But you denied the Holy One and the Just, and asked for a murderer to be granted to you,"* (Acts 3:14).

## Protested

*"Denied"* is one of two main verbs in the sentence. The Greek word "ameomai," translated ***denied,*** is in the middle voice. The middle voice highlights the idea of personal preference. This denial is not their only responsibility, it is their preference. Out of all the choices they could have made, denial is their priority; it pleased them. They felt satisfied with this choice. They were not forced to deny Jesus. They were not in a situation where each choice was undesirable, but they had to choose one. They left patting each other on the back at the great job they did in denying Jesus.

The Greek word "ameomai" is used thirty-two times in the New Testament. One-half of those are in the Gospel accounts.

**Part Two:** Exhortation from the Porch

Paul never uses this word. This verb refers to the expression of the subject's attitude of refusal. These *"Men of Israel"* were rejecting Jesus from the attitude of their nature. They were refusing Jesus in favor of Barabbas. This Greek word "ameomai" pushes the issue to the extreme. To justify their actions as a mistake, did not mean to, or a miscalculation is impossible. "Denial" describes what took place from the inner heart of their being as displayed by their actions.

This verb "ameomai" has two particular aspects in its usage. The word is a statement of an attitude about a claim or demand. In our passage, Pilate presents to this crowd the possibility to release a criminal during the Feast of the Passover (Luke 23:17). Pilate is convinced that Jesus is innocent. He receives pressure from his wife and his own sense of justice to release Jesus. He places Jesus with the worst, most feared criminal he can find, Barabbas. No doubt he expects the crowd to choose Jesus. To his utter amazement, they shout for Barabbas' release and to crucify Jesus (Luke 23:18). They denied, rejected, and refused Jesus.

This verb "ameomai" has a second important aspect in its usage. This aspect comes from the use of the word in Jesus' culture that is to contest something already in existence. The word "ameomai" is not used to deny a false position or the assertion of something incorrect. It denies something true. For instance, Matthew uses this word "ameomai" to describe the attitude of Peter toward Jesus after He was taken from the Garden of Gethsemane. Jesus predicted, *"Assuredly, I say to you that this night, before the rooster crows, you will deny* (ameomai) *Me three times"* (Matthew 26:34). Peter aggressively responded, *"Even if I have to die with You, I will not deny* (ameomai) *You!"* (Matthew 26:35). As Matthew records, three particular times Peter responds negatively to the accusation of being a disciple. He did not deny an untruth. He did not defend himself against false accusations. He renounced, rejected, and denied what was true.

### Denied and Asked | Acts 3:14

In our passage Peter uses this word 'ameomai" about ***the Holy One and the Just.*** You are not just guilty of putting Jesus to death (Acts 3:15). You are not guilty of just selecting Barabbas, the murderer, instead of Jesus, or about just "making wrong choices." We have all heard the statement, "He is a good person, but he just made some bad choices." This is not the position of the "***Men of Israel.***" Jesus was in reality ***the Holy One*** in their cultural setting. He walked their streets in perfect love. Not one act of hatred came from His being. He consistently manifested the nature of God to them. When did He fight, protect, or guard Himself? If Jesus is the true image of the invisible God, would not all humanity scream out, "God loves me?" Yet amid this full revelation, they denied, refused, and rejected this truth, and they proclaimed the reverse. They pointed to Him as a murderer, a person demon possessed, and a criminal.

He was not only ***the Holy One***; He was ***the Just***. This means the love of His nature was manifested in His actions. His actions were aligned with His character. No hypocrisy was present in His life. The ***Men of Israel*** could protest and say that His life was false, but they would be denying reality. His character was manifested, pressed on them, and undeniable in their presence.

This is the case with us as well! We have gone to the extreme in sin. We have not made just some bad choices. We actually took the revelation of God's love for our lives and denied that it was true. God acted on our behalf; we declared that He was not involved and did not care. The reason we went to the extreme of sin is because Jesus went to the extreme of love. Think of the extreme revelation of His love for you. In prevenient grace He came to you. He would not let you go. He revealed Himself repeatedly. He intervened in your circumstances without you even asking. He saved your physical life dozens of times without your consciousness. He healed you of diseases you did not know you had. Jesus placed you amid Divine movement that produced meaning for your life. You went your own way. You and I have consistently pushed Jesus from our lives protecting our sovereignty. We *denied the Holy One and the Just*.

## Prayed

In describing the extremity of evil to which these Jews went, Peter says: *"and asked for a murderer to be granted to you,"* (Acts 3:14). The Greek word "aiteo," translated *asked*, is in the middle voice. The middle voice denotes personal preference. These **Men of Israel** preferred Barabbas to Jesus. Barabbas was a notorious prisoner (Matthew 27:16). He committed murder in the insurrection (Mark 15:7). He was also a robber (John 18:40). We have no other details of his life or of the insurrection in which he took part. How morally twisted were their desires! These Jews actually preferred Barabbas, the criminal, to Jesus, the vision of God.

A strong focus is in this accusation of Peter to the spiritual realm beyond the physical. The act of physically denying Jesus resulting in crucifixion was terrible, but to think of this in the spiritual realm is life shattering. The Greek word "aiteo," translated *asked*, is used repeatedly in connection with prayer (Matthew 6:8; 7:11; 18:19). Although this Greek word "aiteo" is never translated "pray," it is consistently used to ask God for something. "Aiteo" means to ask, request, or beg and is used concerning the lame beggar who *laid daily at the gate of the temple which is called Beautiful, to ask alms from those who entered the temple;* (Acts 3:2). It pictures the seeking of the inferior from the superior.

I am afraid we limit prayer to a meager role in our thinking. We fall into the trap of those who consider prayer done at specific times. They take pride in the length of their prayers and parade themselves in public for all to be equally impressed (Matthew 6:5). Would it not be life shaking to realize that without ceasing we are bombarding the heavenly realm with our desires and prayers? In the Old Testament as the Israelites wandered in the wilderness, they prayed. They not only prayed in the tabernacle, but their complaints, gripes, and whining ascended into the heavenly realm. These came before God as a prayer.

Can you imagine the Israelites crying to God with their fists in the air? They demanded God to release a murderer instead of Jesus. They cried to God to deliver them from and eliminate Jesus from their presence. They do not want His influence in their lives. Do you see the extreme measure of this? All God dreamed of doing in and through Jesus is now happening. The long preparation of the Old Testament hour has come into reality. These Jews prayed to God for a cancellation of that plan. They fought against it with all their might. Peter must have screamed at this point, "Look at yourselves! Even your prayer life rebels against God!"

If you and I could play back a recording of the words we spoke and thought this last week, what did we pray about? We bombarded the heavenly realm by making demands with our complaints. Do we not find ourselves standing with these **Men of Israel** rejecting the dreams of God found in Jesus? I told Him on Sunday that I loved Him. I worshiped and sang songs to Him with great fervor. But my daily prayer life was filled with rebellion. I did not seek His dream but continually proposed my desires. They were selfish and self-sourced.

## Pardoned

The language Peter chose to use in his exhortation is remarkable. He reminded the Jews of their participation in the crucifixion of Jesus. They did stand before Pilate and demanded the release of Barabbas for Jesus. They were physically guilty of all that he says in these verses. But the language is designed

**Part Two:** Exhortation from the Porch

to lift us beyond the physical to the spiritual realities. He uses a word often connected to prayer. Now he uses a word connected to "grace."

*"To be granted"* is a translation of the Greek word "charizomai." The Greek word "charis," translated "grace," forms the base of our word. It means "to show someone favor, to be kind to." The most common meaning peculiar in the New Testament is "to pardon" or "to forgive." Paul uses it repeatedly for forgiveness. *"And you, being dead in your trespasses and the uncircumcision of your flesh, He has made alive together with Him, having forgiven (charizomai) you all trespasses"* (Colossians 2:13).

Peter cries out to the **Men of Israel**. They not only physically rejected and rebelled against the plan of God; they prayed over, begged for a favor, and asked God for grace. No wonder he calls them "ignorant" (Acts 3:17). God's grace walked your streets in Jesus. Oh, the immense and overwhelming favor the Trinity gave you in Jesus. The forgiveness of your sins and the revelation of His Person were in Jesus. But you preferred the hatred and rebellion of Barabbas.

Dear people, what have we done? We live for ourselves, bombard the heavenly realm with our anger and self-will, and demand God to give us the favor (grace) of our desires. He gives us Jesus but we want Barabbas. He gives us love but we prefer our hate. He gives us unity but we want division. He gives us mercy but we want the law. He gives us grace but we want judgment. He gives us a helpmate but we want lust. He gives us food but we want debauchery. He gives us worship but we want emotionalism. He gives us a way out, but we want to remain. He gives us freedom but we prefer bondage. He makes us sons but we want slavery. He gives us destiny but we want meaninglessness. He offers us the eternal but we want the temporal. He gives us Jesus but we want Barabbas. We need to repent!

## Acts 3:15

# SUBSTANCE OF LIFE

*"And killed the Prince of life, whom God raised from the dead, of which we are witnesses" (Acts 3:15).*

The lame beggar who has been healed holds onto Peter; he attracts a large crowd from those gathered at the temple for the hour of prayer and sacrifice. These people need instruction. Peter addresses them not in a sermon but rather in a strong exhortation from the porch. The first half of this encouragement is a series of "paradoxes." We have been slowly walking through these paradoxes and are now approaching the final one.

We began with the "Paradox of Sourcing" (Acts 3:12). The crowd is in awe of the miracle, thinking Peter and John are responsible for it. Peter speaks the words and extends the hand that brings this lame beggar to his feet. But Peter denies that he made any contribution to this miracle; he points to Jesus. In this miracle, God (Trinity) **glorified His Servant Jesus**; it is the "Paradox of Servant" (Acts 3:13). The nature of God manifested through Jesus is the nature of a servant. This nature is what God holds in high esteem. The "Paradox of Separated One" (Acts 3:14) is this Servant who is **the Holy One**. His nature is perfect love, the motivation for service. Linked with this "Paradox of Servant" is the "Paradox of Straight Edge" (Acts 3:14). Being **Just** is the nature of the Holy Servant demonstrated in life. There is no difference between the actions of Jesus and the nature of Jesus.

The final paradox is the "Paradox of Substance of Life" (Acts 3:15).

Keeping this study applicable to with the passage is going to be difficult. The Scriptures linking Jesus with life are many. The New Testament repeatedly describes Jesus as the source of life. John is especially prone to highlight this description. Look at how John begins his Gospel account. ***In Him was life, and the life was the light of men*** (John 1:4). John declares his purpose in writing much later in his account. ***But these are written that you may believe that Jesus is the Christ, the Son of God, and that believing you may have life in His name*** (John 20:31). In his first epistle, John wrote the following. ***God has given us eternal life, and this life is in His Son*** (1 John 5:11). He quoted Jesus on this subject. ***Jesus said to her, "I am the resurrection and the life. He who believes in Me, though he may die, he shall live"*** (John 11:25). ***Jesus said to him, "I am the way, the truth, and the life"*** (John 14:6). Jesus said this in speaking of bread. ***"Most assuredly, I say to you, he who believes in Me has everlasting life"*** (John 6:47).

Our aim is to stay true to the passage in our following explanations.

## Means

My heart and mind yearn to understand the depth of redemption. In a surface view we see only a cultic ceremony, which appeases those people attracted to religion. Animal and even human sacrifices are usual in pagan religions. Is Christianity a glorified expansion of pagan religions appealing to the weak? A deeper look compels us beyond the chants and spells using blood to gain security in an insecure world.

The quandary of redemption is beyond what we can reason with our minds because there are so many aspects. One aspect is the deed of sin that goes from the "little white lie" to the devastating evil of the worst perversion. The nature of sin flows through every deed placing them all in the same category of evil. Was James right when he said, ***"For whoever shall keep the whole law, and yet stumble in one point, he is guilty of all"*** (James 2:10)? If so, the best of us and the worst of us stand before God with equal guilt. This equality of guilt eliminates any thought of degrees of punishment. None of us will have a better place in hell than another. Speaking of hell, will sin really be punished by physical fire? Is there any way to comprehend the depth of separation from God and all sourced by Him?

For our finite thinking to comprehend sinful man is difficult. If we cannot understand the spectrum of being sinful, how shall we understand the spectrum of the punishment for sin? The Bible summarizes it in the word ***death. For the wages of sin is death,*** Romans 6:23). What is the view of this death? Is the death physical? Is the death spiritual? Is the death eternal? The answer to all is "yes!"

The Bible teaches us that physical death results from man's sin. In the Garden of Eden, man was separated from the Tree of Life. The curse of sin brought physical death on the world. Paul dedicated a chapter to physical death and physical resurrection when writing to the church at Corinth. ***For since by man came death, by Man also came the resurrection of the dead*** (1 Corinthians 15:21). But the result of sin is far greater than physical death; it is spiritual death! Man is separated from God and dies in his nature. Everything he experienced in oneness with the nature of God is removed. Man's self-sourcing is the only thing left. To dwell in such a death for a time is devastating, but to comprehend an eternal dwelling is unbearable.

The mystery of redemption is in how God covered all of those aspects of death. He is absolute life. Whatever is happening in Jesus is portrayed by our verse in reaching to the depth of every area of sin with all its destruction. We do not know all, but we do know some. Jesus reversed the effects of physical death.

***Jesus said to her, "I am the resurrection and the life. He who believes in Me, though he may die, he shall live. And whoever lives and believes in Me shall never die"*** (John 11:25-26). Paul proclaimed the following to the Corinthians. ***"If in this life only we have hope in Christ, we are of all men the most pitiable. But now Christ is risen from the dead, and has become the firstfruits of those who have fallen asleep"*** (1 Corinthians 15:19-20).

Our verse goes much deeper than physical or spiritual redemption. The essence of sin that separates us from God is cleansed. We are forgiven and radically transformed! He indwells us. We are united in oneness with His nature and become whole again. The eternal is secure. Look at what Jesus said. ***"Most assuredly, I say to you, he who hears My word and believes in Him who sent Me has everlasting life, and shall not come into judgment, but has passed from death into life"*** (John 5:24). He is the means by which all that is not right in us is corrected. The twist of our nature, the guilt of our past, and the certainty of our damnation is now changed.

Although we may not understand the details of it, we do understand enough to embrace Jesus. I will be His! Beyond all the explanation, beyond the theology, and beyond the organization of the church is Jesus! Nothing can or will take His place. I must spend my time pointing people to Jesus. He is the means of all God designs for me. Redemption is not in understanding; I cannot compensate for my wrong. Jesus conquers my need. I will be His!

## Method

For many, the wonder of Jesus is enough. For others, there is a desire to understand "how" Jesus is all I need. I embrace Him as all sufficient, but I have this burning passion to know Him better. The investigation of who He is brings me to what He has done. This investigation is not wrong or evil in itself.

However, it must never become of greater priority than His person in my life. The investigation of what He has done can become more important to me than Jesus. I quickly become a theologian instead of a "lover of Jesus." I become a student of ideas instead of a passionate seeker of Jesus.

Our passage gives us marvelous insight. Peter reminds the Jews of a recent event. Many of them were present at the secular trials of Jesus. The details of those trials were discussed repeatedly throughout Jerusalem. There was a custom that mercy should be extended to one criminal during the Feast of the Passover (John 18:39). A murderer, robber, and zealot named Barabbas was available. Pilate paired him with Jesus for the Jews to choose. Surely no one would want the feared Barabbas compared with the miracle worker Jesus. The one who destroyed is released; the One who produced "good" is crucified.

**"But you denied the Holy One and the Just, and asked for a murderer to be granted to you, and killed the Prince of life, whom God raised from the dead, of which we are witnesses** (Acts 3:14-15). Isn't this the heart of all that **His Servant Jesus** came to do? He took the place of "*a murderer*." Jesus exchanged places with Barabbas. Jesus now takes on Himself all that Barabbas should experience. He walks the road that Barabbas should have walked. Is it not a mystery?

Perhaps you think Barabbas was just one foul man who got a break. You do not understand the intent of God in all of this. This exchange was accomplished by **the determined purpose and foreknowledge of God,** (Acts 2:23). The **murderer** is far beyond Barabbas. In a heated debate with the leaders of Israel, they accused Jesus. **"We were not born of fornication; we have one Father — God"** (John 8:41). They were referring to His miraculous virgin birth; they believed He was an illegitimate child. Jesus was bold in His response. **"You are of your father the devil, and the desires of your father you want to do. He was a murderer from the beginning, and does not stand in the** *truth, because there is no truth in him. When he speaks a lie, he speaks from his own resources, for he is a liar and the father of it"* (John 8:44). Barabbas, *a murderer*, was fathered by the devil, as were the **men of Israel**. Jesus goes after the father of them all.

Is He playing into their hands or are they playing into His hands? They are going to kill the Prince of life. But listen to this depth of truth. *Inasmuch then as the children have partaken of flesh and blood, He Himself likewise shared in the same, that through death He might destroy him who had the power of death, that is, the devil,* (Hebrews 2:14). God, who cannot experience death, became Man. The Spirit of God sourcing this Man marches into the worst Satan can offer. He will cry, "Give it your best shot!" Satan unleashes all He can muster against this one Man. The principle at the heart of demonic fathering is destruction and death. He will do a work on Jesus. The physical death, the spiritual death, and the eternal death are focused on Jesus. When their work was complete and they were completely exhausted, **God raised** Him *from the dead*!

This Man, through the sourcing of the Spirit of God, cannot be contained. He takes the instrument of destruction and turns it back on Satan. He destroys him with the power of death that he has. The seed of the woman steps on the head of the devil (Genesis 3:15). Satan has no more weapons, no more tricks, and no more power. We are free!

## Motive

What is the motive of the Trinity in such sacrificial act? The motive is contained in the amazing phrase, **the Prince of Life**. The Greek word "archegos," is translated **Prince**, is in the masculine gender, and accusative case, which is like the English direct object. The act of the "killing" is focused on **the Prince**. The Greek word "zoe," is translated **life**, is in the feminine gender, and genitive case, which shows relationship. The masculine gender gives the meaning of concrete, solid, and measurable. The idea of *life* is a mystery, because the feminine gender cannot give the meaning of measured, contained, or mastered. Life is the unending experience of all contained in the heart of God. Jesus calls us in to all that He is. What is He like? He is far beyond a theology or doctrine, and will not be contained in laws or ceremonies of religion. Life is the "mystery" into which He calls us.

*Prince* (archegos) is easier to comprehend. This Greek word is a compound word with overwhelming content and is used four times in the New Testament. The first part is "arche," which means "beginning or rule." The second part is "ago," which means "to lead." The meaning is not simply the one who causes something. One may be the cause of something and not the beginning or originator. Jesus is the beginning or the originator of something. In other words, He is the "beginning" One and He is leading others into it.

The four New Testament verses exclusively use this word as a title for His "Christ" (Messiah) role as the exalted Jesus. He is the first and stands at the head of the parade as a leader. In another encounter with the Jews, Peter makes a bold statement. **"The God of our fathers raised up Jesus whom you murdered by hanging on a tree. Him God has exalted to His right hand to be Prince and Savior, to give repentance to Israel and forgiveness of sins"** (Acts 5:30-31). Jesus is the leader of the new breed of man, people filled with God. He is the founder of a new race! This parallels with the statement of the writer of the Book of Hebrews. **For it was fitting for Him, for whom are all things and by whom are all things, in bringing many sons to glory, to make the captain of their salvation perfect through sufferings** (Hebrews 2:10). Jesus is the *captain*, the pioneer of salvation. He broke a hole in the wall; He made a door where there was no door. He leads us into the heart of God.

**Part Two:** Exhortation from the Porch

The writer of Hebrews calls us to run the race set before us. We are to run as *looking unto Jesus, the author and finisher of our faith, who for the joy that was set before Him endured the cross, despising the shame, and has sat down at the right hand of the throne of God* (Hebrews 12:2). Jesus is the **author**, the originator of our faith. He takes us by the hand and leads us into what He started. We are people filled with the Spirit of God as led by Jesus!

In our passage, Jesus is the **Prince of Life**, and this is intimately tied to *whom God raised from the dead.* Jesus leads us through all the forces of physical death, spiritual death, and eternal death. He pushes back the efforts of the murderer who has the power of death in all phases. He leads us into life, His life! *For if we have been united together in the likeness of His death, certainly we also shall be in the likeness of His resurrection,* (Romans 6:5). I will let Jesus indwell me. I will die to myself that He might lead me into His life!

## Acts 3:15

# A GLORIFIED RESURRECTION

*"And killed the Prince of life, whom God raised from the dead, of which we are witnesses" (Acts 3:15).*

Peter is exhorting the Jews from Solomon's porch. Jesus is the focus of every statement. Paradoxes are the framework by which he presents this focus. A paradox is a statement seemingly absurd and self-contradictory. However, on further investigation we discover it true. In many ways, the Gospel is a paradox. The truth of the Gospel is outside the thought process of our world. Paul realized that **the message of the cross is foolishness to those who are perishing, but to us who are being saved it is the power of God** (1 Corinthians 1:18). The logic of this reality is in **the foolishness of God is wiser than men, and the weakness of God is stronger than men** (1 Corinthians 1:25).

The opening "Paradox of Sourcing" is a focus on Jesus (Acts 3:12). Peter and John violently refuse to take any credit for this miracle. The miracle of the lame man being healed glorifies **His Servant Jesus**. This title, **His Servant Jesus**, becomes the second paradox, the "Paradox of Servant" (Acts 3:13). The Second Member of the Trinity was submissive as is the nature of God. The perspective of God's heart is service. The cross is His nature. Jesus became a man by eliminating everything that makes Him different from you. He joined us in our humanity. In submission to the Trinity, He was filled with the Spirit.

Everything He accomplished was done because He was a man filled with the Spirit of God. God does not delight in our service to Him; He delights when He is able to serve through us!

How did this service appear? He was **delivered up** (paradidomai). Judas betrayed Him. He was **denied** (ameomai). The truth about Jesus was treated as untrue. He was denied as **the Holy One** (Paradox of Separated One) **and the Just** (Paradox of Straight Edge). A murderer was preferred as grace from the evil one (Acts 3:14). All these sufferings are a focus on Jesus. These sufferings are the ingredients of His service. The nature of God is displayed through the life of a submitted Man. These experiences were embraced as the **determined purpose and foreknowledge of God** (Acts 2:23). **The Prince of Life** being killed is the climax (Acts 3:15) and it is the "Paradox of Substance of Life."

The nature of God is the content of **His Servant Jesus** and is displayed through a Man filled with the Spirit. Jesus is the focus; however, the focus of Jesus is on the sourcing by the Spirit. God is glorifying **His Servant Jesus**. Lack of judgment does not explain the death of Jesus. He was not a Man whose dreams were not supported by adequate planning. "Not getting the breaks" does not even closely highlight the truth. The sufferings, including death, are the plan of God; they are the flow of the nature of God through a Man.

But the story is not over! Peter declared, **"Whom God raised from the dead, of which we are witnesses"** (Acts 3:15). If God (the Trinity) is responsible for the death of Jesus, He is responsible for the resurrection of Jesus. If Jesus' death was the result of willing submission to the desire of the Father (Matthew 26:39), so His resurrection results from the same desire. If Jesus refused to take credit for the miracles flowing from His life, He also refuses to embrace the resurrection as His action. God (the Trinity) **glorified His Servant Jesus** in submission and in resurrection. Peter cries, **"Whom God raised from the dead, of which we are witnesses"** (Acts 3:15).

If what we just said is true, let us distinctly and systematically discuss the various elements.

## The Key Person

The key person in the act of the resurrection is **God**. He is the "Focus of the Action." In our phrase, ***"Whom God raised from the dead,"*** the subject is **God** (Theos) in the nominative case. The main verb is ***raised*** (egeiro) in the indicative mood, a simple statement of fact. The subject, in the active voice, is responsible for the action of the verb. This phrase, ***raised from the dead***, is used nine times in the New Testament relating to Jesus (John 21:14; Acts 3:15; 4:10; Romans 6:4; 6:9; 7:4; 1 Corinthians 15:21; 1 Thessalonians 1:10; 2 Timothy 2:8). Four of those nine say that God is responsible for the resurrection of Jesus. The other five strongly indicate this fact by using the passive voice. Many other references that do not have this exact wording are available. Peter says in his sermon at Pentecost, ***"Whom God raised up, having loosed the pains of death, because it was not possible that He should be held by it"*** (Acts 2:24; also see Acts 2:32). In each case, we never consider Jesus to be the source of His resurrection.

In our passage, it is the **God of Abraham, Isaac, and Jacob, the God of our fathers,** (Acts 3:13) who is responsible. This God is the Trinity, the three in one Godhead! The resurrected life of Jesus derives from the Trinity. As He was filled with the Spirit of God and experienced the flow of this nature in His life, so He experienced the flow of this nature in death, the resurrection.

In our passage we find the "Formation of the Approach". One would think everything in the context would be about "life" and "resurrection," but it is about death. The content of being ***glorified*** is about being ***delivered up*** (paradidomai). This betrayal activity gives up or surrenders up. Jesus is handed over to death. The Scriptures say that Jesus is **delivered** by God and by human beings, but a different Greek word is used for each. God delivered (ekdotos) Jesus ***by the determined purpose and foreknowledge*** (Acts 2:23). The Jews **delivered** (paradidomai) Jesus ***and denied in the presence of Pilate,*** (Acts 3:13). "Ekdotos" comes from the Greek word "ekdidomai," translated "to be delivered out of" or "from the heart of." "Paradidomai" means "to deliver over to the power of someone else." Jesus was coming from the heart of God in every circumstance, even His death. The Jews were getting rid of Jesus, and God was embracing Jesus in His death, which was His glorification. Death is at the heart of every action from God and from man. Jesus is going to replace a ***murderer***. The ***Prince of life*** will be ***killed***. Whether the murderer is God or man, death is the core of Jesus' experience.

Peter verifies this action of God, the "Formal Affirmation," by calling on ***witnesses***. God is responsible for the resurrection of Jesus. Let the witnesses testify! We discovered in previous studies of the Book of Acts that the sole role of the "Apostles" was a witness of the resurrection (Acts 1:22). The Apostles were not responsible for planting churches, overseeing organizations, or administration. They were witnesses of the resurrection! Each time they testified they glorified God who raised Jesus from the dead!

## The Key Principle

A principle throughout our passage is in the message Jesus consistently proposed to His disciples (Matthew 16:24-25). This idea is in the heart of every activity of Jesus. The "Focus of the Action" is in a basic assumption, there is no resurrection from the dead without death. This is the difficulty we experience with Paul's statement, ***"that I may know Him and the power of His resurrection, and the fellowship of His sufferings, being*** *conformed to His death"* (Philippians 3:10). We eagerly embrace *the power of His resurrection* while we try to ignore *the fellowship of His sufferings, being conformed to His death*. There is no resurrection without dying.

An "axiom" is a statement or proposition regarded as established, accepted, or evidently true. An axiom is the heart of our passage, **whom God raised from the dead, of which we are witnesses**. This statement in the Greek text is significant. **God** is the subject. **Raised** is the verb. **From the dead** is in the genitive case and not a direct object. In other words, death is not receiving the action of the raising. **Whom** is in the accusative case, the direct object. **Whom** refers to Jesus. God, the Trinity, is acting on Jesus. **Dead**, in the Greek text, does not have an article, so it is not "*the dead*," just "*dead*." The death is of a general category rather than a specific item or area of death. God acts on Jesus in death. A resurrection act would not be without death.

"***From***" becomes an important part of the statement, because it is the "Formation of the Approach." Two Greek words are consistently translated "from." "Apo" focuses on the point of origin being nearby or close. "Ek" focuses on the point of origin being in another object. In our passage, the Greek word is "ek." The action of God is on Jesus in the heart of death. Resurrected life is born in the heart of death.

Death must not be confined to physical death. The nature of God is constantly living in death. Jesus is constantly dying to Himself, and this is demonstrated in the incarnation. He gave up all He had as God to become man. This was the attitude and content of death. He did not become a king, but a criminal accused by the law; this is the heart of dying to self-sourcing. He gave Himself to be crucified in physical death. He took on the sins of the world to experience spiritual death. He went to hell experiencing eternal death. Life thrives in the heart of death.

Peter preached at Pentecost, **"Whom God raised up, having loosed the pains of death, because it was not possible that He** *should be held by it"* (Acts 2:24). Imagine Jesus as the first Man to experience the New Covenant. He is filled with the life of God sourcing Him. All the wretchedness of sin, with all of its punishment of death, is placed on and in Him. But all the sin attempting to destroy Him is redeemed by the power of God in Jesus. Even death that attempts to hold Him is changed. The sting of death is removed. Hades is filled with victory. **Death is swallowed up in victory** (1 Corinthians 15:54). God conquers death by death (Hebrews 2:14-15). We live in death.

Are there any witnesses to this fact? Peter cries, *"of which we are witnesses"* (Acts 3:15), which is the "Formal Affirmation." The writer of the Book of Hebrews speaks of Jesus' link with us. In the same breath, he speaks "life in death," (Hebrews 2:14). Every brother to Jesus can witness of the same life amid death. We are witnesses to the fact that Jesus is alive. We are witnesses to the fact that we are alive in Him. The same Life that could not be conquered in Him cannot be conquered in us!

## The Key Partnership

We do not find life in self-sourcing. The "Focus of the Action" of life is in Jesus. We will never do anything good or great enough to produce life. The farmer who plants the seed is only a partner with the life God places in nature. He simply cooperates with the life of nature. Husband and wife cooperate with the creative power of God's life to produce a new human being. We do not stop life; we do not create life; we do not give life. We are partners with Life. All world religions recognize life in God. But He is removed from us. Oh, the wonder of having the action of Life indwelling us. Suppose we could partner with Life as a glove partners with a hand, which is the message of Christianity.

The life of the Trinity opened itself for us to join its life.

We want to pick what features of the Trinity we will own. Omnipotence, omniscience, and omnipresence are not available. We are invited to partner with the nature of God, which is Life. You and I can be filled with the life of God. He is Life!

This sounds appealing to us. The problem is in the "Formation of the Approach." We only find this partnership in the heart of death. The resurrection is not a reward for Jesus' faithfulness. He did not earn life by dying on a cross. Life is only found in dying. The opposite is equally true. Death is only found in living. When we live for ourselves, we die. A life focused on self is always destructive. Jesus taught, ***"For whoever desires to save his life will lose it, but whoever loses his life for My sake will find it"*** (Matthew 16:25). In our passage, we again find that Jesus lives amongst death.

In a discussion with His disciples about His second coming, Jesus vividly describes His return (Matthew 24:28). Have you ever been driving down the road, jammed on your brakes, and whispered to your children, "Look." They peer around your shoulder from the backseat. You point to buzzards in the street eating road kill. You turn to them and explain the second coming of Jesus, and it is as the buzzards eating on death in the street. Jesus pictures His return this way. The buzzards are living because of death. They feed daily off death. Their survival is death. They must consistently return to death or they do not live.

The second coming is not an absent God appearing to make everything right or an outside God coming to rescue us. The second coming is God, who has never left us, suffering and bleeding amid death. We feed off the dying of Jesus, and we live. As we consistently return to death, losing our lives, we find His life is ours. We find life only in death. No wonder Paul expressed the heart of the Gospel when he said, ***"I have been crucified with Christ; it is no longer I who live, but Christ lives in me; and the life which I now live in the flesh I live by faith in the Son of God, who loved me and gave Himself for me"*** (Galatians 2:20).

**Part Two:** Exhortation from the Porch

Do we not live in death? Our rescue is in death! We are called to absolute death to self-sourcing so Jesus might live through us.

Are there any witnesses to this? The "Formal Affirmation" is found in the multitudes that testify of the life of Jesus indwelling them. In the embrace of His death, we find life. We echo Peter's words: ***"Of which we are witnesses"*** (Acts 3:15).

## Acts 3:15

# THE REVERSAL

*"And killed the Prince of life, whom God raised from the dead, of which we are witnesses" (Acts 3:15).*

The last phrase of verse fifteen resonates like a blast from Gabriel's horn. Peter thunders these words: ***"And killed the Prince of life, whom God raised from the dead, of which we are witnesses"*** (Acts 3:15). I wish I had the dramatic ability to portray the impact of it to you.

In the context of their experiences and culture, it must have been earthshaking. Only a few months had passed since the crucifixion. Perhaps the gossip about the occasion had quieted. The physical results of the earthquakes were still visible. Did they have the veil of the Holy of Holies repaired by this time? Those listening to Peter's exhortation were aware of the rumors of the resurrection of Jesus. The appearances of the resurrected Lord took place over 40 days. Everyone was talking about it. The soldiers were paid to spread the lie that the disciples had stolen the body. The Jewish officials were disagreeing with any talk of the resurrection. The Sadducees did not believe in such "a thing."

Now Peter exhorts them in the context of this miracle. No one disputes the healing of the lame man. This lack of dispute is emphasized throughout two chapters (Acts 3:11; 4:10, 14, 16). This man healed is more that 40 years. Of the many miracles the apostles had taken part in, this healing miracle is the most verifiable. Peter forces them to confront the truth of Jesus!

Let's review Peter's approach. He addresses them as *"Men of Israel"* (Acts 3:12). He then announces: *"The God of Abraham, Isaac, and Jacob, the God of our fathers, glorified His Servant Jesus"* (Acts 3:13). They readily identify themselves as children of Abraham (John 8:39). Their God glorified Jesus through the healing of this lame man.

Peter leaves no question about the person to whom he refers. He tells them about their participation in the recent crucifixion. These details were fresh in their minds. They had joined the crowd in screaming, *"Let Him be crucified!"* (Matthew 27:22). Many of them were possibly having sleepless nights from the memory of His scourging and the brutality of His crucifixion. The event had a sense of demonic presence throughout. Did they not still speak in wonder at the fact that *the veil of the temple was torn in two from top to bottom; and the earth quaked, and the rocks were split* (Matthew 27:51)? Many of them may have witnessed some saints who were raised from the dead at the moment the veil was torn (Matthew 27:52-53).

To deny their participation in the death of Jesus was impossible! They had *delivered up and denied in the presence of Pilate, when he was determined to let Him go* (Acts 3:13). They had *denied the Holy One and the Just, and asked for a murderer to be granted to you* (Acts 3:14). They had *killed the Prince of life* (Acts 3:14). Even though they were amazed when the lame man was healed, there must have been a silence. A cloud of despair, guilt, and conviction through the presence of the Holy Spirit permeated every heart. Heads were hanging, eyes were focused on the floor, and mouths dropped open. They were guilty! They had interfered with the plan of their God. He had sent a Deliverer; this had been their dream for generations. In its fulfillment, they had denied, rejected, and murdered the One sent to save them. This crowd had the same response as the crowd who listened to Peter's sermon at Pentecost. *Now when they heard this, they were cut to the heart, and said to Peter and the rest of the apostles, "Men and brethren, what shall we do?"* (Acts 2:37).

In the low moment of guilt, hopelessness, and fear, the word REVERSAL is sounded. Gabriel's horn will blow the sound of this word at the second coming of Christ. Everything suddenly changes as Peter thunders his message. ***"Whom God raised from the dead, of whom we are witnesses"*** (Acts 3:15). This simple statement of six words overrides all the verses of guilt. Rebellion and rejection are swallowed in the resurrection. The resurrection is a second chance, a renewal. God is not done with us. Hope is not lost. We fight against His plan, and God uses our rebellion in His plan. The worst we can do is conquered in the best God can do! Jesus is alive! This healed beggar is the proof!

## Resurrection

The resurrection is the immediate reversal. A focus on the physical aspect of the resurrection is the beginning. The early church presented the resurrection as the linchpin of the Gospel. If the resurrection is not true, then nothing is true. In Paul's writing to the Church at Corinth, he systematically presents to them this truth (1 Corinthians 15). He begins by saying that he will preach to them the same Gospel he preached to them in times past. They embraced that Gospel and were saved. This message began with ***Christ died for our sins according to the Scriptures*** (1 Corinthians 15:3). But the message continues with ***He was buried, and that He rose again the third day according to the Scriptures,*** (1 Corinthians 15:4).

All this passage was verified by a series of reliable appearances of the resurrected Lord. The interactions with the resurrected Christ create a historic basis for our belief. First, Peter saw Jesus, then the temple crowd encountered His person. Five hundred

**Part Two:** Exhortation from the Porch

followers of Christ saw Him in one setting, then James saw Him. All the apostles interacted with Him, but Paul places himself as the last one to see the resurrected Lord. Paul was *as by one born out of due time* (1 Corinthians 15:8). He declares himself as the least of all the apostles and unworthy because of the way he persecuted the church. In our passage, Peter reminds us, *of which we are witnesses* (Acts 3:15).

These witnesses all preached that *Christ has been raised from the dead,* (1 Corinthians 15:12). Why would any in the Church of Corinth propose there is no resurrection from the dead? The logic is simple. If there is no resurrection from the dead, then Christ is not raised from the dead. If Christ is not raised from the dead, then our witness and preaching is empty. The faith we have is meaningless. In fact, others find us to be liars because we propose something false. The worst is we are still in our sin!

One of the first evidences of sin in the fall of man was the physical effect. Under the curse of sin, the ground brings forth *both thorns and thistles* (Genesis 3:18). Childbirth is painful (Genesis 3:16). Our attitude toward the physical changes; clothes are necessary; sickness and sorrow invade our physical. Physical death is now inevitable.

Rejoice with me in the reality! This physical effect is reversed! Yes, sin *denied the Holy One and the Just*; sin demanded the release of a *murderer* and *killed the Prince of life*. But the story does not end here. *God raised from the dead* the Prince of life! No wonder Jesus shouted at the grave of Lazarus! He said, *"I am the resurrection and the life. He who believes in Me, though he may die, he shall live. And whoever lives and believes in Me shall never die. Do you believe this?"* (John 11:25-26).

You must understand the biblical concept! The resurrection from the dead is not to be viewed as just an event in the future. Jesus establishes a new road; He is the Way (John 14:6). We are walking a deathless road in Jesus. In Him is the reversal of all

The Reversal | **Acts 3:15**

Satan intends for the physical life of man. You must dwell in Him and Him in you. Jesus is our resurrection!

## Redemption

A second aspect of the reversal is the resurrection of Jesus. These are not listed in order of importance or occurrence. They are listed just as aspects of redemption. The English definition of redemption is twofold - "The action of saving or being saved from sin, error, or evil," and "the action of regaining or gaining possession of something for payment, or clearing a debt."

Peter does not disregard the responsibility of the Jews in the death of Jesus. He orally paints a picture that reminds them of the occasion. They were involved in "delivering up" Jesus (Acts 3:13). Were members of the Sanhedrin present at this exhortation? Were those who helped the leaders of Israel in bringing Jesus to Pilate listening to Peter? Did they not support a system of traditions that allowed the execution of their Messiah? The crowd followed the soldiers into the Garden of Gethsemane led by Judas. They milled around the home of Caiaphas as the mock trial was happening. They joined the march. Jesus was dragged down the streets at dawn to Pilate's palace. They screamed for the crucifixion.

Pilate was **determined to let Him go,** and these Jews would not allow it. They stopped every attempt Pilate made to release Jesus. They embraced a ***murderer*** as theirs. Barabbas was released to continue his crimes among them. How could such hatred fill their hearts? From where did the anger arise which consumed their emotions? No wonder Pilate kept asking them "why?" The only reason for their actions was purely sin. The Holy Spirit was doing exactly what Jesus explained. "***And when He has come, He will convict the world of sin, and of righteousness, and of judgment: of sin, because they do not believe in Me; of*** *righteousness, because I go to My Father and you see Me no more; of judgment, because the ruler of this world is judged"* (John 16:8-11).

Pentecost explodes on the world (Acts 2:1-4). The Holy Spirit fills Peter; the Spirit's message goes to the heart of these Jews. They **killed the Prince of life**! **But God raised from the dead** this One they rejected. The Trinity not only reverses the physical effects of the crucifixion, but this resurrection reaches into the spiritual realm. All the hate, evil, and self-will present in their scene is reversed. Physical death is a mere symptom of the spiritual death. Hell cannot hold Him. He embraces the sin represented at the hour of crucifixion. The evil of man encompasses His being. He reverses that spiritual death!

Peter concludes his message with a call to repentance. They must give up a former thought to embrace this new thought of Jesus. He cries, "***Repent therefore and be converted, that your sins may be blotted out***" (Acts 3:19), and it is an amazing message of reversal. All they have been can be changed to all He is! The resurrection of Jesus conquers eternal death. There is no more death. Physical death and spiritual death are reversed.

We strongly say this is not simply "forgiveness." You are forgiven. You ARE NOT going to be forgiven; you ARE forgiven. Will you accept what has been done for you? But it is more than forgiveness. Think of physical death. Think of physical resurrection. Death into resurrection is the reality of reversal. This reversal is also true about our redemption. Peter does not propose a mere forgiveness of the actions of these Jews, as they continue in their hate and rebellion against Jesus. He proclaims a reversal of their state. What they were in hate and rebellion is now reversed in Jesus. They can repent and have their state is reversed! Jesus does not save us "in" sin; He saves us "from" sin.

As He was **the Holy One and the Just**, so we can derive this from His presence. Our nature manifested in our denial, hatred, and murder is brought to death in Him. His life is raised in us!

As His actions aligned with His nature, so He flows through us in our actions. We will be "just." Our state in the spiritual realm and in the practical realm is reversed. He is raised from the dead; so are we! No wonder Peter continues, **"Repent therefore and be converted, that your sins may be blotted out,"** (Acts 3:19).

## Restoration

Peter is clearly not proposing that "Jesus died for me, and I get off scot free." He proclaims something far greater and beyond our wildest dreams. He announces restoration! Let us be sure we understand. According to the dictionary, restoration means "the action of returning something to a former owner, place, or condition."

All three of these are included in our restoration. He created us; we were made for Him. He is the former owner of humanity. Our place is in Him; we are to dwell within the perimeters of His person. We rebel by making our place. Our spiritual condition is not one of emptiness. We were created to be in intimacy with His person. In the embrace of Jesus, the Kingdom of Heaven is formed. This is the restoration. The announcement of the resurrection is not just physical resurrection; it is not just redemption, as forgiveness of our sins. We are not left empty and on our own. We are filled with the Spirit of the resurrected Jesus!

In Peter's exhortation, he speaks of **"the times of restoration of all things"** (Acts 3:12). He explains this with the prophecy given by Moses (Acts 3:22-23). He verifies it as spoken by **all the prophets, from Samuel and those who follow,** (Acts 3:24). He does not call this restoration the second coming of Christ but the first coming. In the resurrection of Jesus, the restoration is complete because the Spirit of Jesus now indwells us. He restores us inside and out. According to the Scriptures, the coming of Jesus ushered in these "last days." We are living in them. The

**Part Two:** Exhortation from the Porch

Spirit of Jesus indwelling us is completing of the restoration.

Peter calls us to intimacy with Jesus, the resurrected One. ***You are complete in Him,*** (Colossians 2:10). Embrace Him, and respond to Him! Let Him fill you! Practice His presence! Let Him be your dwelling place! Receive His mind! Live in His resurrected presence and never die!

Acts 3:15

# IRREVERSIBLE

*"And killed the Prince of life, whom God raised from the dead, of which we are witnesses" (Acts 3:15).*

I am not sure the "celebration of reversal" proposed by our passage can be exaggerated. How can anyone take it for granted? Although the reversal may be complete, it is consistently being revealed in ever unfolding depth. At the heart of all God has done and is doing on our behalf, not a side concern, is the reversal. **"Whom God raised from the dead"** (Acts 3:15) is a simple statement.

Peter presents Jesus in distinct clarity. The nature of Jesus is revealed in the context of Jewish culture. The Trinity God of these Jews and their ancestors planned and progressively warred against sin to present the Messiah to the world. The great war of the Old Testament climaxed in the battle at the cross. Was it a battle or surrender? Did not **His Servant Jesus** again serve according to the nature of God? Jesus gave Himself to be **delivered up**. He surrendered and was **denied in the presence of Pilate, when he was determined to let Him go**. He was **the Holy One**. He experienced the holy nature of God flooding His inner being. He was the first Kingdom Man to be filled with God and derive the holiness of God's nature. He was **the Just**. All His actions were aligned with His derived nature, and there was no hypocrisy. However, these Jews denied Him as **the Holy One** *and the Just*. They preferred a *murderer to be granted to* them. Barabbas was more acceptable to them than Jesus. In fact, they became murderers themselves. They killed **the Prince of life**.

This choice is a full and awful picture of sin! It does not describe a list of evil deeds although acts were involved. It depicts the sinful nature of us all. This sin nature cannot tolerate Jesus. Self-centeredness in all its sourcing power pushed Jesus to the cross. The Jews surely bowed their heads and stared at the floor of the temple porch as a sickish feeling swept over them. Certainly they were gripped by a devastating consciousness of what they had done to the plans of God. Are they not doomed? How can they possibly change or redeem their plight?

Peter does not leave them in this pit of despair! He boldly announces that God REVERSED all that sin achieved. All that sin put in place, God removed. He raised Jesus from the dead, and this one simple act changed everything! The consequence of sin is death. But all is changed when death is changed. Jesus is alive! All has been REVERSED! The physical, spiritual, and eternal aspects of death are all REVERSED. The conquering power of sin and its guilt is REVERSED. Separation from God is REVERSED. Victory is ours in the resurrection of Jesus! We glory in such a message.

However, some elements are not reversed. God is wise in all His movements. Some things must be changed, but there are other things must not be changed! The irreversible things are eternal in the character and nature of God. These are highlighted in our passage.

## Service

A trap is here that we must avoid. The poured out life of Jesus contained in His "obedience to death" is not reversed. Our thinking often develops into a "now" and "then" theology. We are deeply grateful that He came to serve us. The cross, the ultimate sacrifice, was an amazing service Jesus rendered for us. Peter paints a description of the humiliation suffered by Jesus. It included "being denied," "rejected," and "physical pain suffered to death." The Trinity Godhead *glorified His Servant Jesus*. God held this attitude of service in high esteem.

But here is what is so remarkable about our passage. It continues after the resurrection. Jesus sits at the right hand of the Father. Death and hell are conquered. The amazing reversal of death and pain happened. But Jesus still pours out His life in service. Our passage points to the healing of the lame beggar as "glorifying" *His Servant Jesus*. The healing is not just a miracle but also a miracle for the worst of society; one in this cultural status, who deserves the least, but receives the most. This healing is not a movement of God among the Pharisees or members of the Sanhedrin, where you might expect their goodness contributed to such a miracle. But here a beggar, meriting nothing, glorifies Jesus.

The disciples are another example. Jesus poured out His service to them. Think of the hundreds of hours Jesus spent giving Himself to them. How many evenings into the night did He spend explaining and instructing? He spoke to them in parables, performed miracles for their benefit, controlled nature and repelled demons in their presence. Yet, none of them were faithful to Him. How many times would you turn the other cheek to such a dysfunctional group? Isn't it time for Jesus to cease service to them and demand service from them? But even now He reveals Himself to them as the One who serves! He proves it again through the lame beggar. Peter above all others knows this healing is the result of the service of Jesus.

Contained in the statement *"of which we are witnesses"* is the greater service. Did He not labor repeatedly for them to know Him in His resurrection? This statement covers all of the resurrection appearances! Did He not give special attention to

Peter as He instructed Him to *"feed my sheep"* (John 21:17)? Jesus spent 40 days with them after His resurrection (Acts 1:3). He served them again during those days instructing them about the Kingdom of God.

Another example is the Jews whom Peter exhorts. Should they not be dismissed? Should God not stop His dreams for these unfaithful Jews? Have they not acted exactly as their forefathers? Yet the entire intent of our passage is designed to bring them to repentance. Before this story is complete, even the leadership of Israel will receive another chance to embrace Jesus! The healed lame beggar will stand directly in their midst (Acts 4:14). They can say nothing against it. The healing of the beggar is another attempt of Jesus to minister and serve them. His style, the cross style, is the same even after the resurrection.

The cross style was dominant and characteristic of His nature before His resurrection, and it certainly is now. The cross style is the fundamental flow of the Kingdom of God established in the eternal realm. You and I must prepare ourselves for this style. In the Kingdom we will know nothing but service. The Kingdom of God is the embrace of Jesus in the believer until they are one. In this oneness, we know His nature. His nature is still "glorified by being **Servant Jesus**." Caring, loving, and being instruments of redemption here on Earth, are all necessary elements of our relationship with Jesus. Could this be an eternal element? Have we developed a selfish philosophy for heaven? Has it become all about me and what I am going to get rather than Him and all I can give? The nature of service is irreversible! The nature is the nature of **the Holy One and the Just**.

## Spectators

An interesting note is at the end of our verse. Peter boldly says, **"Of which we are witnesses."** The grammar structure is intriguing. "***We***" (hemeis) is the subject of the sentence. We know this because it is in the nominative case. The verb of the sentence is "***are***" (esmen). This verb is the first person plural of "eimi." Being a state of being instead of an action, the focus is not on what we do; it is on who we are. "***Witnesses***" (martus), our word for "martyr," is a noun in the nominative, a subjective complement, and becomes the same as the pronoun.

Peter is not saying they testified about the resurrection. One of the key elements of being an apostle was being a witness of the resurrection. However, no one actually saw the event of the resurrection. Jesus rose from the dead sometime in the early hours of Sunday morning. He did not need the stone to be rolled away so He could exit the tomb. When the two women arrived at the tomb, the angel descended and set the stone aside so they could enter the tomb (Matthew 28:1-6). They did not witness the actual resurrection event either.

They were all, however, witnesses that **God raised** Jesus *from the dead*. They were not witnesses of the noun (resurrection) but of the verb (***raised***). Peter interacted with the resurrected Christ for 40 days. The women saw Him outside the tomb. Five hundred disciples all witnessed Him at once. Paul considered himself a part of this group. Although this appearance was disputed by his enemies, Paul said, *"Then last of all He was seen by me also, as by one born out of due time"* (1 Corinthians 15:8). He was not a witness of the event but of the fact.

I think the Apostle Paul opened the door for me to claim this as well. Could I testify to you that I am a witness that ***God has raised*** Jesus **from the dead**? Did He not fulfill His promise? *"I will not leave you orphans; I will come to you"* (John 14:18)? This One who **God raised from the dead** confronted my life! He entered my flesh to make me His dwelling place. I tell you He is alive! I am not a witness of the event but of the fact!

According to Peter's statement, a witness is a state of being, which you are (esmen), not something you accomplish. The Spirit of God bursting forth in the flesh of Jesus is now permeating our lives as well. The generating, rejuvenating life of the Spirit of Jesus indwells us. Peter did not just tell about the resurrection; he lived the resurrected life as a witness. Is it so with us? Our world must see the life and power that raised Jesus from the dead. To testify of the resurrection event without the resurrection life is foolishness, just information, data, and dead knowledge.

This idea was forceful in the lives of the early disciples. The Greek word for witness (martus) became our word for martyr. As it was first used, it meant witness. It quickly began to mean "giving your life." This meaning is true whether it means physical life in death or in living. Our state of being comes from the action of God raising Jesus from the dead. All that took place in Jesus, which raised Him from the dead, is happening in us. Paul describes the power of God that is working in the believer and producing his life. He relates it to the power **which He worked in Christ when He raised Him from the dead and seated Him at His right hand in the heavenly places** (Ephesians 1:20).

Have you not known His touch? Has He not come to you? Has He brought you into life? Are you a witness of the fact that He rose from the dead?

## Scheme

Another strong statement in our passage is the irreversible plan of God. Peter reveals this to the Jews of his day in a bold declaration. He introduces them as **"Men of Israel,"** (Acts 3:12). This introduction distinctly ties them to the long-range plan of God as revealed in the Old Testament. He declares, **"The God of Abraham, Isaac, and Jacob, the God of our fathers"** (Acts 3:13). They are forced to view the plan in the promises of God to redeem the world through them. God is sending a Messiah. Their temple structure testified this to them daily. Every sacrificial lamb screamed of this reality. Daily they asked, "Could this be the day?" This reference was to the coming of the Messiah.

They have fought against the plan of God, and guilt thunders through their lives. Peter reveals to them that Jesus is the Messiah, the **Servant Jesus**, **the Holy one and the Just**, and **the Prince of life**. They **delivered up** this Messiah as a sacrifice. They **denied** Him **in the presence of Pilate, when he was determined to let Him go**. They preferred Barabbas, the murderer, rather than God's Messiah. They **killed the Prince of life**. They were not indifferent to the plan of God; they fought against it with all their being. How could they have missed it?

But the plan of God is irreversible. In His sovereignty God calculated their disobedience into His plan. In God's redemptive nature He used their rejection to fulfill His plan. The cross was the heart of that plan. We are faced with the interplay between the **determined purpose and foreknowledge of God** and **the lawless hand of men** (Acts 2:23). God planned it; man is guilty of it. This was not a corporate guilt, but an individual guilt. God declared every man, who heard Peter's message, guilty. God not only had a plan for Israel through His Messiah, Jesus, but He had an individual plan for every person in the crowd. Jesus, through Peter, called them back to that plan.

Is He not doing the same with us? We love to measure our lives by the deeds established by the law. To correct a few deeds and adjust our schedule to include more church services is easier than aligning our lives with the burning passion of God's plan for our lives. Are you conscious of the uniqueness of your person? No one has fingerprints or DNA like yours. God created you for a purpose, and you are like no other. Sin is not defined in the content of the deed; it is defined in how that deed relates to the dream of God for your life. An individual may eliminate all deeds of sin (defined by our world) from their life and still be the worst of sinners.

In our passage, those listening are the chosen people of God.

**Part Two:** Exhortation from the Porch

They observe the feast days, hour of prayer, and traditions of Judaism. Their righteousness greatly exceeds a pagan world. But what did they do to Jesus? Every activity they did was against Jesus, the plan of God. The dream of God for your life is in Jesus. We must come back to Jesus! The call of Peter to the Jewish crowd will be to ***"Repent therefore and be converted"*** (Acts 3:19). Repentance is giving up a former thought to embrace a new thought. They are to turn from crucifying Jesus to embracing the risen Lord. The same commitment and determination given to the crucifixion of Jesus must now be experienced in His resurrection presence. The same commitment and determination is the call of God for our lives as well!

## Acts 3:16

# LET'S INVOKE

*"And His name, through faith in His name, has made this man strong, whom you see and know. Yes, the faith which comes through Him has given him this perfect soundness in the presence of you all" (Acts 3:16).*

Peter exhorts the Jews from Solomon's Porch. Standing next to him as a living testimony of the undeniable miracle is the healed beggar. Peter involves recklessness in his approach. He abandons caution in favor of the truth. He will not leap over issues in order to maintain unity with his crowd.

The premise of the Book of Acts is the reality of Pentecost. The first chapter of this book brings us to the event. The second chapter carries us into the event. The rest of the book relates the reality of the event in everyday life. The growth of the Christian Church is explained in the fullness of the Spirit resourcing people, both Jews and Gentiles. The breathtaking events are testimonies of the supernatural movement of God through ordinary people.

Peter is no exception, and we find this in "Refused Credit!" He embraced the Spirit of Jesus and exhibits this in his exhortation to the Jews. The pre-resurrection Peter would have readily claimed the healing of the lame man as his own. He would have basked in the glory of the moment, but he does not seem to be tempted this time. He refuses to accept any personal praise. He highlights the lack of his own power and godliness (Acts 3:12). The fact that he

**Part Two:** Exhortation from the Porch

speaks clearly of his inability to do this miracle depicts this truth. He uses two statements reflecting his inability; he focuses the rest of the chapter (Acts 3:13-26) on Jesus as the miracle's source. This is a real demonstration of a Spirit-sourced man.

Peter also exhibits his embrace of Jesus' Spirit in "Related Jesus!" In the upper room prior to His death, Jesus summarized the ministry of the Holy Spirit. He said, ***"He will glorify me"*** (John 14:16). Amazingly, all the sermons in the Book of Acts are focused on Jesus. They do not speak about the Holy Spirit; they glorify Jesus. Peter's exhortation is about who Jesus is and what was done to Him. He highlights Jesus as the only Source to the lame man's healing.

We must think about the context of Peter's exhortation. These are the same Jews who cried for Jesus' crucifixion. They are loyal to their leaders. The setting of this scene is in the temple at the heart of Jerusalem. The most dedicated and conservative Jews are present. The leaders of Israel are involved; they move quickly to take the apostles into custody at the end of Peter's exhortation (Acts 4:1-3). Peter found the strength to stand faithful before this group because He received the fullness of the Spirit of Jesus at Pentecost!

Peter was not faithful on his own. The reality of his personal denial of Jesus is fresh in our minds. Pentecost is fifty days after the resurrection, and it was only a few days prior to that when Peter denied Jesus three times (Matthew 26:69-75). These denials were not in the presence of Jewish men who demanded Jesus' crucifixion. He denied that he knew Jesus to first a servant girl, then another girl, and finally to a small group who thought they recognized him. All of this happened after he promised Jesus he would be faithful. Now Peter stands before this Jewish crowd demonstrating the power of the Spirit and proclaiming Jesus. The change is that he is now filled with the Spirit of Jesus!

The Spirit of Jesus uses Peter to "Revitalize Faith." The crowd Peter addresses formed the mob that demanded Jesus' crucifixion. He vividly describes their participation, and they cannot help but see themselves. Some of them had also been members of the crowd who honored Jesus on Palm Sunday. On that day they declared Jesus the Messiah. They cried, *"Son of David!"* (Matthew 21:9). The large crowd on that day brought alarm to the leaders of Israel. *The Pharisees therefore said among themselves, "You see that you are accomplishing nothing. Look, the world has gone after Him!"* (John 12:19).

Could this crowd be captured by faith again? Could they have a new vision? The cowering, denying Peter was of no use. Peter had to be sourced by the Spirit! In our passage there is a strong reference to *faith*. Faith is used twice in the verse. Peter says, *"And His name, through faith in His name, has made this man strong, whom you see and know. Yes, the faith which comes through Him has given him this perfect soundness in the presence of you all"* (Acts 3:16). The sentence construction of this verse is difficult to translate. It has to be divided into two sentences. In this study we will investigate the first sentence which boldly states two major ideas: Jesus and faith!

## Focus

"Faith is not the focus!" The word *faith* is used twice in this verse, and it is a dominant idea in Peter's exhortation. The activities in which these Jews participate demonstrate they have no faith in Jesus. Peter calls them to **repent**, which is a new expression of faith. But *faith* is not the focus of Peter's exhortation.

Distraction is perhaps Satan's strongest weapon. He continually attracts us to things that do not matter. We exert our energy to accomplish useless things. Our minds are occupied with thoughts that do not contribute to eternal values. Our money is squandered on junk. Our health is sacrificed on momentary appetites. We cast aside our relationships for selfish

**Part Two:** Exhortation from the Porch

gain. The devil will use anything in our lives that is conducive to distraction.

Even religion can become a distraction. We can be preoccupied with our own self-sourcing. We can focus on our spiritual disciplines. We can put religious programs at the center. We can focus on what attracts the attention of those in our culture instead of their deepest need. We can desperately attempt to solve surface problems and ignore the cause of the chaos. Theology can become our main concern. We can make faith our focus instead of focusing on the object of our faith. We can develop various aspects of faith from positive thinking to denial of doubts. Although faith is definitely an issue in our passage, it is not the focus.

"Form is not the focus." To allow methodology to concern and control us is easy. Knowing how something is done is not more important than doing it. In our passage, Peter does not promote the method of the miracle. Getting the attention of the one who receives the miracle is not necessary (Acts 3:5). His concern is not with the wording. The miracle was not the correct language. A magical formula of the combination of words does not exist (Acts 3:6). Peter makes no reference to the use of the **right hand** (Acts 3:7). He lifts the lame man to his feet, but this was never seen as a standard miracle technique.

Men form denominations from a focus on methods. How sad when the style of music dictates our worship. People are accepted or rejected by their willingness to bow to our methods. Nothing in Peter's exhortation indicates or event suggests the importance of form; it is a non-issue.

"Fix is not the focus." The focus is definitely not on the physical miracle. Everyone who received a physical miracle in the New Testament is now dead. The miracle may help in the temporal but not in the eternal. Miracles are not the standard for judging the presence of God. They are certainly not the way to gauge your spiritual life. Our assurance of salvation is not based on miracles regardless of how numerous. Jesus constantly discouraged and condemned "sign seekers." He said, *"An evil and adulterous generation seeks after a sign"* (Matthew 12:39; 16:4).

Surely we have progressed in our spiritual lives to proper vision. Our sight must not be clouded by apparent success or failure. The will of God is not measured by ease and comfort. Jesus was at the center of God's will while dying on the cross. Those in the Scriptures who considered physical sickness and handicap a result of sin were wrong. This is not the focus. The miracle may be evidence that the focus is correct, but without a correct focus on what matters, there will never be a miracle.

"Focus is Jesus!" The focus is on Jesus. I fear how you might respond to this. Perhaps you are tired of continually hearing this emphasis. Maybe you think all of our sermons are about Jesus. If you do, that is the greatest of compliments. If you demand that we preach something else, it can be arranged. However, to do so, our choice for preaching will have to be something other than the Bible. If we preach based on current events, movies, fashion, psychology, theology, or even denominational history, we can side-step Jesus. My earliest memories of ministry contain a driving passion to be a Biblical preacher. The goal is to allow the passage to dictate the sermon, not my personal surroundings or experiences. I quickly discovered every passage is about Jesus. He is the only focus.

In our passage (Acts 3:16), while the name of Jesus is not used, He is the focus. The word *name* (in my translation) is used twice. The idea of *name* simply focuses on the person of Jesus. Who is this Jesus? He is the One Peter describes to them (Acts 3:13-15). Peter gives strong content to the person of Jesus. They cannot misunderstand his reference. The word *Him* or *His* is used three times. Each time it refers to Jesus. Without Jesus, there is never a miracle. Everything in our lives remains the same and grows worse without Jesus. Wholeness can be only with Jesus. This is not a reference to a theological

**Part Two:** Exhortation from the Porch

or denominational Jesus, but to the real person of Jesus! He is the only chance we have!

# Foundation

The foundation of the miracle Jesus brought to the lame man is found in *faith*. Again this word is used twice in our passage. This means that the act of embracing Jesus is called *faith*. An adequate "focus" on Jesus is *faith*. When I focus on anything else, I do not have *faith* in Jesus; I have *faith* in the "anything else." Faith is not a spiritual word used for only Jesus. Faith is a common experience of life for any and all things embraced.

We can all relate stories of how the organized church has hurt people. Becoming a Christian is not an invitation to believe in the organized church. Will you embrace Jesus? When invited to be a Christian, many people respond with the question, "Which denomination is correct?" They want to know in which denomination to place their *faith*. No one is encouraging you to make your way through the maze of denominational theology. Will you embrace Jesus?

Perhaps you have difficulty believing in the Bible. I have discovered a wonderful thing. You do not believe in the Bible to find Jesus. You must believe in Jesus and then the Bible begins to make sense. The Living Word, Jesus, will unfold the Written Word, the Bible. What about baptism? We must stick to the subject without wavering. The subject is Jesus!

Even the atheist with all of his rejection of God must accept this challenge. Would he dare be open to an encounter with Jesus? If you seek truth without compromise, will you be open to Jesus? Anyone who seeks truth regardless of where it leads him will come to Jesus. He said, *"I am the way, the truth, and the life. No one comes to the Father except through Me"* (John 14:6). Jesus obligated Himself to reveal who He is to the individual who is open and responsive. If you will risk being available, He will bring *faith* to your life!

# Faith

There is an unbending, unwavering definition of *faith*. It leaps off the pages of our passage. It cannot be denied and if you miss it, you do so intentionally. It is "invoking the activity of the Second Party." Invoking is a key word. It points to demanding, wanting, longing, and intense desire. It erupts from an overwhelming need, producing the spirit of desperation. We all experience these kinds of situations in our lives. God allows us to come to the place of tremendous need; He shakes us out of our comfort zone. Self-sourcing quickly finds it is overextended and inadequate. A cry escapes from the heart of the soul.

Out of this great need an activity is requested. At first it may not be properly recognized. It may be thought that someone with adequate resource needs to give that resource to us. If we have a financial problem, someone with wealth needs to pay our bills. If we have a temper problem, someone who has great self-control needs to give us self-control. If we have a hate problem, someone with great love needs to give us an abundance of love. When we focus on what Jesus can do for us, we have the wrong focus. When we highlight the miracle rather than Jesus, we are out of focus. We are passionate about the gift instead of the Giver. The moment this happens the wrong object is the focus of our *faith*. We quickly realize the activity needs His presence. Jesus does not give us what He has; He gives us Himself. Jesus is Jesus in us.

This brings us to the heart of the definition. Jesus is the *Second Party*. He is not second in importance or value. He is supreme. He is second in our choice; we have chosen ourselves first. We are our first choice. Having faith or not having faith is not the problem. We all have an abundance of faith. The problem

**Part Two:** Exhortation from the Porch

is in the object of our faith. Our *invoking* has been focused on ourselves. We have no one to rely on but ourselves. We act on our own behalf. We protect, guard, and source ourselves. We do this naturally and our world promotes and applauds it. We come to the end of ourselves. In sourcing ourselves, we deplete our resource. We come to situations where we are not adequate. Self-sourcing, faith in us, simply does not work. Our faith is not *bad;* it is in the wrong object.

Peter calls these Jews to "invoke the activity of the Second Party." The basis of the call stands before them in the demonstration of the healed beggar. This is what *faith* in Jesus does! He must be the sole object of our faith. He is worthy!

## Acts 3:16

# LET'S LIVE INVOKING

> *"And His name, through faith in His name, has made this man strong, whom you see and know. Yes, the faith which comes through Him has given him this perfect soundness in the presence of you all"* (Acts 3:16).

The greatness of this verse cannot be overemphasized. Although the structure of this verse is difficult, it is a pivotal verse that conveys tremendous insight into the miracle of the lame beggar. The first section of our passage flows into this verse and the last section flows out of it. The verse is divided into two sentences to bring clarity. As we discovered in our last study, *name* and *faith* are the two elements strongly emphasized. In the first sentence, Peter declares that Jesus (*name*) is the One responsible for this miracle. He also declares that *faith* played an important role in facilitating the release of Jesus' power.

In the second sentence of this verse, the same information is offered. However, Peter gives more instruction concerning the element of *faith*. Where do I find *faith*? What is the source of my *faith*? These are the questions Peter answers. He presents Jesus as the power of the miracle and how the power is released into our lives. He leaves no leverage for self-sourcing. No one can say that because Peter and the lame man participated in the miracle, they deserve at least ten percent of the credit. All glory and credit go to Jesus.

**Part Two**: Exhortation from the Porch

This verse can only be understood in clarity through the proper definition of *faith*. At various times in our previous study, we presented our working definition. **Faith** is "invoking the activity of the Second Party." The Second Party is Jesus. He is not second in importance; He is second because we first turned to ourselves. The object of our "invoking" is us, and that is why we need a miracle similar to the lame beggar. He was lame not because of his sin or the sin of his parents, but because of sin in general and the curse of the world. However, he never went beyond his status as a lame man because of his focus on himself. Peter calls this beggar to focus on the Second Party. His life will forever be changed by the state of *faith*.

## Constant

*And His name, through faith in His name, has made this man strong, whom you see and know. Yes, the faith which comes through Him has given him this perfect soundness in the presence of you all* (Acts 3:16).

The Greek text begins with *and* (kai). It continues with *through* (epi). Then the article, *the* (te), appears. Although it is not translated, it is connected to the next word, *faith* (pistis). Notice, it is not *faith* in general, but it specifically relates to the event, the miracle. The interaction between Peter, the lame beggar, and Jesus is contained in the *faith*.

The word *through* appears twice in this verse, and it is a translation of two Greek words. In this first occasion it is a translation of the Greek word "epi." It expresses the meaning of "on or upon." In other words, *faith* is the basis or foundation of the miracle. This miracle is based on *faith in His name*, and *faith* being present is essential; it is self-evident to declare that the miracle would not occur without *faith*.

If you study the miracles recorded in the Gospel accounts,

*faith* is at the core of each of them. A paralytic was lowered through the roof to Jesus. ***When Jesus saw their faith, He said to the paralytic, "Son, be of good cheer; your sins are forgiven you"*** (Matthew 9:2). The woman with a problem of blood touched the hem of Jesus' garment. ***But Jesus turned around, and when He saw her He said, "Be of good cheer, daughter; your faith has made you well"*** (Matthew 9:22). Two blind men cried out to Jesus for help. ***Then He touched their eyes, saying, "According to your faith let it be to you"*** (Matthew 9:29). The same idea occurs in our passage. *Faith* is the basis of this miracle.

Consider Material! To slip into the thought that *faith* is an entity or an actual thing is easy. It is NOT!!! *Faith* does not have substance; it cannot be purchased; there is no store where we can buy *faith*. You cannot build *faith*; you cannot store it. *Faith* cannot be measured, easily accessed, or contained because it is abstract. You cannot rip it from your being as you would a bad tooth. You cannot put it on as you would a coat. You cannot see it; therefore, you cannot evaluate it. The results of *faith* may be inspected, but not *faith*.

When we indicate *faith* is the foundation of the miracle, we speak of a state of being, an attitude permeating the heart. *Faith* is consistent in its view and is not a mood or an emotion that will pass with the circumstances. *Faith* cannot be discussed in amounts except with its object. When we say, "I do not have much *faith* in him," we do not measure the amount of *faith* we have, but we measure the amount of *faith* with which we embrace him. Jesus referred to *faith as a mustard seed* (Matthew 17:20), the smallest seed in the Jewish culture. Jesus discarded any emphasis on the size of *faith*; He highlighted the object of *faith*. He calls us to place all our *faith* in Him!

Consider Movement. To recognize that *faith* is not an activity is important. *Faith* is not something to achieve. We do not practice it and become better the more we do it. As we saturate in the miracle stories, we might think there is an occurring activity that we call *faith*. Can *faith* occur during the miracle, but not occur before and ceases afterwards? NO! We cannot do *faith* as if it were an activity; it is a state of being.

Our definition of *faith* may lead us to think of an activity. *Faith* is invoking the activity of the Second Party. However, the word "activity" is focused on the Second Party, not on *faith*. *Faith* allows the action to come from another who is adequate, not oneself. In fact, *faith* is the ceasing of self-action and the receiving the Second Party's action. We cannot pick and choose when we will have *faith*. What happens in the individual is revealed in their encounter with Jesus. *Faith* is a state of being in which we live, but it is highlighted through physical circumstances.

Consider Relationship. Faith describes an attitude that is within the context of relationship. True, we can have a relationship without *faith*. I have relationships with people whom I do not trust; I do not depend on what they say. I have no confidence in what they do. If I need something done, I do not invoke their activity on my behalf. This relationship is limited, and we should hesitate to call this a relationship.

I may have a surface level relationship without *faith*, but as I engage in the relationship my confidence in the individual enlarges and my *faith* increases. I find I can "invoke their activity" on my behalf without fear or suspicion. It is difficult to discuss this reality without leaving the impression that *faith* has an amount or is a thing. *Faith* is a state of being which exists between two individuals. It will determine the intimacy of their relationship.

Through prevenient grace, Jesus pulls me to Himself. He surrounds me with His penetrating love until *faith* is activity. I invoke His activity in forgiveness of sins. It becomes apparent that I must trust Him for more and more. Our relationship expands with *faith*. The heart of this relationship is stated by this familiar verse, "***I have been crucified with Christ; it is no longer I who live, but Christ lives in me; and the life which I now live in the flesh I live by faith in the Son of God, who***

Let's Live Invoking | **Acts 3:16**

*loved me and gave Himself for me"* (Galatians 2:20). Jesus becomes the total object of my *faith*. I have ceased to have *faith* in me; I invoke His activity in every area and situation of my life. Jesus and I are one. What a relationship!

Consider Rational. You must understand that *faith* is not a feeling, emotion, or hype. You do not talk yourself into an emotional state of *faith*. Ballplayers cheer themselves into an emotional state of readiness to win a game, but this is not a huddle before a ballgame. In other words, the thought process greatly affects *faith*, and if your mind is continually filled with negative doubts and suspicions, *faith* is quickly destroyed. When we focus on only problems, they become all consuming and overpowering.

No wonder Paul encourages us with these words. "***Finally, brethren, whatever things are true, whatever things are noble, whatever things are just, whatever things are pure, whatever things are lovely, whatever things are of good report, if there is any virtue and if there is anything praiseworthy — meditate on these things***" (Philippians 4:8). Jesus consistently reminded us of the devil's deceit. "*He is a liar and the father of it*" (John 8:44). The devil's goal is to blind us; He does not want us to see Jesus. If you know Jesus, you will invoke His activity on your behalf. I want the mind of Christ. As He constantly invoked the activity of His Father while here on Earth, so I want to consistently invoke His activity in my life.

Peter explains the context of this miracle in his exhortation. It is the context of *faith* that invokes the activity of Jesus. Consider carefully what Peter recently experienced. He was still basking in the memories of the resurrection appearances of Jesus. He ate, slept, and traveled with Jesus for 40 days. All he knew about Jesus in the physical became reality in the inner Spirit of Pentecost. Jesus embraced Peter inwardly. He saw Jesus transform the lives of hundreds of Jews. He witnessed many miracles. After all Peter experienced, he knew the lame beggar was not a challenge for

Jesus. He knew the truth. What if you live with Jesus? What if you invoke His activity in everything that touches your life?

Consider Rally. Perhaps this miracle was not simply the *faith* of one man. What if it is the uniting and cooperation of many who have *faith*? In our verse (Acts 3:16), it becomes difficult to distinguish exactly whose *faith* is discussed. Was it the lame beggar who had *faith* in Jesus? Did he hear Peter's sermon when he explained Pentecost? Had he thought about the events and miracles occurring around him? Had some of these early Christians witnessed to him? Or did the *faith* of Peter form the basis of this miracle in the lame beggar's life? It was Peter who confronted him. Peter was the one who grabbed his right hand and lifted him to his feet. Did Peter's *faith* so dominate the scene that this man was affected by it? Did the lame man even have a choice in the matter?

An intriguing story from the ministry of Paul exists. While he was with the Ephesians, **God worked unusual miracles by the hands of Paul,** (Acts 19:11). Some Jewish exorcists decided Paul's method of handling demons might work better than theirs. In one of their deliverance sessions they called **the name of the Lord Jesus over those who had evil spirits, saying, "We exorcise you by the Jesus whom Paul preaches"** (Acts 19:13). They quickly received a response from the evil spirit. **"Jesus I know, and Paul I know; but who are you?"** (Acts 19:15). The demon-possessed man immediately overpowered them. They ran naked and wounded from the scene. The spiritual state of the individual who proclaims the name of Jesus obviously matters!

Each of us must come to our own conclusions. However, consider the truth that both the *faith* of Peter and the *faith* of the lame beggar are both active in this miracle. We must not discount either of them. By the passage, there is no way to prove in the passage from whom *faith* came. Certainly the lame beggar had to respond. He could have refused what God was doing in his life. The rest of his story indicates his embrace through *faith*.

He remained connected though it meant going to jail with the apostles (Acts 4:14). He was one of the vital witnesses to the leaders of Israel.

On the other hand, evidently the *faith* of Peter influenced the lame beggar. This miracle did not happen without Peter invoking the activity of Jesus. No wonder this man holds onto Peter with great strength (Acts 3:11). We must conclude that you and I influence the *faith* of others. What kind of impact does a father have on his son? Consider a son who lives under the influence of a father who always invokes the activity of Jesus for his life. Think of the daughter who sees the demonstration of *faith* in her mother through every situation and trial of her life. Many people come to Jesus in their lives because they have godly parents who invoked the activity of Jesus throughout their lives. What a privilege to be an instrument of faith in revealing its activity and manifesting its reality.

Consider Repentance. The call of the Holy Spirit through Peter demanded response from this large crowd. The only appropriate response is repentance. They must give up a former thought to embrace a new thought. They must admit their former thought of murder; they rejected their Messiah. They must now embrace Jesus who is alive. Five thousand people will accomplish this. In describing this, Luke wrote, "***However, many of those who heard the word believed; and the number of the men came to be about five thousand***" (Acts 4:4). The response of repentance is the reality of *faith*. They are refusing the activity of the first party and are invoking the activity of the Second Party.

This is the call to each of us as well. Wherever we are in our spiritual journey, this response is necessary. We must live a life of repentance, the state of *faith*.

Acts 3:16

# SOURCE OF INVOKING

*"And His name, through faith in His name, has made this man strong, whom you see and know. Yes, the faith which comes through Him has given him this perfect soundness in the presence of you all" (Acts 3:16).*

The self-sourced individual who reads the New Testament will see only what benefits them. A lame beggar is healed; ***so he, leaping up, stood and walked and entered the temple with them — walking, leaping, and praising God*** (Acts 3:8). Who doesn't want this kind of power working in their lives? All the problems that frustrate me would be solved. Blockades in my life would be removed; I could more efficiently fulfill my plans. Nothing is more personally destructive than my self-centered nature. My self-sourcing creates barriers in my life, and I perpetually need resources to overcome these obstacles. I see the power of God as a "fix" to an immediate problem created by my self-sourcing.

Peter's exhortation to the crowd gathered on Solomon's Porch is a report of the miracle's depth. It may appear that the miracle was a simple correction of a physical condition. But this man was more than 40 years of age (Acts 4:22), and his condition was mentally, psychologically, and spiritually crippling. Jesus' miracle was not a quick fix to this man's physical problem. This is true for all Jesus' miracles. His focus is always to bring wholeness. He wants to affect every area of my life. Peter describes the condition of the healed man as one of *perfect soundness*, a translation of the Greek word "holokleria."

The root word for "holokleria" is used only three times in the New Testament. James links completeness with perfection. ***"But let patience have its perfect work, that you may be perfect and complete*** (holokleros)***, lacking nothing"*** (James 1:4). This is an individual who persevered, having suffered loss, and is now complete. Grace abounds in his life. Paul expressed it well, ***"Now may the God of peace Himself sanctify you completely; and may your whole spirit, soul, and body be preserved blameless at the coming of our Lord Jesus Christ"*** (1 Thessalonians 5:23). This Greek word (holokleros) is a compound word. "Holos" refers to all, the whole, and "kleros" refers to a part or share. Thus the whole, having all of its parts, is sound and perfect.

This truth should encourage us all. The presence of Jesus in our lives brings *perfect soundness*. His involvement in my physical opens the door for His involvement in my spiritual. However, if He is the answer for my spiritual life, He will also affect my physical life. I am open to Him. He wants me to retain all initially allotted to me, and I am to want nothing for my wholeness. Praise the Lord!

The wholeness of the lame beggar and the completeness of our personal lives can only be explained in only Jesus. In our passage, it is highlighted in the word *through*. As stated in the previous study, this word is used twice in our passage. ***And His name, through faith in His name, has made this man strong, whom you see and know. Yes, the faith which comes through Him has given him this perfect soundness in the presence of you all*** (Acts 3:16). The first use of the word *through* is a translation of the Greek word "epi." It expresses the meaning of "on" or "upon." In other words, *faith* is the foundation or basis for this miracle. To declare that the miracle would not occur without *faith* is self-evident.

Part Two: Exhortation from the Porch

# Creator

We must begin by examining Jesus as Creator. Jesus is the source of all things. This Greek word (dia) is often connected with the creation of the world. John presents Jesus as **the Word**. He was in the beginning of all things; He was with God; He was God! ***All things were made through Him, and without Him nothing was made that was made*** (John 1:3). Paul expresses the reality of many people having many gods. Yet for us there is only one God! ***And one Lord Jesus Christ, through*** (dia) ***whom are all things, and through*** (dia) ***whom we live*** (1 Corinthians 8:6). In describing Jesus to the Colossians, Paul said, ***"For by Him all things were created that are in heaven and that are on earth, visible and invisible, whether thrones or dominions or principalities or powers. All things were created through Him and for Him"*** (Colossians 1:16). Jesus is the Creator; this issue is easily settled ***through*** (dia) the Scriptures.

Our passage, however, does not describe the creation of the world. Its specific focus is on *faith* in the lame beggar's miracle. In other words, indicated by using "dia," *faith* is created by Jesus. We do not decide what is needed. We do not manufacture, produce, author, or instigate our *faith*. We only recognize and respond to what Jesus creates in us! We can be confident that each person equally receives *faith*. I have encountered many people who say, "I want to believe, but I do not have any faith." Their excuse for living as they want is they do not have any faith. Jesus brings to each of us the element of *faith*.

Because *faith* does not have substance (see previous study), it is not an entity, but the ability to respond. Indeed, no one can live without *faith*. Without *faith,* you can never drive or ride in an automobile. You have *faith* that the road continues beyond the top of the hill. You have *faith* that the brakes will work; you even have some *faith* in those driving toward you. You trust them to stay on their side of the road. Everyone has *faith*; it is a part of our creation.

This means *faith* is not amount, but object. Everyone has enough *faith*; the difficulty comes when we place it in the wrong object. Every Sunday morning you come into church and sit in the same pew. You do this year after year by *faith*. You do not test the pew or ask your spouse to sit first. You are not suspicious or timid about sitting. You have total *faith* in the pew. If one Sunday you sit and the pew collapses, many will run to help you. "Oh, if only you had more *faith*, you wouldn't be sprawled on the floor." What a ridiculous statement. It would not matter how much *faith* you had; that pew was an inadequate object. The issue is not the amount of your *faith*; the issue is the object of your *faith*.

Why am I defeated? Why do my problems overwhelm me? Why do temptations allure me into compromise? Why can't I live above sin? The answer is not lack of *faith*. You and I place our *faith* in an unworthy object. We have trusted ourselves. Through self-sourcing we live in consistent defeat. We will inevitably come to obstacles too big for us. We were never meant to be the solution of our own needs. We invoke the activity of the first party instead of the Second Party. Jesus alone is the adequate object of our *faith*.

## Condition

Jesus creates *faith*, and it is the condition, context, attitude, and response in which I am to dwell. In this condition I find the sourcing of Jesus activated in my life. Again *faith* is not an entity, and it does not have substance. **Faith** is the attitude of reception, openness, and confidence. I must focus my response in Jesus alone. He alone, without dividedness is worthy of my response.

The second sentence says, **"Yes, the faith which comes through Him has given him this perfect soundness in the** *presence of you all"* (Acts 3:16). "***Faith***" is the subject of the sentence. The main verb is "***has given.***" The direct object or accusative is "***perfect soundness.***" Peter highlights the amazing condition of ***faith. Faith*** is the context in which the miracle occurs. God can do anything He desires to do. But He chooses to limit His activity in our lives to the context of the response of ***faith. Faith*** is the atmosphere, tone of my life, response of my heart, and consistent openness of my soul. This allows His presence and the result is ***perfect soundness.***

The surgical room at the hospital is prepared, and it comes with special lights. Its atmosphere and condition is created and awaits a particular activity. Special attention is given to sterilization. It houses carefully selected equipment. Surgery occurs in the confines of these conditions. So it is with the movement of the Spirit of Jesus. God decided to confine Himself to the atmosphere or condition of ***faith.*** Divine surgery cannot happen in the atmosphere of disbelief. The Hebrew writer urges us to enter into the promised "rest." He verifies the existence of such. He points out that the forefathers in the Old Testament received the same promise. The rest is not focused on only days past, but is a reality in the New Covenant as well. God has always dreamed this for us. His appeal is this issue of ***faith.*** The Old Testament forefathers are prime examples of what we should *not* be. They did not enter into this "promised rest." He says, ***"For indeed the gospel was preached to us as well as to them; but the word which they heard did not profit them, not being mixed with faith in those who heard it"*** (Hebrews 4:2). They never experienced the "rest" God wanted for them; they did not have ***faith. Faith*** is the condition, atmosphere, openness, and receptivity necessary for God's movement.

Note, ***faith*** is not focused on results; it is focused on Jesus. Let it be clearly understood that the one desire of ***faith*** is Jesus. We do not decide what we want from God then focus our ***faith*** on the demand. Young believers have often been told, "Just ask

God for what you want and believe He will give it to you; you are to refuse all doubts. Even when it appears you do not have it, you must act as if you do." We are encouraging them to focus on the result. *Faith* is the condition of intimacy with Jesus; we must always depend on Him; we are always open to Him. We do not come demanding; instead we yield to Him. *Faith* must never be an instrument to get what I want. *Faith is* the atmosphere of lying in His arms in total contentment and trust. This is the condition in which He can accomplish *perfect soundness* in my life.

## Cause

If Jesus is the Creator of this *faith*, if it is a condition of intimacy, relaxation, and total trust, how can I experience it? Our immediate response might be self-sourcing. We cannot create it, because Jesus is the Creator. Self-sourcing approaches God thinking, "If He already created it, how can I get it from Him? What do I need to do? Where can I purchase this *faith*? What service must I render to achieve this condition of *faith*?

Our passage states that earning faith is the opposite of what must happen. This thought process destroys any condition of *faith* that might bring *perfect soundness*. You must not think of *faith* as something aside from Jesus like an entity. In our passage, the word *through* is used twice. *"And His name, through faith in His name, has made this man strong, whom you see and know. Yes, the faith which comes through Him has given him this perfect soundness in the presence of you all"* (Acts 3:16). The first use of the word *through* is a translation of the Greek word "epi." It expresses the meaning of "on" or "upon." In other words, *faith* is the foundation or basis of this miracle. This miracle is based on *faith in His name. Faith* being present is essential; it is self-evident to declare that the miracle will not occur without *faith*. We already said this above.

**Part Two:** Exhortation from the Porch

The second use of the word *through* is a translation of the Greek word "dia." It denotes the channel of the action or the how something happens. It describes the agency of the state. Many references are to Jesus. The phrase "through Christ" or some form of the same is in abundance throughout the epistles. Paul said, *"Through Him we have received grace and apostleship for obedience to the faith among all nations for His name"* (Romans 1:5). Scriptures tells us that fruit (Philippians 1:11), comfort (2 Corinthians 1:4), peace with God (Romans 5:1), triumph (Romans 8:37), acceptance with God (Hebrews 13:21), resurrection life (1 Corinthians 15:21), and final deliverance (1 Thessalonians 5:9) come through Jesus (see also Romans 1:8; 2 Corinthians 1:20; 1 Peter 4:11; Hebrews 13:15).

As we investigate these verses, we find a startling reality. In each case the initiative always lies with Jesus. No "verbs of asking" are with this formula *through Christ*. We do not earn, merit, or produce these things; we don't even initiate the idea of having them. These things come from Jesus. We must bring this truth into our passage. The focus is on *the faith that comes through Him* (Acts 3:16). We do not manufacture, produce, or generate *faith*. We do not initiate our *faith*. Jesus is the source of this response.

We have defined *faith* as "invoking the activity of the Second Party." We can only accomplish this as Jesus reveals Himself. He convinces me. Jesus is the initiator of *faith*; He is the Second Party; He produces the activity in response to the *faith*. Therefore, the primary issue is not about *faith*, but Jesus! Do not focus on *faith*; focus on Jesus. He is the solution.

## Acts 3:17

# IGNORANCE

*"Yet now, brethren, I know that you did it in ignorance, as did also your rulers" (Acts 3:17).*

The concept of our passage is highlighted with four situations. *"Father, forgive them, for they do not know what they do"* (Luke 23:34). This is one of the last statements Jesus made from the cross. This raises several questions. Was Jesus asking the Father to forgive the Jews, the Romans, or both? What did they not know? Did they not know they were crucifying an innocent man? After all that Jesus' life revealed, did they not know He was the Messiah?

Paul paints the same picture in his personal testimony. He wrote, *"And I thank Christ Jesus our Lord who has enabled me, because He counted me faithful, putting me into the ministry, although I was formerly a blasphemer, a persecutor, and an insolent man; but I obtained mercy because I did it ignorantly in unbelief"* (1 Timothy 1:13). You can ponder several interesting questions from this statement as well. How can an individual be *a blasphemer, a persecutor, and an insolent man* in ignorance? If Paul had not done these things in ignorance, would he have *obtained mercy*?

The men of Athens gathered consistently at Mars Hill to either *tell or hear some new thing* (Acts 17:21). Paul addresses them concerning their altar *with this inscription: TO THE*

**UNKNOWN GOD** (Acts 17:23). His main focus was on the reality of *"we are the offspring of God."* This should persuade us *not to think that the Divine Nature is like gold or silver or stone, something shaped by art and man's devising* (Acts 17:29). Then he concludes, *"Truly, these times of ignorance God overlooked, but now commands all men everywhere to repent"* (Acts 17:30). Again questions arise. Is the guilt of sin equal to the consciousness of the sin? What is my condition when I am enlightened but refuse to repent?

Now we come to our passage. Peter says, *"Yet now, brethren, I know that you did it in ignorance, as did also your rulers"* (Acts 3:17). All the questions above apply to this situation as well. Peter links this crowd of Jews with their leaders who plotted the crucifixion. Did they not know that Jesus was the Messiah? Did they think that instigating the crucifixion was their only hope? How could they have been so blind? Are they without guilt? If they intentionally crucified Jesus, the Messiah, can they experience forgiveness? Several important aspects to Peter's statement exist. Hopefully as we examine these aspects you will gain clarity.

## Period of Time

Peter begins his statement with, *"Yet now, brethren"* (Acts 3:17). *"Yet"* is a translation of the Greek word "kai." This Greek word is often translated "and." And is a connecting word often with a cumulative effect. In other words, this statement is a climax or the accumulation of Peter's picture of these Jews' sin. He delivers an exhortation under the power and movement of the Holy Spirit. The consequence of this awakening in the Spirit is recorded. *"However, many of those who heard the word believed; and the number of the men came to be about five thousand"* (Acts 4:4).

The Greek word "nun," translated *now*, is a primary particle of present tense, and is an adverb modifying the main verb **know**. Everything described in the previous verses of this exhortation happened in the past. The level of understanding and knowledge then is vastly different from **now**. He establishes a "now-then" picture. Then, one thing may have been true, but now, another thing is true. In other words, things are not as they were. We are at a different level of understanding, and we must respond to this new level.

Peter never implies they are less guilty. The strength of his message presses them with their responsibility for the guilt of their actions. They are responsible for the death of Jesus. He was **delivered up** and they **denied** Him before Pilate. They **denied the Holy One and the Just**, and they are guilty of demanding the release of a **murderer** for Jesus. They actually **killed the Prince of life**. They cannot brush this aside; they are responsible.

The reality is that God brought them into a new position through His mercy. Jesus, through His grace, ushered them into a new revelation of His truth. This is the message for everyone. The guilt of our past is enough to haunt us. Guilt is not eliminated; we cannot act as if it is not there; the depth of this guilt cannot lessen. However, Jesus does not leave us alone. He brings us into a new realm of understanding. In this present moment we are not where we were.

This is the message of "prevenient grace," the grace of God that "goes before." Jesus will not leave us alone. He pursues us. We settle comfortably into our justifications and rationalizations. He will not allow us to dwell in our **ignorance**. This is not an academic awakening about additional facts or intellectual knowledge; it is a spiritual awakening. The Spirit of Jesus distributes light to our inner hearts. We see and know what we have never seen or known. This does not happen to a few individuals; it is promised to everyone. In fact, no person is void of this Divine grace. For this reason, Paul cries, **"So** *that they are without excuse,"* (Romans 1:20). We can stay in our **ignorance** and be damned, or we can respond to His light and have our **sins blotted out**. What will we do now with this extended revelation?

We must note the tone of this exhortation from Peter. You may think he is condemning, being critical, or lashing out. He is brutally honest with these Jews concerning their participation in the crucifixion of Jesus. He certainly does not justify what they did. But this verse (Acts 3:17) brings a ray of hope because it is the beginning of a call to repentance. "Then" you participated in crucifying Jesus, "now" Jesus comes to you with new revelation. Peter embraces this crowd to bring them to full surrender to Jesus.

## Position of Tying

Peter addresses his crowd as **"brethren"** in the opening of his statement. This address was not an accident. He did not do this at first in his exhortation. He identifies with them as an attempt to remove any feeling of personal condemnation or judgment and to create a unity in the new understanding that has come to them all.

Peter links with this identification the main subject and verb, *"I know."* The Greek word "oida" is used, and means to grasp, perceive, or to see. He embraces the crowd as one who understands their situation by experience. Was he not a Jew? He was raised in the same culture. He learned the Old Testament history, sat at the feet of the teachers, and celebrated the feast days. He experienced the domination of the Roman Empire. Peter knew the frustration of paying taxes to the Romans. His heart beat for the deliverance promised through the Messiah. He was one with this crowd in all of those desires.

Peter was one with them in the idea of the Messiah. They

had been taught how to identify the Messiah. What would the Messiah do for them? How would He appear? What strategy would He use? Jesus did not match any teachings they received. They were looking for a military Messiah who would overthrow governments. He thought this even after the resurrection. Jesus appeared to them for 40 days and taught them about the Kingdom of God. Their question was, *"Lord, will You at this time restore the kingdom to Israel?"* (Acts 1:6). They still wanted a national kingdom, a restoring of the pomp and glory experienced in the days of King Solomon.

Peter embraced Jesus as the Messiah, but he still had an incorrect picture of Him. Could this be the basis of his denial of Jesus after the Garden of Gethsemane? Did he really think Jesus would exert His miracle power at the last moment? Jesus was taken in weakness and surrender; He was beaten and dominated. How could He be the Messiah? Peter did not know this dying Messiah.

Peter could easily speak to this crowd; from the depth of his heart he could say: *"Yet now, brethren, I know"* (Acts 3:17). But Jesus came to him with new revelation. The revelation was the physical resurrection, but it was far beyond data and facts. He knew forgiveness from the risen Lord. After what Peter did through denial, how could their relationship ever be the same? Yet, with Jesus there were no walls. He did not hold anything against Peter. In fact, it expanded into the fullness of the Spirit. Jesus came to live in him. *"Now"* there is a relationship of intimacy never experienced. Because Peter has walked in the shoes of these Jews, he can speak to them of the crucified Jesus.

## Posture of Theology

Now Peter comes to the bottom line of the issue. *"You did it in ignorance, as did also your rulers"* (Acts 3:17). Let's

**Part Two:** Exhortation from the Porch

return to one of the passages we referenced at the beginning of this study. The men of Athens gathered consistently at Mars Hill to either **tell or to hear some new thing** (Acts 17:21). Paul addresses them concerning their altar **with this inscription: TO THE UNKNOWN GOD** (Acts 17:23). His focus is on the reality of "**we are the offspring of God**." This should persuade us **not to think that the Divine Nature is like gold or silver or stone, something shaped by art and man's devising** (Acts 17:29). Then he concludes, **Truly, these times of ignorance God overlooked, but now commands all men everywhere to repent,** (Acts 17:30).

Paul seems to reference a time period called **times of ignorance**. With the Athenians, it was the time before the revelation of Jesus. This is the posture of the Old Covenant for the Jews. Several contrasts of this are in the Scriptures. For instance, the Hebrew writer describes it as a **copy and shadow**. In the Old Covenant the priests offered the gifts according to the law. They **serve the copy and shadow of the heavenly things, as Moses was divinely instructed when he was about to make the tabernacle. For He said, "See that you make all things according to the pattern shown you on the mountain"** (Hebrews 8:5).

Paul spoke of the Old Covenant as a **shadow**. He wrote, **So let no one judge you in food or in drink, or regarding a festival or a new moon or sabbaths, which are a shadow of things to come, but the substance is of Christ** (Colossians 2:16-17). The **shadow** is a mere reflection of the substance. You were living in the posture of the Old Covenant. So here is how you operated. You responded **in ignorance**.

The Greek word "kata," translated **in**, means "of an occasion," "by virtue of," "because of," or "through," but you knew what physical act you were committing. This is not about data, information, or simple knowledge. Peter was the same way. He heard everything Jesus said and saw what He did through the eyes of Old Testament understanding. Who could understand what the fullness of the Holy Spirit is like? If your framework has always been the law, how can you grasp intimacy? Once intimacy with Jesus is embraced, everything prior would be *times of ignorance*.

Paul described it in terms of *the natural man*. He wrote, ***But the natural man does not receive the things of the Spirit of God, for they are foolishness to him; nor can he know them, because they are spiritually discerned. But he who is spiritual judges all things, yet he himself is rightly judged by no one. For "who has known the mind of the Lord that he may instruct Him?" But we have the mind of Christ*** (1 Corinthians 2:14-16). Is not the *natural man* ignorant of all spiritual? Does he not live out of his flesh, do the best he can with what he knows, and make decisions based on his natural mind?

But something new has happened. The Spirit of Jesus reveals the mind of Christ. We are ignorant no longer. Jesus spoke, ***"And when He has come, He will convict the world of sin, and of righteousness, and of judgment: of sin, because they do not believe in Me; of righteousness, because I go to My Father and you see Me no more; of judgment, because the ruler of this world is judged"*** (John 16:8-11).

This is what Peter declares to the Jews who crucified Jesus. They lived in the *times of ignorance*. They operated out of their natural mind. This does not eliminate their guilt. They could have known and should have known. They were saturated in their own self-will and traditions of self-sourcing. But now, even as Peter addresses them, the Spirit of Jesus convicts them. The time for excuses is gone. The revelation of the Spirit of Jesus captures their hearts; they now know. Now is the time for response. He calls them to *repent* (Acts 3:19).

The picture of our lives is like this as well. Jesus comes to us. Knowing Bible stories or biblical information is not what it is about, however, it is about the revelation of the Spirit of Jesus. He draws us to Himself in a new way! We are no longer *ignorant*! We must respond.

## Acts 3:17

# I DID NOT MEAN TO!

*"Yet now, brethren, I know that you did it in ignorance, as did also your rulers"* (Acts 3:17).

I want to remind you of the four situations containing this concept (Luke 23:34; 1 Timothy 1:13; Acts 17:23; 3:17). Out of the four, there are three which speak directly to the actions of the participants. The circumstances of these two occasions are significant. While dying on the cross Jesus proclaims, **"Father, forgive them, for they do not know what they do"** (Luke 23:34). Peter, in this exhortation from the porch, says, **"Yet now, brethren, I know that you did it in ignorance, as did also your rulers"** (Acts 3:17). Each of these statements is focused on the activity of Jesus' crucifixion.

The third statement comes from the testimony of the Apostle Paul. He said, **"And I thank Christ Jesus our Lord who has enabled me, because He counted me faithful, putting me into the ministry, although I was formerly a blasphemer,** a persecutor**, and an insolent man; but I obtained mercy because I did it ignorantly in unbelief"** (1 Timothy 1:13). Paul expresses through his actions the same attitude as those crucifying Jesus. What the crowd did to Jesus, Paul was doing to the followers of Jesus. In reality Paul was doing it to Jesus!

In all three of these situations, there is an emphasis on **ignorance**, a translation of the Greek word "agnoeo." This

Greek word means, "not to know." The individual has "a lack of knowledge leading to wrongful conduct." If that person properly understood, they would have acted differently. Jesus and Peter, through the Holy Spirit, thought the Jews who participated in the crucifixion did not understand what they were doing. Paul expresses his dismay over his lack of knowledge. When additional information came to him by the appearance of the resurrected Lord, he changed.

*Ignorance* as an excuse or justification for actions is not indicated in any of these passages. No attempt is made to eliminate guilt for what is done. The crucifixion of Jesus is a heinous crime deserving full punishment. Guilt is not lessened by *ignorance*. Paul acclaims himself a *blasphemer*. It means to speak against God. Do you comprehend how ignorant he was? In holding tight to his belief in Jehovah, he blasphemed the One Jehovah sent. Thus he violated his belief in Jehovah. Paul was *a persecutor. He made havoc of the church, entering every house, and dragging off men and women, committing them to prison* (Acts 8:3). He did this in Jerusalem by placing many saints in prison *and when they were put to death*, he *cast* his *vote against them* (Acts 26:10). He was *an insolent man*, which means he was a violent aggressor. He did not have normal concern for human kindness. He received pleasure from seeing people humiliated and suffering. In each of these situations, there is a sense of "Oh, if I had only known." Once the truth was revealed to Saul of Tarsus, he was radically changed to the "Apostle Paul."

Peter speaks to the crowd at Solomon's Porch. They are guilty of crucifying Jesus. Once the truth of Jesus is revealed to them, they repent. Sins can be forgiven even if done in ignorance. I must be very careful in this discussion. For us to be overwhelmed with our negative, critical, and judgmental attitudes is easy. The purpose of this study is positive, encouraging, and uplifting.

**Part Two:** Exhortation from the Porch

## Intentional or Unintentional

I do not know much about the human heart. I am afraid it may be true of even my heart. Do I know the motive of my being? Almost every Bible scholar approaches this verse by indicating the Old Testament standard of "intentional and unintentional sins." If you have not carefully read the Book of Numbers, chapter fifteen, you need to do so now (Numbers 15:22-31). In eight verses, the concept of "unintentional sin" is used nine times. When you get done reading it, you are left with the distinct impression that God emphasizes guilt for unintentional sin. In each of these verses, He uses the word "unintentional" or "unintended." He views it from a corporate sense of all of Israel or from a view of the individual. He said, *"And if a person sins unintentionally, then he shall bring a female goat in its first year as a sin offering. So the priest shall make atonement for the person who sins unintentionally, when he sins unintentionally before the Lord, to make atonement for him; and it shall be forgiven him"* (Numbers 15:27-28).

The Hebrew word "shegagah," translated *unintentionally,* in this passage is the feminine noun meaning "mistake, inadvertent transgression, error, or ignorance." Its primary use and meaning is an error performed in the daily routine of life. In the Old Testament, this ranged from a slip of the tongue (Ecclesiastes 5:6) to accidental manslaughter (Numbers 35:11 and 15). This Hebrew word "shegagah" also includes acts in which the individual is conscious of what he is doing, but the sinfulness of those acts becomes known after the act occurs. It seems that this word describes the *ignorance* of the Jews in this passage. They were conscious of their acts. They pressured a Roman official. They demanded the death of a man. They manipulated the trial by asking for the release of Barabbas. They did, in effect, kill Jesus by their demands. They were not ignorant of these things.

However, they did not know what they were doing. Peter reveals it to them now.

This ignorance has happened in my life hundreds of time! If I had known before my action, I never would have done it. If I had known the damage that a statement I made would have on another, I never would have uttered those words. I am willing to readily admit stupidity, foolishness, ignorance, mental block, not smart, lack of knowledge, and even slow at times. I have and do experience all these to some degree. This condition causes unintentional sin in my life.

However, does this mean I do not need to worry about it? Are there no consequences to unintentional sins? From God's view, all sins break the relationship between Him and me. This view includes intentional and unintentional sins. Each category requires atonement. This requirement is true in our passage. Although the Jews who crucified Jesus may not know exactly what they did, this does not eliminate or even lessen their guilt. There must be atonement for sin!

In the Old Testament, God provided the means of sacrificial offerings for unintentional sins. In the New Covenant, these sins are more than adequately covered through the blood of Christ. In theological terminology, they fall under the category of "prevenient grace." All unintentional sins in the Christian and the non-Christian are already forgiven through His death. No one stands guilty before God for unintentional sins. What a relief! Without this, we would live in constant tension. We would second-guess every action, thought, and word. Our relationship with God would be "master and slave," a relationship of pressure, suspicion, and stress, instead of "bridegroom and bride." This "master and slave" relationship will destroy intimacy.

The Christian can readily pray the Lord's Prayer. ***"And forgive us our debts, as we forgive our debtors"*** (Matthew 6:12). The Greek word "opheilema," translated ***debt,*** means, "to owe," and is

Part Two: Exhortation from the Porch

a debt as an offense, a trespass requiring reparation. The Greek word "paraptoma," translated ***trespasses*** (Matthew 6:14), and the Greek word "hamartia," translated ***sins*** (Luke 11:4) equals "opheilema." We are forgiven of every unintentional sin; we do not want to take this for granted. Thus we can thank Jesus for His gracious forgiveness for everything not aligned with His desires of which we did not know. We live in His loving forgiveness every moment.

However, in the Old Testament, there was no provision for the intentional sin. These were sins committed ***presumptuously*** or "with a high hand" (Numbers 15:30). Here we begin to understand and sense something of the inadequacy of the Levitical sacrificial system. God gave us His law; we were expected to keep it without error or mistake. God provided for our stupidity and ignorance, but He did not provide for our disobedience and rebellion.

The call of the New Testament is one of forgiveness of all sin. Jesus is the adequate sacrifice for you. Listen to Peter's message, **"Repent therefore and be converted, that your sins may be blotted out, so that times of refreshing may come from the presence of the Lord,"** (Acts 3:19). **"To you first, God, having raised up His Servant Jesus, sent Him to bless you, in turning away every one of you from your iniquities"** (Acts 3:26). In speaking of their sins, Peter mentions only the unintentional sins. In speaking of their guilt, he refers to their entire guilt. Their sins done in ignorance are enough to bring them to repentance. The guilt does not lessen, and there is not an attitude of "it does not matter." In reality, they (and we) fought against the plan of God. Jesus is crucified whether in ignorance or in knowledge. All sin places Jesus on the cross. BUT God provides forgiveness and deliverance.

## Informed or Uninformed

This discussion must also include the availability of knowledge. Could they have known? Were they ignorant because they had no revelation? Why did others in Judea believe and they did not? How responsible are we for knowing? Is there such a thing as voluntary ignorance? All these questions apply to our lives as well.

Peter does not seem to address these issues in his exhortation. Perhaps it is because these questions, whether answered, do not matter. The guilt of these Jews is not worse in one way or another. Look at each side of the issue. Surely they could and should have known Jesus was the Messiah. They could and should have embraced Him as the disciples did. From the beginning of Jesus' earthly appearance, the Trinity broadcasted the truth. It came from a star, in a sky filled with angels, to wise men and shepherds. Could these Jews have witnessed this revelation? Surely they heard about it. Were not these Jews affected by the forerunning of John the Baptist? The powerful movement of the Spirit of God through John should have alerted them. Jesus did thousands of miracles. Nothing He did was done in secret. Was not the Sermon on the Mount enough revelation to command their lives? Does not their positive response of Palm Sunday (Matthew 21) testify to their ability to know and respond? If some Jews knew and believed, why did not all of them? Hundreds of Jews from their setting embraced Jesus. Yes, they could have known, and they are guilty!

Is not this true of us as well? Has not truth come to us all? Are we not all affected by the wonder of God's revelation? Paul is right; we **are without excuse** (Romans 1:20). The creation of the universe reveals His invisible attributes. We have received a revelation "in us" and "to us." We have all had equal opportunity. We are guilty!

But let us view it from the other side of the issue. Did not their culture strongly interfere with the revelation of Jesus? Their leaders, the godliest men of their day, told them Jesus was leading them astray. They incited them to demand the crucifixion. The ones who taught them as children and instructed them repeatedly on Sabbath days led them. How could they have known? His disciples came from the territory farthest removed from the influence of these leaders. But these Jews in Jerusalem had the greatest stronghold.

The law (oral interpretation) told the Jews Jesus was wrong. Should not everyone view the consequence of Jesus' teaching? To understand the overthrow of all the Jews as sacred is inevitable. How could this be right? This teaching must be guarded and protected. These are not passing whims of teaching; they are rooted into hundreds of years of traditions, prophecies, and sacred writings. How could these Jews with an average education understand? They would simply follow their leaders. After all, they are not theological experts. They have families, businesses, and everyday matters with which to cope. Surely they did not know!

Isn't it the same with us? We are bombarded with television and the Internet. A godless program of education, in which Jesus is not allowed, shapes the views of our younger generation. Non-biblical views of sexuality are set forth in the television venue. Every sacred thought is challenged through unlimited access to the Internet. Morals are determined by secular thought instead of biblical truth. Preachers have increasingly less influence and respect in the culture. How may we be expected to know? If we are crucifying Jesus, we must be doing ***it in ignorance*** (Acts 3:17).

So which view is correct? Again, Peter does not address this issue in his exhortation. It simply does not matter. The question is mute, because either way we are guilty! Whether we know or not, we are guilty! Whether we could know or not, we are guilty! Our guilt is not eliminated by lack of knowledge. Our childhood experiences do not eliminate our guilt. Our place of birth, the religion of our parents, and the cultural pressure of our day, does not lessen our responsibility. We have sinned, intentionally or unintentionally, informed or uninformed. We are guilty!

The climax of the truth is that NOW we do know. This is the reality of our passage. Whatever the pasts of these Jews, they know NOW exactly what to do. The Spirit of Jesus brought them to a reality of truth from which they cannot escape. Truth enlightens the prophecies of old (Acts 3:21-22). What will we do with the present truth? According to Peter, they received the revelation *first* for the purpose of **turning away every one of you from your iniquities** (Acts 3:26). He calls them to repentance. Perhaps you did crucify Jesus in ignorance, but NOW you must repent. You know the truth.

What about you and me? Whatever we have known or not known in the past is not the issue. How we responded in the past, in full consciousness or in ignorance, is not the issue. We are guilty; it is revealed; we can be different. Jesus is here!

Acts 3:17

# TWO CAUSES

*"Yet now, brethren, I know that you did it in ignorance, as did also your rulers" (Acts 3:17).*

Are we making too much out of this simple statement in Peter's exhortation? Most Bible scholars propose a pattern to his message. Peter is strong in his rebuke of those who crucified Christ. He describes exactly what they did; are they not guilty? Now in this verse, he begins to soften his approach with them hoping to bring them to repentance. He identifies with them. He says, **"Yet now, brethren"** (Acts 3:17). Peter acknowledges his guilt as he recognizes theirs. After all, they **did it in ignorance** (Acts 3:17). Although they are guilty, God will forgive if they will repent. He extends another chance to them through the Spirit!

Undoubtedly this simple approach is true and acceptable. However, we cannot view this verse as a psychological technique to soften the strength of the guilt to inspire repentance. Peter expresses an aspect of sin that deadens sensitivity to truth and blinds spiritual eyes. Sin can operate only in darkness, ignorance, or blindness. A biblical fact is that **you shall know the truth, and the truth shall make you free** (John 8:32). How will we know the truth? Are we not all ignorant because of the truth we do not know?

To grasp this reality, let's restate the conclusion to which we have come and use this as a springboard for additional truth.

## Two Categories

It seems there are two categories or kinds of sin. The Old Testament teaches us about unintentional sin (Numbers 15:27-28). The fifteenth chapter of Numbers states the concept of unintentional sin nine times in eight verses. God presents this concept from a corporate view for the nation of Israel and the view of the individual. The Hebrew word "shegagah," translated ***unintentionally*** in this passage, is a feminine noun meaning, "mistake, inadvertent transgression, error, and ignorance." Peter places the sin of these Jews in this category. They were not ignorant of their activities; they knew they crucified a man. They aggressively pressured a Roman official to complete this task. They manipulated the trial by asking for the release of Barabbas. They killed Jesus. Their ignorance was in their knowledge that He is "***His Servant Jesus***," "***the Holy One***," "***the Just***," and "***the Prince of Life***."

The second category taught in the Old Testament is intentional sin. These are sins committed ***presumptuously*** or "with a high hand" (Numbers 15:30). In the Old Testament sacrificial system, there was no provision for the forgiveness of such sin. God's law was to be kept without voluntary violation. In the Old Testament, God provided for our stupidity and ignorance, but He did not provide for our disobedience and rebellion.

The Old Testament sin concept is sometimes referred to as the "legal" understanding of sin in contrast with the "ethical" understanding. The "ethical" understanding involves the human will and personal responsibility. It emphasizes the subjective. The intent and motive of the heart must be considered. This reality comes from the consideration of the "fall" of man (Genesis 3). Man was created in the image of God (Genesis 1:26). We can only guess at the capacity of righteousness and holiness found in this perfect image. Man's mental and spiritual awareness were

**Part Two:** Exhortation from the Porch

functioning at total capacity. Man could to know the total will of God, His law; he was also capable of achieving it. In fact, God expected, demanded, and would not tolerate anything less. Man's relationship with God was based on his accomplishment of the law of God.

In the "fall" of man, he lost this ability. Under the curse of sin, he experienced *ignorance*. The capacity of man's mind shrunk to a smaller percentage. He could no longer comprehend the complete law of God; he no longer had the ability to keep it. The story of the Old Testament continually highlights this reality. Man is living in sin. His failures are presented in the tragic events of the Old Testament. God understood and provided for the inability of man's perfect performance of His will. An Old Testament sacrifice for unintentional sin was available. However, God would not tolerate rebellion and voluntary disobedience. This declares to us an amazing truth. God desperately wants a love relationship with us. He wants us to love Him with all our hearts and relate to Him without rebellion.

Although every deed committed contrary to the will of God is technically a sin, there is a distinction between those done in rebellion and those done in ignorance. A leader in the holiness movement, John Wesley, called this distinction "sin proper so-called" and "sin improper so-called." As in the Old Testament so in the New Testament, there is forgiveness for unintentional sins. The death of Jesus provides "prevenient grace" for all sins not involving the will of man. Although every day may contain deeds deviating from the will of God, there is no guilt accrued. No argument against calling such wrongdoings "sin" exists, but these sins must not be confused with willful defiance against God's desires.

Many illustration of this truth are available. A father came home from a business trip. As he pulled into the driveway his young son ran to greet him. In great excitement the boy offered to help his father in any way possible. Could he carry his dad's bags? Could he get him something to drink? Finally, the father asked his son to get him a glass of water. The boy ran as fast as he could into the house, down the hallway, and into the kitchen. He pulled a chair across the kitchen and up to the kitchen sink. He got the biggest glass he could find and filled it to the brim. He ran down the hall and out the door. With an intense sense of accomplishment, he handed the glass of water to his father. His father was very pleased, praised his son for a job well done, and drank all the water. The one detail I failed to mention was that the son had been playing in the dirt. To carry the glass and not drop it, he placed his dirty finger over the lip of the glass. The water splashed over the finger washing the dirt into the glass. The son had mud in his service.

This illustration describes our lives. We have mud in our service. When have we lived adequately before God? When have we performed exactly as we should? Except for the prevenient grace of the cross, we would all be damned. Although there may be mud in our service, this attitude is vastly different from rebellious disobedience. The story quickly changes when a sixteen-year-old responds to his father's request for a drink. This rebellious teenager fills a glass with water and intentionally deposits a fist full of dirt. Each act resulted in dirty water but the motives of each son are entirely different. One is unintentional sin, and the other is intentional sin.

## One Condition

Do unintentional sins have consequences? Above we attempted to discuss the ethical understanding of sin. Now we will discuss the "objective" or the "legal" view of sin. Sin is a violation of the covenant relationship between God and man, whether it is intentional or unintentional. Sins committed in *ignorance* are still sins and require atonement. In other words,

**Part Two:** Exhortation from the Porch

from God's view all sins break the relationship between Him and man. He did not create man for sin. Sin was never intended to be a part of man's life. Sin is an addition and is not necessary for the fulfillment and completion of man's purposeful living.

No one should be flippant about sin. If it is even unintentional, we must never be casual. Even these sins matter because they require the sacrifice of Christ. The wages of sin is death. Our passage is a perfect picture of the consequences of unintentional sin. In his exhortation to the Jews, Peter strongly says that every deed done intentionally or unintentionally crucifies Jesus. No other activities are discussed. These Jews violated the plan of God for which they were created. God established the Israelites as a nation for the entrance of Jesus into the world and they fought against it. This is a picture of the consequences of all sin.

As the New Testament unfolds, the view of sin seems to have only one category. Paul writes about it in his letter to the Romans. *"For all have sinned and fall short of the glory of God"* (Romans 3:23). The atonement of Christ is made for all sin. All stand guilty before Him. John said, "Jesus will **cleanse us from all unrighteousness**" (1 John 1:9). What a relief not to have to worry about categories. We rest in Him.

## One Conversion

Everywhere we look in the New Testament, the Blood of Jesus is the sole solution to sin. Wherever sin is, the blood of Jesus is the single remedy. Peter proposes this in his exhortation. **"But those things which God foretold by the mouth of all His prophets, that the Christ would suffer, He has thus fulfilled. Repent therefore and be converted, that your sins may be blotted out, so that times of refreshing may come from the presence of the Lord"** (Acts 3:18-19). All the prophets foretold the sufferings of Christ. The sufferings caused by sins of the Jews as described by Peter became the solution to their conversion.

The writer of the Book of Hebrews proclaims this truth loudly! *"For if the blood of bulls and goats and the ashes of a heifer, sprinkling the unclean, sanctifies for the purifying of the flesh, how much more shall the blood of Christ, who through the eternal Spirit offered Himself without spot to God, cleanse your conscience from dead works to serve the living God?"* (Hebrews 9:13-14). Listen to these words, *"And every priest stands ministering daily and offering repeatedly the same sacrifices, which can never take away sins. But this Man, after He had offered one sacrifice for sins forever, sat down at the right hand of God"* (Hebrews 10:11-12). We conclude the blood of Jesus is adequate for all sin regardless of its category.

## Two Causes

The cause of ignorance seems to suggest two issues. They are highlighted by two Greek words (poieo and prasso). In our passage, *"Yet now, brethren, I know that you did* (prasso) *it in ignorance, as did also your rulers"* (Acts 3:17) "prasso" is used. We have contrasted these two words in a variety of studies in the past. They become important in understanding the source of sin. Each can legitimately be translated "do, did, or done." However, they are vastly different in the sourcing of the action.

In contrasting these two words, our favorite expression is "painting." The artist who flows with creativity naturally, without effort, can to portray what he sees and feels onto the canvas. The work of an artist is beautiful to behold and amazing to watch. This type of work is "poieo." The barn painter is the opposite side of the spectrum. He is in the hot sun; he looks at his watch desiring a break from his task. He has to do this painting to make his living. He takes little pride in his work. This type of work is "prasso."

God is never the subject of "prasso" as used in our passage. Thus, it is used only with human activity. The general tone of "prasso" is abstract and colorless and is usually connected to human activity, evil or negative, in the New Testament. It most often portrays the idea of continual practice, habit, or routine. It has the tone of "doing something repeatedly" and it is done without thinking due to an established pattern.

Peter suggests the *ignorance* of the Jews who crucified Jesus came from "prasso." They lived their lives in the ruts, patterns, rituals, and ceremonies of their traditions. They could testify to watching for the Messiah, but it was only routine expectation. They were not open, seeking, or searching. They were comfortable with their religious laws and routinely followed their leaders. They missed Jesus as their Messiah. The "signs" of His miracles did not point them to His reality. They plotted along in their legalistic patterns missing the wonder of the new action of God. Should they have known? John the Baptist paved the way; it was an announcement all heard. But in their *ignorance* they did not know. The focus of knowing seems to be on Jesus. I am plagued by what Jesus said in His Sermon on the Mount. *"Not everyone who says to Me, 'Lord, Lord,' shall enter the kingdom of heaven, but he who does the will of My Father in heaven"* (Matthew 7:21). He concluded, *"And then I will declare to them, 'I never knew you; depart from Me, you who practice lawlessness'"* (Matthew 7:23).

In the other two statements (Luke 23:34 and 1 Timothy 1:13) where *ignorance* is suggested, the Greek word "poieo" is used. Jesus said it from the cross, *"Father, forgive them, for they do not know what they do* (poieo)*"* (Luke23: 34). This word indicates a different context of *ignorance*. The context is not of the routine barn painter but the creative flow of their nature. The same word is used for trees "bearing (poieo) fruit." These Jews were motivated by a self-sourcing nature, which blinded them to what God was doing to redeem the world. All they could see was their religious world with its patterns and laws. They thought only about protecting their temple with its rituals and ceremonies. Jesus would change their approach to the worship of God. He would alter their economy and standard of living. They would not see beyond what was driving them (poieo).

Each context of *ignorance* applies to us. How easy it is for us to miss what God wants to do in our lives because we live in established patterns. These patterns become so rigid we cannot see beyond them. Our self-sourcing establishes these patterns and limits our vision. We become ignorant of all that God would do. We must do as Peter instructed **"Repent therefore and be converted, that your sins may be blotted out, so that times of refreshing may come from the presence of the Lord"** (Acts 3:19). We are ignorant no longer. The Spirit of Jesus speaks to us. Will we respond?

Acts 3:18

# ALL HIS PROPHETS

*"But those things which God foretold by the mouth of all His prophets, that the Christ would suffer, He has thus fulfilled" (Acts 3:18).*

Amazing and long lasting effects were from a simple encounter among Peter, John, and the lame beggar. This beggar was not in the list of the most influential men ever. We do not know even his name. The reason this is memorable is simple. The encounter was not about the beggar; it was about Jesus. Jesus always picks such people to affect the world. We do not get distracted with their heritage. Their education or talents do not impress us. We can never say God cannot use us as He did him because we do not have what he had. The Scriptures portrays the lame beggar as having nothing. The message is not cluttered with qualifications and prerequisites; instead it is simply Jesus of Nazareth connecting with a man in desperate need. Jesus is the total resource; the lame beggar has nothing but total need.

Suddenly, the encounter moves from a moment at the Gate Beautiful to Solomon's Porch. Peter and John embrace more than one man; they encounter several thousand people attending the temple. Are they educated? We assume most of them experienced the Jewish educational system. Are they wealthy? Most of them support their families with a respectable level of living. Are they righteous? They have come to the temple at the hour of prayer; this bespeaks their dedication to the Jewish faith. Yet, Peter highlights none of those things.

They are a group of people exactly like the lame beggar. They have a desperate need. The God of Abraham, Isaac, and Jacob foretold through the prophets His solution to the need of their world; they fought against it. They **delivered up and denied**. They rejected **the Holy One and the Just** in favor of a murderer. They **killed the Prince of life**. They were guilty without excuse. If we compare them with the lame beggar, perhaps it would be better to be the lame beggar. Neither of them has any chance of correcting their situation. Each is helpless. The answer for the lame beggar is Jesus of Nazareth connecting to his desperate need. Could Jesus do this for this crowd of Jews as well?

Whatever your qualifications may be, you will never know Jesus until you recognize your desperate need. It is only in absolute helplessness do we find His presence. Otherwise, we are preoccupied with the distraction of our solutions. We miss Him because we are focused on our qualifications. Be assured, we come to a crucial moment when there is nothing but Jesus! The lame beggar made the right choice. Five thousand men in this Jewish crowd made the right choice (Acts 4:4). What will we do?

Saturation in our passage shows us that verses 17 and 18 are intimately linked. They form a transition from the reality of sin and guilt to the call of repentance. The emphasis in the opening section of Peter's exhortation is on what these Jews did (Acts 3:12-15). He climaxed this section with one brief statement about the actions of God (Acts 3:15). God reversed everything they had done by the resurrection of Jesus from the dead. Peter continues this idea revealing several insights into the involvement of God from the beginning. The main subject of our verse is **God**. The main verb is **foretold**. Any additional information in the verse gives content to this one major idea.

**Part Two:** Exhortation from the Porch

# Contrast

Peter opens his statement with the contrasting conjunction *but* (de). In verse 17 the focus is on the *ignorance* of the Jews. In verse 18 the focus is on the knowledge of God. However, it is not just a comparison of what man knows against what God knows. Such a comparison would embarrass us all. We compensate for such belittling with the excuse of being only human. But this is not Peter's argument.

He begins with "The Message." God *foretold* a truth to these Jews. They were not Gentiles with little or no input from God. These were the chosen ones of Israel. They were destined for this moment. The only hope the pagan world had rested with these Jews. They were expected to know. The contrast is in the fact that they lived in *ignorance,* but God *foretold*.

The Greek word "prokatangello," translated *foretold,* is used only twice in the New Testament. Luke uses it each time in this book. Stephen preached this to the Hellenistic Jews. **"Which of the prophets did your fathers not persecute? And they killed those who foretold** (prokatangello) **the coming of the Just One, of whom you now have become the betrayers and murderers"** (Acts 7:52). This is essentially the same message delivered by Peter. It means, "to announce fully beforehand," and it is sometimes translated as "long ago announced."

God proclaimed every Sabbath Day His message to Israel as recorded in their sacred Old Testament. They had this truth in the symbolic prophecies. They observed all the Feast Days proclaiming this message from God. Every sacrifice they made pointed to this message. God overshadowed them with the message to a ridiculous degree. The only possibility of being ignorant would be to willfully embrace *ignorance*.

We might consider that God spoke in ways these Jews could not possibly have understood. Thus Peter proclaims "The Method" of "The Message." ***God foretold by the mouth of all His prophets.*** God did not speak through angels with heavenly language that they could not comprehend. He did not write His message in the clouds using words beyond their knowledge. The message did not come through demonstrations beyond what they could decipher. He chose ordinary men from every economic level, from every section of Israel, from every educational experience, and from every profession. God spoke through the ordinary and understandable language of these people. How could they miss it? And we must ask ourselves how we can miss it in our day? God speaks in the language of our culture, times and through our flesh.

But consider this, "The Message" came through "The Method" of the prophets. The prophets were "The Maximum." They were in abundance proclaiming the message. God did not send forth one or two. Every generation had a prophet handpicked by God to deliver the message. It began with Moses and ended with "The Prophet." In fact, Peter completes his exhortation with this statement, ***"For Moses truly said to the fathers, 'The Lord your God will raise up for you a Prophet like me from your brethren. Him you shall hear in all things, whatever He says to you'"*** (Acts 3:22). The Prophet is Jesus. The message proclaimed by all the prophets climaxed in Jesus. How could they have missed it? What excuse could they give for their *ignorance*?

If so for them, how much more is it true for us? We experience the movement of His Holy Spirit speaking directly to our being. He comes to ***convict the world of sin, and of righteousness, and of judgment: of sin, because they do not believe in Me; of righteousness, because I go to My Father and you see Me no more; of judgment, because the ruler of this world is judged*** (John 16:8-11). How can we miss it? What excuse can we give for our *ignorance*?

**Part Two:** Exhortation from the Porch

# Content

"The Message" of this verse is singular in focus, and it is Jesus. God's aching desire is that we know Jesus. We may be ignorant about many things that do not prompt His concern, but God does not want us to be ignorant about Jesus. God made "The Message" about Jesus so focused and consistent that there was no reason these Jews should be ignorant.

Peter makes statements that declare the deep desire in the heart of God for this knowledge. God *foretold* (prokatangello) this message of Jesus. This is the Greek word "prokatangello," many translate it "announced beforehand," is used only twice in the New Testament, and is one Greek word meaning "pre-proclaimed." God did not wait for the arrival of Jesus to announce His presence. This pre-proclaimed was so important it started at the beginning of man's sin. The "seed of the woman" was "pre-proclaimed" as the single solution to our need (Genesis 3:15).

God's sincere desire for us to know is seen in this statement by Peter, **"by the mouth of all His prophets."** The message of Jesus was not highlighted occasionally or an emphasis of several prophets. "*All*" the prophets pre-proclaimed the message. Hundreds of years were involved in the period of the prophets. They were separated not only by years, but also by distance, backgrounds, and training. If they came from the same "School of the Prophets," we might understand the single focus. But there was no such school. The single message of the prophets was Jesus. The last of the prophets, John the Baptist, was the perfect example. If the message was going to waver, it should have wavered with him. He was four hundred years removed from the previous prophet, Malachi. He had no training; he broke with his culture; his single focus was Jesus.

Although "The Message" is focused on Jesus, the focus of this message is on "The Method." What is it about Jesus that matters the most to God? In this passage, Peter does not refer to the miracles of Christ or highlight His preaching. Peter does not uplift the moral teaching and standard of the Sermon on the Mount. From this verse the conclusion can only be that Jesus' life was about *"that the Christ would suffer."*

Are you not startled that a suffering Messiah is the one thing of which the Jews were ignorant? Their tradition taught them of a conquering, military Messiah. Some even questioned that the Old Testament proclamation of a suffering Messiah. They took the passages related to suffering and applied them to others. That Peter is making this statement is significant because he was the one who rebuked Jesus when He began telling His predictions concerning His death and resurrection (Matthew 16:22). Peter was still confused after the resurrection of Jesus. During the resurrection appearance of Jesus for 40 days, Peter and the other disciples asked, *"Lord, will You at this time restore the kingdom to Israel?"* (Acts 1:6). Surely this validates the reality of the truth; Peter, through the fullness of the Spirit of Jesus, now sees the truth.

The ringing note of finality, conquest, and victory is heard in the last part of this verse. Peter says, *"He has thus fulfilled."* "The Message" is Jesus; "The Method" is suffering; "The Maximum" is completed. The total of all that God spoke through every prophet is completed in Jesus. Jesus accomplished through suffering is necessary. Peter boldly calls these Jews to repentance. They can be forgiven; times of restoration will be theirs; times of refreshing will come from the presence of Jesus. All God spoke through the prophets for hundreds of years is not complete.

We live in such an hour. Everything God needed to do to bring victory to our lives is done. The resources of God are in maximum supply in Jesus. Nothing remains out of place. All is complete.

Part Two: Exhortation from the Porch

# Cure

This brings us to the cure. "The Message" of God to every generation in every culture is Jesus. God does not develop a new message for each situation because the cure is always the same, Jesus. Yes, He spoke the message of Jesus through the prophets of old. Each of them was in a different culture, a different situation, with different problems, and had different enemies to fight and battles to win. Yet the prophets all had the same message, Jesus. The sacrificial lambs of every generation pointed to the Lamb to come, Jesus.

The writer of the Book of Hebrews verified this truth. He lists the heroes of faith. Their victory was all because of Jesus. The writer starts with Abel who offered *a more excellent sacrifice than Cain* (Hebrews 11:4). The more excellent sacrifice was based on Jesus. Enoch found himself in intimacy with God; it allowed him to bypass death and dwell with God. Jesus made such a provision for Him. The list goes from Noah, Abraham, Isaac, Jacob, Joseph, Moses, to many more. Finally, he comes to us. He instructs us to *lay aside every weight, and the sin which so easily ensnares us, and let us run with endurance the race that is set before us* (Hebrews 12:1). "How can I do this?" you ask. The message is the same. *Looking unto Jesus, the author and finisher of our faith, who for the joy that was set before Him endured the cross, despising the shame, and has sat down at the right hand of the throne of God* (Hebrews 12:2).

This brings us to "The Method." The cure is found in the suffering Jesus. The cross is at the heart of the message. Jesus established a Kingdom; the foundation of this Kingdom is the style of the cross. Let it never be suggested that victory is found outside of losing one's life to Jesus who gave His life to us. He calls us to *take up his cross, and follow Me* (Matthew 16:24). The reason for this method is His nature. The physical cross illustrates the nature of God. The suffering expresses who He is. If we are partakers of His Divine nature (2 Peter 1:4), then it will be the nature of the cross. You cannot live for self and be a partaker of the Divine nature.

"The Message" is Jesus; "The Method" is the suffering of the cross; "The Maximum" is total surrender. Partial will not do. Compromise brings only defeat. This total surrender is Peter's call to the Jews of his hour. They must ***repent and be converted***. This call is for a total embracing of how they treated Jesus and a reversal of their lives in embracing Him. No less will it be for us.

Acts 3:18

# GOD FORETOLD

*"But those things which God foretold by the mouth of all His prophets, that the Christ would suffer, He has thus fulfilled" (Acts 3:18).*

The familiar Greek word "de" begins our study. Its primary translation is **but**, presenting a contrasting picture. It introduces something else, whether opposed to what precedes or simply continuative or explanatory. Peter exhorts this crowd of Jews, pointing them to Jesus. They are directly guilty of crucifying Jesus. They **killed the Prince of life** (Acts 3:15). Jesus, this One they rejected, is the source of the miracle. Standing before them is the lame beggar healed. It is this man has **perfect soundness** because of "invoking the activity of Jesus." The miracle occurred because of **faith** in Jesus; Jesus sources this faith.

These Jews did not know the truth about what they were doing. They **did it in ignorance** (Acts 3:17). This does not excuse them or eliminate their guilt. It simply states that what they did not know before, they do know now. This is the foundation of the call to **repent**, the theme of the rest of Peter's exhortation. They must give up a former thought to embrace this new thought.

But there is another important ingredient present in this foundation. **God foretold!** This is why Peter uses the familiar Greek word "de." Perhaps they were ignorant of the truth concerning Jesus, **but** they should not have been! Of all people in the world, they should have known. God revealed His plan through "*all His prophets.*" They were the chosen ones of Israel. They were the nation formed by the covenants of God for this purpose. Through the prophets, God kept the message before them including the last of the prophets, John the Baptist. They should have known, responded, and embraced.

In this verse, Peter explodes the revelation of God to them. They are guilty of the crucifixion of Jesus, and they are guilty of *ignorance*. Let us now look at the details of this.

# God's Plan

Their ignorance is God's plan! The Prime Mover in the passage is **God**. He is the Director who sets into motion His plan. This plan is a product of the dreams of His heart. He is the sole source of what happens in and through Jesus. We did not suggest, add to, or contribute anything to this plan. The plan is born exclusively out of God's heart. The greatest of all realities is that we are at the heart of His plan. We are not an afterthought. We did not appear in the picture because of necessity. You and I are the fiber of His plan.

Let me remind you, the Prime Mover is the Trinity God of the Old Testament. The Hebrew word for "God" is "Elohim," and it is always plural in the Old Testament. This plan is the united effort of the Three Persons in One. Their hearts are united in this single effort of redemption. Each heart burns with this one desire. No One is distracted; there are no other plans. As revealed in the Scriptures, redemption is their one focus. Peter's message to the Jews is a statement of the duration of His plan. The heart of God has been intent on us for a long time. *All His prophets* spoke concerning this one plan for our lives.

This redemption is made known to us through the details of the plan. There is nothing careless about the plan. Even

**Part Two:** Exhortation from the Porch

the details are given special attention. The uniqueness of each individual proclaims the special attention to the amazing plan. Your fingertips and your DNA speak to your personal and unique involvement in His plan. If you were not essential to His plan, why would the Trinity God go to so much trouble over the details of your experience? The greatness of our God determines the greatness of His plan! The greatness of this plan highlights the greatness of our God.

## God's Plan Fulfilled

Peter's message to the Jews is the startling announcement of "fulfillment." Everything in his message is determined by this reality. If this fulfillment is false, these Jews should be congratulated for eliminating a threat to Jewish tradition. But Peter makes an urgent cry. ***"But those things which God foretold by the mouth of all His prophets, that the Christ would suffer, He has thus fulfilled"*** (Acts 3:18). Jesus is the fulfillment of the plan of God. This statement embraces the heart and core of the Gospel plan. It establishes the boundaries; there is nothing outside it.

The Greek word "pleroo," translated *fulfilled*, projects a picture. It portrays a large container with content placed beside it. The content is now put into the container until it is filled. God foretold through all the prophets the wonder of His plan. Peter proclaims that the content of Jesus' life fills up the container of that prophecy. Jesus told His disciples this fact numerous times. His life was a fulfillment of the Old Testament Scriptures. On the Emmaus Road, Jesus spoke these words to two disciples walking with Him. ***"O foolish ones, and slow of heart to believe in all that the prophets have spoken! Ought not the Christ to have suffered these things and to enter into His glory"*** (Luke 24:25-26). In the upper room, after His resurrection, Jesus said, ***"These are the words which I spoke to you while I was still with you, that all things must be fulfilled which were written in the Law of Moses and the Prophets and the Psalms concerning Me"*** (Luke 24:44). Then ***He opened their understanding, that they might comprehend the Scriptures*** (Luke 24:45).

Peter proclaims to the Jews the hour of fulfillment. We are allowed to live in such a marvelous hour. The plan of God is fulfilled in Jesus! We may not have experienced it yet, but it is all in place. Everything has been accomplished. Jesus has done it! Understand thoroughly that Jesus is the fulfillment of the plan of the Trinity God. Everything said by the Old Testament prophets proposes this. The fulfillment of the plan is not accomplished in a governmental structure, the establishment of a religion, or the elimination of evil. We find fulfillment in the person of Jesus!

The last of the prophets, John the Baptist, proposed one thing, Jesus. John was a forerunner to Jesus the Messiah. In stating his purpose, John said, ***"I indeed baptize you with water unto repentance, but He who is coming after me is mightier than I, whose sandals I am not worthy to carry. He will baptize you with the Holy Spirit and fire"*** (Matthew 3:11). The first of the Old Testament prophets, Moses, proposed one thing. He said, ***"The Lord your God will raise up for you a Prophet like me from your brethren. Him you shall hear in all things, whatever He says to you"*** (Acts 3:22; Deuteronomy 18:15). Moses was referring to Jesus; Peter even quotes this in his exhortation to the Jews. Jesus is the fulfillment of the plan of God.

This fulfillment is not only true in the physical appearance of Jesus, the Messiah; it is true in the spiritual provision of the plan of God. Paul continually pushes the idea that we find everything we need in Christ. ***"Blessed be the God and Father of our Lord Jesus Christ, who has blessed us with every spiritual blessing in the heavenly places in Christ,"*** (Ephesians 1:3). He continues to give a lengthy list of provisions; each time he says that they are

**Part Two:** Exhortation from the Porch

"*in Him*." Jesus does not provide the fulfillment of the plan; He is the fulfillment of the plan. What He does is not the completion of the dreams of God; how He ends is all God wants. Jesus is the new revelation now coming to this group of Jews. They thought Jesus was impeding the sacred translations of their fathers. Now they know Jesus is the fulfillment of all God promised through their fathers.

## God's Plan Fulfilled through Suffering

Peter highlights a single aspect about Jesus as spoken by the prophets. He says, ***"But those things which God foretold by the mouth of all His prophets, that the Christ would suffer, He has thus fulfilled"*** (Acts 3:18). The Greek word "pascho," translated ***would suffer***, is used 42 times in the New Testament. Most of the time it is connected with the sufferings of Jesus and His followers. The word means "to experience something that comes from outside." A strong use of the word was attached to experiencing evil. A neutral use for the word was also developed, but a connection with suffering evil is so strong that additional information is required if it is to mean experiencing good.

In the noun form (pascha) the word refers to the Feast of the Passover. Because Jesus is the sacrificial Lamb, this word became intimate with His sufferings. The context of our passage highlights this. Peter declares what Jesus experienced (Acts 3:18). He proposed in detail exactly what Jesus had imposed on Him from the outside. He was ***delivered up and denied in the presence*** before Pilate (Acts 3:13). He was rejected and ***a murderer*** was preferred to Him, ***the Holy One and the Just*** (Acts 3:14). He was ***killed*** (Acts 3:15). These statements are mere suggestions of the additional details of the trials and scourging Jesus experienced. The Jews would have known all these details.

From our passage, we must conclude several factors. One,

"The Plan of God" was for Jesus to suffer. Nothing about the cross was accidental. The cross was not a result of the evil of man and God could do nothing about it. God is not playing a chess game with the devil. The devil moved in the sufferings of Christ, and God had allowed it to win the game. God is sovereign, and the sufferings of Christ will not occur unless planned by God. Let's review the previous sermon by Peter as he explains Pentecost. He said, ***"Him** (Jesus**), being delivered by the determined purpose and foreknowledge of God"*** (Acts 2:23).

The writer of the Book of Hebrews speaks to this truth in the context of Judaism. He declares that Jesus, fulfilling the plan of God, did not have to ***offer Himself often, as the high priest enters the Most Holy Place every year with blood of another — He then would have had to suffer often since the foundation of the world; but now, once at the end of the ages, He has appeared to put away sin by the sacrifice of Himself*** (Hebrews 9:25-26). A sacrificial Jesus is what God foretold through all of the prophets. In addition, every sacrificial lamb offered for the sin of humanity was a symbol pointing to Jesus. In his first epistle, Peter declared. ***"For Christ also suffered once for sins, the just for the unjust, that He might bring us to God, being put to death in the flesh but made alive by the Spirit,"*** (1 Peter 3:18). Peter declares the suffering of Jesus to be the plan of God!

But it is also "The Prophetic Message." Peter definitely says that God foretold this plan of suffering ***"by the mouth of all His prophets."*** Although the Jews to whom Peter speaks may not have recognized it, this was the message of the prophets. The leaders and teachers of Israel sidestepped this truth, which echoed through the prophets. They imposed their plans on the plan of God. This self-planning was a part of the ***ignorance*** of our previous verse (Acts 3:17). How could they have missed the thundering truth of the "Suffering Servant" (Isaiah 52:13 to 53:12)?

A third conclusion is "The Performance Completed." This suffering planned by God and spoken by the prophets is completed in Jesus! Jesus fulfilled the plan. One might relate this suffering to the cross event as described by Peter initially in his exhortation. However, the undercurrent of the truth is the style of the cross. Jesus took the heart of God, the Trinity, and fulfilled it in humanity. The nature of God is that of the cross. His nature is a redemptive flow to others, and is described as "Holy." God's nature is revealed in the humanity of Jesus and continues to flow through Him as He rules the Kingdom. The Kingdom of God is the Kingdom of the cross style.

## God's Plan Fulfilled through the Suffering Your Sin Caused

The crime of the Jews in crucifying Jesus was carrying out God's purpose, which is an amazing mystery and an immense paradox! This was an extreme stumbling block to the Jews (1 Corinthians 1:23). God planned it; man is responsible and guilty of it. These two truths are laid side by side. We must recognize how important these two truths were to the Holy Spirit and thus highlighted by Peter. In his sermon to the Jews about Pentecost, he explained this. The cross was the meeting place of Divine sovereignty and human responsibility. Listen again to this verse. *"**Him** (Jesus), **being delivered by the determined purpose and foreknowledge of God, you have taken by lawless hands, have crucified, and put to death;"* (Acts 2:23). Now Peter repeats this truth in this exhortation at Solomon's porch.

The human mind cannot fully understand such a mystery. God had a plan for all eternity, yet His plan did not force humanity to act against their will. The prophets prophesied the sufferings and death of Jesus, and humanity fulfilled these prophecies without realizing what they were doing. However you reconcile these two propositions will be acceptable. But be sure each truth is equally present in your reconciliation. Peter makes no attempt to reconcile either truth; he simply lays each side by side as Biblical truths. He appeals to the prophets for the proof of God's plan; he appeals to the guilt of man for the proof of our responsibility.

When fully embracing each of these realities, our lives are changed forever. Jesus is the plan of God for our lives. Everything God wants us to have is in Jesus. I must embrace Jesus. In the abandonment of my life to Him, I find the fulfillment of the plan of God for my creation. At the moment I am confronted with Him, I realize my overwhelming guilt. I fought against this plan. I participated willingly and with fervor in His crucifixion. I am not guilty of just some wrongdoings; I am guilty of crucifying Jesus. My ultimate shame is not is stealing, adultery, or lying. I am guilty of crucifying the dream of God for my life, Jesus.

Peter extends a call to the Jews and to me. ***"Repent therefore and be converted, that your sins may be blotted out, so that times of refreshing may come from the presence of the Lord,"*** (Acts 3:19).

# Acts 3:19

# TURN

*"Repent therefore and be converted, that your sins may be blotted out, so that times of refreshing may come from the presence of the Lord," (Acts 3:19).*

The healing of a lame beggar was dramatic. The temple was buzzing with the news as a large crowd gathered at Solomon's Porch. When Jesus moves on a scene, the spiritual life of all is revealed. A dramatic change had come to Peter's life due to Jesus indwelling him. Instead of Peter accepting credit for the miracle, he was deeply disturbed that the crowd even thought such a thing. His entire exhortation is focused on Jesus, the only Source. This crowd, gathered at the porch, experienced the revelation of their spiritual lives and Peter calls them to a dramatic change.

The second word in the Greek text of our passage is "oun," is translated ***therefore***. This Greek word is placed after a sentence or clause to express the external connection of two sentences, one after the other, or the internal relationship of cause and effect that one follows from the other. For our verse, each is probably true. In simple form, Peter says that what he tells them is based on what they have already been told.

Peter calls them to **"Repent therefore and be converted"** (Acts 3:19). He based this call on the content of the exhortation he had already spoken (Acts 3:12-18). Three elements form this base. We will now discuss each of them.

## Proof of Failure

Peter begins this proof with the truth most precious to these Jews. He reminds them that they are *"Men of Israel"* (Acts 3:12). This ties them to the foundation of their nation. The purpose in which their nation was established becomes their purpose. He further highlights this element by saying, *"The God of Abraham, Isaac, and Jacob, the God of our fathers, glorified His Servant Jesus"* (Acts 3:13). As *"Men of Israel,"* they pride themselves in being children of Abraham. This was their supreme defense in an argument with Jesus, *"Abraham, Isaac, and Jacob"* (John 8:39). The reason Abraham, Isaac, and Jacob are highlighted is focused on Jesus. They **glorified His Servant Jesus. Glorified** is the Greek word "doxa." It refers to a perspective that holds something in high esteem. Their forefathers were focused on Jesus. Abraham was saved by faith in Jesus; his salvation unfolded in a plan in which he obeyed by faith (Hebrews 11:8). In fact, *he who had received the promises offered up his only begotten son, of whom it was said, "In Isaac your seed shall be called"* (Hebrews 11:17-18).

Isaac and Jacob were saved by faith. *By faith Isaac blessed Jacob and Esau concerning things to come. By faith Jacob, when he was dying, blessed each of the sons of Joseph, and worshiped, leaning on the top of his staff* (Hebrews 11:20-21). All their forefathers were focused on Jesus. This focus was the foundation of why they were a nation. Jesus, the Messiah was to come through their heritage.

Messiah was not only in their genealogy, but was also in the symbols they used in their worship. The offering of sacrificial lambs, which Peter describes during his exhortation, point to Jesus. They gathered in families of ten or more to celebrate the Feast of the Passover. This feast focused exclusively on the lamb offered as their sacrifice. It reminded them that everything they had emerged from the promise found in this lamb. Their firstborn, land, harvest, family, peace and worship were present because of this lamb. Their hope was placed in the coming of The Lamb of God, Jesus. The Feast of the Passover was a focus on the Lamb, yet it was during this Feast they crucified Jesus. Their faithfulness to the symbols became their biggest deterrent to this reality.

The dream of God from the beginning was to form the nation of Israel through Jesus. In fact, the prophets receive this vision from their forefathers, generation after generation. Peter said, *"Yes, and all the prophets, from Samuel and those who follow, as many as have spoken, have also foretold these days"* (Acts 3:24). This vision was the fiber of their existence as a nation. Peter continues by reminding them they are the *sons of the prophets, and of the covenant which God made with our fathers* (Acts 3:25). How could they have not known?

Contained within the message of the prophets and the covenant was God's promise to Abraham. *"And in your seed all the families of the earth shall be blessed"* (Acts 3:25). They were the platform from which Jesus was presented to the world. Peter, in his final statement said, *"To you first, God, having raised up His Servant Jesus, sent Him to bless you, in turning away every one of you from your iniquities"* (Acts 3:26). The Messiah came to them first; they received the blessing from God first. What a privilege!

How did they respond to this? Although *the God of Abraham, Isaac, and Jacob, the God of our fathers, glorified His Servant Jesus, whom you delivered up and denied* Him *in the presence of Pilate, when he was determined to let Him go* (Acts 3:13). This group denied *the Holy One and the Just* (Acts 3:14). The denial was not simply an act of disinterest, but was rebellious and aggressive. They *asked for a murderer to be granted* to them (Acts 3:14). The contrast is startling. They preferred the criminal, Barabbas, to Jesus, the Dream of God. The *Prince of life* was crucified by their desire. This is a strong description of how they treated the fulfillment of the plan to which God called them. Their guilt is not questioned!

Any feelings of superiority must not arise in us. Any sense of judgment will come back to condemn us. We are as guilty of the crucifixion of Jesus as they were. As God included them in His plan, so He has included us. As the prophets proclaimed this message to the Jews, hundreds of messengers have brought the message to us. We live in a day far superior to the Old Testament hour. The Holy Spirit was released on us in the New Covenant and it was far beyond what they could have ever imagined. Through the provision of Jesus, prevenient grace reveals truth beyond all comprehension. If they rejected Jesus, in our superior position we reject Him more. If they are guilty, we must hang our heads in abundant shame. We have surpassed them in our failures.

***Therefore***, it is time to live in brokenness. "Repentance" must be the consistent attitude found in our positive response to Jesus. Perhaps you did not know the extent of your guilt. This full revelation of who Jesus is and God's plan in and through Him is possibly not fully comprehended by you. You may not have recognized how you have fought against His designs for your life. He moved through the healing of a lame beggar to glorify ***His Servant Jesus***. As He selected a moment of revelation for him, so He selected this moment of revelation for you.

## Provision of Faith

Contained in this revelation of Jesus to our lives is the "provision of faith." Peter does not leave this crowd in the despair of their failure. The Trinity God raised Jesus from the dead (Acts 3:15). Everything we have done in our failure is reversed. Every move blocking the plan of God for our lives is corrected. How can one so guilty begin to believe this truth? For the guilt filled mind, it

**Part Two:** Exhortation from the Porch

is beyond reason. Viewing the crucifixion, embracing it as good, and proclaiming it as victory, is not possible.

This is the wonder of Peter's statement. *"And His name, through faith in His name, has made this man strong, whom you see and know. Yes, the faith which comes through Him has given him this perfect soundness in the presence of you all"* (Acts 3:16). God specifically selected the most helpless among you (from their perspective); He demonstrated His forgiving and restoring love that revealed His true motive. Though you acted against Him, He is not acting against you! **His Servant Jesus** is glorified in this man's **perfect soundness** before your eyes.

Two distinct and important aspects of this faith appear in this statement. One is "focus on Jesus." These Jews had faith in God. They are *"Men of Israel"* (Acts 3:12). They readily embrace the **God of Abraham, Isaac, and Jacob, the God of our fathers,** (Acts 3:13). They can easily quote the Old Testament Scriptures because they have memorized it. The songs of their day are filled with the praises of Jehovah as He acted on their behalf. The feats of deliverances through the hand of God are celebrated in their annual feast days. They carefully train and teach their children in the Jewish traditions and faith. They do not lack faith in God.

However, they did not see Jesus as their God. They did believe in God as "Elohim," which is plural, but they did not see Jesus as a member of this Triune God. They knew the Messiah would come from "Elohim," but Jesus did not qualify. He was not the military leader who would fulfill their nationalistic desires. He was not a legalistic leader upholding their oral traditions. Although He might qualify as a descendent of King David, He had no royal characteristic about Him. Surrounded by the poor, handicapped, and needy did not enhance His image as the One who would deliver them, the Messiah.

Now "Elohim" had demonstrated in this beggar a revelation of Jesus the Messiah. The One they crucified reveals Himself, stimulating faith and extending another chance. They are placed in an undisputable position. How can they deny this demonstration? The lame beggar who has been at the Gate Beautiful for years (more than 40 years of age) stands before them because of Jesus. They must reconsider Jesus!

This is the consistent pattern of what God does in our lives. Most all of us have some belief in God; however, God consistently brings us to a revelation of Jesus. God is generic and non-evasive, whereas Jesus is personally, specifically, and intimately involved. God is creator and is over all. He sits in the sky and watches. But Jesus is here, and He is involved in attitudes, actions, and answers of life. God affects the weather, whereas Jesus affects my thinking. God oversees governments, whereas Jesus wants the ruling position in my life.

But let us not think this is an outward demonstration found in miracles. Something beyond the ordinary transpires in the inner hearts and lives of this crowd. The Spirit of Jesus moves in their inner beings to awaken each individual and reveal Himself. This movement is not the result of Peter's speaking ability or the psychological manipulation of a mob. This is an individual encounter with Jesus who produces the faith in them. Jesus promised the Holy Spirit would do this. He said, *"Nevertheless I tell you the truth. It is to your advantage that I go away; for if I do not go away, the Helper will not come to you; but if I depart, I will send Him to you. And when He has come, He will convict the world of sin, and of righteousness, and of judgment: of sin, because they do not believe in Me; of righteousness, because I go to My Father and you see Me no more; of judgment, because the ruler of this world is judged"* (John 16:7-11).

Jesus went on to promise that the Holy Spirit glorifies only Him (John 16:14). He takes all that is a part of Jesus and reveals them to us (John 16:14). The Holy Spirit brings us to a new realization of Jesus. This does not transpire because of an outward demonstration; we know from in our beings. The outward and inward declares Jesus to us! Paul came to this conclusion. He boldly proclaimed, **"So that they are without excuse"** (Romans 1:20). This proposition is based on **because what may be known of God is manifest in them, for God has shown it to them** (Romans 1:19). Is this not the reality of our state?

**Therefore,** it is time to live in brokenness. "Repentance" must be the consistent attitude found in our positive response to Jesus. **How shall we escape if we neglect so great a salvation** (Hebrews 2:3)? The Spirit of Jesus removes every possibility of misunderstanding, confusion, and ignorance. We are driven to reality! Indeed, we are without excuse!

## Progression of Focus

Peter allows a progression in their understanding and acceptance of Jesus. He is willing to give them the benefit of the doubt. **"Yet now, brethren, I know that you did it in ignorance, as did also your rulers"** (Acts 3:17). Being **Men of Israel,** there was no misunderstanding about a promised Messiah. All the prophets sent by God foretold this truth (Acts 3:18). This was done in the most understandable way. Speaking their language, and being from their culture gave them this message. The message was not given occasionally but was consistently made known throughout the generations and was the resounding theme of all the prophets.

The message was made known daily through all the religious ceremonies in their temple. The candles, the sacrifices, and the feast days all pointed to the coming Messiah. Their educational system revolved around this one event. They memorized the Scriptures proposing this promise. Everywhere they turned they were told of the coming of a Deliverer! This is a fact.

Turn | **Acts 3:19**

The difficulty seems to be in recognizing Jesus as this Deliverer. This demonic technique is nothing new. Causing distractions may be the fundamental of all of the devil's tactics. He wants to distract us from Jesus. If he can confuse us by camouflaging and concealing Jesus, he wins the battle. The distraction does not have to be evil. In the lives of these Jews, the devil used their traditions. They missed Jesus because they were focused on the activities that pointed to Him. We can easily become so involved in religious activities that we miss what is most important. How to pray, how long to pray, and the language of our prayers become more important than Jesus.

But Jesus will not leave us distracted. He moved on a lame beggar demonstrating His presence. This miracle formed the foundation for a message of truth delivered by Peter. This message, united with the internal working of the Spirit of Jesus, clarified the Old Testament prophecies. The message of all the prophets was now understood in a new light. The prophecies were seen as fulfilled in the sufferings of Christ.

This progression goes on in your life. The love of God moves the circumstances of your life to clarify His revelation through His Word. He will not allow confusion to cloud who He is. He will not permit the noise of this world to drown the whisper of His voice. He brings you to Jesus.

***Therefore,*** it is time to live in brokenness. "Repentance" must be the consistent attitude found in our positive response to Jesus.

## Acts 3:19

# REPENTANCE / CONVERSION

*"Repent therefore and be converted, that your sins may be blotted out, so that times of refreshing may come from the presence of the Lord," (Acts 3:19).*

The word **therefore** marks a transition in thought and purpose as Peter moves into the last half of his exhortation to the Jews. As previously stated, it signifies "the instruction I am going to give you is based on the foundation I have already established." In other words, the call to **"Repent ... and be converted"** is not an emotional appeal in an evangelistic altar call. The call is not the result of singing eighteen verses of *Just As I AM*. The call to **"Repent ... and be converted"** is based on the establishment of truth that cannot be denied. Not to respond by repentance to this truth amounts to the denial of reality.

Peter established three basic truths demanding the response to **"Repent ... and be converted."** One is the "Proof of Failure." Their attitude and response to Jesus is beyond question. They do not deny their willing participation in the crucifixion. They are responsible because they **killed the Prince of life**. Barabbas is free, and Jesus is crucified. These are facts. These Jews did this in ignorance, yet in this moment they receive revelation. They understand the prophecies of all the prophets in a new light. **God foretold** through them the sufferings of Christ. They rebelled against the Messiah they dreamed would come! They are guilty.

Repentance / Conversion | **Acts 3:19**

All this is in the context of the miracle of the healed beggar who now stands before them. He is the evidence of a life brought into *perfect soundness*. This miracle has been sourced by the One they so quickly crucified. *Faith* is the context of the miracle that is the context of their guilt. They did not have faith in Jesus and it brought guilt and destruction. The apostles and the lame beggar did have faith and that faith brought *perfect soundness*. Not only was the source of the miracle found in responding to Jesus by faith, but Jesus sourced the faith as well. He is doing this for those listening to Peter's exhortation. As Jesus sources faith in the Jewish crowd, the recognition of guilt greatly increases. This sourcing is "The Provision of Faith."

All this climaxes in "The Progression of Focus." Although they may have been ignorant, that is no longer the case. The Person of Jesus confronts them with clear revelation. The undeniable presence of His Person reveals Peter's exhortation and their knowledge of the prophets' message. What they did not know then, they do know now! You and I must attempt to place ourselves in their situation. Think of the deep, inner, sickening sensation at the core of their beings. This sensation is paralleled with the results of the sermon Peter preached to a similar crowd of Jews during Pentecost (Acts 2:14-40). ***Now when they heard this, they were cut to the heart, and said to Peter and the rest of the apostles, "Men and brethren, what shall we do?"*** (Acts 2:37). In our passage, Peter does not wait for the response from this crowd of Jews. He aggressively continues in the exhortation by delineating exactly how they must respond to the truth. He cries, *"Repent therefore and be converted"* (Acts 3:19).

The statement and context of this passage suggests several responses to us. There is the call to *"Repent."* Our standard definition for repentance holds true in Peter's call. This Jewish crowd must "give up a former thought to embrace a new thought." The Greek word "metanoeo," translated ***repent*** means, "to think differently or afterward." "Meta" denotes a change in location or condition. "Noeo" means to exercise the mind, think, or comprehend. What they thought about Jesus produced their participation in His crucifixion. They must now set that aside. They must embrace the new thought that Jesus is the Messiah! They considered Him a blasphemer, false Messiah, a deceiver of people; this must be rejected for the truth that He is raised from the dead and is the King of the Kingdom of God! They must move from their full rejection of Jesus to fully embracing Him.

In the context of our passage, Luke highlights the element of faith (Acts 3:16). The once lame beggar now stands beside Peter as a healed man. He is the evidence of faith. This healed man is what attracted this crowd to listen to Peter's exhortation. In fact, not only is faith in Jesus the source of the miracle, but Jesus is also the source of the faith. Our standard definition for faith holds true in Peter's call. This Jewish crowd must "invoke the activity of the Second Party." Jesus is the Second Party. Jesus is not the Second Party because He is inferior. He is Second because we invoked our activity first. Therefore, a change must take place. We must turn from our resource (activity) and embrace His resource (activity). This sounds a lot like repentance because each contains the same requirement.

A third response suggested in our passage is "**be converted** (epistrepho)." Two occasions are in the New Testament where "**Repent ... and be converted**" are connected. One is in our passage and the second is also in the Book of Acts. The Jews accuse Paul. He gives his testimony before King Agrippa. He assures the King that he has not been disobedient to the heavenly vision he just told him. In fact, He **declared first to those in Damascus and in Jerusalem, and throughout all the region of Judea, and then to the Gentiles, that they should repent, turn to God** (epistrepho), **and do works befitting repentance** (Acts 26:20).

The Greek word "epistrepho," translated **be converted** or **turn to God** means, "to turn from one direction to another."

Again, there is an obvious connection and similarity among these three responses: repentance, faith, and be converted. If you give up a former thought to embrace a new thought, you are converting or turning to something new. If you invoke the activity of the Second Party, you repent and turn to a new thing. If you are converting and turning to a new thing, you repent and have faith. Perhaps we can be technical and discuss the slight differences between each of these three responses. But all focus on embracing Jesus and allowing Him to be the solution.

Three connections are among these three responses. We will now look at them together.

## Combination

Man can never take sole credit for repentance, faith, or conversion, because there is an interaction of God and humanity in these activities. The source of each response is Jesus. Jesus as the source is distinctly highlighted in our story concerning faith. Peter said, *"And His name, through faith in His name, has made this man strong, whom you see and know. Yes, the faith which comes through Him has given him this perfect soundness in the presence of you all"* (Acts 3:16). The attitude allowing the miracle to happen is "invoking the activity of the Second Party." The ability to change from self-sourcing to Jesus-sourcing is given to us by Jesus.

Peter uses the Greek word "dia," translated **through**. "Dia" is a primary preposition denoting the channel of an act. Faith in Jesus is not stimulated by argument. Faith does not come from theology, and it is not a logical, thought-through decision. Although each of these may play a role in the activity of faith, the source of the faith is the revelation of the Person of Jesus. Jesus, Himself, reveals Himself! In His presence we find faith. Prevenient grace says that Jesus comes to us; we do not come to Him. If He does not reach out to us, we are without capacity of response. We respond in faith because He reveals Himself.

This is the repeated story of our passage. A lame beggar sits daily in the same condition and in the same place. His doom is sealed; he has no hope. What made this day different? Peter confronts him with Jesus. A hand is extended; a command to walk is given. The name of **Jesus Christ of Nazareth** is declared. The lame beggar experiences a new awareness. This man leaps to his feet in newness of life. He is confronted with Jesus, and he finds faith!

Finding faith is only the beginning. A large crowd of more than five thousand men gathers. They are all being confronted with Jesus through this healed beggar. The message is spoken and it is beyond words. They are drawn to embrace Jesus whom they crucified. Arguments do not convince them. The speaking skills of the apostles do not convince them. Jesus comes! Was the lame beggar healed to confront this crowd? Was this the purpose of his healing? Did a lame beggar find Jesus so this crowd could be enlightened? On and on it goes! The common element in all this is Jesus!

However, nothing is forced; no one is left without choice. Peter challenges the crowd to **"Repent therefore and be converted."** **Repent** is in the imperative mood and the active voice. **Be converted** is in the imperative mood and the active voice. Each of these responses is a command. The subject is an assumed "you." The active voice means the subject is responsible for the action of the verb. The people in the crowd of Jews must participate in response to the message. An awakening happens; will they respond? They were ignorant; now they know; will they respond?

We must understand that the participation of God and man in man's conversion is not either/or. Theological terms focused entirely on the action of God on our behalf exist. For instance, regeneration is an act of God when the principle of spiritual life is imparted to man, then the man is in Christ! Conversion consists of the response of man in faith and repentance allowing Jesus to complete His embrace in them. Therefore, conversion is both an act of Jesus and man. Men cooperate with Jesus because they are made willing and able by His Divine grace. Men of old rightly say that a preacher will exhort men, "Turn to God!" Looking back on the act, the convert will say, "God turned me to Himself!"

## Concentration

In each response, there is a final focus; it is Jesus! Faith is a focus on Jesus as the single source for all aspects of life. I am to live in the moment-by-moment involvement of His presence enabling me beyond myself. Self no longer sources the action of life. I am invoking the activity of the Second Party, Jesus! I no longer serve Him, so "doing a good job for Jesus" no longer applies. There is no focus on my faithfulness to Him. He sources a new thing in my life!

The heart of repentance is a new focus. It consists of giving up a former thought to embrace a new thought. Jesus is the new thought and this is evident in our passage. They operated in ignorance. Their ignorance was in the best they could know from their religious structure, culture, and training. They did not see Jesus as He is. Their minds comprehended only the level of their own thinking. In this confrontation with the miracle of the lame beggar being healed and the exhortation of Peter, a new level of thinking is available. In their former thought they were focused on their traditions, sacrifices, and religious structure. Now they are called to focus on a Person, Jesus. He is going to indwell them by His Spirit. They will move beyond the Law to the fulfillment of the Law. The repeated animal sacrifices will move to the fulfillment of all sacrifices (Hebrews 10:12). Jesus is the sacrifice!

The essence of ***be converted*** is a change in focus. The Greek word "epistrepho," translated ***be converted***, is a compound term from "epi" meaning "to" and "strepho" meaning "to turn." A double emphasis, strengthened and emphatic, is on "to." In other words, the emphasis is not on "from" rather it is on "to." Repentance has a focus on "from." One is giving up a former thought of "what was."

The writers declare this throughout the New Testament with abundant examples. The Apostle Paul is a dramatic illustration of this. He describes himself in his former days as a blasphemer, persecutor, and insolent man (Acts 26:11). How could he ever live with himself as an apostle proclaiming his new faith? There had to be a complete turning to Jesus. This must be why he spoke of himself and us as new creatures. In "turning to," something radical happens; it is beyond everything we once were! We are not being invited to just give up "the old;" we constantly struggle to keep surrendering and rejecting "the old." This is an invitation to embrace "the new," and in that embrace "the old" will not matter.

## Completion

Completion is something of the heart of this section. Repentance and conversion are not events anymore than faith is. Conversion is a consistent attitude of acceptance, openness, and focus on Jesus. Whatever is lacking in intimacy and oneness, and focus on Jesus must be completed. The completion is the cry of this experience. The lame man is brought into a place of ***perfect soundness***. This perfect soundness is not just a physical change. Scars, patterns, and thoughts connected with 40 years of being disabled also needed healing. Some perspectives were developed through the constant struggle in begging. The system of his life had to be reestablished in Jesus. ***Perfect soundness*** was far more than a removal of a physical handicap.

Jesus calls for this completeness in these Jews. The patterns of their traditions were deeply embedded in their lives. Their rules and laws were all they had to cling to for security. Jesus threatened their pattern of life and culture; this threat is why they crucified Him. If they embraced Him now, would He do any different? Everything will need to be different in this new Kingdom. Peter is not inviting them to a simple moment of forgiveness for a mistake. To **repent... and be converted,** the core of who they are will need to change. This change is no easy matter. Jesus will embrace the totality of their lives. Nothing will be the same again. Are they willing?

This call is to us as well! We do not mind some adjustments in some areas of our lives. A seminar on parenting is helpful. We can learn some tips on how to better respond to our children. But the call of Jesus is far beyond helpful tips. The claims of Jesus on our lives will not be satisfied until we are complete. We find his completeness is only found in Jesus!

Acts 3:19

# BLOTTED OUT SINS

*"Repent therefore and be converted, that your sins may be blotted out, so that times of refreshing may come from the presence of the Lord," (Acts 3:19).*

To experience the "Exhortation from the Porch" without realizing that God has a PLAN is impossible. We should not refer to it as a general plan; it is "The Plan," a specific plan. You are included in the details. You are not one of the thousands of participants. You are important to the plan and the intricate details of your involvement and His planning highlight your importance. He has calculated the number of hairs on your head; your fingerprints are unique; your DNA is not like anyone else's. You are a "star" in the plan!

If you desire to know the details of the plan, the PROPHETS foretold it. Peter's exhortation is filled with references to the hundreds of years in the past sounding forth the prophetic voice. Peter said, *"But those things which God foretold by the mouth of all His prophets, that the Christ would suffer, He has thus fulfilled"* (Acts 3:18). He continues, *"Which God has spoken by the mouth of all His holy prophets since the world began"* (Acts 3:21). He speaks positively, *"Yes, and all the prophets, from Samuel and those who follow, as many as have spoken, have also foretold these days"* (Acts 3:24). God intended these Jews to experience the fullness of the plan and bless the world with its fulfillment (Acts 3:26). After all, they were *sons of the prophets, and of the covenant* (Acts 3:25).

The message of the prophets focused on one supreme Person, Jesus! All the prophets spoke of the plan of God for Jesus the Messiah. Peter quotes Moses from the Old Testament, *"The Lord your God will raise up for you a Prophet like me from your brethren. Him you shall hear in all things, whatever He says to you. And it shall be that every soul who will not hear that Prophet shall be utterly destroyed from among the people"* (Acts 3:22-23). As spoken by the prophets, Jesus is the fulfillment of the plan of God.

The PROBLEM is these Jews were ignorant of this fact (Acts 3:17). How did they miss it? This ignorance is not discussed; the fact is they did miss it! Ignorance does not negate their guilt. They fought against the fulfillment of God's plan. They *delivered up and denied* Him *in the presence of Pilate, when he was determined to let Him go.* They *denied the Holy One and the Just, and asked for a murderer to be granted* to them, *and killed the Prince of life* (Acts 3:13-15).

What a dismal moment of gloom, guilt, and hopelessness. The revelation of truth comes like a piercing knife to their hearts. What they did not know, they know now! The age of the Messiah, the New Covenant arrived and they fought against it. The days of hope, forgiveness, and intimacy with God are now here. They rejected the One introducing this to them. Pilate washed his hands before this crowd. *"I am innocent of the blood of this just Person. You see to it." And all the people answered and said, "His blood be on us and on our children"* (Matthew 27:24-25). Is there any question of their guilt?

But God gives them a second chance. He desperately wants them to PARTICIPATE in His plan. To show His extreme desire, He demonstrates the power of the Spirit of Jesus now present in this new age. A lame beggar is healed; he stands before them. This crowd can participate as well; they have another chance!

They are called to **"Repent therefore** (give up a former thought to embrace a new thought) **and be converted** (to turn)" (Acts 3:19). The age of the New Covenant is here! They can experience the same presence of the Spirit in their lives, bringing to them what came to the lame beggar. What an opportunity!

Peter begins to list the benefits of experiencing the New Covenant. The first is **that your sins may be blotted out** (Acts 3:19). The heart begins to pound faster at even the thought of such an opportunity. In our state of guilt and dismay, who could dream of such a possibility? Charles Wesley, in his hymn, *And Can It Be,* pictures us in the prison dungeon. In our darkness and hopelessness a quickening ray appears, the prevenient grace of Jesus. We do not come to Him; it is too good to be true, but He comes to us. How can He possibly forgive me? I crucified Him repeatedly. I **killed the Prince of life.** I am being given a second chance!

We want to attempt to go beneath the surface of this statement: *that your sins may be blotted out.* I fear our religious generation takes it for granted; it becomes trivial, casual, and trite. We fall into the trap of "cheap grace." God forgives me; whoops, I did it again. God forgives me, whoops, I did it again. Sin does not matter anymore. It makes the consequences of sin, the crucifixion of Jesus, of little value. Woe to us if we devalue the sacrifice of Jesus' death. Peter focuses the voice of the prophets on **"Christ would suffer"** (Acts 3:18).

## State of Reality

In our passage is a definite attempt by Peter to declare a state of forgiveness. He does not propose an experience of forgiveness as a moment of confession. The Scriptures teaches us of such a moment. John wrote, *"If we confess our sins, He is faithful and just to forgive us our sins and to cleanse us from all unrighteousness"* (1 John 1:9). Every state of being requires an entry moment. The Evangelical Church calls it "being saved." Being saved is a moment of confessing our sins, and then we experience the witness of the Spirit in the depth of our soul that we are forgiven. However, this entry moment is only the beginning, the door into the room of forgiveness.

We must not view forgiveness as something we receive, as if it were a thing. Forgiveness does not have substance, but it is relational. Forgiveness is in reconciliation, two parties embracing. Jesus is not a supply clerk monitoring the distribution of forgiveness. We never have forgiveness as if it were something aside from Him. We experience forgiveness only in the embrace of His Person. He does not give us forgiveness; He is our forgiveness. All that divided or separated us from Him is gone. We are restored. Indeed, "our sins have been blotted out."

This state of being is not something established at the moment of confession or created in the experience of being saved, but this was a part of the message proposed by the prophets. This state of being is brought to pass in the sufferings of Christ. Although in the Old Covenant a sacrifice was required yearly for sins, Jesus came once. The author of Hebrews gives a clear picture of this. *But Christ came as High Priest of the good things to come, with the greater and more perfect tabernacle not made with hands, that is, not of this creation. Not with the blood of goats and calves, but with His own blood He entered the Most Holy Place once for all, having obtained eternal redemption* (Hebrews 9:11-12).

Paul expresses this truth. A provision is given to us in Christ. Provision is a location. God took every good thing He wants us to have and placed them in Christ in the heavenly realms (Ephesians 1:3). He calls them *spiritual blessings*. He highlights when this took place. Actually, *He chose us in Him before the foundation of the world* (Ephesians 1:4), not at our conversion or moment of confession. In fact, we are predestined to adoption as sons and made acceptable in the Beloved (Ephesians 1:5-6). ***"In Him we have redemption through His blood, the forgiveness of sins, according to the riches of His grace"*** (Ephesians 1:7). This state of being was formed *"before the foundation of the world." "Forgiveness of sins"* is only one aspect of the state, but it is importance!

Peter, in his "Exhortation from the Porch" tells us the same truth. ***"Repent therefore and be converted, that your sins may be blotted out,"*** (Acts 3:19). The Greek word "eis," translated ***that***, introduces a purpose clause. It has the idea of motion into any place or direction. Peter could have chosen a variety of words to introduce a purpose clause. In fact, he continues with additional purpose clauses in this exhortation. He uses the Greek word "hopos," translated "*so that,*" to introduce ***"times of refreshing may come from the presence of the Lord"*** (Acts 3:19).

Peter proposes that we should ***"repent therefore and be converted,"*** so we might be ushered into a new location. One of the chief characteristics of this new sphere is the blotting out of sins, forgiveness. Paul said, ***"He has delivered us from the power of darkness and conveyed us into the kingdom of the Son of His love"*** (Colossians 1:13). The Greek word "methistemi," translated ***conveyed***, portrays the idea of transferred. It denotes a change of location or condition.

This new location is an invitation not simply to experience forgiveness for a moment but to enter into a dwelling place of forgiveness. In this state there is no guilt; all accusations are gone. Peace flows within the confines of this location. Relationship and intimacy are freely experienced. Who would not want to dwell in such a place?

## State of Removal

We could spend hours reflecting on what is present in this state of being. Forgiveness, peace, relationship, grace, power, and wisdom are all found in Jesus, our location. But it is also valuable to discuss what is not found in this location. "No sin producing guilt" is found in this state. Peter specifically said this location is a state *"that your sins may be blotted out."* Do not allow the words *"may be"* mislead you. The Greek word "exaleipho," translated *may be blotted out*, is an infinitive. In the English language an infinitive usually begins with the word "to." It often reflects the idea of purpose or for this reason. An infinitive depends on the main verb. It maintains the same subject as the main verb. In this case the subject is an assumed "you," in the passive voice, which means the main subject "you" is being acted on. The Greek word "exaleipho" is a root word with the prefix "ex" meaning "out of." The root word is "aleipho" meaning "to smear or rub." The emphasis of the statement is simple. Through the sufferings of Jesus everything is put into place. Repentance and conversion bring the individual to Jesus, the location of forgiveness. In this state of being sins are removed.

There seems to be a couple of applications to this word (exaleipho). Paul wrote, *Having wiped* (exaleipho*) out the handwriting of requirements that was against us, which was contrary to us. And He has taken it out of the way, having nailed it to the cross"* (Colossians 2:14). This pictures the wiping of ink off a document. Unlike modern ink, in Paul's day ink had no acid content. It remained on the surface and did not penetrate the papyrus or vellum used for documents. It could easily be wiped away with a damp sponge. Jesus penetrates the depth of sin and completely wipes it away. Our sins are gone beyond the possibility of review or recall.

The imagery is also used in the business world. When debtors pay their debt, the practice of creditors canceling or removing the record of the debt is expressed in "exaleipho." It properly refers to writing on tables covered with wax, and then by inverting the stylus, or instrument of writing, smoothing the wax again. It removes every trace of the record. In each of these pictures there is the idea of removal. Sin is seen as something that needs to be removed. Although we do not want to fall into the trap of seeing sin as having substance and being removed like a bad tooth, we embrace the picture of Jesus removing every obstacle stopping us from having relationship with Him!

Think of the circumstances created by the sins of this crowd of Jews. They fought against the plan of God as foretold through the prophets. They **killed the Prince of life**. Their guilt is immense. Yet all sin, despite how small it might be considered, paints this picture. We have fought against the redemptive plan of God, which is the greatest of all miracles. We took His plan and nailed it to the cross. Our rebellion is the means of our redemption. Only God can do this! We caused Christ to suffer; the prophets foretell the suffering of Christ as the plan for our redemption (Acts 3:18). How can it be?

# State of Relationship

There seems to be a purpose in a purpose. Peter makes a strong call, an imperative. *"Repent therefore and be converted."* The main purpose clause follows immediately, *"that your sins may be blotted out."* He calls this crowd of Jews into a "state of being." This "call" applies directly to our personal lives as well! Forgiveness is the state of being in which we dwell; it is not just an experience to remember. In this state of being your **sins** are missing. They are erased along with all the guilt. This seems to be the major purpose in Peter's exhortation. This Jewish crowd is directly responsible for Jesus' death. By the sufferings of Christ, which they caused, their sin of crucifying Him is **blotted out**. God takes the act of your disobedience and rebellion and makes it the way He redeems you.

The purpose in the purpose of all this is then quoted to us. *"So that times of refreshing may come from the presence of*

***the Lord,"*** (Acts 3:19). Understanding this thought will require a complete study, but I want to introduce you to it now. The "state of being" into which he calls us is relationship. The message is that the One we crucified is risen from the dead. Everything we did to Him is reversed (Acts 3:15). We must now embrace Him, as we should have first. I know it is overwhelming. God places us back at the beginning through forgiveness. We can embrace Him in intimacy.

Peter speaks out of his experience. He was not faithful. He denied Jesus three times in the night hours. He is as guilty as the Jews who crucified Jesus. Some might say that he is worse; he was a disciple and knew what these Jews did not know. But the resurrected Lord came after him. Time and again, Jesus called him in to the same place he was before the denial. Now he is filled with the Spirit of Jesus proclaiming the possibility of living in the refreshing presence of Jesus. Jesus is our forgiveness! He embraces us in this moment, and there is only one proper response. ***Repent therefore and be converted.***

## Acts 3:19

# A REFRESHING PRESENCE

*"Repent therefore and be converted, that your sins may be blotted out, so that times of refreshing may come from the presence of the Lord," (Acts 3:19).*

Thousands of Jewish men and women are gathered at Solomon's Porch. The gathering is an unprecedented demonstration of the power and presence of their God. As certainly as God came down on Mount Sinai in thunder and lightning, so He appears in the Temple. He demonstrates Himself through the lame beggar now **walking, leaping, and praising God** (Acts 3:8). He demonstrates Himself through faith. This miracle was accomplished **through faith in His name** (Acts 3:16). Peter and the lame beggar are "invoking the activity of the Second Party!" In fact, the presence of faith is demonstrating His presence; this **faith ... comes through Him** (Acts 3:16).

Peter is demonstrating the presence of God. He lives a testimony of forgiveness, reconciliation, and filling. Pentecost, the outside God coming inside, is demonstrated through Peter's exhortation. The conviction and awakening experienced by this Jewish crowd testifies of His presence. Jesus is alive in this moment; He makes Himself known and felt! This demonstration is laid on the foundation of the Old Testament prophets. **All His prophets** spoke the wonders of this Presence. In fact, everything God foretold through them concerning Jesus, **He has thus**

***fulfilled*** (Acts 3:18). Although they may have crucified Jesus in ignorance, they know now. Revelation left them speechless.

The only thing to do is turn from previous thoughts and actions toward Jesus and embrace Him; it is their only chance. They accused Him of being a blasphemer; they must listen to everything He says; He is the Truth. They crucified Him for being a "false Messiah;" they must bow at his feet as the One sent from God, their Savior. They wanted His death because He broke the Law of God. They must acclaim Him as the fulfillment of the Law. They clung to animal sacrifices; they must now know Him as their only sacrifice. This new thinking is the total turning, **be converted**. They must **repent**, giving up a former thought to embrace a new thought.

In this new reality, there are two purpose clauses. Embracing Jesus instead of rejecting Jesus plants you in a new place. Brace yourself for a radical shift in your life! Things will automatically be different for you. If you do not want to change, keep your attitude of rebellion, legalism, and crucifixion. Turning to Jesus whom you crucified will place you in a flood of newness you cannot contain. Get ready!

**"Your sins may be blotted out,"** (Acts 3:19). Everything involved in your rejection of Jesus will be forgiven in your repentance. Forgiveness is not something that happens in an experience, or something that takes place as an event that you remember from time to time. Forgiveness is a state of being in which you dwell. In this state of being, all guilt is removed. You live blameless before God. In this state of being your actual sins disappear; the record of sin in the past is removed and the sin of the present is cleansed. You are no longer in bondage! In this state of being you embrace relationship with Jesus. In this relationship of oneness with Him, all we have just described happens.

**"So that times of refreshing may come from the presence of the Lord"** (Acts 3:19). This verse segment is the second purpose clause. It describes the relationship of oneness found in ***your***

*sins may be blotted out*. His embrace removes your sins, and your sins are removed so He can embrace you. We find all this *in the presence of the Lord*.

## Agency of Repentance
"so that"

***Repent therefore and be converted*** is the agency by which the presence of Jesus is experienced. Repentance is "giving up a former thought to embrace a new thought." Conversion is "turning to." The sins of these Jews were contained in how they treated Jesus. Peter's discussion was only the crucifixion. He was not concerned about any of their other activities. They rejected Jesus. No sins are outside of this context. Now they must turn to Jesus; they must reverse everything they thought, felt and did toward Him. They must turn from their rejection of Him and embrace Him.

This embrace of Jesus brings them into a new location, ***"that*** (eis) *your sins may be blotted out."* "Eis" is a primary proposition meaning "into." God bringing them into a new state of existence through repentance and conversion is strongly emphasized. "Repent therefore and be converted" is for bringing the individual into a new location. Jesus is the new location. We highlighted this in our previous studies, but it cannot be overstated. The removal of sins is not an experience or event; it is a relationship. We are placed in Jesus where we have no sin or guilt. As He sources our lives, we experience the opposite of self-sourcing, which is the heart of sin.

Once brought into this new location, we come to the second purpose clause. Peter introduces this clause different from the first. Instead of "eis," meaning a change in location, he says, ***"so that"*** (hopos). Some have translated this Greek word "when," but this translation is a bit misleading. It would indicate a time element rather than a distinct purpose. This Greek word (hopos) is found only with the subjunctive verb; it indicates the final purpose, to the end that, or in order that. If this is the "final purpose," the remaining portion of the sentence would be viewed as a continuation of this second purpose. Peter said, *"And that He may send Jesus Christ, who was preached to you before, whom heaven must receive until the times of restoration of all things, which God has spoken by the mouth of all His holy prophets since the world began."* (Acts 3:20-21). The final purpose is found in complete saturation and intimacy with Jesus!

In other words, we must respond to the convicting of the Holy Spirit by repenting and turning to Jesus. This response will move us into a new location, the heart of Jesus. We move from the state of rebellion to the state of embracing. Resistance becomes acceptance. The "lie" becomes the "Truth!" What more could we want? Now we belong to Jesus, and He belongs to us!

## Age of Opportunity
### "times"

There is an interesting element is in this state and is difficult to articulate; therefore, I ask you to think carefully. If this emphasis is found only in the definition of times, it can be dismissed or at least overlooked. However, there are two other ways it is promoted in the text. The subject of *times* is introduced with the Greek word "an," a primary particle normally not expressed in the English translation. If it were translated it would be rendered "perhaps" giving the statement a stamp of uncertainty and mere possibility. It indicates a total dependency on the circumstances. It denotes a supposition, wish, possibility, or uncertainty. It modifies or strengthens the influence of the subjunctive aspect of the verb.

The second promotion of this idea in the text is found in

the subjunctive verb *may come*. The subjunctive mood presents an uncertainty or a possibility, but there is no way to guarantee it. In our passage, Peter wishes it to be true. Everything Jesus provides says that it should be true. Everything is in place for this to be possible. But the uncertainty is present. This element in our passage bothers me. I would like to remove it, however, Peter strongly emphasizes it.

The third emphasis of this as found in our passage is in the Greek word "kairos," translated *times*. No English word equivalent to this Greek word makes it difficult to translate in the English language. It presents a definite period of opportunity, but it is not merely a succession of minutes or a passing of time. "Kairos" must be understood in connection with "chronos," length. "Kairos" is favorable opportunity. In our passage, *times* becomes the opportune time to embrace Jesus.

This approach to the presence of Jesus places such an opportunity of His presence in a different category. One must not take it for granted. If I repent and turn to Jesus, I will receive His presence. I can receive it as a fact; I do not need to think of it again. Embracing Him is a common element in my life like breathing that is automatic. Although this may be true, it is not the approach of our passage. The presence of Jesus is of such magnitude it will not allow such a thought. His presence creates a hunger and thirst; we are continually craving and desiring. The cry of the Beatitudes is ***"Blessed are those who hunger and thirst for righteousness, for they shall be filled"*** (Matthew 5:6). His presence fills us and immediately creates a hunger and thirst for more. We must never settle or take it for granted. A continual awareness of the vastness of His presence calling us to a greater experience must be. His presence is an opportune moment giving way to another opportune moment only to call us to another opportune moment.

## Air of Refreshment
"times of refreshing"

These Jews are described as *"all you who labor and are heavy laden"* (Matthew 11:28). In seeing them Jesus **was moved with compassion for them, because they were weary and scattered, like sheep having no shepherd** (Matthew 9:36). There verses are a picture of exhaustion; it is a long journey with no resting place in sight. Peter proposes the opportune time to this group for *refreshing* (anapsuxis). It means properly "breathing" or "refreshment" after being heated from labor, running, or exhausting activity. It carries with it the idea of "rest," and is used only twice in the New Testament.

This experience is explained with other images. Paul said, **"And you He made alive, who were dead in trespasses and sins"** (Ephesians 2:1-2). The imagery of "death to life" is used consistently throughout the New Testament. John used a great image when he said, **"But if we walk in the light as He is in the light, we have fellowship with one another, and the blood of Jesus Christ His Son cleanses us from all sin"** (1 John 1:7). The light transforms the fear and the danger of darkness! His blood cleanses the filth of our world! We live in the sensation of such an experience!

What a beautiful description of how Jesus affects the human life when He fills it! He comes to us like a fresh artesian well refreshing us in our weariness. He comes like a cool breeze bathing us in a sense of refreshment in the heat of the day. His presence is like lifting of the burden carried on our shoulders. Embracing Him is like stepping from a dungeon cell after years of being without light. Living in Him is like coming home! I belong here. What a moment!

In the early days of ministry, I was consistently warned by more experienced ministers against the possibility of burnout.

Part Two: Exhortation from the Porch

The message was an encouragement for me to pace myself for the long haul. I have become convinced that the single deterrent to burnout is found in Jesus' *refreshing* presence. How can someone say they find Jesus' constant companionship the energy boost for their soul and simultaneously say they are burned out from ministry? Self-sourced ministry soon becomes discouraging and disappointing. Results never measure as large as the effort we think we have invested. But Spirit-sourced ministry is an unfolding adventure of investigating the movement and expansion of His Divine Presence. Jesus is the moment by moment *refreshing* of my spirit!

Oh! The Presence of Jesus! Is He not enough to refresh the soul? Peter is not referring to a *refreshing* that comes and goes. He highlights the opportune moment we enter into intimacy with Jesus who is more than adequate to all life. He blots out our sins and brings the fullness of His embrace, which continually refreshes us! Jesus does not rescue us from a difficult moment to leave us. We live in the consistent flow of His sourcing that brings the *refreshing* of His Spirit into our lives.

## Available to All
### "may come"

Our passage, *"so that times of refreshing may come from the presence of the Lord"* (Acts 3:19), as translated might be misleading. You might consider this in the future tense. Thus, Peter would be saying that **repent therefore and be converted** so your sins may be blotted out (present tense) and in the future there will be times of *refreshing*. However, this is not the case. **That your sins may be blotted out** and **times of refreshing may come** have verbs in the aorist tense, the non-tense. The emphasis is placed on the act occurring rather than on when it is done.

We discovered that this verb is in the subjunctive mood,

giving the sense of uncertainty. A guarantee this blotting or refreshing will happen in the lives of this crowd of Jews does not exist. Peter wishes it would, but he cannot be for certain. Will they sincerely repent and be converted? It is available to all who will be left without His presence. Within the structure of our passage, there are no restrictions or qualifications on those who **repent therefore and be converted**. In other words, we must interpret the word *may* as meaning in the realm of possibilities. Peter urges everyone to experience this **refreshing**; no one needs to be left out.

## Appearance of the Lord
"from the presence of the Lord"

The Greek word "prosopon," translated presence, is a compound word. "Pros" expresses the idea of toward. "Opon" indicates the eye or face, literally the area around the eye. Our refreshment comes from the very face, countenance, or eye of Jesus. He draws so close to us that we are in His face! He is not blessing us from afar. He has not sent us a note. A messenger has not delivered the package of refreshment. Angels are not substituted for Him. He comes Himself; He is the refreshment of the soul.

Has there ever been a greater invitation extended to humanity? Change your mind about Jesus and you will be embraced by His intimate presence. He will cleanse and remove your guilt; the sin that created the guilt will be **blotted out**. His embrace will give you forgiveness and refresh you. This invitation is an opportune moment to change locations. We never need to be estranged from God. To all who will respond in repentance, His embrace is available.

Acts 3:20

# A FOCUS ON JESUS

*"And that He may send Jesus Christ,
who was preached to you before," (Acts 3:20).*

We will forever highlight saturation. We must saturate in His presence and saturate in His Word. This saturation is not a need for those only who preach and teach. Saturation is fundamental for all who want a relationship with Jesus. Intimacy with Jesus is determined by your communication with Him. Indeed, He speaks to us. A prerequisite for saturation in His Word is all preconceived notions must be set aside for the fresh revelation of His speaking. We must not impose our theology on the Scriptures; we must allow the Scriptures to shape our theology.

We have spent many hours soaking in Peter's "Exhortation from the Porch," which is not a sermon as such but an exhortation. The passage (Acts 3:12-26) has two natural divisions. He establishes the guilt of these Jews (Acts 3:12-18). Their guilt is not contained in addictions, broken Ten Commandments, or lack of church activities. Their guilt is in crucifying Jesus; this is found in whatever their activities might be. Sin may manifest itself in a variety of deeds, but guilt is always about rejecting Jesus. The second section is strong instruction on the necessary response to their guilt (Acts 3:19-26).

The required response is ***"Repent therefore and be converted,"*** which is a complete turning to Jesus. The response is focused on the person of Jesus. The Jews rejected Jesus; they must now embrace Jesus with no hint of middle ground. Evidently, every spiritual change in our lives reverts to our embrace of Jesus rather than additional spiritual disciplines or adding another good rule. The response is about our focus on Jesus. Any hesitation concerning Jesus is equal to crucifying Him.

This strong call to *"Repent therefore and be converted"* has a purpose and is contained in several purpose clauses. Peter begins with *"that your sins may be blotted out"* (Acts 3:19). The introductory word *that* is somewhat misleading, because it is the Greek word "eis," which is a primary preposition that has the idea of motion into any place or direction. This word does not give us a focus of Jesus as the new location, which is where sin is removed. We dwell in a state of holiness. This state is not merely an experience at an altar of prayer, but a dwelling place in which we stay.

A second purpose clause is added to this state of forgiveness. Peter declares, *"So that times of refreshing may come from the presence of the Lord,"* (Acts 3:19). *"So that"* is a translation of the Greek word "hopos." It indicates the final purpose. We dwell in a state of forgiveness where intimacy with Jesus is experienced. This state is an opportune moment in our lives. His presence brings the consistent refreshment we need for living. His refreshing presence overshadows discouragement, burnout, and depression. Jesus said, *"I have come that they may have life, and that they may have it more abundantly"* (John 10:10).

This brings us to our consideration for this study: *"and that He may send Jesus Christ, who was preached to you before"* (Acts 3:20). A variety of opinions regarding this verse exist. Many Bible scholars propose this verse as a testimony of the future second coming of Jesus. The verse is tied to the prophetic thought of the repentance of the Jewish nation. Before the Lord returns, the Jews will experience a turning to Christ. Peter calls

**Part Two:** Exhortation from the Porch

the Jews to repentance so Jesus may come back the second time. Although prophecy may teach this truth, is this the essence of the verse?

From my saturation in this passage, I want to propose three basic ideas.

## Present Reality

To note the word *that* is not in this verse is very important. Simply read it as, *"and He may send Jesus Christ, who was preached to you before"* (Acts 3:20). *And* is a translation of the Greek word "kai." "Kai" is a simple conjunction and a primary particle having a copulative and sometimes a cumulative force. It starts a phrase that is not an additional purpose clause; it is a further explanation of the second purpose clause. What is the purpose of the call to *"Repent therefore and be converted"*? First, we are to enter into a new location, a state of being found in the Person of Jesus. The new location is a state of holiness, a state of blotting out all sins and guilt.

We experience this state for a second purpose clause, *"so that times of refreshing may come from the presence of the Lord."* The state of forgiveness gives us a wonderful opportune moment to experience His refreshing presence. He is our new location; He is our forgiveness; He is our victory over sin. His presence repels all sin: His presence refreshes us. He is our strength; He is our new source! There is nothing besides this. In other words, there is not a third purpose clause.

*"And that He may send Jesus Christ, who was preached to you before"* is a continuation of the second purpose clause, and part of the *refreshing* presence of Jesus. This passage is not about the second coming in the future as the world ends. This is about what Jesus wants to do in our lives as we dwell in this new location of forgiveness. We are not waiting for this to

happen; we must experience it now. He is the *refreshing* we are embracing in repentance.

We further see this present possibility in the subject and verb of each clause. **"Refreshing may come"** is the subject and verb of the first statement. **"He may send"** is the subject and verb of the connected statement. Each verb is in the aorist tense, subjunctive mood, and active voice. The subjunctive mood is one of uncertainty; it is a "maybe." We may experience *refreshing*; **He may send Jesus**. His presence and refreshing is determined by our response to **repent therefore and be converted**.

Because these two clauses are linked with a simple connecting conjunction and they have the same tense, mood, and voice, they are proposing the same idea. The idea is the present reality of the new location in Jesus. In turning and embracing Jesus, we experience forgiveness. Sin is blotted out. We are surrounded by His marvelous love and *refreshing* presence. Indeed, Jesus comes to us! His coming is a "present reality."

## Person Reality

Our passage makes it clear that Jesus is the One who comes to us. In the first phrase of the purpose clause, **"so that times of refreshing may come from the presence of the Lord,"** it is not certain to which member of the Trinity Peter is referencing. This non-clarity may be a moot point because the emphasis of the clause is on the *refreshing*. But the second phrase in this purpose clause clearly states that Jesus is the refreshment. The Trinity Godhead is sending the person of Jesus to indwell the believer. We find victory over sin in Him; we find refreshment in Him.

The focus of Peter on Jesus is amazing! He recently experienced the infilling of the Holy Spirit. Now, all he can talk about is Jesus. This focus is so characteristic of the Book of Acts. All the sermons and exhortations in Acts emphasize Jesus. This fulfills

**Part Two:** Exhortation from the Porch

the statement of Jesus. *"But when the Helper comes, whom I shall send to you from the Father, the Spirit of truth who proceeds from the Father, He will testify of Me"* (John 15:26).

In our passage, Jesus is described as *"who was preached to you before,"* (Acts 3:20). **Preached**, a translation of the Greek word "procheirizomai," is not a good translation of what the writer intended. The word is in the perfect tense and middle voice, which refers to something occurring in the past and the results continue into the present. The middle voice highlights the personal preference of the subject doing the action. The verb is in the participle form, which acts as an adjective modifying **Jesus Christ**.

The Greek word "procheirizomai," translated **preached**, is a compound word. "Pro" expresses the idea of "before." The root word of "cheirizomai" is "cheir," which expresses "hand." Thus, the idea of the word is "to cause to be at hand," and has the flavor of "appoint, chose, to destine, or to designate beforehand." Some have translated it "ordain." This Greek word is used by only Luke and found in the Book of Acts three times (Acts 22:24; 26:16). It carries with it the idea of a strong purpose. In other words, Jesus is appointed by the Trinity with strong purpose, and the title **Christ** means Messiah. Jesus is appointed, chosen, and destined to be the Messiah who becomes the new location in which sin is blotted out. He is the refreshment for those who **labor and are heavy laden.**

A strange twist is found in the *"Promise of the Father"* (Acts 1:4). In the Trinity there are three distinct persons. Each member has a personality of His own, yet they are One! Jesus ascended into the heavens, but He is present in the believer. Paul gives us the core of Christianity in the phrase, *"Christ in you"* (Colossians 1:27). Jesus speaks of departing and sending the Holy Spirit, yet He says, *"I will not leave you orphans; I will come to you"* (John 14:18). The Holy Spirit is the very Spirit of Jesus. Now Peter cries that the Spirit of God, **the Promise of the**

*Father*, is fulfilled with the presence of Jesus who was purposed, ordained, and appointed for us.

The call is to **"Repent therefore and be converted."** The response these Jews expressed to Jesus must radically change. Perhaps they were ignorant of the truth in the past, but not now! They must give up a former thought to embrace a new thought in Jesus. They must completely turn in a new direction, Jesus. A feeling of finality, completeness, and totality is in this response. How can they partially respond to Jesus? They held nothing back in the crucifixion of Jesus. Their whole hearts were committed to His destruction. Now the truth has come! This Jesus whom they crucified wants to invade their lives. This is not the invasion of a vague Spirit having no sense of character boundaries. This is the Person of Jesus who demonstrated the character of God before us. The fullness of the Holy Spirit is within the boundaries of the character and life style of Jesus. Jesus defines the fruit of the Spirit, and in Him we know exactly how to respond.

## Purpose Reality

Peter presents to us a distinct "purpose clause." The purpose has never been legalistic. God is not interested in the simple correction of activities. The keeping of rules is not what excites Him. The establishment of organizational functions is not His dream. The temple and feast days were never the desired end. They were always a means to the larger purpose in the heart of God. Even the accumulation of a large group of people applauding Him does not fulfill His purpose. Although each of these items may have their place, they are not the purpose.

Jesus has something so huge going on in Him that it shapes the future of the world. Peter continues in his statement, **"whom heaven must receive until the times of restoration of all things, which God has spoken by the mouth of all His holy prophets** *since the world began,"* (Acts 3:21). This subject will require an entire study of its own, but it must be noted here! As you read this verse, you are struck with the response of the Jews when they heard the Sermon on the Mount. ***The people were astonished at His teachings*** (Matthew 7:28). It means, "knocked out of their senses." Who can comprehend the fullness of what is said?

Evidently this was the purpose from the "start of all things." ***"God has spoken by the mouth of all His holy prophets since the world began"*** (Acts 3:21). This is not a recent desire of God. Things did not get increasingly worse; therefore, God was forced to do something about the situation. The population of humanity did not increase until God was compelled to respond to the need. There has been only one plan from the beginning. God's purpose was fulfilled in the person of Jesus. God's plan was announced at the first sign of sin and is proclaimed by the prophets until Jesus is manifested.

The length of this involvement displays the intensity of God's desire. This plan is "sustained in God's heart." From the sin of only one couple, God began to burn with intensity. That burn for His plan has not increased; the level has always been the same. The Scriptures reveals one consuming plan of redemption, Jesus!

You must yield your life to Jesus. You must embrace Him and allow Him to embrace you. You must be intimate with Him in a moment-by-moment fellowship. He must become your life without distraction or deviation! There must be no distraction or deviations. Everything God wants for you is found in Jesus. Let Him be the boundaries of your life. The call is the same as in years gone by, ***"Repent therefore and be converted.***

## Acts 3:21

# THE TIME OF RESTORATION

*"Whom heaven must receive until the times of restoration of all things, which God has spoken by the mouth of all His holy prophets since the world began" (Acts 3:21).*

The flow of this exhortation is important and is all based on the physical expression of Jesus' activity in the life of a lame beggar. Jesus **"has given him this perfect soundness in the presence of you all."** The new condition is undeniable and undisputable. Even the leaders of Israel are dumbfounded. **"And seeing the man who had been healed standing with them, they could say nothing against it"** (Acts 4:14). Peter begins by establishing their guilt. That they crucified Jesus is a fact. Maybe they did not fully comprehend who Jesus was, but they know now. His appeal is to **"repent therefore and be converted."**

Then he introduces them to two "purpose clauses." These are a part of his appeal for their repentance. The first one is **"that your sins may be blotted out."** Although they are guilty of killing **the Prince of life**, he reassures them they will be forgiven, and it can be reversed. God reversed all they did by raising Jesus from the dead. They can be restored, forgiven, and reinstated. This is another chance. If this other chance was the only encouragement it would be enough to merit repentance.

But Peter continues with a final "purpose clause." **"So that times of refreshing may come from the presence of the Lord"**

(Acts 3:19). The Greek word "kairos," translated *times*, does not refer to a period of time; it presents an opportune moment. The verb *"may come"* is not in the future tense, but is in the subjective mood; it presents the idea of "maybe" or "uncertainty." This verb has the same tense, voice, and mood the main verb in the first purpose clause regarding our forgiveness. Peter refers to the opportune moment of responding in repentance. This response brings them into the state of forgiveness, the state of His presence. Jesus embraces them as He has the multitude of others who live in the fullness of the Spirit of Jesus.

*Repent* (give up a former thought to embrace a new thought) *therefore and be converted* (to turn) is all focused on Jesus. He is the "New Thought" and the One to whom we must turn. We find forgiveness in a new location. Jesus is the New Location and His *refreshing* presence is experienced in the fullness of the Spirit! Peter adds a lengthy statement to this second purpose clause. The next two verses of our passage (Acts 3:20-21) contain this addition. It gives content and further explanation to the idea of His *refreshing* presence.

The first additional statement is *"and that He may send Jesus Christ, who was preached to you before."* We discovered this is not a reference to the second coming of Christ. This statement is a present tense reality giving content to the *refreshing* presence, and is a focus on Jesus. He does not give us the refreshing; He is the *refreshing*. The translation is a bit misleading because He is not *preached* as in a sermon; He is ordained or appointed for a purpose. In other words, this refreshing is an opportune moment when the purpose of God that we find in Jesus can be fulfilled in our lives. We must respond in repentance and turn to Jesus.

The next verse (Acts 3:21) is an additional statement that gives content to Jesus. Peter said, *"Whom heaven must receive until the times of restoration of all things, which God has spoken by the mouth of all His holy prophets since the world began"*

(Acts 3:21). In this statement there are two sections, and in this study we desire to investigate the first.

Much confusion concerning the first statement exists. Most Bible scholars lean toward interpreting the "**times of restoration**" as the second coming of Jesus. They involve the prophetic idea that the nation of Israel will experience a revival before this time. These scholars interpret Peter as calling Israel to repentance so the final return of Jesus will occur. The statement *"whom heaven must receive until the times of restoration of all things"* can easily be understood in this context. Jesus ascended into heaven; He will remain there until He comes again to restore all things. At first consideration, this makes sense. However, after saturation in the passage, the flow of Peter's exhortation leads to a different conclusion.

Consider the subject of the statement, a third-person-singular pronoun indicated at the end of the main verb in the Greek language. In our text, it would be translated "He." The individual to whom this subject refers is in the previous verse, "***Jesus Christ***." The main verb of our statement is ***must*** (dei). It has five aspects in its New Testament usage, but the undercurrent of all of them is the sovereignty of God. It declares in our passage Jesus Christ is under Divine direction. He "ought" or "had to be" because of the sovereign plan of the Trinity. A sense of destiny and purpose exists.

This verb is used with an infinitive. The infinitive is ***to receive***; it depends on and has the same subject as the main verb. It gives purpose and content to the main verb ***must***. ***To receive*** means "to take to oneself what is offered." The accusative or direct object receiving the action of the verb is ***whom heaven***. Further content to this statement is offered with the word ***until***. Something is happening until another thing occurs. ***Times*** (chronos) is a different Greek word from the previous verse (Acts 3:19). In our verse it is "a period of measured time." In the previous verse it is an opportune moment. The Greek word "apokatastasis," translated *restoration*, means, "restoring a thing to its former condition." The Greek word "pas," translated *all things*, is simply all.

*Restoration of all things* is a phrase used in the New Testament that refers to a returning, reestablishment of something lost. A focus is in the Old Testament of the prophets foretelling Israel's restoration as a nation. During the intertestamental period, such hopes became attached to the return of the prophet Elijah (Malachi 4:6). After the Mount of Transfiguration, Jesus told the disciples, *"Indeed, Elijah is coming first and will restore all things"* (Matthew 17:11). Mark, in his Gospel account, records this statement (Mark 9:12). With this as a background, let's investigate.

## Previous Reception

Let's begin with "The Origin of Restoration." Peter says, *"Whom heaven must receive"* (Acts 3:21). In our statement, *heaven* is the direct object of the verb's action, and it must be viewed as the dwelling place of God or the heart of the Trinity. Who can dispute the fact that God instigated this plan? The main verb is *must*. It rings with the sovereignty of God's will and action. The Divine plan spilling forth from the heavenly realms is one of restoration.

He has not given up on us. Generations of effort have continually poured forth from the *heavens* to bring us back. The disaster of the man's fall was complex and complete. It would have been so simple for God to end it then. One couple could have been sent into eternal damnation; God could have started anew. To what extent will God go to renew? How can He possibly bring man back to his original state? The histories will bring some knowledge giving answer to these questions. But the depth of the answer will never be comprehended. *Heaven* is determined to restore.

God will not let you go! His dream is not only for humanity; it is amazingly for you! Every resource of *heaven* will be exploited for your restoration. Your restoration is the only thought expressed in the heavenly conversation. Your restoration is the only topic of every committee. Your restoration is the prayer of the angels and the focus of the demonic hatred. It is the thrill of the Trinity. The Father is longing for the prodigal to be restored, the Savior is dying for his return, and the Spirit is wooing him in his pigpen.

Should we not discuss how far the Trinity is willing to go for such a restoration? How passionate is *heaven*? We find in "The Ordination of Restoration." "Ordination" is the act in which holy orders are conferred on someone. Has not Jesus been ordained by the Trinity for the task of restoration? From where do these "holy orders" flow? Restoration is the nature and heart of the Trinity! Without question all the evidence convinces us that the heart of the Trinity is restoration. God never intends to eliminate or remove us; He never holds us at arm's length. His intent is always to include, redeem, and save us!

We find restoration in the main verb of our passage. Peter said, **"Whom heaven must receive."** The impact of the Greek word "dei," translated *must*, is strong in our passage. The word is soaked with the passion of God's heart. This word states that the restoration is backed up by the sovereign hand of Almighty God. Restoration spills forth from the nature of God! His nature demands this; He cannot help Himself! For God not to restore humanity would mean the destruction of Himself. He is not against you; His nature causes Him to reach out to you. **"God is love"** (1 John 4:8).

What will God do to bring restoration? We must consider "The Order of Restoration." Restoration cannot possibly occur in *heaven*. Although it was birthed there, it must occur on Earth. On Earth is where sin was born; on Earth is where sin must be redeemed. Man got us into this mess and man will have to get us out of this mess. It will require a man IN the mess but not OF the mess.

In Galilee, miracles and crowds were the norm. The popularity of Jesus was strong; the leaders of Israel did not dare touch Him. But Jesus and the disciples came to Jerusalem, where everything fell apart. The Pharisees persuaded the crowds, and Roman influence was the strongest. They should have stayed away from Jerusalem. After the resurrection, the disciples fled Jerusalem and returned to Galilee, but the Resurrected Lord demanded they stay in the seat of their conflict! Things in Jerusalem could not get worse, but they found their solution amid their mess with Him present in His fullness.

He does not allow us to escape our problems. He did not deliver the Hebrew children from the fiery furnace; He simply joined them there. God did not rescue us by staying in heaven; He came to the core of the battle. His plan can only be fulfilled and instituted here! This is the message of the Gospel; restoration will not be given in *heaven*. He has come to us on Earth!

## Present Restoration

Peter's exhortation is an invitation for the Jews to participate in the present restoration. He speaks not about the second coming or the end of the age. He does not urge them to repent because of what will happen in the future; he urges them to repent for what they can experience now.

The heart of his exhortation concerns "The Origin of Restoration." It focuses on one Person, Jesus! This Origin of Restoration is why they must repent (give up a former thought to embrace a new thought). They were guilty of rejecting and crucifying the One who came to restore them. If restoration originated in *heaven* as it flowed from the nature of God, then Jesus is this restoration! If restoration could not occur in heaven, but must occur here in the mess, then God became man; He is here! What did you do to Him? You must repent and embrace Him! Jesus is your only chance for restoration.

The end times is not the discussion; it is a discussion about the restoration of your life. Your family, relationships, character, hope, and dreams can be restored only in Him. Your integrity, discipline, mind, and inner heart can be restored only in Him. He is your only chance. We dare not present any other solution. Jesus is the Restorer and the Restoration. He will be the One who will lead me into restoration; when I arrive in such a state, I will find myself dwelling in Him!

"The Ordination of Restoration" is found in **all things**. We do not understand how great the coming of Jesus is! I do not mean His second coming; I am referring to His first coming! He set into motion a complete restoration for all things. Nothing is left out of His far-reaching touch. His presence is changing everything from the structure of the world, nature around us, and the character of our inner lives. Nothing can escape His redeeming touch. He will restore **all things**.

"The Order of Restoration" refers to the actual sequence of events bringing us to this time. Peter referred to *"the times of restoration of all things"* (Acts 3:21). Again notice that the Greek word "chromos," translated *times*, refers to a definite period. It equals the phrase "the last days" that refers to the end of the age. This time period starts with the appearance of the Messiah, Jesus. This is why Jesus said, *"Indeed, Elijah is coming first and will restore all things"* (Matthew 17:11). He spoke of John the Baptist, His forerunner. John the Baptist laid down the pavement bringing us into the presence of Jesus, the Beginning of the last days. Peter proclaims the One they crucified as the One who ushered us into *the times of restoration*.

This means we have been in this restoration period for more than 2,000 years. One might say that it does not appear things are being restored. In fact, things are falling apart, and chaos is

**Part Two:** Exhortation from the Porch

on every hand. This truth is declared in the parables of the judgment in Matthew's Gospel (Matthew 25). These three parables say the same basic truth attempting to convince us. The main character of each parable is absent when applying the parable to the period in which we now live. The bridegroom is late to his own wedding. We are awaiting his arrival (Matthew 25:5). The man traveling to a far country gave his goods to his servants. He left them in charge while he was gone (Matthew 25:31). He is absent. The Son of Man will come back in all His glory to divide the sheep from the goats (Matthew 25:31). He apparently has been gone all this time. But the thundering message is He is only apparently absent. He has been here all the time working in the *least of these My brethren* (Matthew 25:40, 45). Will we, by faith, embrace Him now like we will embrace Him at His second coming? He is as much here now as He will be then! He is here redeeming and restoring! Will we be embraced by His redeeming, restoring touch?

## Acts 3:21

# WORD OF THE PROPHETS

*"Whom heaven must receive until the times of restoration of all things, which God has spoken by the mouth of all His holy prophets since the world began" (Acts 3:21).*

A realization of the total deliverance this message brings should immediately spark a shout from the depth of your being. It does not need to be psychologically induced or emotionally manipulated. It simply cannot be contained. We find clarity of the message in the simplicity of the message. The message is about one Man. Everything is centered on Him!

Our guilt is centered on Jesus. All sin is focused on how our deeds relate to Him. We **delivered up and denied** Him in the presence of our Roman rulers (Acts 3:13). He was revealed to us as **the Holy One and the Just**, but we would not hear it (Acts 3:14). In our rebellion and self-will, we chose ourselves, **and asked for a murderer to be granted** (Acts 3:14). Is there any doubt we **killed the Prince of life** (Acts 3:15)? All of our guilt is focused on Jesus. Every deed of sin we have committed means we participated in the crucifixion of Jesus.

But God reversed it! He did it in a split second by the power of His Spirit. The roaring life of the Holy Spirit in the being of Jesus conquered death. All to be experienced in the destruction of the eternal soul was endured by this Man! Death could not hold Him. **"Whom God raised from the dead"** is the victory shout (Acts 3:15). Is it that simple? Oh, the complexity we find in this simplicity is enough to engage our discussion forever. The depth of this one Man is beyond the philosophers of any age. Yet when individuals who have not thought it out embrace Him by faith, it is all known! Even a lame beggar is brought into ***perfect soundness*** by this faith (Acts 3:16).

It produces a call to ***"Repent therefore and be converted"*** (Acts 3:19). Repenting is the giving up a former thought to embrace a new thought. Jesus is the new thought and turning to Him brings me into all He is (Acts 3:19). He is a new location, a new dwelling place. The location is a place of ***"sins ... blotted out"*** (Acts 3:19). This location is a place of ***"refreshing ... from the presence of the Lord"*** (Acts 3:19). We actually enter into oneness and intimacy with Jesus. He was ordained and sent for this reason (Acts 3:20). We actually live in the time period when Jesus is restoring all things (Acts 3:21). We are a part of that restoration! What an opportunity! This time is an opportune moment.

Although all this may sound wonderful, how can I know it is true? Many stories, ideas, and theologies are proposed by dozens of religious groups across our world. This proposal is just one more of them. Why do you believe it instead of all the other proposals? We find the answer in the last sentence of our verse. ***"Which God has spoken by the mouth of all His holy prophets since the world began"*** (Acts 3:21). The foundation of all that matters is in this simple statement.

There are three parts to this message. Let us look at each of them together.

## Creation

God did not speak theology, philosophy, or systems of thought. He spoke to us "Jesus!" This is His one, single, and only message! The heart of our statement is ***"God has spoken"***

(Acts 3:21). All the creative force of His voice is in this statement. As we understand creation from the Book of Genesis, God spoke the worlds into existence. Whenever you can find God speaking, you find reality and certainty. You never find emptiness when God speaks. He never speaks ruin or decay. God speaks out of His nature; the results are always equivalent to who He is. **God is love; God is holy!** What do you expect His speaking produces?

The Greek word translated *has spoken* is "laleo." There are three Greek words that could be used. When there is no emphasis on the act of speaking or the content of the speaking, "epin" is used. When placing the emphasis on the content of what is spoken, "lego" is used. When the writer wants to highlight the act of speaking, "laleo" is used. Peter makes a strong emphasis on the reality of the creative speaking of God. The content of what He says is not the emphasis. "God is speaking!" Contemplate the wonder of such a reality. God is not speaking to animals; He is not addressing angels. In our passage He is speaking to us!

The focus of His speaking is **"Since the word began."** The Greek word "apo," translated *since*, is actually "apo" is the preposition "from." The Greek word "aion" used in our passage is in contrast with "kosmos." "Kosmos" refers to people or space, and "aion" refers to age or time. In our passage, the time period under consideration is the "time of the prophets" and is the time before the appearance of the Messiah. It highlights all God did in preparation for this final period. God spoke throughout the Old Testament leading up to the New Covenant.

Again, contemplate the wonder of God actually speaking to us. Let the wonder of His creative speaking grip your thinking. Attempt to comprehend; His entire speaking as revealed is about you. Does this not give you some sense of your value? The focus is not on what God says, but on the fact He is speaking. Peter is telling us God's focus by using the word "laleo." You are the focus of His speaking! This gives clarity regarding your position in His plan.

Perhaps this alone will not be conclusive, but will allow you to see it in the context of the message. Peter uses the Greek word "laleo" to highlight the act of speaking. In doing this he elevates those to whom God speaks. He also does this because the content of what God says is already clearly explained. The content is Jesus. Jesus is the **Word** (John 1:1). The Trinity speaks into existence *"Jesus of Nazareth, a Man"* (Acts 2:22). We see all that God wants through His speaking. The Trinity speaks to us regarding the purpose of our lives. Any attempt to say, "It is impossible," or "The standard is too high," is eliminated by the life of Jesus. Jesus proved the adequacy of the sourcing as spoken by God. This proof of Jesus was not revealed in the heavenly realms, nor was it a theory, but it was revealed in the history of our world. A validated and authentic record is given to us in the Scriptures. Therefore, the Scriptures become our visibility; they are the handle to grip, and investigative display of the speaking of God. The Spirit of Jesus (presence of the Triune God) and the physical record of God speaking interact together to provide the foundation of our belief!

If an individual decides not to believe the Scriptures as the speaking of God, there is no foundation for the life of Jesus. If the life of Jesus is questionable, then God's speaking is uncertain. If God's speaking is confused, we make our way as best we can. We are without a guide and live in uncertainty. But God is speaking; we receive this creative force. His speaking is "Jesus" as recorded in the Scriptures.

## Consistency

God speaks with amazing consistency, *"by the mouth of all His holy prophets since the world began"* (Acts 3:21). The Greek word "dia," translated *by* in our verse but often translated "through," is a primary preposition denoting the channel of an act. In our passage, "*the mouth*" (stomatos ton) refers to utterance, words, or the spoken message. "*His holy prophets*" gives distinction to the prophets. They definitely belong to the God who is speaking. This ownership is verified because they have His nature of holiness. The nature of God is doing something in and through them. They are set apart for His distinct use.

The number of times this word is used in the New Testament denotes its significance. Luke records the prophecy given by Zacharias, the father of John the Baptist. He was mute for nine months before the birth of John; it was because of his laughter at the angel's announcement that his wife would give birth to a son. Zacharias verified his son's name as John and immediately his speech returned. He was filled with the Holy Spirit and prophesied many things to come. He said, *"As He spoke by the mouth of His holy prophets, who have been since the world began"* (Luke 1:70).

Peter strongly references the prophets in his exhortation. Before our passage he said, *"But those things which God foretold by the mouth of all His prophets, that the Christ would suffer, He has thus fulfilled"* (Acts 3:18). Then Peter thunders into our passage. *"Which God has spoken by the mouth of all His holy prophets since the world began"* (Acts 3:12). He continues, *"Yes, and all the prophets, from Samuel and those who follow, as many as have spoken, have also foretold these days"* (Acts 3:24). His final convincing argument is, *"You are sons of the prophets, and of the covenant"* (Acts 3:25). Not only does Peter refer to the prophets but to their consistency. *"All His holy prophets"* are involved in speaking the same thing!

The early church is reported to respond to the threat of persecution by quoting the Old Testament. They begin their praise by saying, *"Who by the mouth of Your servant David have said:"* (Acts 4:25). Many other places record their praise; the language may be different but the emphasis is the same. The

Resurrected Lord appeared to His disciples. *"And beginning at Moses and all the Prophets, He expounded to them in all the Scriptures the things concerning Himself"* (Luke 24:27). He continued, *"These are the words which I spoke to you while I was still with you, that all things must be fulfilled which were written in the Law of Moses and the Prophets and the Psalms concerning Me." And He opened their understanding, that they might comprehend the Scriptures* (Luke 24:44-45).

In all these passages and more, there is an argument of logic that can be applied. Although not all the prophets are in the Scriptures, a crucial content of the Scriptures are the prophets. Jesus summarized the Old Testament into *"the Law of Moses and the Prophets and the Psalms."* The prophets verified Jesus. *"All His holy prophets since the world began"* spoke about Him. Jesus based His existence and validated who He is on the prophets of the Scriptures. Therefore, Jesus connected the message of the prophets to the Scriptures.

*"Which God has spoken by the mouth of all His holy prophets since the world began"* (Acts 3:21) gives us a strong conclusion. The Trinity God spoke *Jesus of Nazareth, a Man* into being. This event was continually spoken through *His holy prophets* as revealed in the Scriptures. Therefore, the Scriptures are the speaking of God revealing Jesus to us! Jesus, before and after the resurrection, relied on the Scriptures, the revelation and speaking of God to His life. If we are to embrace Jesus, we will do the same. If we do not, we have no basis for God's truth but our opinion.

Merely believing the Scriptures is not enough; we must bend our lives under its authority. Jesus allowed the Scriptures to shape and determine His life. He validated His life with the Scriptures. He sought the direction of the Father in the Scriptures. In surrendering to Jesus, I am surrendered to His Word, the Scriptures. The Scriptures are the speaking of Jesus to my life. To be intimate with Jesus is to be intimate with what He says, the Scriptures. I will allow my life to be shaped and determined by His Word!

## Consecration

The phrase *"holy prophets"* is an adjective giving content to the character and expression of the prophets (Luke 1:70; Acts 3:21; 2 Peter 3:2; Revelation 22:6), and it is used in the New Testament four times. In other words, they do not speak in obedience and are holy; they are holy and speak in obedience. The pattern of the prophets is never one of earning, meriting, or achieving a prophetic position. Prophets never offered a resume. God always selects them. No school for training them for this position exists. No common element among them exists. Involved in the selection, is the filling of the Holy Spirit in the Old Testament context of empowering for a task not the New Covenant filling. They become an expression of the nature of God.

The Greek word (hagios) in this context means "to be separated." In other words, the prophets were consecrated and set apart for the purpose of being the mouthpiece of God. They were allowed to speak only what God wanted. Balaam, a prophet, was offered wealth to curse the Israelites. His dilemma was, *"Look, I have come to you! Now, have I any power at all to say anything? The word that God puts in my mouth, that* I must *speak"* (Numbers 22:38).

Peter's exhortation is true for our lives! Forgiveness is ours! We must respond in repentance and conversion. Jesus' nature is a new location. We can dwell in intimacy in this location of His presence. We find everything God wants us to have in Jesus. His presence is the *refreshing* we so desperately need in our lives. The Trinity spoke into Jesus everything we need; there is nothing left to be done.

How can I know this is true! **God has spoken**. He did not

speak through angels, nature, or clever feats. He has spoken *by the mouth of all His holy prophets since the world began*. This speaking is recorded in the Scriptures. Therefore, the Scriptures are the validated speaking of God to our lives. To ignore the Scriptures is to ignore the voice of Jesus. All other methods of communication from God must be validated and thoroughly investigated through the Scriptures. Visions, dreams, signs, and feelings must all come under the authority of the speaking of God through the Scriptures.

I can rest in the security of the Scriptures because God speaks them. I can rest in Jesus. God through the Scriptures speaks Him; I can rest in Him. I can experience forgiveness, peace, and every spiritual blessing; they are all located in Jesus; I am in Jesus. This experience is certain; God in the Scriptures declares it! If God speaks it, will you listen and believe it? Do you know more than He? Is your wisdom greater than His? Has your plan worked better than His? His plan is Jesus; it is revealed in the Scriptures.

## Acts 3:22

# A PROPHECY OF MOSES

*"For Moses truly said to the fathers, 'The Lord your God will raise up for you a Prophet like me from your brethren. Him you shall hear in all things, whatever He says to you"*
*(Acts 3:22).*

After leaving Egypt, the Israelites traveled in the wilderness for three months. They settled into their nomadic way of life under the leadership of Moses. **They came to the Wilderness of Sinai** (Exodus 19:1). They camped before a mountain. The plan of God was to speak to Moses and include all the people of Israel. His purpose was that the Israelites would believe Moses forever (Exodus 19:9). Extensive preparations were made for this to occur. Everything had to be cleansed. Boundaries were established. Relationships between husbands and wives had to be correct.

After two days of preparation, on the third morning, God came. Everyone was frightened. **There were thunderings and lightnings, and a thick cloud on the mountain; and the sound of the trumpet was very loud, so that all the people who were in the camp trembled** (Exodus 19:16). As God drew closer, the intensity increased. Smoke surrounded Mount Sinai; God descended in fire. **Its smoke ascended like the smoke of a furnace, and the whole mountain quaked greatly** (Exodus 19:18). During this time the people said to Moses, **"You speak with us, and we will hear; but let not God speak with us, lest we die"** (Exodus 20:19).

**Part Two**: Exhortation from the Porch

All the other nations of the world had soothsayers, enchanters, wizards, diviners, and witches. They believed in a spiritual world and desired communication from it. The Israelites knew this from their experiences in Egypt. Moses came to Pharaoh. As Jehovah had instructed, **Aaron cast down his rod before Pharaoh and before his servants, and it became a serpent** (Exodus 7:10). Pharaoh immediately called on his wise men, sorcerers, and their secret arts. However, **Aaron's rod swallowed up their rods** (Exodus 7:12).

God did not want to communicate with Israel by this method. God's plan was to speak to the people directly. Involved in the structure of the tabernacle and the times of sacrifice, God spoke directly to His people. Even on Mount Sinai this was true. **And the Lord said to Moses, "Behold, I come to you in the thick cloud, that the people may hear when I speak with you, and believe you forever"** (Exodus 19:9). The Old Testament communication was to be a mere shadow of the real communication God would have with His people in the New Covenant. They would be filled with God; He would communicate directly to each person from within!

But the Israelites were frightened by God's presence as He descended on Mount Sinai. So God gave Israel "prophets!" The two verses from our passage are a quotation of God's promise to Moses for the people (Deuteronomy 18:15-20). Consider the time the Israelites experienced the prophetic role among them. Let's look carefully at our passage beginning with the prophet.

## The Prophet
"The Lord your God will raise up for you a Prophet like me."

The uniqueness of the prophet is highlighted by the absolute selection of God. No one ever applied to be a prophet. In the Old Testament, there was a "School of the Prophets." However, no one was actually trained to be a prophet (1 Samuel 10:5; 11:4; 13:15; 19:19-20; 2 Kings 2:32-5; 4:38). Unlike the priesthood, no prophet was the son of a prophet. The role of the priest was to maintain the temple and to see to the daily ceremonial functions. They were a tribe of people set aside for this purpose. Each priest had the right to be a priest because His father was of the tribe of Levi, but this was not true of the prophet.

Because God selected the prophets, there was no way to predict who would be a prophet. By God's sovereign knowledge, it was determined. No one could plot a pattern to determine when a prophet would appear. God alone understood the future of Israel and the need for the people to hear the voice of God through the prophet. That no prophet could speak unless God placed the words in his mouth was abundantly clear. He was to be sourced by God. It was possible the prophet would not understand the complete thrust of the words given to him.

Jesus divided the Old Testament into three parts: **the Law of Moses and the Prophets and the Psalms** (Luke 24:44). Because Moses is considered a prophet (in the first part) as is David (Acts 2:29-30) the Old Testament Scriptures could be considered a product of God speaking through the prophets. The "speaking of God" is the role of the prophet! Instead of speaking directly to people, God spoke through His prophets. This might be considered the downfall of humanity. We rejected the direct encounter of God to our lives because of fear. God allowed His truth to be heard through a prophet of His selection. However, it is much easier to adjust and compromise the secondhand message of a prophet than it is the face-to-face encounter with God. In speaking to the Jews of His day, Jesus said, **"Therefore you are witnesses against yourselves that you are sons of those who murdered the prophets"** (Matthew 23:31).

Jewish scholars throughout the years considered this statement of Moses to be a Messianic prophecy. Although Moses was saying that there would be many prophets provided by God, there will come the **Prophet**. After the death of John the Baptist, King Herod and many others thought Jesus was John resurrected from the dead. ***Others said, "It is Elijah." And others said, "It is the Prophet, or like one of the prophets"*** (Mark 6:15; also see John 1:21, 25; 6:14; 7:40). Stephen also included the same Scripture quoted by Peter in his sermon to the Hellenistic Jews (Acts 7:37). Jesus would be the final Prophet speaking the complete revelation of God to humanity. He would bring us into the New Covenant where God would again speak directly to and within man.

Within the context of our passage, the Law is emphasized strongly. Moses cannot be segregated from the Law. Peter addresses the Jews whose entire perspective on religion is the Law. However, according to Moses' prophecy, the final **Prophet** will pronounce a new law (Acts 3:23). This new law will be properly understood in the context of "intimacy." The instruction is ***"Him you shall hear in all things, whatever He says to you"*** (Acts 3:22). Even the punishment for not keeping the new law is found in the context of "intimacy." He continues, ***"And it shall be that every soul who will not hear that Prophet shall be utterly destroyed from among the people"*** (Acts 3:23).

Peter's exhortation points us back to Jesus. He is the very One we crucified. We must embrace this new thought and turn to Him. Our attachment to Him is fundamental to our salvation. Outside of Him and His communication we cannot live! Our connection to Him is in the context of being ***"weary, labor and heavy laden"*** contrasted with the ***"refreshing***!" We hear and we are refreshed ***"from the presence of the Lord"***. We are sourced through His "word."

# Parallel
## "like me"

The image of this relationship with Jesus through repentance is found in the history of Moses. The prophecy through

Moses says, ***"The Lord your God will raise up for you a Prophet like me!"*** The Old Covenant and those who participated is a ***copy and shadow of the heavenly things*** (Hebrews 8:5; 10:1; Colossians 2:17). Moses is a "type" of Christ. God established some significant characteristics and patterns in his life that parallel the life of Jesus.

Pharaoh wanted to destroy Moses but the hand of God distinctly delivered him. God intervened in the life of Jesus to deliver Him from the hand of King Herod. The angel of the Lord warned the wise men not to tell Herod the location of Jesus. Joseph, Mary, and the Christ child fled into exile because of the warning of the angel of the Lord. Each event highlights the plan of God and His call on their lives.

God called Moses to be the deliverer of the children of Israel from Egyptian bondage; He called Jesus to be the Deliverer of all humanity from the slavery of sin. Moses came from the wilderness after forty years to bring deliverance. Jesus was in the wilderness for forty days doing battle with Satan for the deliverance of all humanity. Moses participated in various "signs and wonders" before Pharaoh and in the wilderness wanderings, which demonstrated the power of God. Jesus did many "signs and wonders" that pointed to the sourcing of His Father. Moses was the instrument of God giving Israel the Law; Jesus was the fulfillment of all the Law. Moses gave the spoken word of God to the people; Jesus is the Word of God become flesh.

Although it is wonderful to consider all these parallels, they are not the focus of our passage. Our passage relates to communication. The Israelites did not want a face-to-face encounter with God. They were afraid they would die. Moses became a "type" of the real encounter with God experienced in Jesus. As Moses spoke the message of God and demonstrated it to Israel, so Jesus is the message of God to us. He is the love of God. Through the intimacy with Him, I experience God's love. He does not tell me the truth; He is the Truth (John 14:6). He does not stand behind

**Part Two:** Exhortation from the Porch

a pulpit; He indwells me through His Spirit. The fullness of the Spirit is "a new level."

Peter gives us the statement of Moses as a declaration of what he just described. He speaks to Jews who align their lives with Moses and the Law. He calls them to embrace the fulfillment of that prophecy. What was a shadow or copy is now the full reality in Jesus. He comes in the fullness of the Holy Spirit to indwell and communicate with us. Peter calls the Jews to much more than simply recognizing Jesus whom they crucified as the Messiah. They would have understood this prophecy from Moses. The new Prophet will be all that Moses was, only within the context of the New Covenant. He will come to live in them as an intimate guide. His law will be the whispers of a lover caring for His bride. Communication will be on a new level of the fullness of the Holy Spirit experienced at Pentecost.

No doubt these Jews present at Solomon's Porch were aware of the Pentecost event. According to Luke's description of the early church (Acts 2:41-47), those filled with the Spirit of Jesus have a major impact on Jerusalem. They had *favor with all the people* (Acts 2:47). The miracles continued through the apostles (Acts 2:43). This miracle of the lame beggar and Peter's message bring a moment of confrontation to these Jews. Will they move into the fulfillment of Moses' prophecy? The ***Prophet*** has come!

# Pedigree
## "from your brethren"

To include the various emphases Moses uses to surround the appearances of this new ***Prophet*** is important. He says, ***"The Lord your God will raise up for you . . ."*** The Greek word "anistemi," translated ***will raise up***, is closely connected with a resurrection of the dead. Moses may not have intended this emphasis but God who caused Moses to speak did! It must have rung in the ears of this crowd. Peter boldly declared the resurrection to them in his prior statements. After listing all the evil things they did to Jesus, climaxing in *"killed the Prince of life,"* Peter thunders forth with the reversal of it, *"whom God raised from the dead."*

Now Peter takes one of the most influential individuals in their history and highlights the resurrection of Jesus through his words to them. This proclamation was new insight into the meaning of what Moses said. Their Messiah went through the life and death experiences of speaking to them through history; He is not a figure simply of the past. Jesus is not speaking to them about their theology or religious practices; He is not an idea to be thought about. He speaks to them in the present through the Spirit. This approach is the New Covenant. He is raised from the dead!

The Spirit of God expanded the information about this Messiah through Moses. He adds the wonderful knowledge that He is one of us! Jesus comes *"from your brethren."* This presentation is not angelic deliverance; this is not merely Divine deliverance. This is the Divine who becomes one of us. This presentation is the lesson of the "incarnation." This radically changes everything about our redemption. The Messiah is one of us!

Notice carefully the word *from*. In the Greek text, it is translated from the Greek word "ek." "Apo" can also be translated *from*, but it points to the original location as close or nearby. "Ek" means the original location is from within. Our Redeemer is raised from among our ranks. He is one of us! Do you know how startling this is?

This means all that God wants to communicate through the Messiah is on our level. Jesus is not God talking from above; He is one of us; He speaks our language. This communication is not an angel using angelic language. He is one of us; He speaks our language. The writer of the Book of Hebrews uses the example of the Levitical priesthood. The high priest must be taken from among men (Hebrews 5:1). If He was not one of us, He would not understand, lack sympathy, and would have no grasp of our suffering. He has joined us on every level of our existence. He is not one of us in token. He is completely one of us. He is not one of us temporarily; He has become one of us forever. He is not attached to some of us but to all us.

Peter plants his appeal to the Jewish listeners within the context of the prophecy of Moses. Perhaps they do not accept the word of a fisherman who denied Jesus. Would they accept the prophecy of Moses? The Messiah comes **that your sins may be blotted out**. In the new location of His presence, there is no guilt and sin is cleared. Jesus, the Messiah, comes to give refreshing from dwelling in His presence. Will they "**Repent therefore and be converted**"?

## Acts 3:22-23

# THE PROPHET JESUS

*"For Moses truly said to the fathers, 'The Lord your God will raise up for you a Prophet like me from your brethren. Him you shall hear in all things, whatever He says to you. And it shall be that every soul who will not hear that Prophet shall be utterly destroyed from among the people'" (Acts 3:22-23).*

***"For all have sinned and fall short of the glory of God"*** (Romans 3:23). Millions of people have memorized this verse for use in evangelism. These words of Paul expose us all. We can never adjust, compromise, or escape this statement. The first word in the Greek text is "pas," translated ***all***. In the Greek grammar, the writers frontloaded their sentence with what was most important. The emphasis is on ***all***. No one is exempt! Actually, it is worse than it sounds. The phrase ***have sinned*** is in the aorist tense and active voice. The aorist voice focuses on the act of sinning not on when it was committed. The active voice means we are responsible for the action of the sinning. In other words, we are caught in the action of sinning, and we are responsible for this action. In fact, this indictment results in the awful state of ***fall short of the glory of God***. This verb is in the present tense, the indicative mood, and the passive voice. The indicative mood means it is a simple statement of fact. The present tense means it is the state of our lives and will continue to be so. The passive voice means we are acted on by our sinning, which causes us to be far below what glorifies God.

This must be understood within the context of the Law. Paul said, **"Therefore by the deeds of the law no flesh will be justified in His sight"** (Romans 3:20). This statement eliminates any hope of "doing" Christianity. We are all equally guilty; there are no categories in this sin. No one has fallen "shorter" than another, and there are no degrees to sin. This truth is exactly what Peter proclaims to the Jews at Solomon's Porch. In all their religious activity, they crucified Christ. They **delivered up and denied** Him; they **killed the Prince of life**, the content of all sin. Every sin is an expression of rebellion against Jesus. Whatever part of the Law we break is a declaration of our self-will crucifying Jesus. The inward filth of every sin is expressed in the deliberate destruction of Jesus on the cross. Nothing is better or worse than this. We are all guilty!

The call is to **repent therefore and be converted** (Acts 3:19). We do not resource or do this on our own. Jesus comes with His amazing grace. He reveals and makes known; He shows and draws. If we respond, we will experience a new location. In this new location there is no guilt and we are cleansed of all sin. This new location is for Jesus' presence filling us with the refreshment of life. Jesus, ordained for this purpose, will come and indwell us. We will find restoration for our lives. This restoration is what the prophets proclaimed from the beginning (Acts 3:19-21).

In fact, Peter verifies this by quoting Moses, the first prophet, one the Jews held in high esteem. Peter cries, **"For Moses truly said to the fathers"** (Acts 3:22). Then he quotes a statement of Moses to the people of Israel (Deuteronomy 18:18-19). In our previous study we highlighted the subject of THE PROPHET. A common belief was that the end of a long line of prophets throughout the history of Israel would conclude with the Messiah, **"The Prophet."** Peter presents Jesus as this **Prophet**. A PARALLEL between Moses and Jesus exists. Moses said that this **Prophet** would be **"like me."** Moses was the shadow; Jesus was the substance. Jesus would be the Deliverer, Provider, Guide, High Priest, and Word. But above all, Jesus is the Law. He is the fulfillment of the Law. His Spirit indwells the believer; the Law is found in the embrace of "*Christ in you.*" The amazing element of it is PEDIGREE. Jesus, the Messiah, did not come from without but from within, "*from your brethren.*" "*God will raise up for you a Prophet*" (Acts 3:22). It points to the resurrection. Jesus is not a prophet of the past; He is the *Prophet* of this hour, one of us!

Will we "*Repent therefore and be converted?*" Will we cease crucifying Him with our acts of self-sourcing? Will we allow Jesus to be all He intends to be in us? Moses in his prophecy outlines for us the position of this *Prophet*.

## Proclamation
"Him you shall hear in all things, whatever He says to you."

In his prophecy, Moses said, "*Him you shall hear in all things, whatever He says to you*" (Acts 3:22). One of the first noticeable issues is that the "Context of the Prophecy" demands progression. Moses communicated this prophecy in the circumstances of the Ten Commandments. Israel was going to receive her governmental structure in this same setting. This setting was the formation of Israel as a nation for a long-range purpose. This prophecy was fulfilled through hundreds of years into the time of Christ. The timespan and the number of prophets from Moses until Christ are overwhelming. Each prophet is used by God to contribute another step in the progression. The progression would not have been so long or painful if Israel had obeyed the message of their prophets.

Progressive revelation is one of the great principles of the Old Testament. God did not reveal all His truth at once, because humanity was not prepared for such a revelation. Therefore, God used the prophets to speak, each revealing part of His purpose.

Jesus is the conclusion of the entire revelation. The prophetic line comes together in its highest and best Representative. If any confusion was in the revelation of the former prophets, it was made clear in Jesus. All their pieces were united; a picture of the heart of God is now seen. **He is the image of the invisible God** (Colossians 1:15).

Paul said, **"But when the fullness of the time had come, God sent forth His Son, born of a woman, born under the law"** (Galatians 4:4). **Fullness** is a translation of the Greek word "pleroma." This Greek word means, "to fill as a container." Paul refers to a container as a period of time (chronos). God worked in the Old Testament through the prophets to fill the period of time, the Old Covenant. At the completion of this revelation, Jesus came! He is the completion of all God did through the prophets.

We must also understand the "Communication of the Prophecy" envelops "*all*," a complete revelation. We are to **hear** Jesus **in all things, whatever He says to you**. Unquestionably, Jesus is the One speaking; He is the One to whom we listen. The Greek word "laleo," translated **"He says,"** is focused on the act of speaking. The Greek word "lego" would be used to focus on the content of His speaking. In other words, in this statement of Moses', content of the final revelation is not under consideration. The emphasis is on the entirety and finality of the One speaking.

The Greek word, translated ***in,*** is "kata." This Greek word means "down." It indicates a motion from a higher level to a lower level. Whatever Jesus proposes, we should heed as the complete truth. The New American Standard Bible translates this, **"to Him you shall give heed in everything He says to you"** (Acts 3:22 NASB). The words ***in everything*** (NASB) and ***all things*** (NJKV) are a translation of the Greek word "pas" meaning "all, any, every, or the whole." The impact of Moses' statement is strong. Jesus, **the Prophet**, will speak. His speaking will be the climax of all the revelation of the past period, the Old Testament.

Whatever He says will be the complete revelation of God to us, and no indication any other word is needed. Nothing can be added; there is no further revelation.

Involved in the statement is all inclusiveness. The speaking of this final **Prophet** will encompass every area of life. In other words, Jesus is not speaking of religion. He does not specialize in specific areas of philosophy. Jesus is the complete revelation of who man is to be in every area of his existence. All relationships are clearly seen in His person. The business world must bend to His speaking. The arts must listen to His voice. Athletic endeavors must be conducted according to His dictates. Our finances and materialism finds fulfillment in Him. All our body drives must bow to His direction. The farmer, schoolteacher, student, construction worker, banker, fashion model, plant manager, scientist, wife, husband, child, movie star, manufacturer, taxi driver, and lawyer are all addressed. Who is not included? What area of activity and involvement is not contained in Him?

Matthew carefully selects specific miracles to include in his Gospel account (Matthew 8-9). These miracles represent various areas of human existence. He includes Jesus' physical touch when He delivers a man from leprosy; Jesus speaks the word and a servant in another location is healed. Jesus calms a raging sea, and He casts out demons. He touches the internal heart and soul of a paralytic man making him whole inside and out. Jesus reaches into Matthew's life and delivers him from the self-focus of materialism and power. He raises a man's daughter from the dead, and a woman with an issue of blood touches the hem of His garment and is made whole. He opens blinded eyes; He delivers a demon-possessed, mute man, and he suddenly speaks. This **Prophet** is the completed revelation of the heart of God for humanity!

The completed quotation from Moses says, ***"And it shall be that every soul who will not hear that Prophet shall be utterly destroyed from among the people"*** (Acts 3:23). This statement contains the "Condemnation of the Prophecy" which points to a final Word! Jesus is embraced as the truth or there is no truth. We are presented with two options: "**hear that Prophet**" or "**be utterly destroyed**;" there is no other alternative. This is extremely narrow in its approach. But this approach is not an isolated case. ***Jesus said to him, "I am the way, the truth, and the life. No one comes to the Father except through Me"*** (John 14:6).

The previous verse is a plea for you to be intimate with Jesus. You and I must know Him in His fullness. This is not about theology but about a Person. This is not about an adjustment in activities, but a relationship of intimacy with your Bridegroom. He is **that Prophet**!

## Purpose
"Him you shall hear in all things, whatever He says to you."

God had a purpose for the people of Israel when Moses spoke this prophecy. From the beginning God's intention was to communicate with man directly, one on One! Communication is the heart of intimacy. God did not want to belch out laws and have men comply as robots. From the creation of Adam to the redemption of your soul, His purpose is intimacy.

No wonder the "Command of the Prophecy" is certain. As you view the statement of Moses, "***you shall hear***" is in the future indicative, and indicates a simple statement of fact. The future tense relays something to come. However, in the Greek language, the future indicative, as in this statement, is often considered an imperative. This statement is not just a nice one for consideration, and it is not one suggestion among many. This statement is a command coming from the heart of God. *"**The Lord your God will raise up for you a Prophet like me.**"* Do you hear the love in this statement? God is not doing something just to get His own way. He is doing this "***for you***!" He designed redemption in Jesus because He cares about you. This kind of love and focus requires a positive response. This command has a great purpose.

The "Content of the Prophecy" is complete in a Person, Jesus. The purpose is not found in a doctrine, theology, in a set of laws, or ethics. The content of the prophecy is found in relationship with Jesus. This relationship is discovered within the boundaries of what He says." Moses said it, *"Whatever He says to you."* The Greek verb, translated *"He says,"* is in the subjunctive mood. Often, this means "uncertainty or maybe."

The uncertainty is not found in the occasion of His speaking. In other words, there is no uncertainty regarding the fact of His speaking. The prophecy is not "the Prophet may speak to you." If He does will you respond to Him? This prophecy is as sure as God is sure and is based on the sovereignty of His Person. He promises a climatic and final **Prophet**. This **Prophet** will speak to you. He will speak in language you can understand because He will be raised *up for you* and will be *from your brethren*. No one can declare that they did not hear or understand Him.

The uncertainty of the verb is found in the content of the speaking. In other words, what will He speak? We often go to another and say, "Will you do me a favor?" They respond by saying, "Before I say yes, tell me the favor." In other words, we ask the question, "What is the favor?" The uncertainty is in the favor. What is this **Prophet** going to say to you? He does not tell us. We already discovered the Greek word "laleo," translated *"He says,"* is focused on the act of speaking, not on the content. Our response to the **Prophet** must be, "Yes, I will hear and respond; speak to me!" Our response is to Him not to what He says. We embrace Him; we are intimate with Him; we trust Him! Whatever He says will be good for us. Of course, we will hear Him and respond fully to the content of His speaking.

Notice our "Compliance to the Prophecy" is childlike. The prophecy says, *"Him you shall hear in all things,"* and *"every soul who will not hear."* In each case, the Greek word, translated *hear,* is "akouo." The word is used in a variety of ways determined by the context. In this prophecy it focuses on listening and responding to the **Prophet**. Paul wrote to the Ephesians concerning submission to each other in family. He said, *"**Children, obey your parents in the Lord, for this is right**"* (Ephesians 6:1). The Greek word "hupoakouo," translated *obey*, is the same as in our passage with a prefix "hupo." This prefix means "under." Paul instructs the children to come under the influence of their parents. To simply do the actions required is not enough. They are to listen to, be influenced by, and allow their parents to shape their lives.

The call in our passage is for us. Intimacy of relationship brings a depth of communication that must shape our lives. It determines our attitudes, responses, and relationships with others. We come under the influence of the **Prophet**. He is the influential force of our lives. He determines everything. I must know Him more. I must be closer to Him. Peter's message is that the **Prophet** has come; will we listen to Him?

## Acts 3:23

# TO BE REMOVED

*"And it shall be that every soul who will not hear that Prophet shall be utterly destroyed from among the people" (Acts 3:23).*

When interpreting any Scriptural passage, the context ultimately shapes and influences the interpretation. Peter quotes an Old Testament prophecy stated by God through Moses. He did not choose Moses or this prophecy accidentally. No other prophecy applies to the Jews more than this one. No one disputes the prophetic status of Moses; God Himself gave him this rank. God spoke the words of our passage directly to Moses (Deuteronomy 18:18). Moses received his call to be a prophet at the burning bush (Exodus 3:4). He is accredited as the first prophets. Jewish scholars call him the "Father of the prophets."

The Jews listening to this quotation could quote it from memory. Peter was not the only one to give this abbreviated version. Stephen also partially quoted this passage in his address to the Sanhedrin (Acts 7:37). Even the Gospel writers alluded to these words many times (Mark 6:15; John 1:21-25; 6:14; 7:40). Although the exact wording differs from the Hebrew text and the Septuagint, the meaning is basically the same.

Moses said that God would raise a **Prophet** like him, and he quoted what God promised (Deuteronomy 18:18). God spoke to Moses face to face (Numbers 12:8). The Jews considered Moses the greatest prophet in their history. The Book of Deuteronomy

## Part Two: Exhortation from the Porch

closes with a tribute to Moses. *But since then there has not arisen in Israel a prophet like Moses, whom the Lord knew face to face, in all the signs and wonders which the Lord sent him to do in the land of Egypt, before Pharaoh, before all his servants, and in all his land, and by all that mighty power and all the great terror which Moses performed in the sight of all Israel* (Deuteronomy 34:10-12).

But as great as Moses might have been, Jesus is greater! He surpasses Moses in every way. The writer of the Book of Hebrews captured the truth when he wrote the following. *And Moses indeed was faithful in all His house as a servant, for a testimony of those things which would be spoken afterward, but Christ as a Son over His own house, whose house we are if we hold fast the confidence and the rejoicing of the hope firm to the end* (Hebrews 3:5-6). The supremacy of the New Covenant found in Jesus is beyond comparison to the Old Covenant started by Moses. The writer of the Book of Hebrews called the Old Covenant *obsolete* (Hebrews 8:13).

The PROCLAMATION proclaimed in Jesus is far superior. In our previous study, we discovered the "Context of the Prophecy" is one of progression. Jesus emerges as the climax of the Old Covenant. The content of the Old Testament formed the foundation for the New Testament found in Christ, and there is nothing beyond Him. The "Communication of the Prophecy" is stated as *all*. The communication is a complete revelation of all God wants us to know. In fact, the Holy Spirit will indwell us to guide us into this full revelation of truth in Jesus (John 16:13). The "Condemnation of the Prophecy" quickly reveals this completeness. Jesus is the only truth; there is no other choice. If you deny Jesus, you deny reality!

The PURPOSE of the "proclamation" in Jesus is plain. The "Command of the Prophecy" is found in the call. Moses said, *"Him you shall hear in all things"* (Acts 3:22). Although the main verb of this statement is future indicative, in the Greek language this verb is often considered an imperative. The focus of all God is doing in Jesus is *"for you."* A forceful love is motivating this New Covenant. In fact, the "Content of the Prophecy" is complete in a Person. The purpose is not found in theology, a doctrine, or a belief system but in the Person of Jesus. All the dreams of God for you are fulfilled in Jesus. The "Compliance of the Prophecy" is absolutely essential. We must come under the influence of Jesus and listen. This brings us to the final section of Moses' statement.

## Prohibition
"shall be utterly destroyed from among the people"

The "Contrast of the Prophecy" is evident. Moses reports, *"And it shall be that every soul who will not hear that Prophet shall be utterly destroyed from among the people"* (Acts 3:23). Our statement begins with *and*, translation of the Greek word "de." The primary translation of this Greek word is "but," a contrasting conjunction. It introduces the negative side (Acts 3:23) of the prophecy contrasted to the positive (Acts 3:22).

We highlighted the positive emphasis in our previous study. How important is the order of statements as recorded in the Scriptures? Is it significant that the positive is given first? The positive is the primary mover of our hearts. Some preachers use scare tactics to motivate people to respond to Jesus. They speak of wrath, judgment, and damnation, promoting Old Testament illustrations of destruction while by-passing Jesus' loving death.

To this day, I remember an evangelist preaching from a text found in the Book of Proverbs. Solomon wrote, *"I also will laugh at your calamity; I will mock when your terror comes"* (Proverbs 1:26). The evangelist painted a vivid picture of God standing on the edge of heaven laughing in glee and delight as damnation comes to my life. The tragedy for the listening congregation was the lack of a complete picture of the passage. The verses leading up to that statement tell of the immense love and concern of God. His counsel, His loving rebuke, His outstretched hand, His call, His revelation, and outpouring of His Spirit are all proclaimed (Proverbs 1:20-25).

Even in the Gospels we see this contrast. Jesus does speak of hell. He paints a vivid picture of the damnation of a lost soul. However, the only time He mentions hell is to self-centered religious Pharisees and disciples. In proportion to the love of God, redemption, and forgiveness, Jesus mentions hell little. If you preach on hell as Jesus did, you will never mention it to motivate surrender to Jesus.

Moses begins with a positive appeal. Think of what God has done for us! *"The Lord your God"* is such a marvelous statement. He is ours, and we are His! He is not a foreign god who fights against us. We are birthed by His power, called by His voice, and directed by His prophets. We are His people. *"The Lord your God will raise up for you"* is too much to comprehend. He acts on our behalf. He channels His power and wisdom for our benefit. He is not against us; He is for us! He does not plot our destruction; He plans our success in Him. *"The Lord your God will raise up for you a Prophet like me from your brethren."* No one fully understood the wonder of this statement until Jesus came. Even now, we barely scratch the surface in our comprehension of such a provision. He continues, *"Him you shall hear in all things, whatever He says to you."* If God speaks to us with a wise plan, why would we not listen? His speaking comprehensively includes every area of our lives. His guidance is sure; He always promotes our best!

Do not overlook the reality of this truth! *"Or do you despise the riches of His goodness, forbearance, and longsuffering, not knowing that the goodness of God leads you to repentance?"* (Romans 2:4). The Greek language in this passage is beautiful. The Greek word "ago," translated *leads*, means "to lead, induce, incite, or guide." God does not scare us, condemn us, or repel us; He entices, pulls, and woos us. How is He doing this? He does this with **"the riches of His goodness."** The Greek word "eis," translated *to*, is actually "into." He brings us into the midst of giving up a former thought to embrace a new thought. He makes it clear, presenting goodness, and offering love we cannot refuse.

Now let us consider the negative side. "The Content of the Prophecy" continues to be a state of existence. We find a positive and a negative in this state of being. This negative side is an old message for us; it is hammered out in nearly every passage we study. We do not deal with just an act that results in a consequence. We deal with a state of mind, the intent of the heart, or the motive of our soul. This condition is not the response of a moment, but the state of existence in which we dwell.

We saw this in the positive statement of the prophecy. Although the Greek grammar does not specifically indicate a state of being, it is suggested. He does not speak of definite activities, ceremonies, or commandments. You are going to live in a state of listening, coming under the influence, to the loving communication of His presence. He will influence you and guide you *in all things*. He does not guide in specific areas of life that affect only His interests. Does He care about other areas? He wants to live in a state of love and intimacy with us where He is involved in our total lives. This is His state of being.

In our passage, Moses said, **"And it shall be"** (Acts 3:22). The verb is the future tense, active voice, indicative mood of the first person singular or "eimi." It can be translated "I am," a state of being. As the positive aspect of this contrast is a state of being, so the negative is not an action of God but a state of being in which we will exist. This is not a statement of punishment for one's lack of hearing. "Not listening" results in a state of being. This verb is the first word in the Greek text. This means it is the focus of the statement.

Let's now view this in the context of Peter's exhortation. These Jews are guilty of crucifying Jesus (Acts 3:12-15). God marvelously reversed everything they did to Jesus by raising Him from the dead (Acts 3:15). Now through faith in Him, repentance, and conversion, they can enter into a new location (Acts 3:16-19). This new location is a state of being. In this state, guilt is gone and sin is cleansed (Acts 3:19). This state of being allows the *refreshing* presence of Jesus to saturate your life. This refreshing is not a touch, experience, or an event; it is a state in which you dwell (Acts 3:19-20). When in this state, His presence restores you (Acts 3:21). In fact, Moses, held in high esteem by these Jews, verified this state of being (Acts 3:22-23). If they believed all Moses proposed, how much more would they hold to all Jesus proposes? Moses recognized Jesus as the climax of the prophets knowing he was the beginning.

Now let us view carefully the state of being that results from not listening. If the **Prophet** is not heard, "The Consequence of the Prophecy" is severe. The statement is about who is included in the consequences. The Greek word "pas," translated *every*, is the word "all." The statement is black and white; there are no gray areas or loopholes. You either dwell in the state of listening or in the state of not listening. Again, this is not about activities. That is why **Jesus said, "Not everyone who says to Me, 'Lord, Lord,' shall enter the kingdom of heaven, but he who does the will of My Father in heaven"** (Matthew 7:21). You must not interpret this as your accomplishment of the Father's list of desires. The Greek word "poieo," translated *does*, is a state of being that is a nature flowing in you. The word is used for trees bearing fruit. "Poieo" is not an activity but a nature creating results through you. The category of listening or not listening is not about activities; it is about the flow of God's nature.

The consequence is "***shall be utterly destroyed***." This phrase is a translation of the Greek word "exolothrouo." In the Old Testament Greek translation this word is used many times;

however, the only use in the New Testament is our in our passage. Our passage is a reference to several Old Testament verses. One of them is, *"For any person who is not afflicted in soul on that same day shall be cut off from his people"* (Leviticus 23:29). In this passage, our Greek word is translated *shall be cut off from his people*.

The word means "to destroy completely." The definition is strong; however, contained in the word is the idea of remove. The idea proposed in our passage is "anyone who does not dwell in the state of listening shall be destroyed and so removed from the people." It refers to a type of severe ostracism. Remember, this is a quotation from the Old Testament giving it an Old Testament context. The usual mode of punishing such offences was to cut the offender off from among the people (Exodus 12:15; 30:33; 31:14; Numbers 15:31; 19:13; Leviticus 7:20-21, 25, and 27).

The statement *from among the people* is added. This further describes the action of the preceding verb. The Greek word "ek," translated *from among*, is a movement term. It indicates that the original location was "within the people" but they are now removed "from the people." The statement is clear; they are to be excommunicated, deprived of the privileges of a people. For the Jews, this communication was the most severe punishment that could be inflicted. They would be cut from the privileges of sacrifice and worship in the temple and in the synagogue. They would be regarded as a pagan and an outcast.

Our verb (exolothrouo) in the passive voice is significant. This means those who do not listen are not responsible for the removal or for being cut off. Again Luke confronts us with the two "states of being." One is a state of dwelling in which we are guilt free and cleansed from sin (Acts 3:19). The presence of Jesus refreshes and restores us. We hear Him, come under His influence, and are in intimate communication with Him. At the same time, there is the state of being guilty. We crucified Him; we are not refreshed nor restored. We do not have intimate communication with Him. We are removed from everything that brings life, health, and peace.

This picture is of the vine and the branch (John 15:1-6), not of a God angry with us because we did not do what He said. He is not punishing us. If we abide (state of being) in Him, we live; this is not an activity. We intimately connect with Him, experience His life, and bear His fruit. We cannot help ourselves because we live in the state of intimate connection. If we do not abide but are cut off, we wither and die. The vine does not cause this death; it is a result of not abiding in Him, a state of being. Peter and Moses bring us back to Jesus! We must give our lives to Him! We must be intimate with Him! We must live in His presence moment by moment! We must repent and be converted! Jesus is our state of being.

## Acts 3:24

# THE PROPHETS AGAIN

*"Yes, and all the prophets, from Samuel and those who follow, as many as have spoken, have also foretold these days" (Acts 3:24).*

Looking at this verse, I shook my head and asked myself this question. What is the point of doing another study on the prophets? Surely this subject has been exhausted. In this exhortation from the porch, Peter refers to this group repeatedly. He first mentions the prophets in the middle of his exhortation. **"But those things which God foretold by the mouth of all His prophets, that the Christ would suffer, He has thus fulfilled"** (Acts 3:18). He continues by ending the purpose clauses with this affirmation. **"Which God has spoken by the mouth of all His holy prophets since the world began"** (Acts 3:21). He cannot resist quoting the first of all the prophets, **"For Moses truly said to the fathers"** (Acts 3:22). The quotation is a promise from God to bring about a line of prophets ending with Jesus. Now he gives us one more verse, restating what he said previously. What is the point?

Are these random statements concerning the prophets? Is Peter merely exhorting? The first thing coming to his mind is what he says. Is this exhortation pronounced by the Holy Spirit, placed into the Scriptures, and inspired through Peter? Peter is not repeating because of a lack of knowledge; these are all key statements designed by the Spirit of Jesus to affect the thousands

**Part Two:** Exhortation from the Porch

of Jews gathered at the porch.

We must view the first statement that refers to the prophets. *"But those things which God foretold by the mouth of all His prophets, that the Christ would suffer, He has thus fulfilled"* (Acts 3:21). This statement is focused on SUFFERING. Suffering is the result of our sin. Jesus turned this suffering on itself to redeem us from sin. The product of sin proved as the solution to sin itself is an amazing truth. The destruction of sin is used by Jesus to make us alive in Him! The writer of the Book of Hebrews said it like this, *Inasmuch then as the children have partaken of flesh and blood, He Himself likewise shared in the same, that through death He might destroy him who had the power of death, that is, the devil"* (Hebrews 2:14). How can we possibly describe it? The penalty or wages of sin is death. Jesus took the chief weapon of sin and used it to destroy the source of sin.

In this exhortation, Peter describes the terrible sin and guilt of these Jews. The problem is not the activity of the deed; the problem is how that deed relates to Jesus. The focus of their guilt is on their rejection and crucifixion of Jesus. Every deed of sin is sinful because of its rebellion against Jesus. Peter highlights the suffering of Jesus. He was *"delivered up and denied"* (Acts 3:13). They *"denied the Holy One and the Just, and asked for a murderer to be granted,"* (Acts 3:14). In fact, they *"killed the Prince of life,"* (Acts 3:15). This death is the suffering the prophets foretold and *"He has thus fulfilled"* (Acts 3:18). This suffering is the core of our redemption and is how *"sins may be blotted out"* and *"times of refreshing may come."*

The second statement related to the prophets is the climax of the two purpose clauses expressing SALVATION. Repentance and conversion open the door to a new location. *Sins may be blotted out* in this new room. In this location Jesus cleanses sin and removes guilt. However, there is a second and greater purpose, and it is that *"times of refreshing may come from the*

## The Prophets Again | Acts 3:24

*presence of the Lord."* Once in this new room, the walls begin to come in on us. We realize that this new location is not a room at all; it is the person of Jesus embracing us. We dwell in Him. He is **refreshing** and brings **restoration** to our lives! All this *"God has spoken by the mouth of all His holy prophets since the world began"* (Acts 3:21). The prophets gave constant expression to the heart of God; He wanted to restore us from the beginning of our rebellion. The prophets are His voice expressing His plan! The prophets are the voice of God expressing the "suffering" that brings "salvation."

Then Peter quotes the first prophet, Moses. This quotation focuses on the SAVIOR JESUS. We rejected Jesus, producing His suffering, which in turn became our instrument of deliverance. God ushers us into the new location of Jesus' presence that brings refreshment and restoration through His embrace. Moses clearly told us this would come through a *"Prophet like me from your brethren. Him you shall hear in all things, whatever He says to you"* (Acts 3:22). Jesus is the One who suffered for us; Jesus is the new location where sin is cleansed and guilt is removed. Jesus is the refreshing for our souls and the restoration of all we lost.

Now Peter thunders into this last statement about the role of the prophets, the SUM OF ALL THINGS. Peter says, *"Yes, and all the prophets, from Samuel and those who follow, as many as have spoken, have also foretold these days"* (Acts 3:24). In the Old Testament Scriptures there are sixteen prophets in two sections, the major and the minor prophetic writings. There are four Major prophets: Isaiah, Jeremiah, Ezekiel, and Daniel. There are twelve Minor prophets: Hosea, Joel, Amos, Obadiah, Jonah, Micah, Nahum, Habakkuk, Zephaniah, Haggai, Zechariah, and Malachi. A proper view of the prophets is found in their location. The prophets of the Northern Kingdom include Hosea, Amos, Joel and Jonah. The prophets of the Southern Kingdom are Isaiah, Jeremiah, Obadiah, Micah, Habakkuk, and Zephaniah; the prophets of the Captivity are Ezekiel and Daniel; the prophets of the Return are Haggai, Zechariah, and Malachi.

This is not an exhaustive list of the prophets. This list includes only those who wrote the Old Testament. According to our study in the Book of Acts, we need to include Moses and Samuel in this list. Each wrote in the Old Testament and are considered to be prophets. David, the writer of the Psalms is called a prophet as well (Acts 2:30). Although we may not have an exhaustive list of the prophets, there is an emphasis on including every one. In his exhortation, Peter says, *"all His prophets"* (Acts 3:18 and 24). We now want to view all that they had in common.

## Same Subject

Peter declares that the prophets all spoke on the same subject. This truth is revealed in the previous two verses about the prophecy of Moses (Acts 3:22-23). Again, this prophecy is considered a Messianic prophecy. All the prophets are going to speak for God; however, the final Prophet will be the Word of God. A room in this prophecy for all the prophets exists. Every generation or time period will have a prophet. But ultimately, the subject of every prophet will appear. Jesus will be the final Prophet of which Moses is a type.

Peter verifies this when he first mentions the prophets in his exhortation. *"But those things which God foretold by the mouth of all His prophets, that the Christ would suffer, He has thus fulfilled"* (Acts 3:18). Again, the emphasis is on *"all the prophets"* telling us about the same subject. Obviously, the subject of the prophets is Jesus; but in this verse, more is focused toward the suffering of Christ. The emphasis startled the Jewish congregation. Their image of the Messiah was a conquering military Ruler. How could they have missed it?

Peter pinpoints the subject again in our verse for this study.

## The Prophets Again | Acts 3:24

*"Yes, and all the prophets, from Samuel and those who follow, as many as have spoken, have also foretold these days"* (Acts 3:24). His emphasis is *"**all the prophets**.*" The subject is *"**these days**.*" He refers to the appearance of the Messiah. He came! Peter says this as a fact that cannot be denied. No one in this crowd, including the scribes, can deny this truth.

Peter learned this from his Jewish training in the school at the synagogue. The Resurrected Lord had recently taught this truth to him. Jesus appeared to all the disciples in the upper room. Then He said to them, ***"These are the words which I spoke to you while I was still with you, that all things must be fulfilled which were written in the Law of Moses and the Prophets and the Psalms concerning Me." And He opened their understanding, that they might comprehend the Scriptures*** (Luke 24:44-45). Jesus presented the Scriptures as a product of the writing of the prophets. Moses, the author of the "***Law of Moses***" is a prophet; David the writer of "***the Psalms***" is a prophet. Jesus based His life's revelation on the Scriptures written by the prophets.

Jesus is the only subject under consideration. Peter presents only one subject, Jesus, to the Jewish crowd. Their salvation is declared in one context, Jesus. They are called to ***"Repent therefore and be converted,"*** a change of mind about Jesus. *"Refreshing"* and *"restoration"* are both ***"spoken by the mouth of all His holy prophets since the world began,"*** (Acts 3:21). Peter frames all this in the context of Jesus. All messages from the prophets flow into or come from Jesus. No one can hear the prophets without being confronted with Jesus. They spoke the same subject!

## Same Source

If the prophets spoke the same subject, they must have had the same source. To even consider that all the prophets had the same source for their speaking and writing stretches our minds. Some controversy about the time period of Moses' deliverance of the children of Israel exists. Based on an Old Testament statement, the deliverance was four hundred and eighty years before the fourth year of King Solomon's reign (1Kings 6:1). That places the date during the year of 1447 BC. God positioned these prophets throughout this long spread of history. They did not meet, come from the same school, or write from the same research books. Therefore, the consistency of their message about Jesus is astounding! This consistency can be explained only by the fact that these prophets were not responsible for this message. They could only speak what God placed in their mouths.

The first Greek word in our text is "kai," and it is cumulative in its use. Peter takes the prophecy of Moses (Acts 3:22-23) and adds important information to it. The second Greek word is "pas," which relates to "*the prophets*" (the fourth and fifth English words). In the Greek language, the author front-loaded the sentence with what he considered most important. The emphasis of this statement is on "pas," translated "all."

Peter emphasizes this again with "de," the third Greek word in our text, translated "*yes.*" The primary translation of this conjunction is "but." It is a contrasting conjunction. Peter establishes the prophecy of Moses about The Prophet. He will be a prophet like Moses. He will deliver the final word on which all will be judged. BUT now in our text, Peter highlights all the prophets between Moses and the final Prophet. He speaks of Samuel who followed Moses as a prophet. A timespan was between the two without a prophet. He links Samuel with "*those who follow,*" a translation of the Greek word "kathexes." The word has the idea of consecutiveness. In other words, there will be prophet after prophet who will follow consecutively producing one message.

After referring to this consecutive line of prophets, Peter

says, *"as many as have spoken."* Each time Peter refers to the prophets in this exhortation, he remarkably highlights "speaking!" Listen to verse 18. *"But those things which God foretold by the mouth of all His prophets"* (Acts 3:18). Peter concludes the call to repentance and the two purpose clauses with *"which God has spoken by the mouth of all His holy prophets since the world began"* (Acts 3:21). Even in his reference to the prophecy of Moses, he says, *"hear in all things, whatever He says to you. And it shall be that every soul who will not hear that Prophet"* (Acts 3:22). Now in our passage for this study he says, *"as many as have spoken, have also foretold these days"* (Acts 3:24). The consistent reference to *"mouth," "hear,"* and *"spoke"* is too remarkable to ignore. The consistency is a direct reference to the source of the prophets. They were chosen, empowered, and sourced by God. No wonder they spoke the same message, Jesus!

## Same Sum

Each prophet gave the complete picture of Jesus not just one part. Some scholars attempted to discover a progressive pattern of the unfolding picture of the Messiah throughout the prophets. Three hundred and thirty-three prophecies from the prophets embracing every aspect and feature of Christ's coming are in the Scriptures. His life, sufferings, death, burial, resurrection, glorification, the Kingdom, and other aspects are all covered. Although each prophet gives a complete picture of Jesus, each one adds details, giving some argument to a progressive pattern Many of them spoke of things not heard of during their time. For instance, the manner of Jesus' death was prophesied before the crucifixion was invented (Psalms 22:16).

However, even with this understanding of the difference in details, each prophet gave the complete picture of Jesus. No generation was left in the dark; all are without excuse. The message came to them all! Peter highlights this in the final words of the text, "***these days***" (Acts 3:24). The Greek words, translated "***these days***," are nothing extraordinary. "Hemera" is the Greek word for a 24 hour period. "Tautais" is most often translated "***these***." However, this phrase is significant in light of the context in which it is spoken. "Christ's suffering," "the blotting out of sins," "Jesus giving restoration," and "the times of restoration" are content of "***these days***."

The picture of a redeeming Messiah, revealed now in the Person of Jesus Christ, clearly presented by all the prophets. Eliminate all reason for these Jews not knowing. If so for them, how much more it must be true for us! We have the period of the prophets besides the period of "***these days***." The cumulative grace of the outpouring of the Spirit of Jesus comes to us in the context of a two thousand year span. The radio and television waves are filling the air with His message. The prevenient grace of God brings you and me to the clear message of Jesus, and it is necessary that we respond in repentance.

We must set all else aside, and must embrace Jesus. We are pressed with the call to be intimate with His presence. We must die to ourselves and the core of our selfish will. Yes, the prophets have spoken to us as well!

Acts 3:25

# WHO ARE YOU?

*"You are sons of the prophets, and of the covenant which God made with our fathers, saying to Abraham, 'And in your seed all the families of the earth shall be blessed'" (Acts 3:25).*

In the early days of my ministry, Jesus developed in me desperation for Himself. Throughout my upbringing my parents exposed me to the activities of religion, filling our weeks with religious doings. My father was a pastor, so our schedule revolved around the church. Those were the days of Sunday morning, Sunday evening, Wednesday night prayer meetings, two revivals a year, special children's activities, and then youth meetings. Participation in those activities and religion was endless. God called me to full-time ministry that prompted a development of sermons and Bible studies, thus adding to the religious things I did.

Jesus held an important place in all this activity. But I found that often the activity overshadowed His presence. As a teenager, He created in me a hunger for Himself. This hunger resulted in my saturating in His presence. Developing a consistent consciousness of Jesus in my life became a priority. Saturating in the Scriptures created an awareness of His voice speaking to me. Christianity became defined not by doing religious deeds but by the awareness of His presence.

This shift did not result in inactivity or lack of doing. As

### Part Two: Exhortation from the Porch

I preached this concept, many accused me of prompting laziness. Focusing on His presence did cause many activities in my life to stop. I began to desire only the activities He sourced. If the "doing" is not a result of His sourcing, it is empty and meaningless. This focus on His presence quickly moved me from a religion that I "had" to a relationship with Jesus that I "embraced." It became who I was in Him. Instead of imposing and forcing my inner person to conform to an activity, the activity became an expression of my heart.

Living focused on His presence is the amazing concept of the final statement of Peter's exhortation at the porch! He says, **"You are sons of the prophets, and of the covenant which God made with our fathers, saying to Abraham, 'And in your seed all the families of the earth shall be blessed'"** (Acts 3:25). Being sourced by Jesus is the new level of the New Covenant, which God proposed. These Jews came so close to missing it! They crucified Jesus. But God raised Him from the dead to give them another chance. His suffering resulted from their disobedience and is the platform for the redemption from their sin of disobedience. Will they repent?

Peter does not propose new religious activities to replace old ones. We will enter a new location where there is no guilt and sin is cleansed (Acts 3:19). The purpose of the refreshing of the Spirit of Jesus becomes the internal cooling system of our existence. In fact, He restores us back to the Father's original dream for our lives. Because this restoration is the consistent message of all the prophets, none of this is new news! Moses said this as the first prophet. In fact, from Moses to Samuel, through every successive prophet, it is the message. Jesus, The Prophet, is the climax of all that should be heard! He is the complete and final revelation of Truth! The hour of revelation is upon us in Jesus!

Now we move into the climax of Peter's exhortation (Acts 3:25-26).

## Everything is based on WHO YOU ARE in Him
"You are"

Peter gives a clear description of this crowd gathered around Solomon's Porch. It begins with a STATE OF BEING. The Greek word "humeis," translated *you*, is often used as an emphatic and can be translated "you, yourselves." The first word in the Greek text is this, which means it is the focus of the statement. It becomes personal in this usage. Peter addresses the Jews who gathered around the porch. He is not speaking in general but specifically to these Jews. In fact, the Greek verb also contains this pronoun. Therefore, in our sentence it is there twice, giving it double strength and focus. The Gospel message is like this. It cuts through all the obstacles to the heart of each person.

The Greek word "este," translated *are*, is the second-person plural of "eimi," which means, "to be" and is translated "I am." This word definitely delineates the "state of being," and is in sharp contrast with the beginning of Peter's exhortation. His focus describes their activities toward Jesus. They *"delivered up and denied in the presence of Pilate."* They *"denied the Holy One and the Just and asked for a murderer to be granted."* They *"killed the Prince of life"* (Acts 313-15). These were all activities carried out in response to the presence of Jesus. It constitutes their guilt and sin! This crowd of Jews could not possibly deny any of these activities.

If the Gentiles committed these terrible deeds toward Jesus, it would be evil and sinful. The Romans who participated in the scourging and carried out the will of the Jews were guilty. The pagans of the world by their demonic involvement established the basis for this terrible event. They could be labeled "wicked." But Jews did these awful, sinful, and aggressively barbaric deeds. They dwell in a state far beyond the Gentiles; they are privileged beyond anything others can imagine. We must view their guilt through the lens of the "state of being." What is that state?

They are SONS OF THE PROPHETS. The Greek word "huios," translated *sons*, is often translated "children." The indisputable meaning intended by Peter in this message is simple. These Jews are the product of generation after generation of Israelites to whom the prophets spoke. They readily embrace Moses, Samuel and all the prophets as a part of their history. The prophets are an intricate part of their historical DNA.

But more specifically, they are sons of the prophets because their belief in the coming Messiah is shaped and controlled by the prophets. Peter relentlessly highlights this in his message to them. He said it was **"foretold by the mouth of all His prophets"** (Acts 3:18) and Christ suffered. The dream of the New Covenant including refreshing and restoration, **"God has spoken by the mouth of all His holy prophets since the world began"** (Acts 3:21). Peter reminds them of Moses as the first prophet who spoke about Jesus, The Prophet (Acts 3:22-23). He continued, **"Yes, and all the prophets, from Samuel and those who follow, as many as have spoken, have also foretold these days"** (Acts 3:24). The prophets birthed these Jews! They have a staggering privilege as sons of the prophets.

Peter connects this with one additional element. They are SUCCESSORS OF THE COVENANT. The prophets continually reminded them of the covenant. The image of covenant is the primary way the Bible portrays the relationship between God and His people. If God's message through the prophets is not enough, the unconditional promises of God through the covenant relationship with them are. The focus of Peter's message is much more than the promises of physical land and prosperity, and is focused on Jesus, the Messiah. He is the embodiment of the New Covenant. Peter calls it **"these days," "times of restoration of all things,"** and **"times of refreshing."** God promised this to their fathers, and is fulfilled it in their presence.

The unilateral quality of the covenant is astounding. Most

covenants in the Old Testament are bilateral. This means two equal parties contribute to the covenant. How is this possible with God when no one is His equal? In fact, we have nothing to contribute that will benefit Him. God's covenant with us is one sided. He makes all the provisions; He experienced the great sacrifice for the covenant. We have no part in the covenant except to respond to His provisions.

Peter calls us to view ourselves. We participated in the rebellion against Jesus that resulted in His crucifixion. But this rebellious nation is not who we were intended to be! God includes us in the heritage of the Jews. We are blessed through all He plans in the New Covenant. Come on! We need to embrace Jesus in greater intensity!

## Everything YOU ARE is based on WHO JESUS IS
### "And in your seed"

Peter's logic is simple. The Jews he addresses are a product of the movement of God through the prophets. Their theology, religious practices, and national heritage are all shaped through the message of the prophets. In fact, this can be summarized in terms of the covenant God made with Abraham. The prophets started with Moses and the proclamation of the Law. However, according to Paul, the covenant started four hundred and thirty years before the Law. He strongly stresses that the Law given later could not annul the covenant, a promise from God (Galatians 3:17). Therefore, the real source of who they are is found in the covenant given to Abraham.

Peter states the covenant simply. *"And in your seed all the families of the earth shall be blessed"* (Acts 3:25). Immediately notice, it is SINGULAR IN FOCUS! God speaks specifically to Abraham. The promise is to his *seed*, a translation of the Greek word "sperma," which is singular not plural! God said, *"And I will*

**Part Two**: Exhortation from the Porch

*make your descendants multiply as the stars of heaven; I will give to your descendants all these lands; and in your seed all the nations of the earth shall be blessed;"* (Genesis 26:4). The Hebrew word translated *seed* is singular. You can interpret this to mean the "posterity" of Abraham.

However, the Apostle Paul clarifies this. **"Now to Abraham and his Seed were the promises made. He does not say, 'And to seeds,' as of many, but as of one, 'And to your Seed,' who is Christ"** (Galatians 3:16). Jesus is the focus of the covenant! Everything the Trinity God worked and planned through the Old Testament focused on Jesus. He is the fulfillment and completion of all the promises!

This means Jesus is SUPERIOR IN NATURE. Here is his reasoning. God made a covenant with Abraham focused on **"his Seed,"** Jesus. Four hundred and thirty years later, the law appeared. No one could keep the law. It acted as a **"tutor to bring us to Christ"** (Galatians 3:24). The law taught us the futility of righteousness by doing the Law. Jesus is the only One who became flesh and not only kept the Law, but fulfilled it. God gave the covenant for a relationship with Him through faith; the Law taught us we could not have relationship with Him through doing; in Christ we are back in relationship with Him through faith. He is the only one dwelling in such a relationship. He is intimate with the Father; the Spirit sources Him. Whatever the Father wants Jesus wants! They are One.

The message to these Jews becomes, "Jesus is the SAVIOR OF OUR SOUL." They took the One, the Seed of the covenant, and crucified Him. They did not just **"deny, delivered up,"** but they **"killed the Prince of life."** But God reversed everything they did by raising Jesus from the dead. He is back and alive. They have another chance! Will they embrace the essence of the covenant in Jesus? Everything God intended for these Jews, beginning with Abraham, is found in Christ.

## Everything JESUS IS and YOU ARE is for the PURPOSE OF OTHERS
"all the families of the earth shall be blessed"

This is good news for the Jews, but I am a Gentile. I have no identification with the Jews in race, religious practices, or religious heritage, but this is astounding news for us. We must see the impact of this in light of the prejudice of the Jews. Peter is not fully conscious of what he is saying now. God will deal specifically with him regarding his exclusion of the Gentiles (Acts 10). The Christian Jewish leaders conducted a council in Jerusalem to change the course of all Christianity by embracing the Gentiles (Acts 15). However, even without knowing it, Peter pronounces the truth. He uses the Greek word "pas," translated *all*. To adjust this word to mean "partial," is impossible. He continues with the Greek word "patria," translated *families*, and it is used only three times in the New Testament (Luke 2:45; Acts 3:25 and Ephesians 3:15), and is used to designate the origin of individuals from the same father or ancestor. It suggests God as the Creator and Father of all peoples of the Earth.

Concerning the subject of the covenant given by God, we are remarkably SUBMITTED INTO THE COVENANT. This submission was not an addition to the covenant later. In the mind of God, the covenant did not expand to become this. God did not change His mind. His intent from the beginning was to include everyone. He said this to Abraham. Every man, every race, every culture would be planted into Jesus, the ***Seed***. The prejudice of the Jews with the oral interpretations of the Law focused on the exclusion of everyone except Jews. In Christ, this exclusion was redeemed.

In fact, this brings us to the SUBSTANCE OF THE COVENANT. The heart of the covenant is Jesus. He is the covenant. The focus of Jesus is the focus of the covenant.

**Part Two:** Exhortation from the Porch

Whatever Jesus desires is the desire of the covenant. Jesus burns with the heart of the Father. The Trinity is not divided on anything.

Before His crucifixion, Jesus made an appointment with His disciples (Matthew 26:32 and 28:7). It would occur at a specific time in Galilee after His resurrection from the dead. This is the only scheduled resurrection appearance of Jesus to the disciples, and is significant that it was to be in Galilee, an eight to ten-day trip from Jerusalem. The disciples experienced the crucifixion in Jerusalem; many of the resurrection appearances were in Jerusalem; they were to stay in Jerusalem for the outpouring of the Holy Spirit. To keep this appointed schedule, they would need to make the long trip to Galilee. All this highlights the importance of this meeting. This scheduled encounter with the Resurrected Lord was the "Great Commission." He commanded, ***"Go therefore and make disciples of all the nations, baptizing them in the name of the Father and of the Son and of the Holy Spirit,"*** (Matthew 28:19).

The SUPPLY OF THE COVENANT is no surprise, and it was at this meeting that Jesus said, *"All authority has been given to Me in heaven and on earth"* (Matthew 28:18). This verifies the statement of our passage (Acts 3:25). The blessing the families of the Earth will experience is found *"in your seed,"* Jesus. He is the blessing! This brings us all into the scene at Solomon's Porch. We are guilty of crucifying Jesus. But God raised Him from the dead. He is back; what will we do with Him? We must repent and be converted. He wants to refresh and restore us. We can live in Him without guilt and sin.

## Acts 3:25

# A REMAINING PROMISE

*"You are sons of the prophets, and of the covenant which God made with our fathers, saying to Abraham, 'And in your seed all the families of the earth shall be blessed'" (Acts 3:25).*

The Old Testament is filled with the reality of covenants. The writers present the idea of covenant two hundred and eighty times in its pages. A variety of covenants were between men; even marriage was considered a covenant. However, the news of a covenant between God and humanity is the most startling. This covenant broke the pattern of all other covenants. The covenant between men was a covenant of two equal parties. Each member contributed to the covenant. This type of covenant is a bilateral covenant. However, God does not have an equal. Man has nothing to contribute except ***"filthy rags"*** (Isaiah 64:6). God's covenant is a unilateral covenant. He is the only one who contributes to the covenant. He provides all provisions and benefits. Our sole responsibility is to experience, accept, and respond to the provisions. Jesus is the sole provision!

God established a covenant with Abraham. The first record we have of this promise sets the direction of Abraham's life. ***Now the Lord had said to Abram: "Get out of your country, from your family and from your father's house, to a land that I will show you. I will make you a great nation; I will bless you and make your name great; and you shall be a blessing. I will bless those*** *who bless you, and I will curse him who curses you; and in you all the families of the earth shall be blessed"* (Genesis 12:1-3). The promise is amazing. Abram is not an equal partner in the covenant because he can contribute nothing. God makes all the promises. God is the One who will bless. Abram is in a winning situation. God only requires that Abram accept the covenant and relationship with Him as offered.

Although it may seem this encounter was the first knowledge Abram had of God, it is not. Terah, his father, actually reared him in the faith of one true God. Abram was surrounded by polytheism and idolatry, but accepted the call of God on His life. He was at a mature stage in his life, 75 years of age, when God proposed this covenant. As stated above, a specific land was promised; it was later revealed as the land of Canaan (Genesis 12:7). Abram was to produce a great nation. God promised, *"And I will make your descendants as the dust of the earth; so that if a man could number the dust of the earth, then your descendants also could be numbered"* (Genesis 13:16). Also God promised tremendous blessings to all. Abram was to be blessed; those blessings Abram would be blessed, and *all the families of the earth* would be blessed.

Now hundreds of years later, Peter speaks directly to the descendants of Abraham. What had been mere words spoken by God to a man had already proved true. Peter reminds them of the covenant, *which God made with our fathers, saying to Abraham, "And in your seed all the families of the earth shall be blessed"* (Acts 3:25).

## Faith – The Issue

The context of this statement is faith. Although Abram is participating in a pagan culture, God speaks to him. Will Abram believe the promise of God? Faith means "invoking the activity of the second party." Will Abram come under the influence of this new covenant and participate in all its benefits? That obedience is not the condition of the covenant must be said; it is faith. The action of faith will be obedience; Abram will obey because he believes. But the context of the covenant relationship with God is faith! Hundreds of years later the writer of the Book of Hebrews proposes Abraham as a supreme example of faith. He wrote, *"By faith Abraham obeyed when he was called to go out to the place which he would receive as an inheritance. And he went out, not knowing where he was going"* (Hebrews 11:8).

Faith was not a moment or at the beginning of the covenant experience. Faith was the continual condition and attitude of Abraham's relationship with God. The Scriptures seem to highlight four important encounters between God and Abraham showing this faith. It begins with the call of God to migrate to a strange country. He must leave all he has known including family, job, friends, and homeland (Genesis 12:1). He must invoke the activity of God, a step of faith, more than the plans and security of his own making.

But faith must expand into all areas of his relationship with God. Great friction occurs between the herdsmen of Abram and Lot, his nephew. Abram and Lot grew so wealthy that land would not support their flocks. Abram must part company with Lot, and he behaved generously in allowing Lot to choose the territory that he preferred (Genesis 13:8-11). In response, God renewed His promises of land and a great nation to Abram.

A third occasion highlighting faith was when the covenant was confirmed. God changed Abram's name to Abraham. He promised Abraham a son (Genesis 17:16); this son would be named Isaac, and he would inherit the covenant (Genesis 17:19 and 21). Abraham had provided Ishmael to be the fulfillment of the covenant. He was 99 years old at this time. Would he accept the activity of God, the second party, instead of his own plans?

The most serious test of Abraham's faith was found in God's order to offer his son Isaac as a sacrifice; the covenant was to be perpetuated through Isaac (Genesis 22:1-2). Without questioning, Abraham followed the proper sacrificial ritual; at the culminating moment God intervened and Isaac was spared (Genesis 22:11). Abraham passed the test; he was a man of faith.

Peter proposes this proposition to the children of Abraham. They stand in the same place Abraham stood hundreds of years earlier. However, they have more information, history, and evidence for faith. Will they invoke the activity of the second party and accept Jesus? Everything God promised to do through Abraham and His descendants is now hanging in the balance. The fulfillment of the covenant is found in Christ. What will these Jews do? Will they, by faith, *"Repent therefore and be converted"* (Acts 3:19)? A relationship with Jesus except by faith is possible. The tone and atmosphere of His involvement with us demands the acknowledgment of His authority. *For in it the righteousness of God is revealed from faith to faith; as it is written, "The just shall live by faith"* (Romans 1:17).

## Face – The Impossible

Perhaps acknowledging His authority is the foundation for the demand of faith. We face with the impossible. If we were capable in ourselves, faith in Jesus would not be required. Abraham is confronted with a proposition of which he is incapable. Abraham is captured by the dream of being the father of a nation. Yet, he has no children. His name, Abram, means "exalted father." It must have been embarrassing to meet a new acquaintance; once they heard his name they immediately asked, "How many children do you have?" In shame Abram replied, "None." Then on the renewal of the covenant, Abram's name was changed to Abraham. His new name means "Father of the Multitudes." The father of the multitudes had no children.

Sarah, Abraham's wife, was barren. Abraham faced an

impossible situation. He was 86 years of age. Sarah decided to rescue God and Abraham from embarrassment. She offered her Egyptian maidservant, Hagar, to Abraham (Genesis 16). Sarah would have a son through her maidservant. Self always desires to source the answer, the opposite of faith. Indeed, a son, Ishmael, was born. But Sarah's heart was captured by jealously. Self-sourcing always creates chaos.

When Abraham was 99 years old, God spoke to him again. He renewed His promise of the covenant. By this time, Ishmael was 13 years old. Abraham thought he had the child situation under control. God announced that Sarah would have a son; Abraham fell on his face and laughed. He said in his heart, "Will a child be born to a man who is 100 years old, and will Sarah, who is 90 years old, bear a child?" (Genesis 17:17). Abraham pleaded with God to accept Ishmael as the fulfillment of the promise. But the works of self-sourcing are not acceptable in God's sight.

Peter exhorts the Jews in the same situation as Abraham. They are barren. They repeatedly make plans to satisfy the requirements. They face impossibility. Their traditions, law keeping, and ceremonies do not satisfy. Their nation is crumbling under the pressure of Rome. They are truly doing the best they can. God provided the answer, Jesus, but they crucified Him. They are guilty because they **killed the Prince of life**! Surely, this is an impossible scene. All is lost!

But the answer is so simple! God raised Him from the dead. In a moment of time, by the thought of His mind, God reversed everything we did in our self-sourcing. Jesus is back! What will we do with Him now? He is the Son of Promise. We must, **"Repent therefore and be converted."** Jesus will relocate us into a room where there is no guilt and no sin. The walls will begin collapsing on us; only they are not walls, but His arms. We are in Him. He is refreshing and restoring us. The impossible becomes reality through faith.

**Part Two:** Exhortation from the Porch

In our lives we face impossible situations. God allows us to reach this place. We have exhausted our self-sourced attempts. We are like the woman with the issue of blood (Matthew 9:20). We have gone to many doctors and spent all our money. We are empty of all resource. We are the picture of the first Beatitude, **"Blessed are the poor in spirit"** (Matthew 5:3). But God does something impossible not only for us but to us! It began in Genesis. Abraham embraced it by faith; the prophets proclaimed it by faith. The lame beggar was given **"perfect soundness"** among of this crowd of Jews (Acts 3:16). He received it by faith. We should be next!

## Focus – The Individuals

Amazingly, the situation is impossible, and it drives me to faith. No amount of self-effort will accomplish the task. I must "invoke the activity of the second party." But if Jesus is going to be involved, it will always be focused on others. Abraham's life became a life of dependence on the movement and direction of God. He was living by faith. But in every circumstance it was never only about Abraham but others.

God calls Abraham to sacrifice his son Isaac. Isaac is the seed of promise; he is the only possibility of a fulfilled promise. Abraham did not act without thinking and preparation. The fire had to be prepared; the equipment had to be gathered. Preparation for the journey to the mountain had to be made. A three-day trip with a campfire and resting place each night was necessary. He fellowshipped with his son, because he was conscious these were his final hours with him. Isaac was a young lad; Abraham loved him dearly. How could God require this? Yet by faith, Abraham offered Isaac. Then, at the last moment God intervened on Abraham's behalf. The Scriptures say that God was pleased that Abraham did not withhold his son from

Him. He caused Abraham to look behind him and see a ram caught by his horns in a thicket (Genesis 22:13). He offered it as a burnt offering instead of Isaac. *And Abraham called the name of the place, The-Lord-Will-Provide; as it is said to this day, "In the Mount of the Lord it shall be provided"* (Genesis 22:14).

God did provide for Abraham. He did provide for Isaac. But it was beyond the scope of their lives. God promised, *"In your seed all the nations of the earth shall be blessed, because you have obeyed My voice"* (Genesis 22:18). Is this always the large view of men/women of faith? God is not blessing only their moment, but His purpose is for others in all generations. God's action is never about the individual and his/her needs but always about others.

The pressing reality of this prophetic statement, *"And in your seed all the families of the earth shall be blessed"* (Acts 3:25), recognizes the *seed* of Abraham as Jesus. Carefully view His life and discover this truth. Everything God did for Abraham was for the purpose of Jesus, *your seed.* Everything God did for Jesus is for *the families of the earth.* God filled Jesus with His Spirit (Matthew 3:16). The filling was not to make Him feel accepted and loved, or empowered for success. It was about others. During the wilderness temptation, Jesus did battle with Satan. The Father gave Him victory after victory. Finally, the angels came and ministered to Him (Matthew 4:11). This was not a personal victory simply for Jesus. This victory was a provision for us all. The resurrection was not limited to benefit Jesus; it provided life to all *the families of the earth.*

A lame beggar over 40 of age begged daily at the temple beside the Gate Beautiful. He claimed the best spot for begging for himself. Peter and John were going into the temple at the ninth hour, the three o'clock hour of prayer, and was also the hour of sacrifice. This time was a moment of destiny. Jesus intervened in this beggar's life. By the flow of the power of the resurrected Lord, this lame man was on his feet. The demonstration of his healing was so significant that *all the people saw him walking and praising God* (Acts 3:9). God certainly blessed a lame beggar. But it is not about just this man. God used this man to create an opportunity for evangelism in the structure of the temple. Peter exhorted this large crowd, and five-thousand men became disciples of Jesus (Acts 4:4). Through this healed beggar, the Sanhedrin was again confronted by the power and person of Jesus (Acts 4:14). The early church again knew the filling of the Holy Spirit and went forth with boldness to testify of His greatness (Acts 4:31).

This Divine approach is true for all our lives. We often cry to God about our problems. Indeed, our problems are pressing and God is deeply interested. But when He intervenes, it is an intervention beyond our need. In affecting your life, He will have in mind *the families of the earth*. This must be the focus of our lives as well. Spirit-sourced activities can never be focused on us. The church must not create programming for its own benefit. We must not become a people who use God for our own personal benefit; He wants to use us to benefit others. Will we allow Him?

Acts 3:26

# WHO IS FIRST?

*"To you first, God, having raised up His Servant Jesus, sent Him to bless you, in turning away every one of you from your iniquities"* (Acts 3:26).

As we begin our study, I assume that we agree on several facts. One is PASSION of the Trinity God to bring redemption to humanity. This priority cannot be disputed; the Scriptures consistently verify it. **"For God so loved the world that He gave His only begotten Son, that whoever believes in Him should not perish but have everlasting life"** (John 3:16). His passion has never been judgment or destruction. He said, **"For God did not send His Son into the world to condemn the world, but that the world through Him might be saved"** (John 3:17). The mission statement for Jesus proclaimed by the angel at His birth was, **"And she will bring forth a Son, and you shall call His name Jesus, for He will save His people from their sins"** (Matthew 1:21). Jesus defined His own life when He said, **"For the Son of Man has come to seek and to save that which was lost"** (Luke 9:10).

This mission is the conclusion Peter presents to this Jewish crowd. Is it possible Peter did not realize the full ramifications of what he said? An expanded view came later in his encounter with Cornelius (Acts 10). This view compelled him. Everything God did through Abraham and the prophets was for *"all the*

***families of the earth"*** (Acts 3:25). The prophecy communicated by Moses refers to ***"every soul"*** (Acts 3:23). Although this may have been considered only for those in the Jewish community, could it be for everyone? God never intended to come only to the Jews. In the suggestion of God coming to the Jews ***first*** (Acts 3:26) is the indication that He will come to others as well. To have a ***first***, you must have a second then more, which would include all humanity.

A second assumption is that the only instrument of redemption is a PERSON. If there were any hope of being saved by the Law, it was smashed hundreds of years ago. Paul concluded, **But that no one is justified by the law in the sight of God is evident, for "the just shall live by faith"** (Galatians 3:11). If any man contemplates he can save himself, he is a fool. **For by grace you have been saved through faith, and that not of yourselves; it is the gift of God, not of works, lest anyone should boast** (Ephesians 2:8-9).

The self-sourcing carnal nature of humanity continually resists this grace. If we cannot save ourselves, we at least want to contribute to our salvation. But our salvation and spiritual life depends on Jesus. He does not give it to us; it is what He is! All biblical illustrations point to this. Jesus is the vine and we are the branches (John 15:1-6). Life is found only in attachment and surrender to the vine. We are the soil; He is the seed, the Word. He provides the life and produces the fruit of my life (Matthew 13:3-9).

The exhortation from the porch is focused on the person of Jesus. He is the one they crucified (Acts 3:13-15). He is *"His Servant Jesus"* whom God glorified (Acts 3:13). The healing of the lame man is accredited to *"His name, through faith in His name,"* (Acts 3:16). The message of the prophets is about Jesus' suffering (Acts 3:18). Embracing Jesus is the issue of repentance (Acts 3:19). *"Refreshing"* will come from His presence (Acts 3:19). He is the One who will be sent and bring restoration (Acts 3:20). He is the *Prophet* who will be like Moses (Acts 3:22).

The detailed and great PLAN of God is the third assumption. Peter consistently points out God's plan in his persistent reference to the prophets. He almost overstated it. Every statement Peter makes in this exhortation is followed by and based on the voice of the prophets. The redemptive suffering created by the disobedience of these Jews is *"foretold by the mouth of all His prophets"* (Acts 3:18). Repentance resulting in *"sins may be blotted out,"* *"times of refreshing,"* and *"times of restoration of all things,"* are all *"spoken by the mouth of all His holy prophets since the world began"* (Acts 3:19-21). Moses, the first and greatest Old Testament prophet, proposed a succession of prophets. This succession concluded with the *"Prophet"* (Acts 3:22-23). In fact, Samuel and a consecutive line of prophets all *"foretold these days"* (Acts 3:24). The timespan of these prophets is nearly 1500 years. The Trinity God is working a plan!

In this plan, there is a natural sequence of events and involvement. God established a high priority in this progression. This progression has already been noted in the consecutive line of the prophets. Each appeared in the proper order, giving the message, and contributing to the climax of the plan.

The necessity of this process did not rest on God. In other words, His power, wisdom, or ability was not a requirement. God was quite capable of doing it at once with one thought of His mind. The necessity is in the character of humanity. God went through this process for our benefit. Peter refers to this in his last statement in the exhortation. He said, *"To you first, God, having raised up His Servant Jesus, sent Him to bless you, in turning away every one of you from your iniquities"* (Acts 3:26).

Part Two: Exhortation from the Porch

# Precondition

Peter proposes the reality of *first* in the sense of PRECONDITION. The Greek word "proton," translated *first*, is an adverb used 60 times in the New Testament. From the definition of the word, there is little to be gained in understanding. New understanding comes mainly from the various ways it is used in the New Testament. The precondition usage is dominant in the Scriptures.

Jesus used this word frequently. When discussing the contrast in relationships among people in the New Covenant with the Old Covenant, Jesus established a sequence of responses in the New. It must spring from a heart with no hate. The Old was content with not murdering; the New called for no hate. How would this manifest itself in daily life? If you come to God with a gift while you have division with someone else, you must leave your gift and go to be reconciled with your brother. Jesus said, **"First be reconciled to your brother, and then come and offer your gift"** (Matthew 5:24). Reconciliation is a precondition to the acceptability of your offering to God.

In the same Sermon on the Mount, Jesus spoke about judging others. He used the exaggerated picture of a man with a large plank in his eye attempting to remove a little speck from his brother's eye. His instructions are, **"Hypocrite! First remove the plank from your own eye, and then you will see clearly to remove the speck from your brother's eye"** (Matthew 7:5). A proper procedure or a precondition in helping your brother exists.

We must bring this idea into our passage. God's passion is to win the world. He longs for and loves *"all the families of the earth"* (Acts 3:25). He places His focus on the person of Jesus to bring families to Himself. He carries out a distinct plan within the structure of time to achieve this goal. In that order or plan, events and items must precede other events and items. Peter speaks this truth. Jesus must *first* come to the Jewish nation before the Gentiles (all non-Jews) can be won.

An interesting controversy took place in Antioch. Upon Paul's arrival in Antioch, he followed his typical pattern of going to the synagogue on the Sabbath day. He read the Law and the Prophets and was invited by the rulers of the synagogue to exhort the people. Paul used the Old Testament to present Jesus to the Jews. As the Jews left the synagogue, *the Gentiles begged that these words might be preached to them the next Sabbath* (Acts 13:42). Then *on the next Sabbath almost the whole city came together to hear the word of God* (Acts 13:44). The Jews were filled with envy and began to contradict and blaspheme; *they opposed the things spoken by Paul* (Acts 13:45). *Then Paul and Barnabas grew bold and said, "It was necessary that the word of God should be spoken to you first; but since you reject it, and judge yourselves unworthy of everlasting life, behold, we turn to the Gentiles* (Acts 13:46). It seems that Paul consistently preached to the Jews first in all his missionary journeys as a precondition to ministering to the Gentiles.

Many Jews brought accusations against Paul. King Agrippa heard the testimony of Paul's conversion and mission. After clearly describing *the light from heaven, brighter than the sun, shining around me and those who journeyed with me,* Paul shared the message Jesus gave him, to minister to the Gentiles. Paul testified, *"Therefore, King Agrippa, I was not disobedient to the heavenly vision, but declared first to those in Damascus and in Jerusalem, and throughout all the region of Judea, and then to the Gentiles, that they should repent, turn to God, and do works befitting repentance"* (Acts 26:20; see Romans 1:16; 2:9-10).

The message of Peter to the crowd of Jews in and around Solomon's Porch is one of responsibility. God followed His one precondition for winning the world. Jesus has come to the Jews. What will they do with the message? Their rejection of Jesus hindered the plan of God. God will complete His plan in spite of them, but what could have taken place because of them? Instead of becoming a part of the evangelistic movement of God's heart, they become a part of those who needed to be evangelized.

Let me declare to you fathers, "Jesus has come to you *first*." Do you not have the place of authority and influence over your family? Are you not responsible for the revelation of Jesus to your children? Has Jesus not placed you in your vocation in order to win **the families of the earth**? Did He not come to you *first*? Your job or career is not simply an activity to earn money. Jesus placed you in a place of ministry. He comes to you *first,* and you are responsible! Has He not ordained us to be in this town and given us this location for the declaration of His name? We receive the message *first*! Every preacher should tremble as he approaches the pulpit of the church. Jesus has given the message to you *first* for others.

# Priority

Peter proposes the reality of *first* in the sense of temporal PRIORITY. Added to this precondition is the idea of "first of all, or above all." In the Sermon on the Mount Jesus addresses worry. How our worry focuses on what we eat, what we wear, and our materialism is interesting. Jesus recognizes the world around us is focused on such matters. He admonishes us with the following words. **"But seek first the kingdom of God and His righteousness, and all these things shall be added to you"** (Matthew 6:33). Jesus brings everything into sharp contrast with the Kingdom of God. Therefore, exclusive value or priority is stressed. How can the value of an intimate relationship with Jesus be compared to anything temporal?

Although Jesus said this in the Sermon on the Mount, it is soon revealed in the activities of His life. The miracles of Jesus attract all manner of people. One individual enthusiastically said, ***"Teacher, I will follow You wherever You go"*** (Matthew 8:18). He had no idea of the suffering, denial, and cross bearing required in belonging to Jesus. He simply wanted an easy path of miracles. Then another of His disciples said to Him, ***"Lord, let me first go and bury my father"*** (Matthew 8:21). Any hesitation on belonging to Jesus nullifies that belonging. Such a precondition cancels a relationship with Jesus because it devalues the Person of Christ.

Please allow our passage to be understood in light of this significance. The Jews do not receive the revelation of Jesus *first* because they are more important than the Gentiles; they are important because they received Christ *first*. Jesus gives them their status. Paul is clear about this as he writes to the Romans. He writes, ***"For I am not ashamed of the gospel of Christ, for it is the power of God to salvation for everyone who believes, for the Jew first and also for the Greek"*** (Romans 1:16). This statement from the Greek text should not be translated "then for the Greeks." The phrase must be translated ***"also for the Greeks."*** The Jews are not of greater priority because they are Jews; their value is found in the coming of Christ to them in the proper sequence of time.

As a Christian, I often wonder how I have received the revelation of Jesus in my life. I see many times in the past where I could have been bypassed, but it is almost like I have been selected. The right person at the right time said the right thing, and then Jesus embraced my life. Am I more important than others? You are a temporal priority. He came to you for others. This responsibility must grip your life. It appears our generation is content to receive the blessings of His presence and float their way to heaven. They do not burn with the heart of God who comes to us *first* for others.

**Part Two:** Exhortation from the Porch

# Purpose

Peter proposes the reality of *first* in the sense of PURPOSE. In one sense, he says the purpose several times. Jesus comes *first* to the Jews so **all the families of the earth shall be blessed**. However, in the purpose is an interesting method. Jesus did not come to the Jews and give them a revelation of Himself with the expectation they would share it with the world. This method would contain the supposition that the Jews were better equipped for this responsibility than were the Gentiles. The Jews were smarter, financially stable, and stronger in character; therefore, God chose them for the task and came to them *first*.

But this method has a false supposition. God chose the Jews simply because He had to choose someone. He had to come to someone *first*. The Jews have no superiority. In fact, God did not choose them to do something for Him; He chose them so He could do something through them. God did not love them more than the Gentiles; He did not prefer them to the Gentiles. The wonder of the Jews is not what they did, but what God did through them. They formed the genealogy through which the Messiah was born; they formed the culture in which the Sermon on the Mount was preached and demonstrated. They became the foundation for the Kingdom to step into our world. The dream of God was never about the Jews; it was always about **all the families of the earth** being blessed.

This inclusiveness is the method of the Kingdom of God. You and I cannot hide behind a lack of talent, education or proper personalities. This Kingdom is not about us; it is about Him. "I cannot do anything significant for Him" is a false and demonic statement. He chooses us to do something through us. Matthew begins his Gospel account with a genealogy. It contains a list of 42 generations. None of them fully understood the role they were playing in the dreams of God. They married, had children, and did business like Gentile families. But God was doing something through them to redeem a world. He came to them *first*. This unselfish role is the call of the Kingdom for us. We want to assume specific tasks, accomplish specific programs, and fulfill specific obligations for God. He is looking for lives totally submitted, filled with His Spirit, and resting in His plan. Are you one?

## Acts 3:26

# A CLIMACTIC STATEMENT

*"To you first, God, having raised up His Servant Jesus, sent Him to bless you, in turning away every one of you from your iniquities" (Acts 3:26).*

Peter has come to the end of his exhortation from the porch. In his final sentence he reaches into this exhortation and highlights many of his major thrusts. For instance, he expresses, **"God, having raised up His Servant Jesus,"** (Acts 3:26). This reference to the resurrection is used two other times in Acts (Acts 3:15 and 22). In this statement Peter presents the overwhelming idea of **"His Servant Jesus."** Peter opened his exhortation with this title for Jesus (Acts 3:13). He emphasizes the intimate relationship between **"The God of Abraham, Isaac, and Jacob, the God of our fathers"** with Jesus. He outlines the service Jesus renders in His servanthood. He is a suffering Servant. All these Jews were reminded of the picture painted by Isaiah, the prophet (Isaiah 53). He calls them again to **"Repent therefore and be converted,"** (Acts 3:19). Jesus' purpose is to turn **"every one of you from your iniquities."**

We can clarify the verse if we diagram the grammar. **God** is the subject of the sentence. But Peter gives content to this God! He is the God who elevated, established, or **raised up** Jesus. We discovered this same phrase in two other places in Peter's exhortation. A definite tone of reference to the resurrection in the other two exists. However, in the statement in our verse the resurrection is doubtfully indicated. **God** is the prime mover. He is the Trinity God who not only gives life, but also establishes positions. The Greek word "anistemi," translated **having raised up**, is a verb used as an adjectival participle, giving content to **God**.

The prime action of God in our verse is **sent**, the main verb. The Greek word is "apostello," the verb form of apostle. The action of God in our verse is focused on the direct object, **Him**. The action denotes that one is sent on a specific mission. The mission is quickly described with an infinitive, **to turn away** (apostrepho). **Everyone** (hekostos) is the focus of the infinitive. An infinitive always requires and depends on a main verb. It always has the same subject as the main verb. This presents an amazing truth we will expound later. Involved in the action of God sending is the act of turning us away from our iniquities. We do not turn from our iniquities and He comes; He comes and we are enabled to turn. This turning is not true for only a few, but it is true for **everyone**.

In our English translation of this verse, there appears to be another infinitive, **to bless**. However, when we investigate the Greek text, we discover it is a verb in the participle form. It modifies and gives content to **Him**. The Greek word "eulogeo," translated **to bless**, means "to speak with purpose of good intervention." Jesus is the Word; He speaks of God and intervenes on our behalf. It appears the word **iniquities** (poneria) gives a broad view of all wickedness. He cleanses all depths of evil. He will straighten any twist of carnality. All the demonic forces tremble in His presence. The evil system is abolished in Jesus!

This verse is the climax of Peter's exhortation. **God** is the Prime Mover. Peter describes Him as the One who establishes positions, puts things in their place. This Prime Mover **sent** Jesus to save everyone from all wickedness. He can do this because He is **to bless you**. He is God speaking good things about you and to you. Understanding the flow and heart of this statement, we must place it in Peter's exhortation.

Everything Peter describes in this climactic statement is found in the position in which Jesus abides. He is **His Servant Jesus**. The title **Servant** applied to Jesus is remarkable, but not a common title for Jesus in the New Testament. It occurs twice in this exhortation from Solomon's porch (Acts 3:13 and 26). It also appears twice in the following chapter (Acts 4:27 and 30). The difficulty with the term is that the Greek word (pais) from which **Servant** is translated is more often translated "son." It seems in our translation that the "son of God" idea became so dominate that this translation of **Servant** was seldom used. What is remarkable about this passage is its apparent connection to the prophecy of Isaiah. Isaiah presented the coming Messiah as "The Suffering Servant" (Isaiah 52 and 53). Peter refers to the prophets foretelling that Jesus would suffer (Acts 3:18), and the most likely prophecy for this reference is Isaiah.

I want to encourage you to read the prophecy of Isaiah (Isaiah 52:13-53:12). Many Jewish scholars ignored this prophecy of the Messiah. It did not fit their desires; they could not comprehend a "suffering Servant" bringing any kind of deliverance to Israel. Some Jewish scholars attempted to include this prophecy by proposing there would be two Messiahs. Still, their focus was on a military Messiah who would bring political freedom. They missed **His Servant Jesus**. Is this why they crucified Him? Was this the ignorance that had them (Acts 3:17)?

We must carefully note THE SOURCE of His service! Although Peter clarifies this many times in his exhortation, he feels compelled to do so once more. He said, **"To you first, God, having raised up His Servant Jesus"** (Acts 3:26). The Greek word "anistemi," translated **having raised up**, is a verb in the participle form, used as an adjective to modify and give content to **God**. The **having raised up** God sourced Jesus as a Servant! Peter refers to the **"God of Abraham, Isaac, and Jacob, the God** *of our fathers,"* Jehovah, the Trinity God (Acts 3:13).

This Greek word "anistemi" is a compound word. It consists of "ana," translated "again," and "histemi," translated "to stand." This does not relate to the resurrection, instead it relates to the appointment of Jesus to serve in this position of Servant! This definition is verified by its same use in verse 22, where Moses is quoted speaking for God. He said, *"The Lord your God will raise up for you a Prophet like me from your brethren. Him you shall hear in all things, whatever He says to you"* (Acts 3:22). God, the Trinity, is going to cause Jesus "to stand" in the position of *a Prophet*. Although this statement may emphasize a different perspective on the servant role, it verifies the sourcing of the role.

Being sourced by God is fundamental to everything God planned for humanity. Whenever we stray from this reality, we enter sin and destruction. It characterizes the first sin of Adam and Eve against God to the rebellion of the devil. It produces our anxieties and despairs and causes destruction of our relationships. Sin can only be written with the self-sourcing "I" in the middle. Redemption is described as *"I have been crucified with Christ"* (Galatians 2:20). God's sourcing the Man who redeems us is not a surprise. He is an instrument of God-sourced service. This establishes the pattern for us is not a surprise. Oh, how God wants to source us! We are not to be independent from Him, but dependent on Him. We are to be united with Him, produced by Him, and an extension of Him.

We must carefully note the service He renders is not an activity but He is THE SEED. The Trinity God sources Jesus in the position of "the Seed." Think of the history involved in the fulfillment of such a promise. God promised the serpent in the Garden of Eden. *"And I will put enmity between you and the woman, and between your seed and her Seed; He shall bruise your head, and you shall bruise His heel"* (Genesis 3:15). God moved in this direction by beginning a nation through Abraham. On renewing the covenant with Abraham, God made a promise. *"In your seed all the nations of the earth shall be blessed, because you have obeyed My voice"* (Genesis 22:18). Now hundreds of years later Peter proclaims God's original promise to the descendants of Abraham. *"And in your seed all the families of the earth shall be blessed"* (Acts 3:26).

Let me remind you that Paul proposed that Jesus is the Seed. ***Now to Abraham and his Seed were the promises made. He does not say, "And to seeds," as of many, but as of one, "And to your Seed," who is Christ*** (Galatians 3:16). The Trinity God appointed Jesus to replace Abraham to bless ***all the families of the earth***. When Peter tells us that God ***raised up His Servant Jesus,*** the reference is not to the resurrection from the dead, instead it refers to the appointment to serve as the offspring of Abraham.

Jesus is the ***Seed*** through which all humanity will be blessed. The details of birthing an entire nation through hundreds of years were all designed to usher Jesus into this position. No wonder the angels filled the sky with praise at His birth (Luke 2:13). No wonder the star in the sky shone brighter than before the announcement (Matthew 2:2). No wonder the devil went on a rampage of killing baby boys (Matthew 2:16). Jesus is the single blessing of God to all humanity. The blessing is not the solution of our immediate problems or financial benefits. The blessing is not to simply heal physical difficulties or provide for our comfort. Jesus is the blessing, the Seed. He is not activity oriented but relational. ***His Servant Jesus*** serves in and through relationship. The focus is on His person. The Good News of the Gospel is Jesus.

Peter's final call to the Jews is to come to Jesus. What a turnaround this would be for them. They *"delivered up and denied in the presence of Pilate, when he was determined to let Him go"* (Acts 3:13). They *"denied the Holy One and the Just, and asked for a murderer to be granted"* (Acts 3:14). They *"killed the Prince of life,"* (Acts 3:15). The only hope they ever had they eliminated. The plan of God from the beginning was rejected at the end. Can they have another chance? *"God raised from the dead,"* and reversed everything they did! Jesus is back; He gives them a second chance. What will they do with Jesus now?

As Peter's exhortation comes to an end, there is a third element to consider; Jesus is THE SUMMATION. We must reconsider it. This truth is presented repeatedly throughout the Scriptures. Although this third element is indicated and suggested in the previous two ideas, it must be highlighted again! Everything comes together in the person of Jesus.

This third element is presented from the beginning of the exhortation. While the healed beggar holds onto Peter, they make their way into the temple. His entry is the first time he has been allowed to enter. Handicapped people were not allowed to worship in the temple. You would think he would have been awestruck with the beauty and magnitude of this place. Surely the healed beggar would spend time investigating the various porches and pillars of the temple area. But he is focused on Peter, as if Peter is responsible for his miracle. Peter will not allow such a conclusion for even one split second. He immediately focused this crowd on Jesus, the source of the miracle. He leaves no room for misunderstanding about the identity of Jesus! He is the One they denied, rejected, and killed. He is the One God raised from the dead. Let it be known, *"And His name, through faith in His name, has made this man strong, whom you see and know. Yes, the faith which comes through Him has given him this perfect soundness in the presence of you all"* (Acts 3:16).

Then Peter establishes a foundation of prophecy for this single focus on Jesus. *"God foretold by the mouth of all His prophets, that the Christ would suffer, He has thus fulfilled"* (Acts 3:18). The potential for forgiveness and cleansing from sin, which allows refreshing and restoration, will happen through only Jesus. God spoke this *"by the mouth of all His holy prophets since the world began"* (Acts 3:21). Moses, the first prophet, spoke this message. God was going to raise up The Prophet who would be Jesus (Acts 3:22). ***"Yes, and all the prophets, from Samuel and those who follow, as many as have spoken, have also foretold these days"*** (Acts 3:24).

Even the covenant beginning with Abram was focused on Jesus. God promised, ***"And in your seed all the families of the earth shall be blessed"*** (Acts 3:25). Paul clarifies that the *Seed* is singular and refers to Jesus. The sole purpose of Abraham and the nation of Israel was a lineage through which Jesus would be born. Jesus is the focus. Because the genealogy of Jesus was found in the nation of Israel, it was natural He would appear in this nation first (Acts 3:26). But the intent in the heart of God from the beginning was to bless *all the families of the earth*.

What is the blessing Jesus grants? Peter describes it as ***"turning away every one of you from your iniquities"*** (Acts 3:26), a call to repentance and conversion as Peter has already said (Acts 3:19). However, in this statement there is an added encouragement. The additional good news is that Jesus will be instrumental in the process of turning us away from evil, a pure statement of "prevenient grace." Peter is not simply presenting a logical and historical point of view for these Jews. This is not an argument to be combated with more debates. This is not a philosophy to think about and perhaps act on later. God raised Jesus from the dead. He is back. He confronts these Jews in this moment as Peter speaks. Jesus acts on and in their lives to give them the ability to believe; He produces the faith to grasp the truth. He provides the strength to walk into the new location of forgiveness and cleansing. Will they respond to Him?

This is the way Peter concludes His appeal. But should not every sermon we preach bring us to the same conclusion? We must focus on Jesus. He is the goal toward which we travel. He is the road on which we proceed to get to our destination. He is the resource by which we find the ability to make the journey. He is the One who gives us the insight to begin the trip. He is all there is! He is the One we seek for salvation. He is the One who calls us to seek. He is the One who gives us the ability to respond by seeking. He is all there is! He is the One in whom all things make sense. He is the wisdom by which we see the supreme issues of life. He alone can bring the revelation of truth; when truth is revealed it is Him! He is the sum of all things.

Don't let anything or anyone distract you from Jesus. Do not let the good or the bad, the institution or the organization, the theology or the program, the ceremony or the rules, or the emotions or the mind become a substitute for Him. Let us come back to Him. You must be intimate with Jesus!

# ABOUT THE AUTHOR

Stephen Manley has found through the saturation of the Word the message of the cross. It is beyond an event; it is a style. Thus, the cross is not a piece of wood or an emblem, but it is the heart of the person of Christ. Cross style is the Christ style. He must be central. As an international evangelist, Stephen has taken this message to the world.

After 41 years in itinerant evangelism, Stephen Manley felt a clear call from God to come off the road for the purpose of starting the Cross Style School of Practical Ministry. In 2009, Stephen launched and became the lead pastor of Cross Style Church in Lebanon, Tennessee to create the ministry platform for future students.

The Cross Style School of Practical Ministry was launched with a desire to not only train up men and women in the Word, but to give them practical hands-on experience in ministering to a lost and dying world.

Stephen's life, testimony, and preaching has been used throughout the last six decades to touch, influence, and transform the lives of countless people around the world. For Stephen, his life is wrapped up in a total saturation of Jesus and the Word of God. Time in the Word is more than an activity or duty to schedule in his day. It is the delight of his heart and the focus throughout his day because it draws him deeper into intimacy with Jesus Christ. He wants his "moment-by-moments" saturated with the Person of Jesus and the Word. He longs for Jesus to ever increase and expand in and through His life. As he once wrote:

*"Jesus is present in every situation of my life. There is no conversation in which I do not feel His presence.*
*He participates in all my recreation. He is everywhere I go. Who would want to be without Him? He is the protection for my life. He is the fragrance I constantly smell. He is the flow of my spiritual blood giving me life.*
*He is my constant nutrition making me healthy.*
*I cannot survive without Him. I am a Jesus pusher!!!!*

*I want to push Him on you.*
*I want you to join me in this obsession.*
*You do not have to work at it; it is not a discipline.*
*It is as natural as breathing.*
*Please let Him pull you to His heart."*


Learn more about Stephen Manley and the ministry of Cross Style at: **CrossStyle.org**

www.ingramcontent.com/pod-product-compliance
Lightning Source LLC
Chambersburg PA
CBHW020940230426
43666CB00005B/93